CLEVELAND
GARDEN CENTER

FROM
CLEVELAND
ROSE SOCIETY

# American Rose Annual 1959

FRANK H. ABRAHAMSON, Editor

MARGARET E. COON, Assistant Editor

## AMERICAN ROSE SOCIETY

4048 Roselea Place

Columbus 14, Ohio

Buckeye.................HAROLD H. ALLEN, Chillicothe, Ohio
Illinois-Indiana...........DAVID T. GOLDEN, Elmhurst, Ill.
Great Lakes .............FRANK J. HOWELL, Detroit, Mich.
North Central............CARL J. HOLST, Minneapolis, Minn.
Central..................EARL THOMAS, Des Moines, Iowa
South Central.............ROGERS C. MARTINI, Amarillo, Tex.
Rocky Mountain ......... ROY T. LITTLEJOHN, Wheatridge, Colo.
Pacific Southwest......... MRS. GEORGE DOOLITTLE, Albuquerque, N.M.
Northern California-Nevada.MARTIN J. MARTIN, San Francisco, Calif.
Pacific Northwest.........MRS. DANIEL HEFFNER, Portland, Ore.

## Gold Honor Medal
### Awarded To
DR. J. HORACE McFARLAND
For his long devotion to this society and his unstinted effort to the
advancement of the rose in America.   1933
MRS. HARRIET RISLEY FOOTE
For the beautiful rose gardens she has made.   1933
ROBERT PYLE
For his untiring effort and invaluable service to the rose.   1933
DR. JEAN HENRI NICOLAS (posthumous)
For outstanding achievements with the rose.   1937
THEODORE WIRTH
Founder of municipal rose gardens.   1938
L. B. CODDINGTON
For his origination of new roses.   1941
FRED H. HOWARD
For outstanding work in hybridizing and introducing
new varieties of roses.   1941
DR. WALTER E. LAMMERTS
For his outstanding work in rose hybridization.   1945
L. C. BOBBINK
For outstanding achievements and service to the rose.   1945
FRED EDMUNDS
For preëminence in judging roses and inspiring love for them.   1946
DR. LOUIS M. MASSEY
For invaluable research on rose diseases and distinguished service to
the society.   1947
DR. T. ALLEN KIRK
Ideal American rosarian.   1948
ARTHUR F. TRUEX
For loyalty and distinguished leadership.   1949
E. S. BOERNER
For producing better roses through hybridization.   1951
HERBERT C. SWIM
For the hybridization of better roses through scientific methods.   1951
GEORGE A. SWEETSER
For his untiring effort in promoting the American Rose Society and laying
the groundwork for its present success.   1952
HARRY L. ERDMAN
For unselfish devotion to the rose and to the society.   1953
ROY E. SHEPHERD
For distinguished service to old roses and their history.   1954
C. EUGENE PFISTER
For his ability to inspire others to grow roses.   1956

# Contents

# Illustrations

COVER: Starfire (Gr), Walter E. Lammerts; introduced Germain's, Inc., Los
Angeles, Calif. Plant patent 1742. Described page 258.

# Sixty Years of Progress

John R. Patterson

Moline, Ill.

LITTLE DID THE founders of our great society realize when they first met in March 1899 that we would progress during the next 60 years until we now have more than 17,000 members from every state, as well as most of the other countries of the world.

Only a few roses that were popular in those days are still being grown today. Although rosarians had many more problems that we face today, they still managed to stage many fine rose shows. The same diseases and insects plagued these rosarians, and they only had a soft soap emulsion and tobacco dust with sulphur to combat them. Nevertheless, enthusiasm ran high, as was demonstrated during a sensational exhibit on March 25-27, 1908, at the Art Institute in Chicago. The promises of the exhibitors were more than realized. "The West wins with *American Beauty* and *Richmond,* but the East is on top with *Killarney.* President Simpson of the American Rose Society was astonished with what the Chicago exhibition has shown," the records state.

Today, we are all indeed fortunate in having thousands of new roses, insecticides, fungicides and fertilizers to practically eliminate all of these past troubles, so that we can now grow beautiful roses the easy way. Many members of our society have contributed to this marked advancement. Everyone now has access to a wealth of information through our publications, national and district meetings and in their own respective local clubs.

"How much for so little" should indeed be our story to the new prospective member who is just starting to grow roses. With the Proof of the Pudding and other features of the yearly American Rose Annuals, the monthly American Rose Magazine and our large lending library, no one should lack thorough cultural information.

As your president during these two years, I have enjoyed the privilege of meeting many of you, attending some of your fine rose shows and visiting both the little and large rose gardens that you so proudly own.

# Roses Have A Universal Appeal

George A. Stingle
Morongo Valley, Calif.

THE rose has held an important place in our lives for untold ages.

It has been used to infuse a tone of harmony in our music and arts. We lilt My Wild Irish Rose, Roses of Piccardy, Roses and You, The Last Rose of Summer and other lyrics selected from a list of an estimated 4000 songs about the rose.

It would be impossible to guess how many times the rose has been tied in with girls' names, such as Rose, Rosalie, Rose Marie, Rosella, Rosanna and Rosellen.

Even family names, like Roosevelt, Rosecrans, Rosamond and Ross, had their origin in some ancient activity connected with rose culture.

Roseburg, Santa Rosa, Montrose, Rosedale and many other towns and cities owe their names to the popularity of the rose.

Cemeteries carry names like Rose Lawn, Rose Dale and Rose Crest in order to sweeten their somber atmosphere.

Love for the rose has carried it into the names of many plants, such as Rockrose, Rose of Sharon, Rose de Montana and many others, none of which are in any way related to the rose. Even the very attractive Christmas rose is a hellebores, and the Confederate rose is a hybiscus.

## WHEN YOU ENTER A STORE

You may ask for a rose when you buy a rosette for your shoe, a perforated nozzle for a water pipe, a card for a mariner's compass or a host of other gadgets. Then we have rose slugs, rose rash, rose quartz, rose nails, rose engines, rose burners and a great number of other items identified by the name rose.

Poets have always had a soft spot in their hearts for the rose. The famous Greek poetess Sappho in her writings called it the queen of

8

flowers instead of the king of flowers as it had generally been termed.

All over the world where roses are grown, the rose design has been used to adorn religious vestments. It has been woven into tapestries and inset in stained glass cathedral windows. It has been imprinted in the trappings and regalias of monarchs, potentates and dignitaries. It is universally found in rugs, carpets and other floor coverings, draperies, dress patterns, jewelry, pottery and on down to the lowly match book.

## In Song and Legend

Almost since the beginning of history, the rose has been a symbol of love, charity, friendship and honor. In fact, the rose has always represented the finest and noblest phases of life in all countries.

Thousands of legends have sprung up around the rose, all dealing with acts of kindness or the evidence of love and honor. Most of these legends originated long ago in Europe. But we in this country have our rose legends, too. One deals with the Cherokee Indians, who regard the beauty of all flowers as a reflection of love. This legend tells of a handsome young brave who returned from a hunting trip to find his settlement in ruins and his sweetheart missing. In searching for her, he learned that she had been slain and her spirit had been changed into a beautiful rose. This rose was the ancestor of the lovely Cherokee roses which we find growing along our fences today.

In early days when people had different gods for fire, war, sea, etc., they also had a god of love called Eros, whose name is a rearrangement of the word rose.

Down through the ages the rose has been used as a symbol of secrecy and silence. Until recent years, certain European groups of people wore roses behind their ears to indicate that they heard everything and told nothing. In legislative halls, secret documents were placed under a rose to show that they were confidential. To this day, we use the expression "subrosa," meaning secret or hush-hush.

In early Roman and Grecian days, no festivities were complete without a lavish display of roses. Cleopatra loved the flower, and when she entertained Mark Antony, she had the floor of the great hall covered about 1' deep with rose petals.

Rose water and various medicinal rose concoctions have been "sure cures" for an endless number of ailments, including mental troubles. The basis of some of our highest-priced perfumes today is rose oil, or attar. Since it takes the petals from about 60,000 roses to make one ounce of attar, you can easily see why it is so expensive. Its production is a complicated process requiring careful growing, picking, drying, distilling, etc. A number of European countries manufacture attar, but Bulgaria is considered the largest producer.

Distillers use roses in an emblem advertising their liquor. While it might not always be complimentary, the rose nevertheless represents jollity and good fellowship.

Rose apples, or hips, are supposed to contain 400% more vitamin C than oranges. During World War II, English women and children gathered several hundred tons of rose hips annually to supply vitamin for their soldiers.

Monarchs, kings and other nobility spend fortunes on rose gardens. Napoleon's wife Josephine had the most magnificent rose garden of her time. She imported roses from all rose-growing countries in an effort to have plants of every variety. For hundreds of years, public and private rose gardens have graced every rose-growing country. Many of them are world-famous. A great many castles, cathedrals and ducal estates are richly adorned with them.

Growing rose bushes for the trade is big business in this country. Many rose-growing firms have rose fields containing from 5-10 million plants. Roses represent over 30% of the nursery stock in the United States.

Hybridizers all over the world constantly produce new varieties. This may take 10 years, and cost around $50,000. If and when a hybridizer creates a real top-notcher, a revenue edging up to a million dollars is in sight.

The rose is the national flower of Honduras, Roumania, Bulgaria, Poland, Czechoslovakia, Iran, Turkey, England and there is a campaign on to make it our national floral emblem.

It is not known just how long a rose will live. The oldest rose known today is at Hildesheim, Germany. It is estimated to be about 1000 years old. Geologists tell us that roses were growing on this continent 35 million years ago. The largest rose bush in the world today is at Tombstone, Arizona. The story is that it was planted by a bride from Ireland 50 years ago.

When you take a rose in your hand, take a good look at it and remember that it represents everything beautiful in life. It stands ever-ready to carry your message of love and good will to the farthest corners of the earth.

# Roses Respond
# to the Midnight Sun

Louise M. Marx

Anchorage, Alaska

A LASKA'S PRESENT-DAY rose gardens might well be called "Arteries of New Garden Beauty," for here in Anchorage, where the Chugach mountain range forms an impressive backdrop, grow many of the rose treasures of the north.

A familiar sight in many local gardens is the so-called *Sitka* rose. Its origin still remains a mystery. Old-timers say that a priest brought a rose bush from Russia to Sitka in the early days. He grafted it to a local wild rose bush. From this union grew the rose that we now know as *Sitka*. Its blossoms may be single or double, in colors of pink, deep pink, purple-red or white. The blooms of the single rose seldom last more than a day. Each has an appealing fragrance. Leaves are wrinkled, gray green in color, and grow in sets of seven. The stems are very thorny. *Sitka* is virtually pest-free, and it endures much cold, excessive moisture, dryness, heat and even poor soil. It grows to a height of 6-8'. Large, round, red hips form after the petals fall. I make jam and syrup from them.

The Greater Anchorage area is proud of its five garden clubs which actively promote gardening in the newest state in the Union. An annual mid-August event of great interest to residents and tourists alike is the annual Garden Tour and Flower Show sponsored by the Anchorage Garden Club. Last year, my husband and I opened our garden for the second time to tour visitors. Many rosarians from our sister states (and from other countries) were genuinely surprised to find Hybrid Teas and other less-hardy roses growing here. My favorite Hybrid Tea, *Shades of Autumn,* put on an especially fine show on the day of the tour by partially unfolding many richly-colored buds (trying, it seemed, to convince visitors that "gold grows here").

During the past 10 years, rose enthusiasts have been battling with our local "mother nature" to achieve the so-called impossible by growing less-hardy roses. Tea, Hybrid Tea, Floribunda, Polyantha and Climbing roses are no longer strangers in local gardens.

In the Summer of 1948, my husband and I lived in a small apartment close to downtown Anchorage. The space allotted to me for my gardening projects measured 3′ x 5′. By using 16″ rough boards, my husband built a raised flower bed. Here I planted *Show Girl,* my first Hybrid Tea rose.

By mid-June, *Show Girl* had become the community conversation piece. Friends, neighbors and strangers frequently stopped by to admire her. "Do you mean to say that roses like that grow outdoors in Alaska?" was the question that pleased me most. It created an incentive to grow many other kinds of roses.

Our present home took shape in May, 1951. Before the building debris had been cleared away, *Queen o' the Lakes,* another Hybrid Tea, was displaying an array of velvety red blossoms in her new home along a south wall.

Today, I stop frequently to convince myself that all I see is real. An edging of deep blue lobelia and a backdrop of white gypsophelia set off a mass of exciting blossoms in a long, narrow island of roses, the home of such favorites as *Chrysler Imperial, Eclipse, Peace, New Yorker, The Doctor, Talisman* and *Shades of Autumn.* I added *Nearly Wild,* a Shrub, to my rose family last Spring. Clusters of pink blossoms, centered with white, kept the 2′-high bush covered with color throughout the Summer. The blooms are fragrant, and always the first to be admired by our many visitors.

*American Pillar,* a Rambler, was a St. Patrick's Day gift from friends in Seattle. Planted outdoors in March next to a cement wall, and protected only by newspaper, the small "sprout" adjusted quickly, grew to a height of 3′ and bloomed through September.

Alaska's Midnight Sun shines down from a northern sky all day (and most of the so-called night) during early and mid-Summer. Roses respond to these long hours of daylight and produce exceptionally beautiful flowers and foliage.

The local temperature rarely reaches 80°, even during what we term "hot summer." 55-70° is more like it; ideal, it would seem for growing many shrubs and flowers.

My rose garden enjoys a southern exposure, in position for full morning sun. A growth of spruce trees near the rim of the canyon serves as a windbreak, yet the rose bed enjoys free air circulation.

The top soil in our area is no more than 16″ deep. Sand and

fine gravel lay immediately beneath it. Roses prefer a slightly acid soil, and local gardeners have little trouble in maintaining it. Peat moss is available in great quantities in nearby areas at no cost to anyone who can use a hand-shovel. Most of it is intensely acid. Since it is necessary to remove the soil to a depth of 3' before planting roses, I put the good soil in a wheelbarrow in order to save it for the backfill. I fill the bottom 12" of the hole with a mixture of equal parts of compost and peat moss, followed with about 6" of an equal mixture of sand and loam which I form into a cone-shaped mound that I fit the roots upon. I place the graft union of the rose plant about 1" below the soil level. For the remainder of the backfill, I use a mixture of 1 part peat moss to 2 parts loam, adding 2 cups of bonemeal for each rose plant.

I leave a deep, permanent basin around each plant; equal in size to the anticipated spread of the rose branches, and about 2" deep. The water and fertilizer that I place in this type of reservoir during the growing season seep down directly to the roots of the plant.

There are few cattle raised near Anchorage. The nearest dairy herds are in the Matanuska Valley, 50 miles away. So, cow manure is expensive and often hard to get. Hundreds of gardeners must, of necessity, look to other types of fertilizers to meet their needs. My soil lacks organic matter, so I fill the basins around my rose plants twice a month during June, July and the first two weeks in August with a quart of my basic fertilizer solution which I make by mixing 1 tablespoon of Alaska Fish Fertilizer and 1 teaspoon of Hyponex in a gallon of water. After that, I do not use any kind of fertilizer because our roses have an early bedtime. This food combination has done more for my roses than anything that I have tried in the past.

Our beautiful Alaskan birch trees serve as the breeding and feeding grounds for a well-known brand of "wildlife" called aphids. Home owners who have tried to preserve the native trees and use them in their landscape pattern find it necessary to spray them once or twice during the season with malathion. Then, in order to control the aphids in their gardens, they also have to spray shrubs and flowers weekly all during the Summer. The labor and money involved are no small items. Imported lady bugs appear to be the answer to our aphid problem. During the past Summer, we bought packages containing 30-40,000 of these insect bugs. They did an excellent cleanup job. "Miss Bug" moves on to greener pastures once she has eaten the first crop of insects at home, so gardeners have learned that it is wise to release a thousand or so at a time, and to keep the others in the refrigerator in a dormant condition until needed. When the bugs are exposed to warm air, they become active and start feeding on other insects immediately.

Winter protection for roses is another perplexing problem for far-north gardeners. Some people replace their roses with new ones each year, but this often results in red figures in the garden allotment column. One method is to bury rose bushes each Fall (just before the final hard freeze) in a pre-prepared 2'-deep x 2'-wide trench, with markers at the head and foot for identification in the early Spring. The labor involved discouraged me from using this method a second time, and encouraged me to look for an easier one. Last year, I saved all of my 30 rose bushes by placing 8" cone-shaped mounds of dry sawdust around the base of each bush in the very late Fall, after the ground was firmly frozen. Then I drew the canes as close together as possible and wrapped them well with a heavy-weight foil tied around the bottom and top, leaving a small opening at the top for ventilation so that the canes would not mildew. We had a very mild Winter, however, with the temperature dropping to 22° for a very short period of time in mid-December. Since we know that the freezing and thawing of the soil in early Spring is greatly responsible for most of the winter injury to rose bushes, I believe that this method is the answer to wintering-over our plants safely. The sawdust keeps the ground from thawing too quickly in the early Spring, and helps the roots to remain dormant until the freezing and thawing period is past.

As the ice that forms in the sawdust gradually thawed out, I removed it and the foil. Then I pruned the canes down to the point where they were still showing green. New shoots started to grow quickly, and the rose bushes developed healthy, sturdy canes which produced an abundance of blossoms all Summer.

Tundra meadows and forests are rapidly giving way to hundreds of newcomers. From them, as in the past, we will learn new ideas in gardening technique, and will welcome their new introductions to our local gardens. To have been numbered among the early Alaskan rose pioneers fills me with a deep inner satisfaction and joy. My cherished dream is to have Anchorage become known as the Rose City of the 49th State.

# The Search
# For Better Roses

Dr. Robert N. Stewart and Peter Semeniuk*
Beltsville, Md.

THE Ornamentals Section of the Department of Agriculture's Agricultural Research Service has initiated a long-term project on rose genetics at the Plant Industry Station at Beltsville, Md. Our methods and goals differ in several respects from those of amateur and commercial breeders since we do not intend to put finished varieties on the market in the next few years. Moreover, we are not confining the study to research dealing with the inheritance of fragrance.

Our evaluation of the various organized rose breeding programs now underway elsewhere indicated that modern roses are being adequately-explored for the genetic variations of commercial value that they may contain. The number of seedlings of Hybrid Tea and Floribunda parentage flowered each year probably approaches one million. The great stimulus for this mass breeding and selection is the demand for new outdoor roses for home gardens.

Various factors force hybridizers to use only a limited number of modern roses as parents in their crosses. Commercial breeders and many experiment station workers are under pressure to produce finished products that can be used immediately. Most amateur breeders hesitate to undertake the long program that would be necessary if they were to utilize the various desirable characteristics which many species roses possess. Perhaps the greatest deterrent to their use is the fact that no one knows what to expect from crosses involving them, and has no idea how many generations it would take to transfer these desirable characteristics from species to acceptable and useful garden or greenhouse rose varieties. The polyploidy (large number of chromosomes) of modern roses undoubtedly contributes to some of the sterilities which occur when they are crossed with species roses. This same hybrid, polyploid characteristic of modern roses has made the segre-

---

*Horticulturists, Crops Research Division, Agricultural Research Service, United States Department of Agriculture.

15

gation of genetic characters so complex that no one has been able to describe any clear-cut examples of Mendelian inheritance. Therefore, any prediction of breeding behavior with reference to specific desirable characters is impossible, and so is a breeding program planned on this basis. Because of this situation, the many developments in the science of genetics have had little or no effect on the methods of breeding roses, and modern roses are still the product of the rather old-fashioned method of mass selection.

We are trying to solve these and other problems that confront rose breeders. Perhaps the greatest need is to find new sources of disease and insect-resistant parent stock that have good keeping quality and fragrance.

A second question that we eventually hope to answer is of great theoretical, as well as practical interest. We must find out how genes, identified and described on the basis of their behavior within a single diploid species (one that has twice the normal number of chromosomes), express themselves when introduced into interspecific hybrids (developed by crossing species roses with themselves) and into the complex genetic background of the modern roses.

## Work Well Underway

During the past three years, we have collected species, diploid forms of all kinds and old-fashioned roses from many sources (private collections, experiment stations, arboretums and the wild) and planted them on their own roots so that there will be no problem of the understock sprouting and taking hold. We are now working on problems like pollination control, seed germination, handling seedlings, induction of flowering in seasonal bloomers, embryo culture, inoculations with disease organisms, measuring fragrance, etc.

One of our first steps has been to self-pollinate our roses. Many have proved self-sterile. We are crossing these with their nearest relative. Seedling populations from successful selfing of individuals of the various species are extremely uniform. Several show no obvious variation in populations of 100 or more. However, several instances of segregation into two or three clear-cut classes (including white vs. pink flowers, fused vs. divided style, double vs. single flowers, fragrant vs. non-fragrant flowers, ever-blooming vs. spring-blooming, and dwarf vs. normal habit of growth) have indicated simple Mendelian inheritance of the differences observed. Final proof of this awaits the flowering of at least another generation of seedlings.

Where we find parallel variation in two species that will cross, we want to see whether the similar characters in the two species are due to the same gene (in other words, whether inheritance is the same in hybrids as in the parent species). We have done this in only a very few genera, and found only one clear-cut case where genes in two different species were actually the same. We must extend this work with diploid forms (in which inheritance is still relatively simple) before we can tackle the complex problem posed by the polyploid Hybrid Teas and Floribundas whose parentage involves as many as seven or eight species.

## KEEPING BLACKSPOT ALIVE

We are presently working on the problem of maintaining cultures of blackspot fungus in a virulent (live) condition over a period of time, since in order to breed for blackspot resistance, we must be able to maintain the individual races of the causal fungus in an unchanged state over a good many years so that we can test inheritance of any resistance we may find in successive generations. We are anxious to test every seedling that we raise against a representative sample of races of the blackspot fungus. A number of Dr. W. R. Jenkins' cultures are still viable and produce abundant spores in test tubes. But, the spores either do not germinate on rose leaves, or the germination tubes do not penetrate the leaves. Dr. Jenkins used these cultures four years ago to show that there are many different kinds of blackspot, just as there are many different kinds of colds. We are anxious to use these races since we already know quite a bit about their host range. In some experiments, giving the spores various cold treatments during and before inoculation showed some promise. However, since the virulence (ability to produce a disease) is greatly diminished, we are gathering new isolates from roses grown in different parts of the country and planning to store them under different conditions and on different media to see whether we can maintain virulence as well as viability. A second possible way to keep a continuous supply of virulent inoculum of the same races is to re-isolate and identify each one by testing against a constant host spectrum each year.

Our first problem in respect to fragrance has been to develop a measuring system for this elusive character. At this point, we are relying on a "fragrance panel" of two (the authors). We agree about 95% of the time, and our differences are only slight. We are not trying to differentiate the thousand and one qualities in fragrance that have been ascribed to roses, but are gradually educating our noses and preparing a "scent chart" of everblooming plants which possess the distinct qualtities that we begin to recognize. On several occasions, we took six or eight roses to local garden clubs and asked each member to rate them as "very fragrant, slightly fragrant or not fragrant." We chose roses which were either very fragrant or not fragrant to us to use. Approximately 80% of the people in these groups put each rose tested at the same end of the scale (15% put it in the middle, and 5% at the other end). So, we have always agreed with the majority (except in the cases where we included a *Sutter's Gold* with the petals removed. Only a few garden club members have ever called this rose fragrant, but it is very fragrant to us). We must face the fact that however fragrant a rose may be, 5-10% of the people will not be able to smell it. People differ in their ability to smell, just as they do in their ability to taste.

Self-pollinations of both fragrant and non-fragrant Floribundas and Hybrid Teas have produced both fragrant and non-fragrant seedlings in the first generation. Many of these first-generation plants have proved self-sterile. However, we did get several different second-generation progenies from *Ma Perkins*. These have been just as variable as the previous generation, so we conclude that fragrance in Hybrid Tea and Floribunda roses is determined by the interactions of a number of genes.

The real question is whether the answers to our current rose problems may be found in the present-day varieties. No rose will grow well in all parts of the country unless you follow a regular and thorough pest control program. Nearly all varieties could be improved with respect to fragrance and cut-flower keeping quality. If all the characters needed to make an "ideal" rose are scattered through the modern varieties, then the commercial breeders are doing everything possible to get the right combination.

We feel that major improvement must come from germ plasm or breeding material which is not now being utilized. We are looking for this, and trying to find out how to use it when and if we do find it.

# Rose Growing in Hawaii

Amy Greenwell

Captain Cook, Hawaii

I am a nut! So is every other rose grower in the Hawaiian Islands! I learned this not-so-astounding fact through correspondence with a well-known California rosarian. She got the word from her brother who lives on the island of Maui. There are times when I think his is too mild a term to describe rose growers in Kona on the island of Hawaii!

Kona is on the steeply-sloping west side of the largest island of the group. It is sheltered from the strong prevailing north-east trade winds by the enormous 13,000 foot bulk of the active volcanic mountain, Mauna Loa. This, in combination with one taller and two smaller mountains, gives Kona a climate that has the Weather Bureau forecasters fascinated. They always guess incorrectly!

We normally have beautiful dry, cool days from October to April. The rest of the year is cloudy, warm and wet. We depend on Summer rains to give us our water supply, which we must catch off our roofs and store in tanks or cisterns. The past two years have been very dry, and those of us who have access to brackish water wells have been more than fortunate. Most of Kona's population lives at an elevation of 1300-1500', two to four miles from the ocean. Our average rainfall is 60-80". The soil is produced from lava flows, ranging from recent to very ancient ones, which decompose to form humusy clay.

Wind is not usually a problem in Kona. Mauna Loa protects us and gives us gentle land and sea breezes. However, to keep up her reputation at the Weather Bureau, she sometimes gives Kona private gales like one we had last Summer. We were relieved that a tropical storm had passed us by with only fog. The fog lifted late in the day to expose a white ocean below us. Mauna Loa caused the wind to backlash. In 10 minutes, the gale struck and lasted for over three hours. The next morning, I found my anticipated rose show strewn everywhere; 10-12' Hybrid Perpetual canes were entangled with each other, and leaves and thorns were stripped off.

Worst of all, salt spray had blown up from the ocean, burning leaves and killing young shoots. Winter storms bring strong winds, but if we prune our bushes and allow the wood to harden, little damage is done.

One peculiar Kona problem (and one I haven't had to cope with as yet, but know that I will have to sooner or later) is a lava flow. No one can definitely state where the flow will originate, or what its path will be, but the most frequent location for the past 100 years has been some miles south of central Kona. Anything in its way is destroyed. If the flow reaches the ocean, vast columns of sulphurous, salty steam rise and blanket the land with a plant-killing smog. Our native plants are not injured, but all "exotics" are defoliated or killed by this acid cloud.

The steep rocky slope with its odd weather pattern and climate proved to be ideal for coffee (not roses), so all life here revolves around its culture. But, 100 years ago (before coffee got the upper hand), every home was surrounded with rose bushes whose parents came from China, New England and Europe on the hundreds of sailing ships which put into Hawaii. You can still see remains of some of these hardy shrubs bursting colorfully out of great tangles of grass and weeds along the highway.

## COFFEE BROUGHT THE TEA

With the advent of the coffee industry came the Hybrid Tea rose and improved living standards. Soapy bath, laundry and dish water began to flow underground instead of over the roses. Beetles, grasshoppers, red spiders, aphids, rose chafers, blackspot and mildew found the Hybrid Teas more succulent than the old roses, especially without the soap flavor. Roses which could not be moved died, and so did interest in growing them until after World War II when DDT was put on the market. Now, interest increases with every new chemical, and Kona will soon be decorated with roses again.

Before my mother's bushes died completely, she dug them up in 1928 and moved them to our newly-built mountain cabin at 5000′ elevation where insects are few and far between. Today, 31 years later, they are producing one of their best displays of bloom in spite of virtually no care and absolutely no spray.

I built my house six years ago on a weedy ¾-acre lot. I had been told that roses would not grow in my locality, and not to waste

TAPESTRY HT
Gladys Fisher; introduced Conard-Pyle Co., West Grove, Pa. Described page
257.

WHITE QUEEN HT
E. S. Boerner; introduced Jackson & Perkins, Newark, N.Y. Plant patent 1762.
Described page 259.

money on expensive imports as they would only last for a year or two. Nevertheless, I wanted to use them in the five-year landscaping plan that I had in mind. The first two roses that I planted (*Soeur Therese* and *Mme. Cochet-Cochet*) looked like horrid, waxed five-and-ten cent store specimens. At this crucial period of their lives, I took an extended trip of one and a half years. When I returned, the two bushes were flourishing and covered with blossoms, much to my surprise.

## START WITH OLDER ONES

That Fall, I took the plunge and ordered a catalog from a nursery specializing in old roses. I thought that they would be hardier and less demanding of my time, especially as my five-year plan progressed. I have found this true, but since I do like having Hybrid Teas in the house, I have set aside an easy-to-care-for section for them.

My first order arrived in March, coinciding with the normal beginning of the rainy season. We had had no rain during the previous month, and none was yet in sight. To conserve water from my nearly-emptly tank, I planted *Mrs. John Laing, Paul Neyron, American Beauty* and *Red Favorite* together instead of in their planned locations. Close by were my new red, orange and yellow daylilies. This planting remains intact today. It is a very gay, though unorthodox one, and is definitely improved by volunteer browallia and nigella among the lilies. Now I order one color at a time.

The following year I planted in January, February, March and April. The Winter was even drier than the previous one, but by that time I was on a brackish water line. The young bushes of the first three months' plantings started their Kona life on water containing 100 parts of salt per thousand, and they did very well! The April bushes drank pure rain water and did much better, though.

I have to use fresh water for spraying since the brackish mixture is salty enough to burn the leaves. Dry weather brings mildew and grasshoppers. Our local stores have none of the new mildew preparations, because coffee is not troubled with this disease. Dusting or spraying with wettable sulphur (the only available control here) burns the leaves. The only remedy is to remove all diseased leaves. That is a nasty job to perform on a robust Damask or Moss! DDT and malathion quickly control the grasshoppers.

Winter is mulch time. Coffee husks are good for our rocky land;

they will form new soil in time as they sift between the stones. They do keep the ground from becoming too wet, and do an excellent job of keeping down weeds, but their fungus threat diminishes their value as a mulch for me. Too, they are worse than useless on real loam, since they pack down and only permit a little moisture to permeate (even from a 2" cloudburst). Since I have good soil and no rocks, I use a good top dressing of chicken manure covered with wood shavings or sawdust. The sawdust keeps raindrops from spattering on the low leaves, and does not mold the way that coffee husks do.

## LOADED WITH ORGANICS

With the rainy season (beginning with two solid weeks of fog and drizzle) come blackspot, thrips, beetles, weeds and malnutrition. The copper and sulphur sprays I had been using were worthless. Until I found a tiny expensive packet of captan on the store shelf last Summer, I was on the verge of giving up. With my every-other-day spraying program, I soon bought up every package of captan in the district. Once I finally controlled the blackspot and saved the bushes, I relaxed. Then, to my horror, all of the hard-fought-for new leaves turned to lace. So, I added DDT to my weekly captan spray. To keep red spiders from taking over, I add malathion to the spray every other week. Some of my neighbors who have only a few bushes go out each night with a flashlight to catch and squash the beetles. Another lives near a streetlight, and therefore does not have this problem since the pest only eats between 6 and 10 p.m. Nothing can be done about the thrips, but their worst damage is done only at the beginning and the end of the wet season.

June, July and August are our wettest months. The plants literally grow overnight; and so do the weeds. With all this active growth from 1" or more of rain a week (or even a day), the bushes get hungry far sooner than those growing in an area which must be irrigated. I live on a cattle ranch, and have found from sad experience that pasture grass takes over the garden enriched with the best organic fertilizers. The only reasonable fertilizer that we have is called "Koffee Grower" (a 10-10-10, which could be nicknamed "Rose Grower"). I feed my established plants about two cupfuls, and recently-planted ones one handful each month in ever-widening diameters to lure their feeder roots outward. In the middle of the month, I add foliar fertilizer to the spray and hope that the roots can get some benefit as it washes off if the leaves cannot consume it before the afternoon's rain.

August and September are the months to prowl abandoned house sites for old rose cuttings. Chinas and Hybrid Chinas are the most common. Green roses (*Rosa chinensis viridiflora*) are found only in cultivated gardens, but are still cherished for some reason. This rose has a very melodic hula song written about it—far lovelier than the flower itself! Another old favorite, and possibly the earliest rose in Hawaii, is *Rosa damascena*. It was brought in about 1800 by Spanish cowboys who came to teach Hawaiians to wrangle cattle. The standard Hawaiian cowboy uniform used to include a fresh lei, or wreath of these "Castillian" roses every day. This pretty custom has unfortunately died out, except for rare festive occasions. There are many other old roses that I am trying to identify as I see them, but I still have no idea of many of their names.

## CATALOGS ARE LITTLE HELP

Aside from the usual and unusual problems we have in Kona, the last one is shared by all Hawaiian rosarians; choosing varieties and ordering them. Without the benefit of any public or private rose gardens to view, we are at the complete mercy of catalogs. Roses either are all-too-frequently described in Hollywoodian terms, or are so well-known and satisfactory on the mainland that the description merely reads "pink," or "old favorite." We are left to wonder why the rose is so special. That happened to me with *White Knight,* and to a neighbor with *Careless Love*. Nevertheless, if they produce enough flowers to make spraying worthwhile, we keep them and hope that they will improve with age.

The thrill and anticipation of ordering roses is also sometimes dulled by a polite form letter from the nursery stating that it sells its bushes only in the United States. We Hawaiians do not like being considered "foreigners" (after all, we have been part of the Union for the past 60 years), so if we can curb our indignation enough to write back that we **are** a part of the United States, we find that apologies are in order because that particular rose has sold out, "but please do not hesitate to order early next year." We do that and go through the same rigamarole again! On the whole, though, our experience has been more than pleasant. Most nurseries write us special notes inquiring about their plants on arrival and

later. I have had, and will continue to have considerable correspondence as result of my orders.

## CHINAS ARE BEST

The Chinas are, of course, among my most satisfactory roses.
Miniatures and Polyanthas are great favorites, and do very well.
Harsh-leafed Hybrid Perpetuals, like *Paul Neyron* and *Mrs. John
Liang,* fare better against the beetles than soft-leafed varieties, but
they all do very well as far as vigor is concerned. Hybrid Teas
definitely need more attention, but they are well-worth the bother
as they produce flowers for cutting all year. So far, the best
of these are: *Nocturne, Soeur Therese* (if mine isn't a mislabeled
*Peace*), *Lady Elgin, Tiffany, Forty-niner, Dean Collins, Grey Pearl,
Peace* and *The Doctor.* Grandifloras *Queen Elizabeth* and *Montezuma* are fine. I think that Floribundas are not grown because at
least three are needed to make a decent showing. We would rather
dig three holes in the rocks for three different varieties than for
three identical unknowns which we may not like. Damasks do very
well. So do Hybrid Musks. *Cardinal Richelieu* has proven to be
the hardiest of all varieties—untouched by insects and blackspot.
My other Gallicas were almost lost from blackspot. Many more
roses should do well here. It only takes some trial and error, plus
some extra cash and a love for experimenting with different types
and varieties to discover them. If a variety likes Kona, we are more
than rewarded for our efforts.

It does seem idiotic to struggle with too much and too little rain,
too many insects and fungus diseases, rocks and possible lava flows,
to say nothing of ordering blindfolded. I guess we are nuts! But,
after reading innumerable articles on growing roses elsewhere, I
wonder if we Hawaiians are the only ones?

By the way, who can tell me where to find the rose *Mauna Loa?*

# What I Look For In Roses

## Mrs. Nat Schoen
## Vancouver, Wash.

Roses can "fill the bill" in your garden, whatever the landscaping problem, *if* you select them with a definite purpose in mind.

In the past decade or so, great strides have been made in developing rose types for every conceivable purpose, and for every type of climatic condition. If you find less than complete satisfaction with the results obtained in your own garden, it may well be the fault of your selection rather than roses as a whole. With over 6,000 varieties in commerce, it is not surprising that a rosarian could err in making the proper selection. However, there are certain basic features to look for in each type which will create a garden of great beauty and infinite satisfaction.

Before you order any plants, spend some time studying the needs of your particular garden. First, figure out the types of roses that you need for mass planting, edging the walks, shrubbery background, ground cover and, of course, roses for the display garden.

Now let's set down the minimum requirements for each of these types of roses. Keep all of them in mind and ask your rose-growing friends and local nurserymen specifically about them when you make your purchase. You will eliminate many disappointments.

### FLORIBUNDAS FOR MASS

In the order mentioned, Floribundas provide the most satisfaction for mass plantings if they are carefully selected (or the most disappointment when carelessly purchased). Consider the economic standpoint; since these roses are usually purchased in groups of 3-30 or more, an error can prove costly. What should Floribundas provide? (1) They should be free-blooming. We plant them for abundant color, and that doesn't mean just in June and September. (2) They should clean themselves well. The petals should drop as they fade, leaving the plant attractive while new blooms form. We do not mind clipping spent Hybrid Tea blooms, since this operation does not require a great deal of time, but if we have to clean myriads of withered blooms from masses of Floribundas, we soon find our interest as dulled as our shears. This is perhaps one of the most important factors to look for in a Floribunda. (3) Colors should be clean and hold well in sun or rain. Burnt reds, faded oranges or weak yellows add nothing to the garden and leave the rosarian discouraged with roses in general. With so many varieties in every color class to choose from, it is not hard now to find the desired color with the stability needed for whatever climate in which you live. (4) For mass planting, we need plants which are well-branched and regular in growth habit. Long arching trusses or sprawling canes have no place in this type of planting. (5) Last of all, the foliage should be attractive and disease-resistant. Rosarians will devote unlimited effort to spraying the exhibition prima donnas, but resent having to take more time to keep the Floribunda beds healthy and attractive. This factor must be "built-in."

Floribundas also play an important role as edging. Choose varieties for this purpose which have a very compact growth habit. If they must be constantly pruned to keep within bounds, they will produce little bloom and lose their purpose in the garden. Varieties which are fairly dwarf in some areas may not prove compact enough for this purpose in others. Some of the Miniature varieties serve better in these cases.

## Grandifloras in Back

Grandifloras come into their own in the background. The tremendous vigor of these roses accompanies that of the shrubbery. Since the classification is left to the introducer, it is up to us to check carefully to see if the varieties truly measure up to what we have come to expect of the class. They must be free-blooming, disease-resistant and carry their blooms in long-stemmed trusses. Lower growing, bushier types are better-suited to the specimen beds in many cases.

Some of the outstanding older types (such as the Rugosas) also fit well in the shrubbery background. The lovely foliage and repeat-blooming habit of several of these roses lends them well to base plantings as well. Overlooked by many rosarians, these so-called "old roses" have much to offer. Some of the Hybrid Rugosas produce golden foliage in the Fall to add additional color in the garden when it is so much appreciated. A colorful array of large rose hips is an extra bonus that these types provide.

## GROUNDCOVERS OVERLOOKED

We haven't heard much about varieties that are suitable as ground covers. Where the climate permits, nothing could be lovelier than *Mermaid,* that golden-yellow single Climber, trailing over an embankment. Look for plants that require little pruning or personal attention, since they may be nearly inaccessible. They should be somewhat remontant (repeat-blooming) and have attractive foliage (probably glossy for the best effect). If they insist on sending out stiff upright canes that require pegging down, they are not proper subjects for this purpose.

Now for the "meat" of the subject, the display garden. Let's divide this into two types to help us ease the job of selection: decorative and exhibition-type roses. While it is possible (and usually desirable) to have a combination of both factors in one variety, it is not always essential. Remember that even though some varieties in question will produce few blooms or poor plants, they may be outstanding for exhibition.

From the standpoint of the average rose enthusiast, the ideal Hybrid Tea should have the following desirable qualities: good color stability, disease resistance, attractive foliage, freedom of bloom and the ability to produce roses suitable for decoration in the garden and home (and at least an occasional one of exhibition quality). It seems like too much to hope for all these, but they are now within the realm of possibility.

In making selections, it is most important to first know the problems of your own climatic conditions. There is no universally-perfect rose. Even the best or most popular ones find unhappy homes in certain areas. If you know in advance what some of your local conditions require, you can safely eliminate trouble-makers. For example, heavy-petalled varieties do not open well in areas which have considerable rainfall throughout the growing season. The shape, as well as the number of petals determines a rose's ability to open well. Roses with long overlapping petals will pack together and form a sodden mass when they are wet. Where these conditions do not exist, this type unfurls its petals beautifully. Certain colors do not develop properly under these same conditions. Peach and apricot tones look dismally buff in many instances. Where Summers are long and hot, brilliant fleeting colors are not worth growing. Under these same conditions, varieties with only a few petals will "blow" almost before opening. There are exceptions, of course, but generally these facts hold true. Some sections of the country have special fungus disease problems (for instance, rust). If yours is one, bypass those varieties which have proved definitely susceptible and pick one of a similar type which does not carry this characteristic.

## PICK RIGHT LOCATION

The location of your garden as related to sun and shade should also help in determining your choice. Some roses perform to perfection in full sun. Others give best results only when they receive a bit of afternoon shade. These are questions to which you need answers before you make an investment in garden beauty by purchasing roses. Personal observation, plus the advice of local rosarians (both professional and amateur), will provide the answers to nearly every problem. Once you are aware of these regional factors, selection becomes considerably simpler.

Now decide what you expect your roses to do for you. If you belong to the majority who want both decorative and exhibition blooms on the same plant, avoid those varieties labelled "for the exhibitor only." Catalogs are an excellent source of information. Keep in mind, however, that the colors illustrated may not coincide with those produced in your own garden. Some information regarding plant habit and flowering may be included, but only enough to make a list of suggested varieties. Check this later with local results in nearby gardens.

Be sure to pay attention to height and plant habit when you lay out your display garden beds (unless you don't mind constantly changing the position of plants later on).

Now you can see that any complete list of satisfactory varieties for every use is impossible. I will suggest a few in each category, however, which have proved themselves most adaptable throughout the country.

## Roses for Mass Plantings

| | |
|---|---|
| Little Darling | Floribunda |
| Circus | Floribunda |
| Ivory Fashion | Floribunda |
| Red Wonder | Floribunda |
| Cocorico | Floribunda |
| Pinkie | Floribunda |

## Roses for Borders

| | |
|---|---|
| China Doll | Floribunda |
| Chatter | Floribunda |
| Garnette | Floribunda |
| Josephine Wheatcroft | Miniature |
| Margo Koster | Polyantha |

## Roses for Ground Cover

| | |
|---|---|
| Mermaid | Climber |
| Max Graf | Hybrid Rugosa |
| Creeping Everloom | Shrub |
| Little Compton Creeper | Large-flowered Rambler |

## Roses for Shrubbery Borders and Background

| | |
|---|---|
| Queen Elizabeth | Grandiflora |
| Audie Murphy | Hybrid Tea |
| Montezuma | Grandiflora |
| Carrousel | Grandiflora |
| Blanc double de Coubert | Hybrid Rugosa |
| Governor Rosellini | Grandiflora |

## Roses for Display Gardens
(produce both decorative and exhibition bloom)

| | |
|---|---|
| Peace | Hybrid Tea |
| Eclipse | Hybrid Tea |
| Charlotte Armstrong | Hybrid Tea |
| Pink Favorite | Hybrid Tea |
| Montezuma | Grandiflora |
| Burnaby | Hybrid Tea |
| New Yorker | Hybrid Tea |
| Tiffany | Hybrid Tea |
| Sutter's Gold | Hybrid Tea |

## Roses for the Exhibitor

| | |
|---|---|
| Sam McGredy | Hybrid Tea |
| Uster Monarch | Hybrid Tea |
| Eden Rose | Hybrid Tea |
| The Doctor | Hybrid Tea |
| Charles Mallerin | Hybrid Tea |
| Show Girl | Hybrid Tea |
| Bridal Robe | Hybrid Tea |

# Garden Roses
# When You Want Them

## Dr. Richard F. Stinson*
## East Lansing, Mich.

GARDEN ROSES usually produce their first flush of bloom during the second week in June in areas having a latitude and altitude similar to that of East Lansing. Few blooms follow this heavy flowering period until late July (about seven weeks later). However, by removing flower buds developing from mid-May until late July on given dates last year, we were able to produce blooms within a few days of a predictable date. This work will help growers who need flowers for display or show competition when unpinched shoots are not ready.

The pinching technique for inducing a heavy crop of greenhouse roses for Christmas, Easter and other holidays has been a standard greenhouse practice for many years,[1,2] but has never been suggested for timing garden roses.

A "soft pinch" is made when you can clearly see the flower bud in its whorl of surrounding foliage by removing the stem tip to the second 5-leaflet leaf. This results in a long straight stem with only a little "tab" to mark the position of the pinch (Figure 1).

Make a "hard pinch" when the bud has emerged from the surrounding leaves and is about the size of a pea, removing the stem tip to just above the second 5-leaflet leaf. A small stem stub remains to mark the position of this "hard pinch" (Figure 2).

When you remove an open flower from a rose plant, leave two 5-leaflet leaves on the plant. The axillary buds will start to grow and produce new flowering shoots which will take as much time to develop blooms as those from a pinch. Therefore, a "cut" is equivalent to a "pinch" for timing purposes. Figure 3 illustrates the stub

Although it takes the same length of time for a flower to develop from a "soft pinch," a "hard pinch" or a "cut," the "soft pinch" leaves an almost-undetectable tab, while the other two methods leave a stub that is usually referred to as a "hook." These "hooks" are especially objectionable if you want extra-long cut flowers.

We "hard pinched" and "soft pinched" and tagged eight varieties

* Assistant professor of horticulture, Michigan State University.
Journal Article 2352, Michigan Agricultural Experiment Station, East Lansing, Mich.

**Figure 1.**

"Soft pinch" and effect. Right: Remove stem tip just above second 5-leaflet leaf when flower bud is visible. Left: Resulting straight stem with tab at point of pinch.

**Figure 2.**

"Hard pinch" and effect. Right: Remove stem tip just above second 5-leaflet leaf when flower bud is pea-size. Left: Resulting small stub remains at the point of pinch.

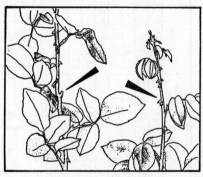

**Figure 3.**

Result of a "cut." When fully-developed flower is removed, new shoot develops with a heavy stub at base.

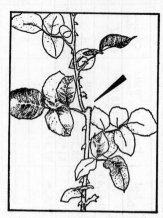

## TABLE 1. Garden Roses; Days to Flower From Bud Removal Date

| Date bud removed | Varieties | | | | | | | | Average days to bloom | Average days to bloom by types | | | Pinch to-bloom groups |
|---|---|---|---|---|---|---|---|---|---|---|---|---|---|
| | Red Duchess | Konrad Adenauer | White Swan | Comtesse Vandal | Queen Elizabeth | Rounde-lay | Spartan | Ma Perkins | | Hybrid Tea | Grandi-flora | Flori-bunda | |
| May 19 | | | 48,86* | 47,47 | | 47 | 48,45,45 | 48 | 47 | 48 | 47 | 47 | |
| May 26 | 40,42,43 | 43 | | | 35,43,54* | 45,42,42 | 41,41 | 46,48 | 43 | 42 | 52 | 45 | 45 days |
| June 2 | | | 40,39 | | 43,44 | | 42,42 | | 42 | 40 | 44 | 42 | |
| June 9 | 38,38 | 38,38,38 | 37,b,b | 54,57 | 52,b | 37,b,b | 32,32,38 | 47,b,b | 41 | 42 | 45 | 37 | |
| June 16 | 39,49 | 51*58* | b,b,b | 38,38,38 | | 37,38,b | 51*56*55*R | 49,56* | 41 | 40 | 38 | 49 | 41 days |
| June 23 | 37,53* | 37,37 | 38,41,b | 31,35 | 32,36,b | 42,b,b | 44,b | | 37 | 37 | 37 | 44 | |
| June 30 | 31 | | | | 35,44,53* | | | 38,38 | 37 | 31 | 40 | 38 | |
| July 7 | | | | | 51* | | | 37,37,43 | 39 | | | 39 | 36 days |
| July 14 | 32,32 | | 35,35,39 | 32 | 38,38,38 | 30,30,32 | | 38 | 35 | 34 | 34 | 38 | |
| July 21 | 28,50,26 | 41,80* | 32,38,b | 23,40 | 38,43,43 | 49 | | 43,89* | 38 | 35 | 43 | 43 | |
| July 28 | 18,23,38 | 30,b | b | 32,37,71* | b | 38,b | 54*83*b | b | 31 | 30 | 38 | | |
| Aug. 4 | 51,43,82* | 38,38,39 | b | 37,37,74* | 64,73* | 39 | 35,69*b | 49,50,74* | 44 | 42 | 52 | 45 | 44 days |
| Aug. 11 | 45,45,59 | 59,59 | 62 | 43,43,56 | 64 | 44,57,67 | 49,57,65 | 65,b,b | 55 | 52 | 58 | 59 | |
| Aug. 18 | 51,52,59 | 52,59,b | 51,51,60 | 44,60 | 57,57 | 52,53,60 | 56 | 53,b | 55 | 44 | 56 | 55 | 55 days |

*-omitted from averages, unusual delay; b-blind shoots; R-severe red spider infestation.

## TABLE 2. Garden Rose Flowering Timetable

| Week of bud or flower removal | May 3rd week | May 4th week | June 1st week | June 2nd week | June 3rd week | June 4th week | July 1st week | July 2nd week | July 3rd week | July 4th week | July 5th week | Aug. 1st week | Aug. 2nd week | Aug. 3rd week | Aug. 4th week |
|---|---|---|---|---|---|---|---|---|---|---|---|---|---|---|---|
| Week of flowering of pinched shoot | July 1st week | July 2nd week | July 2nd week | July 3rd week | July 3rd week | July 4th week | July 5th week | Aug. 1st week | Aug. 2nd week | Aug. 3rd week | Aug. 4th week | Sept. 3rd week | Sept. 4th week | Oct. 2nd week | Oct. 4th week |

of Hybrid Teas, Grandifloras and Floribundas at weekly intervals during the Summer of 1958. We tried to make three pinches on each variety each week, but in some instances there were insufficient buds at the right stage for pinching. Then we recorded all flowering dates.

The results are presented in Table 1. Some shoots took unusually long to develop blooms. In an effort to include as many shoots as possible, we pinched some weak shoots (these were the ones that developed slowly). This points out the importance of using only strong shoots on healthy plants for timing purposes.

The delaying effect of a heavy red spider infestation is seen in the June 16 pinching of the Floribunda *Spartan*.

Some varieties showed a marked tendency to produce blind (non-flowering) shoots.

Unusual weather conditions may cause deviations from the expected time of flowering. Cool weather extends it, hot weather decreases it.

Timing for Fall flowering is less precise than during the Summer.

All three types of roses required about the same length of time to produce blooms from a pinch. The pinch-to-flower time for May pinches was about 45 days; for the first three weeks in June, 41 days; for late June through late July, 36 days; for the first week in August, 44 days; and for the second and third weeks in August, 55 days. Pinches made the third week in August produced flowers in mid-October—past the date that rose blooms are usually destroyed by a hard frost in East Lansing. Flowers bloomed within four days (plus or minus) of the average number of days for the "pinch-to-bloom group" to which they belong. This indicates that if you pinch shoots on Wednesday of a certain week, you can reasonably expect these shoots to flower during the week in which the predicated date would fall.

By using Table 2, you can determine the appropriate pinching date for producing flowers any week from the first of July through the last of August. For example: if you want to have an especially-large number of blooms during the third week in July, pinch all shoots in either the "soft pinch" or "hard pinch" stages on Wednesday of the third week in June.

[1] Laurie, A., D. C. Kiplinger and K. S. Nelson, Commercial Flower Forcing, McGraw-Hill, New York, 1958.
[2] Post, K., Florist Crop Production and Marketing, Orange Judd, New York 1949.

# Growing Roses in North Dakota

Ester A. Schrimpf
Fargo, N. D.

I N my travels about this great country of ours, I have found that many people think of North Dakota as a very cold and unpleasant place to live. When I tell them that we often cut roses late in October, they don't believe me. True, we often have very cold Winters, but our Fall season is unsurpassed. Our September bloom is really remarkable.

We live in what is known as the Red River Valley, where the soil is the best in the world. It is a little on the heavy side, though, so I add compost to break it up. An unused fish pool behind two big evergreens makes an ideal place for my compost site. Into this goes everything from the yard: leaves, vegetable scraps and tops and grass clippings.

## 15 Years of Experience

I have grown roses for the past 15 years or so, and have about 100 bushes and a few Climbers. They perform better each year as I learn more about them. Most of my Hybrid Teas grow to a height of 5-6' and often produce several dozen blooms and buds at one time. Floribundas do very well too, as do the newer Grandifloras, which as a rule are taller than any Hybrid Teas. Our blooming season usually gets a good start by the end of June or first part of July. From then on, we have almost-continuous bloom until early October.

Our biggest problem is winterkill. This usually happens in the Spring when we have a few real warm days alternating with freezing weather. If we could just find some way to avoid this, I know that we would not suffer the losses that we do. This factor has discouraged many an enthusiast. As for myself, my plants' performance in a single season is rewarding enough, and I don't feel too badly when I have to replace some of my favorites. On the other hand, I do have a number of hardy roses (including *Fashion* and *Tallyho*) that have survived for 12 years or longer.

In the Spring, I keep my protective cover on well into April, since this is that tricky time of the year when anything can happen. But if I notice new growth, I have to start removing the hay or flax straw mulch. Later, I remove the soil hill, usually by easy stages.

Once the weather has settled, I cultivate lightly and work in some complete plant food around each plant. I also start my spray program early and try to spray every two weeks (or oftener if I notice thrips).

## WATER SUPPLEMENTS RAIN

If we don't get enough rain, I give my roses plenty of water (in the morning so that the plants will dry in the sun).

This past Summer, I mixed a foliar fertilizer in with the spray, and did the two jobs of fertilizing and controlling pests at the same time. I do believe that my plants were taller and huskier than in the past, and this foliar feeding program may have been a contributing factor. I stop feeding about the middle of August as I want my plants to harden early if possible.

As soon as our nights are cool, we start having trouble with blackspot and mildew. I have not found a spray that will stop blackspot, but am glad to notice that some roses are not as susceptible to it as others.

## EASE OFF IN SEPTEMBER

I ease off on the watering in September, too, since we usually get plenty of Fall rain (which often makes it hard to get the hilling and covering done when it should be). I try to finish hilling about the middle of October, and then wait until we have had a few real hard freezes before I put a mulch cover on. Then I can say "adieu" to my roses for another season.

It is a constant source of pleasure to grow this wonderful flower for the home, to give to friends and neighbors and to use in arrangements and flower show competitions. I do have many other flowers, but the roses are by far my favorites.

What pride I assume when friends come to see what's growing in my back-yard. I hope that I will continue to be curious, for in that way I may discover an easier way to grow roses in this wonderful far-north-state, and encourage others to do likewise.

# 1958 Fungicide and Insecticide Tests on Garden Roses

Dr. L. M. Massey, J. S. Melching
and Dr. J. A. Naegele*

Ithaca, N. Y.

W E conducted fungicide and insecticide tests in the Cornell University rose garden again in 1958.[1]

Because of winter injury to the old rose bushes, we set new plants in 10 beds last Spring to provide a uniform vigorous planting for testing. Four beds (labeled "A") contained 12 plots each. The remaining six beds (labeled "B" and "C") each contained 10 plots. A plot consisted of 18 individual plants; three each of the following six varieties: *Goldilocks, Kaiserin Auguste Viktoria, Diamond Jubilee, Crimson Glory, Pinocchio* and *President Herbert Hoover.* The field plan (Table 1) shows how we arranged the plots at random within the beds. We repeated treatments in the A beds four times, and in the B and C beds three times.

## FERTILIZATION

Before planting, we applied 20 pounds of 6-6-6 mineral fertilizer and spread barnyard manure on each bed, then mixed it in thoroughly with a Rototiller. We added 20 more pounds of the 6-6-6 fertilizer to each bed at mid-season.

## INOCULATION

We used the same inoculation method as in 1957, putting blackspot fungus spores in the A beds on July 31, in the B and C beds on August 1 and again in the A, B and C beds on both August 5 and 23. We noticed a natural infection of powdery mildew in all untreated control plots by July 20. This disease continued to spread and intensify in most of the beds throughout the season. We grew bean plants in the greenhouse and infested them with two-spotted mites before

* Professor emeritus of plant pathology, assistant in plant pathology and associate professor of entomology, respectively, for the New York State College of Agriculture at Cornell University.

## Table 1

**Field plan of rose garden experimental plots showing plot locations in each bed, and location of beds.**

| Bed B-1 | Bed C-1 | Bed B-2 | Bed C-2 | Bed B-3 | Bed C-3 |
|---|---|---|---|---|---|
| 13 | 24 | 14 | 25 | 20 | 29 |
| 22 | 26 | 18 | 29 | 13 | 23 |
| 15 | 29 | 19 | 32 | 16 | 28 |
| 21 | 30 | 15 | 27 | 17 | 24 |
| 17 | 32 | 21 | 31 | 18 | 27 |
| 19 | 28 | 13 | 24 | 22 | 30 |
| 16 | 31 | 16 | 23 | 19 | 31 |
| 20 | 27 | 22 | 28 | 14 | 32 |
| 18 | 25 | 17 | 30 | 21 | 26 |
| 14 | 23 | 20 | 26 | 15 | 25 |

| Bed A-1 | Bed A-2 | Bed A-3 | Bed A-4 |
|---|---|---|---|
| 2 | 4 | 8 | 6 |
| 5 | 10 | 3 | 1 |
| 12 | 11 | 9 | 7 |
| 7 | 3 | 1 | 4 |
| 9 | 1 | 6 | 5 ——————→ N |
| 1 | 2 | 12 | 8 |
| 3 | 7 | 4 | 9 |
| 6 | 5 | 10 | 3 |
| 10 | 9 | 11 | 12 |
| 8 | 12 | 7 | 2 |
| 4 | 1 | 5 | 10 |
| 11 | 6 | 2 | 11 |

transplanting them into the rose plots (between rose bushes, in contact with the foliage in order to let the mites transfer to the rose plants) about July 15.

Our methods of watering and applying chemicals, the equipment we used and our method of recording data were the same as in 1957.

Because of an unusually cold, wet Spring, the new plants did not produce foliage until relatively late in the season. As a result, we applied the first chemicals on July 4 and 5, and thereafter at approximately 7-day intervals through September 28.

The materials that we tested, and the concentrations at which we applied them are given in Table 2.

The summation of the data taken, and of observations made during the season is given in Table 3. This includes the relative efficiencies of the formulations in controlling blackspot and powdery mildew, along with ratings of plant response to each treatment. The treatments are arranged in descending order according to their ability to control blackspot.

## DISCUSSION

The 1958 growing season in Ithaca was by far the wettest one since we began the current series of tests in 1950. Only the 1956 season could equal this one in coldness.

The artificial blackspot fungus spore inoculations resulted in uniformly-severe infections in the unsprayed plots, and provided a stringent test of the experimental control materials.

There was enough powdery mildew in all the control plots and the A and B beds for us to evaluate the chemicals that we tested for its control. This was the first year we were able to do this. The cooler weather and numerous days of high relative humidity, coupled with the availability of viable mildew spores from the many rose plants in the display garden next to the test plots may explain the prevalence of the disease last year.

On the other hand, the unusually cool season and frequent rains kept two-spotted mites from transferring from the bean to the rose plants, and they caused little or no damage on the roses in the control plots.

Cyprex gave complete control of blackspot and powdery mildew at the two concentrations used (treatments 5 and 6), but we noticed excessive discoloration, severe distortion and stunting after two or

## Table 2

Materials tested on garden roses in 1958.

| Treatment | Material and/or Formulation | Concentration |
|---|---|---|
| 1 | Jackson and Perkins Rose Spray, 1958 formulation | 6#/100 gal. |
| 2 | Phaltan<br>Phosphamidon | 1# Active<br>.5 pt /100 gal. |
| 3 | Phaltan | 1# Active/100 gal. |
| 4 | Phaltan<br>Sticker-spreader | 1# Active<br>.5 pt /100 gal. |
| 5 | Cyprex | 1# Active/100 gal. |
| 6 | Cyprex | 1.5# Active/100 gal. |
| 7 | Maneb | 1.05# Active/100 gal |
| 8 | Zineb | 1.3# Active/100 gal. |
| 9 | Ferbam | 1.14# Active/100 gal. |
| 10 | Maneb (Sprayed in sequence, one following the other at 7-day intervals)<br>Glyodin Acetate<br>Ferbam<br>Zineb<br>Captan | 1.5#/100 gal.<br>1.5 qt./100 gal.<br>1.14# Active/100 gal.<br>1.3# Active/100 gal.<br>1# Active/100 gal. |
| 11 | Maneb<br>Zineb<br>Ferbam | .5# Active<br>.5# Active/100 gal.<br>.5# Active |
| 12 | Untreated control | |
| 13 | Jackson and Perkins Rose Dust, 1958 formulation | Dust |
| 14 | Captan 50% w.p. | 1# Active/100 gal. |
| 15 | Captan 80% w.p. | 1# Active/100 gal. |
| 16 | Aramite 1% Active<br>Lindane .25% Active<br>DDT 5% Active<br>Dieldrin .25% Active<br>Captan 7% Active<br>Karathane .75% Active<br>Soluble carriers A and C | Dust |
| 17 | Same as 16, but Eastern Magnesium Talc substituted for soluble carriers A and C | Dust |

| Treatment | Material and/or Formulation | Concentration |
|-----------|------------------------------|----------------|
| 18 | Aramite 2.5% Active<br>Lindane 2% Active<br>DDT 7.5% Active<br>Dieldrin 1% Active<br>Captan 15% Active<br>Karathane 2% Active<br>Soluble carriers B and C | 6#/100 gal. |
| 19 | Same as 18, but Eastern Magnesium Talc substituted for soluble carriers B and C | 6#/100 gal. |
| 20 | Same as 18, but Kelthane substituted for Aramite | 6#/100 gal. |
| 21 | Same as 16, but Kelthane substituted for Aramite | Dust |
| 22 | Untreated control | |

| 23 | Ferbam | 12% Active | |
|----|--------|-----------|---|
| | Maneb | 3% Active | |
| | Am. Cy. #23441 | 3% Active | |
| | DDT | 5% Active | |
| | Dieldrin | 1% Active | 6#/100 gal. |
| | Diazinon | 5% Active | |
| | Karathane | 2% Active | |
| | Urea | 1% Active | |
| | Aluminum Stearate | .25% Active | |
| | Vatsol OTB | .2% Active | |
| | Carriers | | |

| 24 | Ferbam | 12% Active | |
|----|--------|-----------|---|
| | Maneb | 3% Active | |
| | Urbazid | 3% Active | |
| | DDT | 15% Active | |
| | Dieldrin | 1% Active | |
| | Meta Iso Systox | 3% Active | 6#/100 gal. |
| | Sulfur | 25% | |
| | Aluminum Stearate | .25% | |
| | Urea | 1% Active | |
| | Vatsol OTB | 2% | |
| | Carriers | | |

| 25 | Glyodin Acetate<br>(34% solution) | 44% | |
|----|-----------------------------------|-----|---|
| | Meta Iso Systox | 5% | |

| Treatment | Material and/or Formulation | Concentration | |
|---|---|---|---|
| | Givaudan Cedar | | |
| | Bouquet | 3% | 2 qt./100 gal. |
| | Actidione | .04% | |
| | Emulsol #500 | 10% | |
| | Isopropanol | 40.66% | |
| 26 | Ferbam | 6% Active | |
| | Maneb | 2% Active | |
| | Captan | 3% Active | |
| | Dieldrin | .1% Active | |
| | Kelthane | 2% Active | Dust |
| | Diazinon | 2% Active | |
| | Sulfur | 25% | |
| | Urea | .25% | |
| | Vatsol OTB | .25% | |
| | Carriers | | |
| 27 | Ferbam | 6% Active | |
| | Maneb | 2% Active | |
| | Captan | 3% Active | |
| | Dieldrin | .1% Active | Dust |
| | DDT | 5% Active | |
| | Chlorothion | 5% Active | |
| | Sulfur | 25% | |
| | Urea | .25% | |
| | Vatsol OTB | .25% | |
| | Carriers | | |
| 28 | Glyodin Acetate (34% solution) | | 1.5 qt./100 gal. |
| 29 | Zineb (sprayed according to weather conditions) | | 1.3#/100 gal. |
| 30 | Ferbam | 5% Active | |
| | Kelthane | 1.5% Active | |
| | Malathion | 5% Active | |
| | Zineb | 3% Active | Dust |
| | Karathane | 1% Active | |
| | T.D.E. | 5% Active | |
| | Sulfur | 15% | |
| | Carriers | | |
| 31 | Copper Carbonate | .6# | |
| | Ammonium Hydroxide (sp. gr. .9) | 3 qts. | |
| | Arsenate of Lead | 3# | 100 gal. |
| | Sodium Oleate | 3.9# | |
| 32 | Untreated control | | |

three spray applications. We then cut the dosages listed in Table 2 in half during the latter part of the season and the plants recovered somewhat from these injurious chemical effects and were still disease-free at the end of the season. Further investigation of this material at concentrations ranging from 1/4-3/4 pounds active per 100 gallons seems warranted.

Phaltan (treatments 2, 3 and 4) gave equally-good, nearly-complete control of blockspot and powdery mildew, and we did not notice any adverse chemical effects. Good plant growth was evident in all these plots. However, many people would object to the very heavy white residue which the material leaves. The addition of a small amount (1/4 to 1/2 pound) of ferbam to the spray might reduce this visible residue significantly without affecting the efficiency of the Phaltan.

Treatments 8, 11, 9, 10, 14, 20, 15 and 24 gave good control of blackspot, good or fair control of powdery mildew, and produced no undesirable plant effects. Most of them are single ingredient sprays, containing such fungicides as zineb, maneb, ferbam or captan. It is interesting to note that, although these fungicides are generally not considered particularly effective against powdery mildew, they provided adequate control during this season, while the appearance of a heavy infection of the fungus disease was noted in the unsprayed control plots.

The other formulations did not control blackspot (which is by far the most serious rose disease in this area) satisfactorily last year, although many of them might have been adequate if the weather had been less favorable for disease development.

Thanks to the American Cyanamid Co., California Spray Chemical Co., E. I. DuPont de Nemours and Co., Rohm and Haas Co., Stauffer Chemical Co., and Union Carbide Chemicals Co. for supplying materials for the tests. Also to the Plant Products Corp. for formulating some of the combinations used, and to the Jackson & Perkins Co., Conard-Pyle Co. and Melvin E. Wyant for supplying the new roses for replanting. Grants of $500 from the American Rose Foundation and $400 from the California Spray Chemical Co. covered part of the expense of maintenance, labor and other necessary items.

---

[1] For information on earlier tests in this series, see page 37 of the 1958 American Rose Annual.

## Table 3

Relative Ratings of Materials Tested on Garden Roses—1958

| Treat-ment No. | Disease Control Rating Black Spot | Powdery Mildew | Chemical Injury to Foliage Distortion | Discoloration | Burning | Visible Residue |
|---|---|---|---|---|---|---|
| 6 | Good | Good | Excessive | Severe | Slight | None |
| 5 | Good | Good | Excessive | Severe | Slight | None |
| 7 | Good | Good | None | None | None | None |
| 2 | Good | Good | None | None | None | Very Heavy |
| 4 | Good | Good | None | None | None | Very Heavy |
| 3 | Good | Good | None | None | None | Very Heavy |
| 8 | Good | Fair | None | None | None | None |
| 11 | Good | Good | None | None | None | None |
| 9 | Good | Fair | None | None | None | None |
| 10 | Good | Good | Slight | None | None | None |
| 14 | Good | Good | None | Slight | None | None |
| 20 | Good | Good | Slight | None | None | Slight |
| 15 | Good | Good | None | None | None | None |
| 24 | Good | ....* | Slight | None | None | None |
| 31 | Fair | .... | None | Moderate | Slight | Heavy |
| 29 | Fair | .... | None | None | Slight | None |
| 26 | Fair | .... | None | None | None | Moderate |
| 17 | Fair | Good | None | None | None | Heavy |
| 27 | Fair | .... | Moderate | Slight | Slight | Moderate |
| 19 | Fair | Good | Slight | Slight | None | Slight |
| 23 | Fair | .... | None | None | None | None |
| 1 | Fair | Fair | None | None | None | None |
| 18 | Poor | Good | None | None | None | Slight |
| 13 | Poor | Good | None | None | None | Moderate |
| 21 | Poor | Good | None | None | None | Heavy |
| 28 | Poor | .... | None | None | None | Slight |
| 25 | Poor | .... | None | Slight | None | None |
| 16 | Poor | Good | None | None | None | Moderate |
| 30 | Poor | .... | None | None | None | Slight |
| 22 | Plants | Poor | Poor | None | None | None |
| 12 | heavily | Poor | None | None | None | None |
| 32 | defoliated | .... | None | None | None | None |

*In the beds containing treatments 23 through 32, the incidence of powdery mildew was too slight to provide control evaluations.

# You Can Grow Fine Roses

### A. S. Beinhacker
### Angola, Ind.

WOULD you like to grow beautiful roses? All you need to do to grow prolific plants is follow these simple steps:

First, decide how many rose bushes you wish to plant to start with. Visit the municipal rose garden in your vicinity whenever you can to get acquainted with various varieties and colors of rose plants. You should be able to buy No. 1-quality, three-year-old plants with three to four sturdy branches for about $1.25 each.

There are two types of rose plants: the bush type, which grows to 4' in height; and the climbing type, which grows up to 20'. Plant the bush type in the open, the climber against a wall, pillar, post or fan-shaped trellis that you can spread and fasten the branches to. Rose bushes should have at least six hours of sunshine each day, preferably morning sun.

### CHOOSE YOUR FAVORITES

Decide whether you want June-blooming types like Hybrid Perpetuals, or monthly blooming kinds like Hybrid Teas, which will produce new blossoms from June to November. With these, you can have as many as five crops of bloom in one season. No other flower is so prolific in bloom and beauty. If you live in a cold climate, plant only June-bloomers; they are more likely to survive extremely cold Winters.

Try some of these monthly bloomers. I have tried and tested them for many years. They are prolific and hardy, and have strong disease resistance. *Radiance* (red), *Gruss An Teplitz* (crimson), *Columbia* (pink), *Sunburst* (yellow), *Talisman* (variegated), *President Herbert Hoover* (golden), *Frau Karl Druschki* (white). The June-blooming *Paul's Scarlet Climber* has red blooms. You can buy these varieties in any reliable store selling rose plants.

The best planting time is in the Spring; as soon as the frost is out of the ground, but not later than April 30.

Dig a hole 18″ in diameter and 2′ deep. If you plant more than one bush, space them 18″ apart. If the soil is lumpy, break it up. Place the roots of the rose plant in a bucket of water, then remove the covering under water to keep wind and sun from drying out the fine, sensitive feeder roots. They are the lifelines of the plant. Now remove the rose from the bucket with one hand and lower it into the hole, letting the roots hang loosely straight down until the crown is level with the ground. Fill the hole with your soil mixture, then tramp it down with your foot to remove air pockets in the ground. Pour the bucket of water into the hole slowly until it soaks into the ground. Then add more soil until you have a 2″ mound which will protect the plant until it is established.

## Take Off Your Wraps

Remove this mound when it gets warmer. In the meantime, water every morning for six days. Mount the name plate you receive with each plant on a 2′ stake driven into the ground in front of the plant so you and your friends will have the satisfaction of knowing what you have planted. Then relax and let nature take its course.

As a preventive against disease, use an inexpensive rose dust or spray that you can buy in any store. The directions on the package will tell you when and how to apply it.

Plants, too, must eat to thrive. Spread 5-6 tablespoons of your commercial fertilizer around each plant after each blooming period until October, then stop feeding. Keep it about 2″ from the plant itself, and apply water to soak the fertilizer into the ground close to the feeder roots.

Cultivate the soil after each rain; it helps to let oxygen penetrate into the ground.

Water your plants three times each week, after sunup. Remove the sprinkler, lay your hose on the ground and let the water run until the ground is thoroughly soaked. When foliage is wet, it has a tendency to mildew and blackspot.

Growing roses is a most satisfying back-to-nature hobby. The thrill you feel as you watch the first rose bud develop in the Spring and the glorious colors unfold will compensate you for the small cost and effort you devoted to make this possible.

# The Rosarian's Guide To Birds

## Don Evans
## Overland Park, Kan.

I AM NOT THE KIND of a bird watcher who goes tramping out in the dewey morning with binoculars and notebook to search in covert and swamp for feathered creatures to spy upon.

In fact, I have always watched bird watchers rather closely. Why? Because I'm suspicious of any character who thinks that a bobolink can be as beautiful and thrilling as the bloom of a rose kissed with morning dew. But, in order to watch for the *unfeathered* birds of the garden, you must have something in common with the true birdwatcher: you must know the calls or fieldmarks by which the "birds" that you seek can be identified.

One bird that we all see (although some of us may not have identified him yet) is the **Slippered Grouse**. This bird plants some roses in the Spring, then sits around in his slippers and grouses because they are beset by midge, thrip, blackspot and mildew. His call varies, but it can be recognized by its whining tone.

Here are some of the other birds that haunt the rose garden:

**Scissor-Billed Slasher**—gets his kicks out of pruning his rose bushes Spring, Summer and Fall. His call is "Snip—Snip—Snip."

**Crested Disbudder**—disbuds his roses all Summer long—show season or not. He even takes off a few single buds. He has fine bushes, but not many blooms.

**Oblique Complimenter**—know for his call, "My! You have beautiful roses. But . . ."

**Avid Spadewielder**—digs in his rose bed all the time. He never gives feeder roots a chance to live.

**Red-Billed Hoeswinger**—sub-specie of the above specimen, who digs with a hoe or other sharp instrument.

**Purple Dowager**—thinks the word "society" is *the* important one in the phrase, rose society.

**Grey-Bearded Hasbeen**—won't admit that a good rose has been introduced since 1903.

**Tufted Ribbonsnatcher**—his fieldmark is the ribbons that he carries home from the show. He thinks more of a blue ribbon than of all of the blooms in his garden.

**High-Sounding Phraser**—seldom seen in the garden, but this is the bird who writes the descriptions of roses for the catalogs. To him, all roses are all-time All-Americans.

**Golden-Winged Experimenter** — believes the High-Sounding Phraser. His field mark is his check book.

**Back Row Chatterer**—there is one in every rose society.

**Adept Disorganizer**—too many societies have one of these. He can't lead, and won't follow.

**Needle-Eyed Gadgetfinder**—his fieldmark is the array of tools, trick sprinklers, sprayers and dusters that he has gathered around him.

**Wide-Eyed Believer**—harkens to the call of any fertilizer salesman, and believes any claim he makes, no matter how fantastic.

**Organic Preacherbird**—believes that anything which does not come from a cow or compost heap is bad for everything and everybody.

**Arranging Nestbuilder**—abhors a single rose. Builds "nests" all Summer in all kinds of crockery. He lays no eggs, except when his masterpiece fails to win a blue ribbon.

**Happy Presider**—organizes rose societies, then keeps them running.

**Eager Joiner**—joins every rose society that he can find, but lives in an apartment and grows no roses.

**Five-Toed Color Abhorer**—hates roses of a certain color, and looks askance at any one who does like that color. A sub-specie likes any rose, as long as it is red.

**Silver-Throated Gush**—known by its call, "Oh! Isn't that lovely? What is it—a Rugosa or a rhododendron?

**Gimlet-Eyed Leafpicker**—thinks blackspot will go away if he picks off all of the infected leaves.

**Migratory Lobbysitter**—gathers at each annual convention of the American Rose Society to renew acquaintances and enjoy himself. A real happy bird.

Anyone knows that birds of a feather flock together, and I am happy that I have found so many other birds who loves roses, too.

# Roses For Chicagoland Gardens

### Frank H. Stewart
### Chicago Heights, Ill.

T HIRTY-FIVE million years ago there were roses growing on the earth, according to fossil evidence. They got along without man very well. Everybody has different ideas about their care, but whatever we do to them, they're pretty tough and will likely survive.

Planning should be the first step in starting or adding to rose beds. Suggested methods of planting roses in beds are shown in figures A and B (page 51).

Bushes may be placed 15-72" apart in Chicago. Some varieties get bigger than others, and there is considerable variance in size of plants of the same variety, depending upon sun, soil and culture. I used to plant 18" apart, but I am now using 24" to keep blooms from tangling in other bushes, or being torn by thorns. This is a problem in the Windy City. Some people recommend closer planting for a more solid mass of color, to avoid the sight of bare dirt and to shade the ground in the Summer. On the other hand, in addition to alleviating the tangling and tearing problem, planting farther apart gives each bush more queenly individuality, costs less and provides more "working space" between bushes. Besides, a little well-kept soil or mulch is, in my opinion, attractive between the greenery of the bushes. So, I recommend about 24" between Hybrid Teas, Grandifloras and larger Floribundas; 15" between Floribundas used as a hedge; 6' between Climbers; and 3' between old-fashioned or Shrub roses. However, do anything you want, depending on your own purposes and desires.

Plant your roses where they'll get at least six hours of sun a day. Morning sun is better, as it dries the dew sooner, lessening the opportunities for blackspot. It also is not as hot as the afternoon sun, which causes blooms to fade fast. However, these factors are not all-important, so plant the roses where you have to without worrying.

Drainage is important, but not a problem in most areas around Chicago. If you fill a 12-18" hole with a few buckets of water and the water drains away in a couple of hours, you're all right.

Avoid planting near trees or large shrubs. If you must plant near them, cut the tree roots near the rose bed every Spring and Summer by digging deep with a spade.

Other factors to be considered in your plans are the height and color of the roses. My experience is that you can never be sure about height; so much depends on the location. At least, plant the bushes which are supposed to grow taller in the back instead of the front row.

As to color, most roses harmonize, but be a little careful. For example, a coral-peach *Fashion* is not advisable next to a clear pink *Frolic*. The American Rose Society's Buying Guide indicates the color as well as the height of each modern variety. You'll find plenty of differences of description between various catalogs and publications about this, but what can you expect? In your own yard, color depends on the amount of shade, heat, rain, etc. Two bushes of the same variety planted side by side will even vary greatly. Most authorities recommend planting several reds together, then several yellows, and so on, rather than mixing each color singly. There's nothing wrong with planting one each of a color, however, especially in a small garden. You might be different and have a garden of all white roses. This is very attractive with green grass and a green background, especially at night. But, be sure to use plenty of Floribundas, like *White Bouquet* or *Summer Snow,* as many of the white Hybrid Teas are not prolific bloomers.

All the "modern" roses (Hybrid Teas, Floribundas, Grandifloras) bloom from early June into November in Chicago. Most of the Climbers, old-fashioned, species and Shrub roses bloom only once here, but the abundance and beauty of their June bloom is so great that they deserve a place in your garden.

As you do your planning, also bear in mind your pocketbook, time and, above all, enthusiasm. When you finish, you're ready to dig up and prepare your bed in advance of planting (preferably in the Fall if you intend to plant in the Spring). This is one step that can discourage you completely, and, as an amateur, I can tell you not to worry about it unless you want something to do. If you do it for your first bed, you probably won't for your second. A lot of people don't find that their roses grow any better after this fancy soil preparation. I find that a Winter of freezing and thawing breaks up my clay soil nicely. Some people insist on being technical. For their benefit, let me say that roses (so I read) like slightly acid soil (pH 6.0-6.5), 7.0 being neutral. You may send samples of your soil to the university, or test it yourself. If it is acid (below 5.0), add ground limestone; if alkaline (7.5 or higher), add sulphur.

Now sit down and order your roses. Most roses are grown on the West Coast, in Arizona, Texas or on the Lake Erie shore of Ohio. It makes no difference where the rose was grown, as long as it is a healthy, No. 1 bush with at least three husky canes. It is not frugal to pay less for a No. 1½ or No. 2 bush with fewer canes. Various nurseries bud their roses on different rootstocks. *(Dr. Huey, Rosa multiflora japonica* and so on), but unless you're an "eggspert" or a "nut," you won't care. What the misguided sadist does to them in his yard will make more difference than the rootstock will.

Whether or not a rose is patented has nothing to do with its merits. After the United States Plant Patent Act was passed in 1930, the popular Climber *New Dawn* was the first rose to be patented. The originator of a new variety previously received no monetary gain for his accomplishment. Now the propagator pays a royalty to the patent holder, and we pay a little more for the bushes. The availability of a patent has provided an incentive to hybridizers both in the U.S. and Europe, and the larger nurseries have since added research departments with professional personnel.

The symbol AARS (All-America Rose Selections) is a sign of merit. The AARS was founded in 1938 by the country's leading rose growers to test new varieties in 25 official test gardens under varying soil and climate conditions before they are introduced to the public. At the end of a two-year period, a few varieties considered nearly-perfect are selected for the AARS award.

In ordering, you can save some money by comparing prices between nurseries. Although the prices of patented roses are fixed, you can often save by buying from a nursery which offers a quantity discount. You'll go nuts making this comparison on a lot of varieties, but if you feel that there are several equally-good nurseries, and you're buying a lot of roses, you *can* save money.

**A. Proper way to locate roses in a two-row bed**

**B. Proper way to locate roses in a three-row bed**

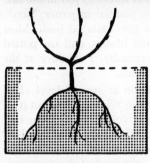

**C. Planting: Roots spread out naturally over earth mound; bud union at ground level**

**D. Pruning: Clean slanting cut just above a good outside bud, going in same direction as bud (1) and (2). Leave no stub in cutting off dead or unwanted cane (3)**

**E. Cutting blooms**
  (a) never cut here
  (b) remove dead bloom here at 5-leaflet leaf
  (c) cut flower for house here, leaving at least 2 5-leaflet leaves

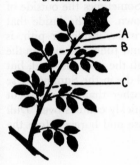

**F. Disbudding**

pinch off bud

pinch off bud

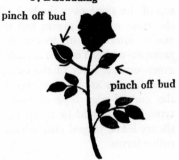

If you don't want to order bare-root roses from nurseries by mail, you can buy roses from a local department, garden or grocery store. If the roses are labeled two-year-old No. 1, and you get them early in the season (not after they've sat around for weeks and dried out or wasted their strength sending out pale yellow shoots which will die when exposed to the sun), go ahead (although I wouldn't buy them myself). Most roses are sold to the public this way, actually.

You can also buy potted roses. These are roses which are bought wholesale from the West Coast or other growing areas and shipped bareroot to a local garden center, instead of direct to you in the first place. At the garden center, the roots are planted in paper "pots". You pay a little for the extra labor, but get a started bush. Most people consider it better to plant bare-root bushes, and use potted plants to fill in later. Opinions vary. Personally, I shudder at the possibilities of root damage in the potted plants.

I recommend planting with the bud union at ground level (Figure C). It may be better protected during the Winter if you put it 2" below ground level, as some recommend, but you risk having the bud union rot from dampness, and weakening the bush by letting hair roots form from the canes. If you can do it, it's a good idea to have the surface of the rose bed about 1" below the level of the surrounding turf for easy watering.

Early April is pruning time in Chicago. Fall pruning is a waste of time, as you'll have to prune again in the Spring (because of winterkill). Then, too, callus formation at the end of the cut cane is slow in the Fall, and borers and fungi may enter the cut ends.

We don't have to worry about how low to prune, because Winter takes care of that in Chicago. Just cut slightly below the brown part of the cane, not over $\frac{1}{4}$" above an outside bud, on a slant with the top of the slope over the bud (Figure D). Sometimes the outside of the cane may be green, but the inside brown. It's the inside that you're interested in, so cut down to where the inside, or pith, is greenish-white. You can actually get leaves and June blooms from the green outside layer of the cane, even though the inside is dead, but these blooms are inferior and the leaves will die in the Summer. Use the curved-edge type of pruning shears rather than the snap-cut type. They should be sharp. A clean cut quickly calluses over. Dull shears leave jagged cuts which invite disease and borers before the callus forms.

PINK CHIFFON F

E. S. Boerner; introduced Jackson & Perkins, Newark, N.Y. Plant patent 1564.
Described page 255, 1958 American Rose Annual.

GREEN FIRE F
H. C. Swim; introduced Armstrong Nurseries, Ontario, Calif. Plant patent
applied for. Described page 247.

Prune to an outside bud to promote outward, rather than inward growth which produces an unshapely bush. Remove crossing canes and tangling blooms which halt air circulation and thus encourage mildew and blackspot. Cut off weak, straggly growth, and any aged canes which have seen their best days. Suckers will occasionally grow speedily up from the roots of the bush. Cut them off as soon as you find them, or they will take the strength away from the grafted plant, and instead of your favorite Hybrid Tea you'll have an ordinary plant of whatever understock was used. This is usually what has happened when people say that their rose has ceased to bloom, or that the blooms have changed color. Cut the sucker off right at the root below the soil line. Otherwise it will grow back fast. Every year, about 1% of my roses throw out suckers. That's a small percentage, but 1% of the millions of roses in the United States is a lot of bushes, and every rose grower can expect a sucker every year or two.

Remove dead wood from Large-flowered Climbers like *Paul's Scarlet Climber* and *Blaze*. Also cut back side shoots that have flowered. Most of these roses bloom only in June, and often not the first year, so don't cut canes unless they are dead. Ramblers (small-flowered, flexible-caned climbers like *Bloomfield Courage* and *Chevy Chase*) bloom on the previous year's growth, so cut the old canes to the ground each year after the June bloom, and leave the new growth, which will be next year's bloom. In general, Shrub and old-fashioned roses also bloom on the old wood, so cut dead and very old canes back to the ground and shorten laterals and canes after the June bloom to keep the bushes within bounds and encourage better blooms the following year. Prune these higher than Hybrid Teas. They do not freeze back generally, but they will get straggly and leggy unless pruned back to about 4' occasionally.

Fertilizing is something that I would like to avoid, but it is unfortunately necessary. Authorities and directions differ, so all I'll say is this: follow the cheapest and easiest method recommended, which is: (1) if you prepare your new bed several months in advance, mix in fertilizer when you do it; (2) regardless of whether or not you prepare the bed in advance, don't use any fertilizer when planting; (3) fertilize when the new growth starts in April, then again in early June, right after the heavy June bloom and finally in early August (absolutely not later than August 15). Later applications will promote growth too late in the season to harden and withstand the Win-

ter weather. It invariably dies. You can probably do more to kill a
bush by late fertilizing than by any other means. What fertilizer? Any.
You won't notice any difference. If you do notice a difference when
you change fertilizers, it is probably not due to the fertilizer. How
much fertilizer? Whatever the directions say.

Spraying is necessary to control diseases and insects. Weekly spraying is best, starting when the leaves first come out in April. But don't
worry if you don't get around to it. I've gone two months without
spraying without disaster. Any good rose spray or dust is satisfactory. Follow the directions. Use an all-purpose spray or dust to save
work and thought. The following chart briefly covers the main problems in Chicago:

| Symptoms | Cause | Comments |
|---|---|---|
| Pink and green lice on new shoots | Aphids | Everybody has them. Why shouldn't you? Follow a weekly spray or dust program. |
| Skeletonized leaves | Rose slugs & sawflies | Don't get hysterical. |
| Leaves yellowish or reddish or with brown areas, mealy on the underside, many may drop | Red spiders | Careful, or you'll kill yourself instead of the spiders. |
| Black spots with fringed margins, leaves often turn yellow and drop | Blackspot | Don't commit suicide. Some of the nicest people have it. This year's most blackspotted bush may be next year's best one. Clean up old leaves and pick off and give the garbage man the first infected leaves. Spores enter leaves only after 6 hours of continuous moisture, so don't get the leaves wet in the evening. Use a mulch so rain won't splash spores around so much. Weekly spraying or dusting is the best protection. |
| Yellow leaves | Chlorosis | May be due to lots of things; deficiency of nitrogen, manganese, magnesium, iron or poor |

| | | drainage—take your pick. Send in a soil sample for testing or just change fertilizers. Maybe you haven't been fertilizing at all. Shame on you! |
|---|---|---|
| Browning of tips and edges of leaves | Chemical burn | I know, you didn't do it. Did you? |
| Black and crooked buds | Midge | The little whitish-orange maggots have been gorging themselves. July and August is picnic time for them. But you had a nice time on your vacation, so why worry? Start spraying again. |
| Buds don't open, petals have brown edges | Thrips | Give these buds to the garbage man, too. |
| Holes in buds | Rose chafers, rose budworms, various beetles | Spray |
| Holes in ends of canes | Borers | Larvae of carpenter bees and sawflies bore into the pith. Cut infested canes down to the end of the hole. Paint ends of large canes after pruning with orange shellac or tree wound paint. Don't prune in Fall. |
| Precise ovals cut out of the edges | Leaf cutter bees | The bees cut these out to line their nests in logs and stems. Since they don't swallow the pieces, there is no control. Just close your eyes and relax. |

Mulching is good for both the roses and you. You may use buckwheat hulls, peat moss, sawdust, ground corncobs or almost anything. Manure which has been used in mushroom houses is an excellent mulch. If you use corncobs or sawdust, you'll have to add a little nitrogen. May is a good time to put on your mulch. It prevents most weed growth, holds moisture in the soil so that you don't have to water much in the Summer, keeps the soil from baking, eliminates cultivating and forms a barrier against transmission of blackspot spores from the soil to the bushes during a rain. The mulch should be 1-2″ deep. Don't pile it too deep around the bush, or it may rot the canes. If you mulch, water fertilizer down through it instead of cultivating it in. If you do cultivate, don't go deeper than 1-2″ or you will disturb the roots.

A rose bed should have a neat edge. Cut the turf with a spade. Go along a string tied between stakes, then pull the grass clumps out by hand. Don't dig a ditch. You will injure the roots and leave the roses growing on a "hillside", with their roots too near the surface.

Remove dead blooms rather than letting them fall onto the ground or stay off-color on the bush. Don't just pluck them. Cut them with shears just above the top five-leaflet leaf (Figure E).

For bigger blooms, pinch off the side buds (disbud) when small (Figure F). You probably will not get fewer blooms in the long run, because the bush will throw all of its energy into producing new blooms sooner than if you let the side buds stay on and bloom after the main center bloom.

In Chicago, formal winter protection is largely a matter of superstition. If your bushes are healthy and you don't fertilize after August 15, they'll live through the Winter with no protection. If you want to protect them, just hill 6-8″ of dirt around the base of each plant—nothing else. People who play around with additional protection are killing their bushes with kindness, shutting off air circulation, rotting the canes. Be lazy and brave, and you'll have better success and save money. Armistice Day is a good time to hill up.

If you have tree roses, dig them up by November. Lay them flat and bury them completely just under the surface in a well-drained part of the yard. Mark the spot carefully. Next April, wash the dirt away with a hose so that you can lift the tree up easily without breaking it, and replant.

Climbers (if you're strong enough to wrestle with them) will be better off if you tie them down to the ground for the Winter.

Be sure to either use markers to identify the varieties that you plant, or make a map of your beds. I do both, as the kids may pull up the markers. You pay much more to get roses which are true to name, so don't throw your investment away by losing track of their identity.

Now let's get down to the kinds of roses for Chicago. In general, all kinds will do well here except Teas, Climbing Hybrid Teas, and "weeping" tree roses.

Plant some Large-flowered Climbers. Beware of the "everblooming" varieties if you want really vigorous plants, 10-20′ tall. They usually don't grow that much, because they put their energy into blooms rather than growth. If you want beauty in June and plenty of height, stick to *Silver Moon* and *City of York* (white); *Mrs. Arthur Curtiss James* and *Doubloons* (yellow); *New Dawn* and *Mary Wallace* (pink); and *Dr. Huey* and *Paul's Scarlet Climber* (red). There are more, of course. *Bloomfield Courage* and *Chevy Chase* are among the few Small-flowered Ramblers which are not overly susceptible to mildew.

Don't be scared of tree roses. They bloom at eye level, and are easy to carry through the Winter if you do as I mentioned under winter protection. They'll last for years in Chicago.

Most of your roses in beds will be "modern" varieties: Hybrid Teas which produce large blooms from June to November; Floribundas which have clusters of smaller blooms from June to November and are especially good for borders, hedges and masses of color; Polyanthas, which are much smaller than Floribundas, but otherwise similar; and Grandifloras, which, being crosses of Hybrid Teas and Floribundas, have generally more, but slightly smaller blooms than Hybrid Teas. The latter are new, but they can be used for any purpose. Indeed, all of these types of roses can be used anywhere.

As to what kinds of these "modern" roses to buy, the best thing for you to do is to look at the American Rose Society's Buying Guide. Any rose rated 7.0 or better is a good risk. These ratings are obtained from amateur growers throughout the United States.

A garden of only modern roses is not complete, however. Older roses have charm and beauty which withstand changes in fashion. Yes, there are fashions in roses, like in ladies' dresses. Growing only modern roses is like eating only hamburgers and milk shakes. There is an increasing trend toward including the older roses in gardens to avoid a bourgeois appearance. Briefly, a species rose is a wild rose, rather than a horticultural variety. The blossoms are usually single and abundant in early Summer, followed by ornamental seed pods. Let's look at a few of them and their hybrids:

*Rosa foetida bicolor.* Noted for its brilliant coloring. An ancestor of the modern yellow, orange and copper Hybrid Teas. Don't prune.

*Rosa multiflora.* Widely advertised as a living fence, but not recommended for small lots as it gets too big. Better for farms and the Toll Road Commission. Much used as an understock. White blossoms.

58 AMERICAN ROSE ANNUAL:

*Rosa hugonis.* Very early-flowering, with long, graceful branches. Native to the rocky, semi-arid regions of north central China. Does best in poor soil.

*Raubritter* (Robber Baron). A Rambler. Does best in full sun. Distinctive pink blooms.

*Rosa chinensis viridiflora.* A queer rose, entirely sterile. The green "flowers" are composed of what appear to be green leaves edged with bronze which make interesting corsages that go perfectly with tweeds.

*Rosa eglanteria.* The sweetbrier of "Midsummer Night's Dream". The foliage perfumes the garden with the scent of ripe apples. Pink single blossoms. Produces orange-red hips in the Fall.

*Rosa omeiensis.* Young canes bear wing-like thorns which glow like fire. Especially effective if planted with the setting sun behind it. Tall. Single white blooms. One of the very few roses with only four petals.

*Rosa roxburghii.* Unopened blooms resemble small chestnut burrs. Leaves resemble those of the locust tree. Attractive pink flowers. Blooms more than once.

*Rosa moyesii.* Reddish terra-cotta color, unlike that of any other flower. Difficult to establish, so don't buy it unless you're willing to gamble.

*Rosa moschata.* Masses of white bloom in the Spring. Highly fragrant, especially in the evening.

*Belinda.* A Hybrid Musk. Blooms profusely in large trussses similar to phlox. 4-6' tall, suitable for a hedge, pillar or shrub. Blooms more than once.

*Cornelia.* Copper-pink. Does well in part shade, as do most Hybrid Musks.

*Kathleen.* This Hybrid Musk's blooms resemble apple blossoms.

*Hon. Lady Lindsay.* Pink blooms of Hybrid Tea-form. Many of these Shrub roses make much larger plants, and produce perhaps three times as many flowers as the average Hybrid Tea. This one grows about 3' tall and 3' wide, and is good for a dooryard planting or in front of taller shrubs.

*Nevada.* Another Shrub with white blossoms, often splashed with red like a camelia.

*Fruhlingsgold* (Spring Gold). Pale yellow single flowers, not repeat-blooming. A good Shrub.

*Coupe d'Hebe.* Large pink flowers on a vigorous Shrub.

*Rosa rugosa.* The hardiest of all roses, with wrinkled or rugose foliage. The Japanese made perfume from it early in the 12th century.

*Hansa.* A Hybrid Rugosa with double, large, red flowers. Makes a good hedge. Plant 2′ apart.

*Blanc Double de Coubert.* A pure white Hybrid Rugosa. Used extensively to make the finest French perfume.

*Sarah Van Fleet.* Fragrant pink flowers come all Summer and Fall on a 5-8′ plant. Likes full sun. Another Hybrid Rugosa.

*Rosa rugosa rugosa.* Almost purple blooms. 4-5′ tall.

*Mrs. Anthony Waterer.* Maroon, almost purple in some seasons. Still another fine Hybrid Rugosa.

*Delicata.* A mauve-pink Hybrid Rugosa. Compact growth.

*Rosa gallica.* Very hardy.

*Cramoisi des Alpes.* Red, brushed with purplish-black. For those who like an unusual Gallica.

*Belle des Jardins.* Crimson-purple, occasionally striped white. A wonderful Gallica to use in old-fashioned bouquets featuring pink to deep purple shades.

*Commandant Beaurepaire.* A spectacular striped Gallica.

*Rosa centifolia.* Also known as "cabbage" rose because of the incurved globular form of the blooms. Will grow up to 7′ tall in Chicago. I wouldn't be without it.

*Rosa centifolia muscosa.* Very hardy in Chicago.

*Rosa centifolia cristata.* Unusual fringe of mossy growth along the edges of the sepals. One of the most popular of the old roses. The pink blossoms are especially attractive when about one-quarter open. Your grandma had it, and so should you.

*Comtesse de Murinais.* Pale pink.

*Gloire des Mousseux.* Especially noted for the handsome foliage from which the globular pink flower emerges.

*Deuil de Paul Fontaine.* Unlike most mosses, this dark red variety will repeat its bloom for you. No sissy—I broke my garden fork digging it up to relocate it one year after planting.

*Mousseline.* Everblooming after established. Does fine in Chicago. These roses bloom on the old wood, so don't whack them down. You get more bloom by pegging the canes (that is, forcing them to arch over by staking the ends of the canes to the ground). If you lack room for this, just cut each growth cycle 3 or 4 eyes above the preceding growth, but do not prune again until after the Spring bloom. Pegging increases the bloom of any of the old roses that grow long canes as much as five times. Otherwise, you may get more height, with only a tuft of bloom on the end of the cane.

*Rosa damascena.* Wonderful.

*Mme. Hardy.* The finest white Damask. Very hardy. Spring bloom only.

Hybrid Perpetuals are a result of crossing Bourbons with *Rosa chinensis.* They link the roses of the early part of the 19th century with those that are fashionable today. They are big, sturdy plants, but the canes will freeze back in Chicago Winters. If you don't care to peg the long canes down to a horizontal position, you may cut them back to about 18″ after the June bloom. They bloom each year on shoots which grow from canes of previous years. Therefore, it is important to try to carry the canes through the Winter. So, I suggest more earth covering in the Winter for these than for the Hybrid Teas.

*Barone Prevost.* One of the finest Hybrid Perpetuals. Rose-pink, with sweet fragrance

*Roger Lambelin.* One of the most unusual Hybrid Perpetual roses. The dark red petals are sedged with white. Best in full sun. Roses like this one are not grown in abundance, and sometimes it takes three or four years to get one.

*Marchioness of Londonderry.* Very tall growing. Large flesh-tinted blooms, sometimes 6″ across.

*Mable Morrison.* Blue-green foliage with light pink blossoms. Compact grower.

*American Beauty.* This famous old rose is little-grown today, but the name lingers on. Very fragrant.

*Reine des Violettes.* Queen of the violet shades. Tall. Almost thornless. Heavily perfumed.

*Henry Nevard.* One of the best Hybrid Perpetuals.

*Baroness Rothschild.* Crushed strawberries and cream.

*Black Prince.* Famous black-red rose.

Polyanthas.

*The Fairy.* Produces masses of small pink blooms all Summer and Fall.

*Paul Crampell.* Orange-scarlet.

Floribundas are crosses of Hybrid Teas and Polyanthas, and are excellent for borders and hedges. They produce larger flowers than the Polyanthas.

*Gruss an Aachen.* One of the oldest Floribundas, and still one of the best.

Hybrid Teas resulted from the crossing of Hybrid Perpetuals with Tea roses, which are not hardy in the North. Today most people mean Hybrid Tea when they say "rose."

*Kathleen Mills.* A single Hybrid Tea with blooms likened to a flight of pink butterflies.

*George Dickson.* A large, fragrant Hybrid Tea.

*Blanche Mallerin.* A very good white Hybrid Tea. Fragrant.

You will want to plant mostly modern roses, because they are all ever-blooming and because they are the fashion. But, I think that many of the older roses are as beautiful, if not more so, and certainly more interesting. So I hope you will find an appropriate place in your garden for some of them.

Just as you fit some old-fashioned roses into your garden, be sure you fit your modern rose beds properly into your yard. If you really want to have a well-balanced garden, perhaps you may wish to consult a landscape architect, as I did with my new house, small as it is. A plan, whether made by a professional or by yourself after study, is necessary if your roses are to fit in with the rest of your landscaping for a beautiful overall effect.

Finally, once you get your roses planted, devote whatever time you have to proper pruning, spraying and fertilizing. And don't kill them (and yourself too) with a lot of excessive winter covering.

# The Importance of Rose Rootstock Selection

A. N. Roberts*

Corvallis, Ore.

Most rose varieties today are budded on a selected rootstock of another variety or species, although some grow as well and produce as many flowers on their own roots.

*Rosa canina* is the most popular rootstock in Canada and Europe. In this country, approximately 80% of the roses are propagated on *Rosa multiflora* roots. *Dr. Huey* (Shafter Robin), *Gloire des Rosomanes* (Ragged Robin), and *Rosa odorata* are used in warmer sections of California and the South. Many other types are currently being tested.[1]

Research to date has shown that seedlings of given rose species may vary greatly in their influence on scion varieties when they are used as rootstocks. Hence, we selected 15 northern types of *Rosa multiflora* from commercial mixtures to compare with three Texas strains in our initial tests. We hope to expand our eight-year-old program in the future to include certain European, as well as domestic clones of this and other species.

## BUD FAILURE STUDIED

In our first tests (1948-50), we grew a total of 20,000 cuttings of the 15 *Rosa multiflora* strains, budding them to *Mme. Henri Guillot* and *President Herbert Hoover* in an attempt to find the answer to the nurseryman's bud failure problem. There are two types of bud failure in the nursery row. In one case, the bud shield fails to unite with the cambium of the stock, so that the bud dies shortly after the budding operation. The other type of bud failure, commonly referred to as "pinch-off" in Pacific Northwest rose growing areas, does

---

*Horticulturist, Oregon State College.

[1]For information on some of these projects, see page 27 of the 1957 American Rose Annual, and page 18 of the January and page 5 of the November 1957 issues of the American Rose Magazine.

not appear until growth starts during the Spring following Summer or Fall placement of the bud. This delayed failure is not a result of a poor union of the bud shield with the cambium of the stock, but is a rupture of the bud itself from the shield, resulting from an apparent anatomical and/or mechanical weakness of the rapidly-expanding shoot formed by the bud.

In this first test, we studied the influence of variations in (1) rootstock, (2) scion variety, (3) time of planting, (4) method of growing, (5) time of budding and (6) treatment of the stock at budding time on the incidence of the two forms of bud failure (tables 1 through 5).

## PLANT PERFORMANCE

Rootstock variation and treatment of the stock (topping) at budding time had the most-pronounced influence on bud failure. The percentage of bud failure was significantly different between the several selections of *Rosa multiflora* rootstock used. The practice of "topping" the rootstocks at budding time decreased the incidence of the "pinch-off" form of bud failure more than any other factor studied. Spring planting of the cuttings likewise decreased, while Fall and/or shallow planting increased bud failure of the "pinch-off" type. Although the cause of this form of bud failure was not determined, the most vigorous strains of *Rosa multiflora,* and cultural practices which favored heavy growth and development of the cuttings prior to budding, produced more of it.

In 1953 and 1954, we budded a total of 6,000 *Etoile de Hollande, Mrs. Sam McGredy* and *President Herbert Hoover* plants on the 15 original selections of *Rosa multiflora.* In 1955 and 1956, we budded 6,000 more *Shining Star, Ena Harkness, Crimson Glory, Kaiserin Auguste Viktoria, The Doctor* and *Mrs. Pierre S. du Pont* roses on the five rootstocks which performed best during the previous year. In 1955, and again in 1957, we planted sample plants of the various combinations from the nursery in typical rose garden fashion for further evaluation.

We judged the performance of the plants in the nursery row on the basis of (1) degree of "fall-forcing" (premature elongation of the newly-placed scion-bud soon after union has occurred. This contrasts with what is considered the normal sequence of events; where

## Table 1
## ROOTSTOCK INFLUENCE

| | Per Cent Bud Failure | | |
|---|---|---|---|
| | No Union | "Pinch-off" | Total |
| Ore. III | 13.4 | 4.1 | 17.5 |
| Ore. I | 22.6 | 1.1 | 23.7 |
| Texas Clark | 22.9 | 4.6 | 27.5 |
| Texas Tate | 21.7 | 7.7 | 29.4 |
| Ore. IX | 36.7 | 2.5 | 39.2 |
| Ore. VIII | 37.5 | 5.6 | 43.1 |

## Table 2
## TIME OF PLANTING CUTTINGS

| | Per Cent Bud Failure | | |
|---|---|---|---|
| | No Union | "Pinch-Off" | Total |
| Fall | 5.7 | 24.5 | 30.2 |
| Spring | 7.5 | 16.2 | 23.7 |

## Table 3
## METHOD OF GROWING CUTTINGS

| | Per Cent Bud Failure | | |
|---|---|---|---|
| | No Union | "Pinch-Off" | Total |
| Soil Mounded | 15.9 | 11.9 | 27.8 |
| Shallow Planted | | | |
| 20" Paper Mulch | 1.8 | 28.9 | 30.7 |
| 12" Paper Mulch | 2.1 | 24.8 | 26.9 |
| No Paper Mulch | 6.6 | 15.7 | 22.3 |

## Table 4
## STOCK TREATMENT AT BUDDING TIME

| | Per Cent Bud Failure | | |
|---|---|---|---|
| | No Union | "Pinch-Off" | Total |
| Topped | 5.9 | 12.5 | 18.4 |
| Not Topped | 7.3 | 28.2 | 35.5 |

## Table 5
## PER CENT OF PINCH-OFF

| | Time of Budding | | |
|---|---|---|---|
| | July | August | September |
| Mme. Henri Guillot | 24.9 | 26.3 | 18.1 |
| President Herbert Hoover | 25.9 | 23.3 | 23.9 |

## Table 6

### PER CENT OF FALL-FORCED SCION-BUDS

| Rootstock | 1953-54 | 1955-56 |
|---|---|---|
| Ore. VIII | 0.8 | 0.5 |
| Ore. VI | 0.5 | 6.5 |
| Ore. 1 | 4.0 | 6.7 |
| Ore. V | 1.9 | 7.1 |
| Ore. III | 9.7 | 18.0 |

## Table 7

### PER CENT YIELD OF NO. 1 PLANTS (ALL SCION VARIETIES)

| Rootstock | 1953-54 | 1955-56 |
|---|---|---|
| Ore. III* | 44 | 47 |
| Texas Clark | 36 | .. |
| Ore. 1 | 33 | 53 |
| Oregon V | 33 | 49 |
| Ore. VI | 31 | 56 |
| Ore. VIII | 30 | 53 |
| Ore. 8 | 22 | 53 |
| Ore. IX | 18 | .. |
| Ore. 9 | 16 | .. |

## Table 8

### SUCKERING OF ROOTSTOCK

| Rootstock | Number Sucker Below Bud Union |
|---|---|
| Ore. III | 14 |
| Ore. VIII | 16 |
| Ore. V | 18 |
| Texas Tate | 30 |
| Ore. VI | 33 |
| Ore. 1 | 35 |
| Ore. 9 | 36 |
| Texas Clark | 44 |
| Ore. 8 | 50 |
| Texas Welch | 71 |

---

*More susceptible to November 1955 freeze because of tendency to "fall-force" its buds. Reason for poor showing in 1955-56.

## Table 9

## NUMBER OF FLOWERS PRODUCED BY SEVERAL ROSE VARIETIES ON SELECTED STRAINS OF ROSE MULTIFLORA, 1957-58

| Variety | Rootstock | Total Production Per Season (average blooms per plant)* | |
|---|---|---|---|
| | | 1957 | 1958 |
| Crimson Glory | Ore. 1 | 69 | 143 |
| | Ore. III | 64 | 146 |
| | Ore. V | 63 | 161 |
| | Ore. VI | 67 | 157 |
| | Ore. VIII | 63 | 141 |
| Kaiserin Auguste Viktoria | Ore. I | 62 | 91 |
| | Ore. III | 48 | 89 |
| | Ore. V | 35 | .. |
| | Ore. VI | 47 | 98 |
| | Ore. VIII | 62 | 117 |
| Mrs. Pierre S. du Pont | Ore. 1 | 76 | 145 |
| | Ore. III | 69 | 135 |
| | Ore. V | 75 | 157 |
| | Ore. VI | 96 | 176 |
| | Ore. VIII | 73 | 159 |
| Ena Harkness | Ore. I | 71 | 133 |
| | Ore. III | 64 | 134 |
| | Ore. V | 75 | 163 |
| | Ore. VI | 73 | 169 |
| | Ore. VIII | 72 | 153 |
| The Doctor | Ore. I | 29 | 75 |
| | Ore. III | 32 | 77 |
| | Ore. V | 37 | 83 |
| | Ore. VI | 33 | 69 |
| | Ore. VIII | 42 | 88 |
| Shining Star | Ore. I | 52 | 91 |
| | Ore. III | 52 | 90 |
| | Ore. V | 56 | 131 |
| | Ore. VI | 59 | 110 |
| | Ore. VIII | 59 | 113 |

*Average of 12 plants—3 plants per plot replicated four times

the scion-bud remains dormant after placement until growth starts the following Spring), (2) grade of plants produced, (3) rootstock suckering below bud union and (4) flower production in the rose garden (tables 6-9).

These and other data not presented support the following conclusions: (1) superior strains of *Rosa multiflora* for rootstock purposes *can* be selected, (2) rootstocks best-suited to nursery operations, and which produce the "best" nursery plants (smooth appearance), do not necessarily produce the best garden specimens, (3) some rose varieties are more subject to rootstock influence than others and (4) there is no one superior rootstock for all scion varieties. Genetic variation in the *Rosa multiflora* rootstock species showed up in both the nursery and garden performance of the rose varieties budded to them.

While observations of root characteristics in the nursery favored *Texas Vlark, Ore. I, III* and *VI* (smooth, uniform, fibrous and pliable), garden performance records showed that *Ore. V, VI* and *VIII* produce somewhat more vigorous plants and more flowers. However, no one stock was superior for all varieties.

*Ore. V* has the undesirable characteristic of forming its roots on one side of the cutting, thus giving the bareroot plant a lopsided appearance. *Ore. VIII* is a very thorny type of *Rosa multiflora,* which is undesirable in nursery operations. *Ore. VI* is a thornless type that performs quite well in both the nursery and garden. It does not make as good cuttings as *Ore. I* or *Ore. III,* but is satisfactory. It produces new roots rapidly after transplanting, which may be an advantage. *Ore. I* and *Ore. III* produce the best wood for cuttings, and even though the plants do not perform quite as well as the other three stocks in the garden, they are acceptable.

The solution to the problem of rootstock selection seems to be a compromise in finding stock which lends itself to large-scale nursery production, and at the same time performs well in the garden. A great deal of testing will have to be done before superior rootstocks can be selected for the numerous varieties and types of roses being grown today. It may be possible to accomplish this by grouping varieties suited to a given rootstock.

Rootstock, like scion selection, will have to be done on a regional basis to find the stocks best suited to local soil and climatic conditions and to the scion varieties being grown.

# Good Roses
# For Fall Bloom

## Dr. John P. Rankin
## Elyria, Ohio

ALTHOUGH my garden has become a mere ghost of its former self, I still love and grow roses.

"Dunridge Garden" (located east of town on US Route 20) formerly contained a 30 x 200′ bed planted with about 2400 Hybrid Teas, Polyanthas, Chinas and Teas, representing hundreds of varieties. Two equal areas to the east and west (shielded by a screen of 400 lilac varieties) were filled with what I roughly call "semi-climbers" (a mixture of Hybrid Perpetuals, Shrubs and species roses that are too tall or vigorous to use with the others). Two giant double arbors (which, if planted end-to-end would make a trellis about 800′ long) surrounded the garden. They were filled solidly with about 400 Climbers.

Unfortunately, many of these roses have succumbed to environmental conditions of soil, location, climate and neglect. But, I am gradually transplanting the remainder to another plot in town to make way for new construction at the old site.

I built and opened Dunridge in 1932 with the help of some of my patients who were anxious to "work out" their medical bills rather than part with their scarce funds. I had grown roses in a small way previously, and in fact still have a few of the plants that my mother brought with her in 1894 when my parents moved here after the first great Johnstown flood.

The list in Table 1, which I prepared during a long frost-free Fall, gives a rather comprehensive idea of the varieties which will produce a continuity of garden delight lasting almost until Christmas here in northern Ohio where Lake Erie tempers our climate and where we have a perfect colloidal clay soil.

Still, it takes plenty of patience and work to raise these roses. For instance, I found it necessary to crowd many "tender" beauties (like *Mermaid, Emily Gray, Paul's Lemon Pillar, Apeles Mestres, Gloire de Dijon* and *Marechal Niel*) into a 10′x30′ peaked-roof cold house in order to keep them alive through as many painful Winters as possible. I laid others down on the ground and covered them with earth, straw and tar paper. I wrapped still others in an upright position.

After all these years, I am sure that I may know more about how *not* to raise roses than anyone else in America. And yet, after growing, loving and losing most of the catalog offerings since 1919, I am still thrilled and sustained by the belief that I have enjoyed better luck than my efforts deserved. This has been sufficient comfort and reward.

Our gardens are really not ours "for keeps." With Providence, Mother Nature and Father Time on our side, we keep up, dig and delve away in them to provide a haven for myriads of plant creations which strive for a place in the sun. Here we walk humbly and act wisely, painfully learning that precious gift called appreciation and becoming (in a borrowed phrase) "artists in awareness."

## TABLE 1. Fall-Blooming Roses

| | |
|---|---|
| Allen Chandler | Climbing Hybrid Tea |
| Allen's Fragrant Pillar | Climbing Hybrid Tea |
| Amelie Gravereaux | Hybrid Rugosa |
| Arnold | Shrub |
| Auguste Kordes | Climbing Floribunda |
| Ausonius | Hybrid Musk |
| Australia Felix | Hybrid Tea |
| Billy Boiler | Climbing Hybrid Tea |
| Birdie Blye | Shrub |
| Bishop Darlington | Hybrid Musk |
| Black Boy | Climbing Hybrid Tea |
| Blanc Double de Coubert | Hybrid Rugosa |
| Blaze | Climber |
| Bloomfield Fascination | Recurrent Semi-Climber |
| Bonfire | Rugosa |
| Candeur Lyonnaise | Hybrid Tea |
| Captain Christy | Hybrid Tea |
| Captain Thomas | Climbing Hybrid Tea |
| Cascadia | Shrub |
| Ceres | Hybrid Musk |
| Chaplin's Crimson Glow | Large-flowered Rugosa |
| Chaplin's Pink Climber | Large-flowered Rugosa |
| Christine Wright | Climbing Hybrid Tea |

| | |
|---|---|
| Cl. Cecile Brunner | Climbing Polyantha |
| Cl. Clotilde Soupert | Climbing Polyantha |
| Cl. Columbia | Climbing Hybrid Tea |
| Cl. Etoile de Hollande | Climbing Hybrid Tea |
| Cl. Hadley | Climbing Hybrid Tea |
| Cl. Helen Gould | Climbing Hybrid Tea |
| Cl. Meteor | Climbing Hybrid Tea |
| Cl. Mme. Edouard Herriot | Climbing Hybrid Tea |
| Cl. Mrs. Henry Bowles | Climbing Hybrid Tea |
| Cl. President Herbert Hoover | Climbing Hybrid Tea |
| Cl. Souv. de Claudius Pernet | Climbing Hybrid Tea |
| Cl. Summer Snow | Climbing Floribunda |
| Cl. Talisman | Climbing Hybrid Tea |
| Clio | Hybrid Perpetual |
| Comet | Climbing Floribunda |
| Conrad Ferdinand Meyer | Hybrid Rugosa |
| Countess of Stradbroke | Climbing Hybrid Tea |
| Crimson Conquest | Rugosa |
| Daphne | Hybrid Musk |
| Deschamps | Noisette |
| Dr. Eckener | Hybrid Rugosa |
| Dr. Huey | Rambler |
| Dr. W. Van Fleet | Large-flowered Rambler |
| Druschki Rubra | Hybrid Tea |
| Ednah Thomas | Climbing Hybrid Tea |
| Emile Fortepaule | Rugosa |
| Eugene Jacquet | Rugosa |
| Eva | Hybrid Musk |
| Fisher Holmes | Hybrid Perpetual |
| F. J. Grootendorst | Shrub |
| Flower of Fairfield | Rugosa |
| Frau Karl Druschki | Hybrid Tea |
| Gartendirektor O. Linne | Polyantha |
| General Baron Berge | Hybrid Perpetual |
| Gloire de Dijon | Climbing Tea |
| Gloire des Mousseux | Moss |
| Gloire des Rosomanes | China |
| Golden Dream | Hybrid Rugosa |
| Golden King | Hybrid Rugosa |

| | |
|---|---|
| Grace Wayman | Climber |
| Gruss an Teplitz | Shrub |
| Henry Nevard | Hybrid Perpetual |
| Hiawatha | Rugosa |
| Hon. Ina Bingham | Hybrid Tea |
| Hon. Lady Lindsay | Shrub |
| Hugh Dickson | Hybrid Perpetual |
| Indian Summer | Climbing Hybrid Tea |
| Inermis Morlettii | Shrub |
| J. B. Clark | Hybrid Tea |
| John Russell | Hybrid Tea |
| Julia, Countess of Dartrey | Hybrid Tea |
| Juliet | Hybrid Perpetual |
| Kathleen Harrop | Bourbon |
| Kitty Kininmonth | Climber |
| Lessing | Hybrid Musk |
| Lyon Rambler | Rugosa |
| Mabelle Stearns | Shrub |
| Marguerite Carels | Climbing Hybrid Tea |
| Marie Leonida | Climber |
| Marquise de Castellane | Hybrid Perpetual |
| Martha Lambert | Shrub |
| Maxime Corbon | Rugosa |
| May Queen | Rugosa |
| Mermaid | Climber |
| Miss Marion Manifold | Climbing Hybrid Tea |
| Mme. Albert Barbier | Hybrid Tea |
| Mme. Georges Bruant | Shrub |
| Moonlight | Hybrid Musk |
| Mrs. George C. Thomas | Climbing Hybrid Tea |
| Mrs. John Laing | Hybrid Perpetual |
| Nelly Custis | Shrub |
| Nevada | Shrub |
| New Dawn | Climber |
| Norah Cunningham | Climbing Hybrid Tea |
| Old Blush | China |
| Oskar Cordel | Hybrid Perpetual |
| Paul's Scarlet Climber | Large-flowered Rambler |
| Penelope | Hybrid Musk |

| | |
|---|---|
| Pink Grootendorst | Hybrid Rugosa |
| Pink Profusion | Shrub |
| Princess Van Orange | Rugosa |
| Prosperity | Hybrid Musk |
| Queen of the Musks | Hybrid Musk |
| Red Explorer | Climbing Polyantha |
| Reveil Dijonnais | Climbing Hybrid Tea |
| Roger Lambelin | Hybrid Perpetual |
| Ronsard | Hybrid Tea |
| Rosa spinosissima altaica | Species |
| Rosella | Climbing Hybrid Tea |
| Roserie | Rugosa |
| Rudolph von Bennigsen | Shrub |
| Sammy | Hybrid Musk |
| Sarah Bernhardt | Climbing Hybrid Tea |
| Sarah Van Fleet | Hybrid Rugosa |
| Scarlano | Shrub |
| Schoener's Nutkana | Shrub |
| Scorcher | Climbing Hybrid Tea |
| Sierra Snowstorm | Shrub |
| Silver Moon | Large-flowered Rambler |
| Skyrocket | Hybrid Musk |
| Souv. de Claudius Dennoyel | Climbing Hybrid Tea |
| Souv. de Mme. H. Thuret | Hybrid Tea |
| Stanwell Perpetual | Shrub |
| St. Ingebert | Hybrid Tea |
| Summer Snow | Floribunda |
| Symphony | Hybrid Tea |
| Thisbe | Hybrid Musk |
| Turkes Rugosa Samling | Hybrid Rugosa |
| Ulrich Brunner Fils | Hybrid Perpetual |
| Urdh | Hybrid Tea |
| Vanity | Hybrid Musk |
| Victor Hugo | Hybrid Perpetual |
| Victor Teschendorff | Hybrid Tea |
| Von Liliencron | Semi-climber |
| Von Scharnhorst | Shrub |
| Waltham Climber | Climber |
| Zephirine Drouhin | Bourbon |

# The Comprehensive Flower

Gladys Zoetman
Cleveland, Ohio

Is anything quite as lovely as to awake on a lovely Summer morning and open the French doors, revealing a beautiful garden of roses, their lovely fragrance blending with the beauty of a silken butterfly caressing their petals?

This is what we have waited for, the enchantment of a full-blown rose, after hours of nourishing the earth and coaxing a lovely specimen to the zenith of its ultimate beauty.

Down through the ages, the rose has been used as a symbol of all things beautiful. A dark red rose is said to have bloomed at the Saviour's crucifixion where His drops of blood fell, its silken petals the same deep color.

For the sweetest token of love to his beautiful Juliet, Romeo chose one lovely rose.

Jose touched to his lips the rose thrown by vivacious Carmen.

The artistic jeweler seeks to copy the rose. His beautiful interpretation is the 24-facet diamond.

The designer of dresses appliques a lovely yellow rose on a deep green velvet background.

The proud bridegroom presents his bride with the most beautiful of all flowers—a ribboned bouquet of pink roses.

The tiny new baby is welcomed with sweetheart rose buds.

A lovely May queen is even more lovely with the traditional crown of roses in her hair.

The silken white rose is treasured in memory of a beloved mother.

The influence of the rose is found in the rose-splashed drapes of a happy sun-room, in the rose-colored velvet drapes of the library and in a coat of arms: a lion's head, gauntlet and golden rose. Pink roses on a blue background have been used as a carpet in the White House Blue Room.

California, with its pageantry of roses, and the loveliest roses of Florida's "Venice of the South" simply confirm that the rose is truly the comprehensive flower.

# Ten Years of Success with the Rose

Agnes B. Hamblen

Durham, N.C.

**M**ORE books have been written about the rose than about all other flowers combined. This is due to its antiquity, unrivaled appeal and popularity, and to the unique and almost inexhaustible store of facts, lore, legends and traditions concerning the romance, history and culture of the flower whose world prevalence is attested by its one-syllable name being practically identical in all languages, both ancient and modern. Indeed, the genus Rosa is a cosmopolite among plants.

Since there are more than 5,000 known named varieties, my experience with several hundred is obviously definitely limited. At the same time, I believe that I have proven enough, regarding selection of varieties, sources of supply and planting and cultural methods, to draw reliable conclusions which may aid others in rose growing.

Eight years ago, our rose garden consisted of 650 plants. The vicissitudes of time, family illness and the realization that approximately 200 plants, if given attentive care, will provide all the rose blooms any family and its friends could want from a wide range of different varieties in the several classes, have reduced our rose garden to the latter size.

The average person's concept of a rose is a Hybrid Tea in bud stage. To a rosarian, a bud is only a potential bloom, growing more beautiful and interesting as it unfolds.

One of the rose's greatest charms is the wide range of its classes, adapting it to an equally-wide range of uses.

Roses may be used in mass planting for color and landscape effect. Shrub and bush roses may be planted singly and very effectively in prepared holes to serve like any other specimen plant. Those with climbing or trailing tendencies can cover banks, walls, trellises, arbors and fences. Others are grown to produce flowers to use in corsages, informal bouquets and the most formal arrangements. Many older roses are grown for their historic and/or sentimental value. We are doing all of the above.

Confining one's interest to Hybrid Teas exclusively is like eating only meat as a diet. Verily, Hybrid Teas are the standby and the glamorous darlings of the rose garden, yet oftimes they are temperamental prima donnas. Assuredly, there would be no rose shows without Hybrid Teas, which are the best exhibition type of the genus. Visitors to shows want and expect to see Hybrid Teas occupying at least half the show tables, the remainder divided among Floribundas, Grandifloras, Climbers, "other roses not listed above" and arrangement classes.

We prefer to depend primarily on the old "tried and true" varieties, awaiting the verdict of more adventurous souls who try the new introductions, all of which are costly and many doomed (like Broadway theater openings) to early rejection. As nearly as we can, we also confine our selections to fragrant varieties, though oftentimes the color, disease resistance and profusion of bloom will make a nonfragrant variety irresistible. Here are our favorite Hybrid Teas, grouped according to color: coral, peach, salmon, apricot, pink-blend range—*Tiffany, Angels Mateu, Mrs. Sam Mc-Gredy, Comtesse Vandal, President Herbert Hoover;* yellow and yellow blend—*Sutter's Gold, Golden Dawn, Peace;* red—*Crimson Glory, Rubaiyat, Rose of Freedom, Christopher Stone, Etoile de Hollande, Heart's Desire;* pink—*The Doctor, Dainty Bess, First Love, Picture, Show Girl, Curly Pink.*

No white Hybrid Teas have high national ratings or have done well for us for an extended period except *Frau Karl Druschki* which is still conceded by rosarians everywhere to be the best white rose, though lacking fragrance completely. Also known as White American Beauty, it gives profuse bloom in May, a lesser amount in the Fall, and might be termed a "too-vigorous grower." The most effective way we ever used "the Frau" was to peg the canes to the ground with wire. Vertical shoots sprouted from the arched canes, grew high, bore many blooms, and bowed with their weight. The whole effect of the six plants so treated was that of a hedge; a blanket of white bloom on arching canes.

Five years ago we abandoned Climbers, finding that they did not produce repeated bloom. Though providing a gorgeous display in May, the labor and expense of keeping them pruned, fertilized and dusted and sprayed were out of proportion to their rewards.

Arbors or trellises must be kept in repair and painted, constant tying-up is required, and if grown on a white toolroom, garage or home, stain from the protective chemicals used soon turns the white paint to a spattered yellow or brown.

There are two exceptions that we keep. Both are yellow and practically evergreen. *Mermaid* is a vigorous climber or trailer, with large, single, fragrant pale-yellow blooms with amber stamens, that blooms constantly and is very disease-resistant. *Rosa banksiae* climbs 20′ or more, and blooms at the same time as wisteria, Carolina jessamine, azaleas, camellias and flowering fruit trees. Our particular vine came as a rooting from our "old family place" in Mississippi, and therefore has great sentimental value to us. It does not require dusting or spraying.

Many of the so-called "old-fashioned" varieties have always been conspicuous in our rose garden. We grow and love the "Common Moss" and the Crested Moss *(Chapeau de Napoleon)*, finding them fragrant and uniquely beautiful in the garden and in "period arrangements" where they seem to belong. They bloom for about three to four weeks late in April and into May, and do not repeat. *Rosa chinensis mutabilis*, with its single-formed bloom varying from yellow to orange to crimson, climbs 20′ into a tree and is constantly in bloom, requiring no care.

Of the Damask roses, *Kazanlik*, from which the Balkans made attar of roses for generations, is my favorite. Growing to 6-8′, it produces clusters of very double, highly-fragrant, rosy-pink blooms over a period of three to four weeks, also in late April and early May. *Louis Phillippe*, a China rose, is a constant bloomer for us, producing a hardy rosy-red bloom on a 4-5′ plant which is suitable for a hedgerow.

*Cardinal de Richelieu*, a double, rich violet Gallica, is interesting as a collector's item, though its fragility constitutes a drawback for this purpose. The plant makes a bushy shrub of 3-4′, with branches tending to shower earthwards.

A famous and influential variety in rose genealogy is my favorite of all "old" roses: the Bourbon *Souvenir de la Malmaison*. Quite a large bloom, very double, flesh-pink with a deeper rosy center, a free-producer and repeater on a 2-3′ bush, it is a must for rose collectors, possessing a great deal of unique character, age and beauty.

*Rosa Mundi* is a Gallica with semi-double form, wild rose fragrance and petals that are white or pale pink, broadly striped with red and deep pink, all white or all red.

*Rosa centifolia,* the Cabbage Rose or Rose of Provence, pink and fragrant, has a cupped form, overlapping petals and nodding head. It is the rose most frequently seen in paintings and prints of Flemish still-life and Georgian "period pieces."

More like an "old" rose in character, *La France,* the first Hybrid Tea (introduced in 1867), is a pale pink, fragrant, husky, vigorous bush. It repeats monthly, and since it blooms in Summer and looks like an "old" rose, I combine it with other Summer flowers in the Victorian manner, often turning it backwards. With an attractive reverse side, this practice creates an effect reminiscent of the "pieces" of bygone days.

We admire Hybrid Perpetuals. This class lacks a good yellow variety, but has many husky favorites in its ranks, including *Paul Neyron,* with its huge, very-double, cupped, fragrant, clear pink blooms (occasionally recurrent). It grows into a vigorous 5' plant.

I would hate to imagine a rose collection without *Rosa hugonis,* also called Father Hugo's Rose and the Golden Rose of China. No good for cutting, it has 2" fragile, single, pale-yellow blooms with very slight fragrance, borne singly on long, drooping branches. It ushers in the season for us, showing its first blooms by mid-March. It blooms for several weeks, but does not repeat. It is a shrub rose and should be given plenty of "elbow room."

Equally important as a shrub, or on a pillar, are the members of the *Rosa rugosa* family, so called because of their rugose, shining, dark-green foliage (a great addition to arrangements). White and pink species, both single and fragile, develop into 8' plants. The lovely Hybrid Rugosa *Sir Thomas Lipton* is an indispensable pillar rose, as is *Dr. Eckener,* which grows high into a tree. It has a large, semi-double, fragrant, coppery-yellow bloom which turns pink as it ages. Blooming intermittently, it is so hardy and satisfactory that we are planting another this year.

Modern rose gardens are incomplete without a variety of Floribundas, which have so much to offer in color range and diversity of form. Our favorite among the red ones is *Geranium Red,* which has a consistent habit of blooming singly, and is so large and so handsome with its multi-petaled formation that we would like to see it transferred to the new Grandiflora class. Very fragrant, a delightful orange-red, it is a constant bloomer and combines successfully in arrangements with the following other Floribundas which we grow successfully: *Fashion* (a truly gorgeous coral-peach, semi-double, possessing a wild rose fragrance on a vigorous 3' bush), *Orange Triumph* (actually a coral shade, small blooms clustered on a compact, bushy, 2-3' plant), and *Margo Koster* (a dwarf, fine for edging, with small salmon clustered blooms, no fragrance, but no thorns). Among red Floribundas, we also have a hedge of semi-double *Glorious* which blooms profusely in May, in spite of neglect (little pruning, no dusting or spraying) on 3' plants. Light red flowers, shaded with orange, have a slight fragrance. The foliage is dark and leathery.

The new Grandiflora class adds more size of plant and colorful bloom to our garden than anything which has happened lately. We are getting great success and much pleasure from two red varieties: *Roundelay,* tall grower (5') with extremely dark red, velvety-textured petals of typical Hybrid Tea number and form; and *Carrousel,* 6' high, huge, peony-like blooms (handsomer in their wide-open stage) and the longest-lasting cut flower that I know of. A coral, *Montezuma,* is 7' tall, with a handsome, urn-shaped bud. A slow opener, of Hybrid Tea quality, its color is very eye-catching. A pink of deep intensity, *Dean Collins* also has Hybrid Tea quality, and is a husky 6' bush. These four varieties lack fragrance completely, but have every other characteristic desired in an "ever-blooming" rose.

Most Southern rosarians who make room for all classes of roses believe that no garden is complete without planting Tea roses. We feel that they do not add enough to "pay their way." Being ever-blooming, they must be cared for during the entire season. We still have a *Duchess de Brabant* in our garden, but I do not consider it indispensable.

Roses are like people: We choose one for some characteristic, knowing that it lacks others which are desirable. None is perfect, embodying every attractive quality. In our garden, selected from all available classes or types, we have all desirable traits, each one compensating for those another lacks.

Problem number one in growing fine roses is securing good plants. Like producers of any other agricultural crop, rose nurserymen experience good and poor seasons. Secure your plants directly from reputable rose nurseries which either grow the plants they sell or buy them from such dependable growers that they can afford to guarantee the stock they sell, replacing it if the home gardener reports that he planted and tended it properly but it failed to prosper.

There is no such thing as a "bargain" rose plant. We steer clear of, and advise others against plants which can be loaded on a grocery store cart or sold in a department store basement. A certain amount of expense, two years of time, and much labor are required to grow, harvest, properly pack and ship No. 1 rose plants. All reputable nurseries charge essentially identical prices for the same varieties. Newer varieties are always higher, becoming cheaper as the supply increases. After patents on roses expire, the price is always reduced, too. A No. 1 plant should always have three strong green canes, 14-18″ long. The wood should appear alive, and there should be an ample root system, none of which should ever be cut off when being planted, unless it is already broken. Instead, adapt the hole to the extent of the longest roots. We do not buy or recommend paraffin-coated plants because the wax keeps the canes green, no matter how long the plants have been dug, and the roots may be dry and dead, concealed from the purchaser's view by a colorful paper bag.

So-called "bargain" roses are not guaranteed to be true to name, either, and the purchaser has no redress on this basis. A reliable nurseryman guarantees the plants he sells to be true to name, as well as to live and produce according to claims and the customer's expectations.

A reputable nurseryman also packs his stock for shipment so well that the plants will be moist when opened. We always soak our roses overnight in deep tubs of water before planting, no matter how damp their roots seem when unpacked, for they have usually been in transit many days and will be grateful for a thorough soaking. If weather does not permit immediate planting, we "heel" them into a deep pile of sawdust, with only the tops of the canes showing, until we can plant them. We usually ask for delivery late in February, knowing that eastern-grown roses have been harvested in the preceding Fall, but properly stored till delivery-time, and that California roses are not harvested till late December and January and stored till the time requested for delivery to the customer.

It makes no difference where a rose is grown as long as it is raised under proper conditions, carefully handled to prevent cuts and breakage and then kept in cold storage until packed for delivery. We would really prefer to plant in the Fall, but have had so many disastrous experiences with the "false spring" of January, which forces new growth destined to be killed by the colder weather which invariably follows, that we have learned to favor Spring planting. Obviously, since California roses are not harvested till Winter, you could not plant bushes from that area in the Fall if you preferred.

A regrettable aura of mystery seems to surround several facets of rose growing. One of these is planting. I find nothing mysterious about the procedure. Find a location where at least a half day's full sun is guaranteed and which provides good drainage, as roses do not tolerate "wet feet." To assure proper drainage, many growers place rocks, coarse gravel or tile in the bottom of their beds. We have not found this necessary.

The best soil is a rich slightly-acid clay loam with high humus content. Roses have been said to flourish in any soil which will grow good beans and potatoes. A certain amount of sand is helpful for drainage. Some rosarians find it easier to prepare holes, spaced as desired, rather than digging and preparing entire beds, since the prepared soil between the plants is then wasted. We, however, always prepare beds, digging to a minimum of 18″, then mixing topsoil, old cow manure and a generous layer of raw bone meal with a rotary tiller about two months before we plan to plant our new roses. Otherwise, we might burn the roots.

When we are ready to set in any shipment of roses (after soaking in water overnight), we place them in a large galvanized tub of water in the garden to prevent exposure of roots to air and wind. We have already placed our labels bearing name, year of planting and nursery from which procured, spacing them in accordance with the growth habit of each plant. Contrary to catalog instructions which always appear to be written for colder climates where bushes do not grow as large, we never place any plants closer to each other than 36″, and we plant many which we know to be husky growers from 40-48″ apart. Between every two rows of plants, we allow a service path of 48″, permitting easy access for applying dust or spray, fertilizer and in all other ways caring for the roses.

Before digging the hole for any plant, we examine its root system thoroughly for extent and formation, because we must allow enough space to set the roots as they grew in the field. The height and shape of the cone of soil which we build up in the center of the hole must conform to the individual plant. After fitting the plant down over the cone, with the crown or bud union a little above ground level, we shovel about half the soil back into the hole, then step in and tamp the soil gently but firmly on the roots, holding the plant with gloved hands to keep it straight and centered. Then we pour a bucket of water in and let it settle and soak in while we set another plant. This is most necessary, no matter how moist the soil is from recent rain, or plant roots won't completely settle.

Then we add the remaining soil, tamping it down firmly also. We hill-up the plant with a heaping spade of clean soil next to the crown and canes, then place a bushel of old sawdust (ground corn-cobs, buckwheat hulls or whatever mulch material you use may be substituted) on the plant. This is left until we believe Spring has come, then pulled down gradually, day by day, using gloved fingers as gently as possible to prevent breaking off new buds and tender growth. The sawdust now spread between the plants helps to mulch the bed, but is not thick enough to be a complete mulch.

We keep our rosebuds mulched in Winter as well as in Summer to keep down the growth and spread of chickweed (our worst weed pest), conserve and hold moisture and make a neat-appearing, well-groomed bed.

We do not hill up our old, well-established plants in this area; temperatures do not drop low enough to require their protection.

Pruning is also surrounded by an aura of awe and mystery. We do not understand this, since the purpose and method seem very simple to us. To comprehend how and when to prune, you know what you hope to accomplish.

In the first place, after all buds are killed by frost (usually in December), we top our plants to prevent damage to long canes from lashing winds, sleet, etc. We prune our old plants when the swelling leaf buds appear, usually in early March. Certain equipment is necessary to do a good job with least damage to the swelling plants: a pair of strong, sharp, pruning shears, gloves and a small amount of orange shellac with which to paint the cuts. This keeps borers from getting into the wounds and going down into the plant, which, if allowed to happen, is fatal. We formerly applied this with a small brush, but last year a smart rosarian friend showed us how to use a medicine dropper to apply the shellac. This saves splashing, waste and does the neatest job imaginable. Orange shellac is preferable to clear, because it is easier to see readily where you have been.

Pruning results in well-balanced bushes with four to six evenly-spaced branches. This calls for the removal of unwanted canes, twiggy or spindly growth, dead or near-dead, old, gnarled canes that will not produce new shoots and canes growing awkwardly or crossing. In pruning, we direct the sap into canes which promise to produce quality bloom, encourage new basal growth, good air circulation, allow light to reach the center of all plants, permit the wood to ripen more rapidly and reduce fungus disease.

Each rose plant presents its own problems, calling for individual treatment. Pruning is a very tedious and time-consuming operation, amounting to plant surgery with all the above purposes in mind. The usual result is that we prune vigorous, strong plants less, and weaker growers more heavily. Uniform pruning is an utter impossibility in a rose garden. Pruning is either light, moderate or hard. We practice moderate pruning, always cutting just above an outward-slanting eye, so that new shoots will grow out from, rather than into, the plant. Leaving stubs above the eyes where new growth begins is an invitation to canker, the worst stem disease of roses.

Pruning goes on all season. As the plants grow, they tend to produce some unwanted canes. Others die or appear unhealthy. Cutting blooms is actually a form of pruning and should always be done carefully and judiciously, just above an out-pointing eye so that new growth will not extend toward the center of the plant. Permitting a friend or neighbor to have "cutting privileges" in one's rose garden while on Summer vacation may, and often does, do more harm than allowing the blooms to remain and die on the plants. Proper cutting of blooms is a very integral part of caring for plants. Continue to use orange shellac all season to heal cuts.

It is not advisable to fertilize newly-planted bushes until after the peak of bloom in May, since the nutrients in the well-prepared soil are sufficient. After the May bloom, however, we treat them as "old" plants, and fertilize them every three or four weeks through August. It is not wise to apply fertilizer after this because early frosts may kill new growth stimulated by the plant nutrients and cause serious damage. I push back the mulch around each bush, gently work one teacupful of a well-balanced fertilizer into the soil making sure to keep it several inches from the plant to prevent possible burning. Then I pull back the mulch. If there is no rain for several days, I irrigate the beds using flat, plastic hoses with water outlets only on the downside, twined snake-fashion through the rose beds, under the mulch, where they remain until worn out. I hook an ordinary garden hose to each in turn, turn the faucet low and soak for several hours. By this method, there is no water waste. The mulch does not have to be wet, but holds the moisture in the soil which becomes thoroughly soaked under it. Roses should be watered weekly in a drought.

Unfortunately the genus Rosa, particularly the fancy new hybrids, is as attractive to disease and insects as it is to humans. The most destructive disease which besets our plants is stem canker, which is as insidious as cancer in the human. It appears in a blotchy fashion on apparently-healthy canes, turning them a cinnamon color, finally killing the cane and eventually the plant. The only remedy is surgery. Cut the cane to a point below the canker; ofttimes a whole cane has to be severed at the base. Always paint the wound with orange shellac.

Blackspot of rose foliage is the most talked-about disease, but does not cause us as much sorrow as canker. It is a fungus, which is carried in in the air and thrives particularly in damp or rainy spells. Practice good garden hygiene. Pick off and burn affected leaves. Better still, prevent its formation by weekly applications of dust or spray. In 1956 we saw almost no blackspot and no powdery mildew, another fungus disease which causes great disfigurement to the foliage, and to the bloom as well. It is generally conceded that if a preparation will control blackspot, it will control mildew at the same time.

Some insects may damage roses in our area. Aphids appear early in Spring, but are readily controlled by any insecticide containing nicotine sulphate. Thrips appear particularly and uncannily on the white and yellow varieties. Red spider mites can cause as much defoliation as blackspot. A defoliated plant cannot produce roses, because all food is manufactured and stored in the leaves. A regular and thorough application of a protective material containing the chemicals which prevent infestation by the known rose enemies is essential. This is preventive, rather than curative.

We used spray in years past, but found that we can apply a thorough coating of dust in the time required to mix a spray. Ofttimes a hurried job must be done when rain is imminent, for one of the credos of good rose care is: "Never permit a rain to catch your plants without a fresh, thorough coating of protective materials on them." Of course, whatever is used must be applied on the undersides of the leaves, as well as the top. If ever in doubt about whether to dust today, the answer is unequivocally "Do." The time to start disease and insect prevention is when the first leaves begin to form, and though it is difficult to continue applications after all bloom buds have been frost-killed, it should be done. Protection should be provided as early and as late as there is foliage on the plants.

We apply a dormant lime-sulphur spray in January to disinfect the plants, causing all leaves to drop in a few weeks. Rake these from the Winter mulch and burn.

Contrary to common belief, the rose is not difficult to grow. When you consider the blooming period which stretches in Piedmont, North Carolina, from mid-April to mid-November at least, the rewards far exceed those from any other plant. In the cases of camellias, lilies and hemerocallis, for instance, enthusiasts must prolong the period of bloom by planting early, medium and late-blooming varieties, whereas we may expect repeated blooms for seven or eight months of the year from the same rose plants.

Often one hears the comment, made critically, that "he" or "she" spends so much time on his roses, when the actual fact is that the happy rose grower is spending the time *with* his roses. They are satisfying and rewarding companions, with the joys and dividends in direct proportion to the effort and attention expended. It is true that it is not advisable for individuals who take lengthy Summer vacations to attempt rose growing, but on the other hand, one who grows and loves roses does not want long separations from them. As soon as I return from a five-day absence during the blooming season, I check on the amount of bloom and whether it appears to have rained, necessitating an early coverage with protective dust or spray.

One of the charms of growing roses as a hobby is that it offers a

Ivory Fashion F
E. S. Boerner; introduced Jackson & Perkins, Newark, N.Y. Plant patent 1688.
Described page 248.

CANDY CANE
MIN.
Ralph Moore; introduced Sequoia Nursery, Visalia, Calif. Described page 241.

LITTLE SCOTCH
MIN.
Ralph Moore; introduced Sequoia Nursery, Visalia, Calif. Described page 249.

limitless number of side-benefits or dividends. For me, one has been that of being an accredited judge of the American Rose Society, of which there are only nine in the Carolinas. This activity works reciprocally: I become a better grower by judging annually in the rose shows in North and South Carolina, and the more I grow and live with roses, the more competent judge I can become.

Helping to organize societies devoted to the love of the rose, both in Durham and other towns in North Carolina, and giving programs to these groups on different aspects of rose lore and culture, has also contributed to my enjoyment of this hobby and to the sum total of my knowledge of the genus Rosa. By meeting with the small local groups and by attending the national conventions, held throughout the United States, I have grown to realize that rosarians in general are a wonderful and dedicated group of people (the largest devoted to the love of a particular flower) and the rose has been the basis of many new and fine friendships for my family and for me. My horticultural knowledge and experience have thereby been enriched, and the horizons of my life have been widened.

Rose geneology is another facet of the subject which appeals to me. I have made a small beginning by, for instance, tracing the progeny of the variety *Charlotte Armstrong*. A superior rose itself, with a high national rating and frequently chosen as "Queen of the Show" due to its exhibition form and other qualities, it has also been used with great success in hybridizing other fine and popular roses.

Roses, save for the dark red ones, dry successfully and therefore lend themselves to handsome Winter arrangements. They are generally conceded to be unsurpassed for arrangements in their fresh state. These aspects add to the attractiveness of growing roses as a hobby and constitute a large part of my enjoyment of the quantity of blooms which we have available from April through November of each year.

The rose is incontestably the most universally-beloved and the most versatile of flowers. It makes an ideal hobby plant because of the challenge offered by the care and know-how it requires, and by the wide range of its classes, varieties and their uses.

The genus Rosa offers greater opportunities than any other flower for study, research, experimentation and side hobbies.

# The Effect of Plant
# Patent Protection
# in the United States

John F. Lemon*
West Grove, Pa.

$P$UBLIC INTEREST and well-being has been served and advanced so greatly by the rapidly-increased introduction of new and valuable plants in those countries which give plant breeders protection and incentive that world-wide government interest in the subject is now wide-spread. Commissions from both the British and Canadian governments are in the midst of intensive studies right now. The United States system stands out in the spotlight. Court decisions upholding "patent rights" or similar (but differently-named) "growers rights" affecting new horticultural and agricultural varieties have recently been made in Belgium, Holland, France, Italy, Austria and America. These laws vary from country to country as to the type of plant that can be protected, the length of time of protection and in many other details.

Plant breeders in the United States had no form of protection until the early 1930's. Since plant breeding (if properly done) is an expensive procedure requiring a great deal of care and detail to carry out tests to insure valuable selections, only those enthusiasts who could afford it as a hobby engaged in this activity. I speak with feeling in this matter, since my grandfather, father and uncle (E. G. Hill, Fred Lemon and Joseph H. Hill, respectively) poured much of the profit from their rose business into creating new varieties during their lifetimes. Far too-few men could do so, and plant breeding in general was at a low ebb. Government experiment stations did most of the work with grains and cereals. New vegetables resulted from the efforts of two different groups: the very big seed dealers (who needed a con-

*Vice-president, The Conard-Pyle Co.

86

stant flow of new named varieties to brighten their sales lines of trade packaged goods), and the great canners and processors (who wanted improved varieties for their own purposes and did everything possible to keep the results of their efforts secret). Fruit, like ornamental breeding, was negligible. The United States was very much behind the rest of the world in developing and introducing new rose varieties. The quality of the plant and flower of those which were put on the market was low. Most good roses came from Europe.

Then in the early 1930's, Congress decided that the inventors of new asexually-reproduced horticultural products deserved the same protection and advantages as the inventors of new mechanical and chemical ideas, methods and products. So, it established the plant patent.

## BASED ON COMPETITION

The whole idea of patents in the United States is based upon the constitutional provision which gives Congress the power to encourage new products for the eventual good of the general public. It was written as an inducement to promote study, experiment and spending money, time and effort in attempts to produce new and better things for everyone. The incentive offered to plant breeders gives them a relatively-short (17 year) period of monopoly, and they cannot extend their patents. Patents are also limited to those varieties and species which are reproduced *only* asexually (by cuttings, budding, grafting, layering or any other method which involves taking a piece of one plant to make another exactly like it), not by seed (which is produced by sexually crossing two plants, and which will in turn develop into an unpredictable offspring when it sprouts). As a result of this law, every patented plant in the United States is actually a "piece" of the one original seedling plant. Every *Peace* rose growing in the gardens of America is truly a "part" of the original bush.

The sudden change in conception of the property value of a horticultural variety from an open "public ownership" status (similar to that of open public lands or unbranded livestock) to that of a legal title and ownership (even for only 17 years duration) took the trade and public a little time and education to get used to, just as the initial establishment of private land ownership, fences and individual rights did. Nevertheless, a great majority of nurserymen accepted the plant Patent Act as law, and endeavored to understand and abide by it from the start. Today, it would be difficult to find many nurserymen who object in any way to it.

Rather, every good nurseryman believes that it is a good thing both for the trade and for the general public. In the law's earliest stages, the general public jumped to the erroneous conclusion that any plant that was patented had to be very good. A very large group still does not realize that certain plants are patented. But, from their experience in buying patented articles in other lines, they accept a patent tag as an indication that the owner was at least willing to spend money on a patent. A much smaller buyers' group considers a patent tag or notice only as evidence that they are getting the genuine article (but not as a guarantee of the excellence of the product). We still need to firmly impress these latter facts in the mind of the general public (for its own protection). The only people who still object to the plant patent are those who believe in communal instead of private property rights of any kind.

## ENCOURAGED BREEDERS HERE

Today, less than 30 years later, more than half of the finest rose breeders in the world are at work here in America. The royalties and purchase monies earned by a few hybridizers outside the United States whose roses have met the standards set by competition here have enabled them to continue to improve the quality and quantity of their work and thus contribute to the betterment of the rose throughout the world. A study of plant breeding in those countries which have adopted some form of protection for their plant breeders, as opposed to those countries which have not, gives impressive weight to the value of protection for plant breeders. In almost all of Europe where protection is at last possible, the tremendous increase in interest, effort and productiveness on the part of plant breeders is quite evident. Great Britain and Canada (where the breeders have no protection at present) used to lead the field, but now plant breeding has fallen into the doldrums, is little practiced and the results are exceedingly ineffective (in fact, backward). Only those English and Canadian breeders who market their products in patent-protected areas are working with any assurance or enthusiasm.

This market-wide improvement of quality evolved as a result of the restrictions which patent owners were able to place on the quality of plants bearing their patents which are offered to the public. This is not a *requirement* of the patent law itself, but it is right given by the law of which, I am happy to say, almost every American rose patent owner takes advantage. Almost without exception, they require every licensee to market only those plants which meet the standards set by the American Association of Nurserymen to qualify them as Number 1 or 1½ roses. All undergrades may not be sold. In order to meet this competition, producers of non-patented plants must offer roses of the same general quality to the public if they are to stay in business. So you see that the rose-growing American public has profited tremendously as a result of the plant patent law.

## Spurred Public Interest

The tremendous increase in interest by the general public in the ornamental field in the United States is largely the result of the advance in the garden rose industry, made possible by the enormous increase in public promotion and information paid for by the royalties earned by the patents. In order to be of eventual profit to the owner, a surprisingly-large part of royalties has to be spent upon acquainting the general public with the new invention and its advantages. It is not enough just to develop or invent a fine new thing. No one knows about it. It is not enough to patent and achieve a monopoly control of it for a short period of time. Nobody knows about it, so few want it. Everyone must hear about it and its advantages before they can buy and use it. The last 30 years of plant patent protection in the United States have proven this beyond question.

Breeders of fruits and nuts are beginning to profit by the example set by the rose. The delay in these fields was caused by the much longer time needed to grow and test new seedlings, and then propagate and grow them on a large enough scale to put them on the market.

In short summary, then, the Plant Patent Act in the United States has immeasurably helped the general public, the nursery industry and the hybridizer at the same time. It has created an interest and resulted in an effort to breed new plants which have been introduced years before they might otherwise have been available. It has also supplied the wherewithal to see that the public is advised of the availability of these fine new varieties.

# Roses Bring Much Joy

Mrs. I. R. Mercer

San Antonio, Tex.

I WAS PLACED in an orphanage in New York City at a very early age. When I was 9 years old, I was adopted by a German family in the wonderful state of Texas. We lived three miles from the little town of Schulenburg and a mile and a half from a small settlement called High Hill. High Hill consisted of a church, school, graveyard and a general store. Forty-eight years ago, this was way out in the country. I walked to school in High Hill from there. Although I was meant to care for this family's 8-month-old boy, I was put to work in the fields. This is not meant to sound pathetic, because that was the most wonderful thing ever to happen to me. I did not realize until a few years ago that in this way I was taught the art of horti-culture. When a person has this kind of experience, I believe that he or she is wonderfully blessed.

Twenty years ago my late husband and I bought and built our present home on a two-and-a-half acre lot. My experience at High Hill was all in the field with cotton, corn and vegetables. So, vege-tables were what I grew until 1948 when I switched to flowers, shrubs and roses.

I purchased my first dozen roses from an itinerant agent who "hap-pened" along almost before the water facilities were connected.

Only one lived—a *Radiance*—but it out-grew, out-bloomed and out-lived many varieties planted later. In fact, it stayed for nearly 20 years and was the source of inspiration that fired my ambition to grow roses as a hobby.

The years have taught me that "life is no bed of roses," but I have learned that a bed of roses will do much toward making life more enjoyable. The work involved in tending roses is a labor of love —an outlet for suppressed emotions, also recommended for stiff joints, sore tonsils and mental mesmerism.

To me, half the fun of growing roses has been collecting and experimenting with different types and varieties and observing their various characteristics and habits at close range.

I now have 74 choice Hybrid Teas in an ideal location, and I must say that they have been a great joy for me. I give them the same care as the cat and the canary, and they show it too. I have beaten the theory (in this locale) that roses must be replaced every three or four years if you want healthy, hardy blooms.

Without question, the Hybrid Teas are the aristocrats of the modern garden. *La France,* the original Hybrid Tea, has a special place in my heart and garden. The enormous blooms of *The Doctor* and his competitor, *Dr. Debat,* are truly sensational. The latter is a seedling of the reliable *Radiance,* and time will tell whether it has inherited some of the vim and vigor of the old-timer. For extra-long-stemmed buds of perfection, I have found *President Herbert Hoover, Charlotte Armstrong, Grande Duchesse Charlotte, Sutter's Gold* and *Buccaneer* all very capable of supplying my bud vases. Some of the others that have done especially well for me are *Crimson Glory, Comtesse Vandal, Rubaiyat, Colin Kelly, Yours Truly, Texas Centennial, Santa Anita, Picture, Tallyho, Nocturne, Eclipse, Peace, Forty-niner* and *Chrysler Imperial.*

Unrivaled for their ever-blooming clusters and sprays of sparkling colors are the small-flowered Polyanthas and their hybrids, the large-flowered Floribundas. They are ideal for creating a scene of color and show up to better advantage when planted in borders or in groups. My favorite Polyantha, *Crimson Rosette,* is a rather small bush with excellent foliage right down to the ground. Every spray is a bouquet of unfading red roses. I once counted 52 blooms on one spray! *Goldilocks* is a good yellow Floribunda that is bushy and a prolific bloomer. *Red Ripples* and *Ming Toy* grow tall.

Shrub roses are the toughest of all. *Mabelle Sterns* grows low but spreading, and soft pink blooms come in clusters. *Kathleen* has many slender canes which need support and bear flowers in clusters that resemble glorified apple blossoms. *Rosa roxburghii* is the most unique rose in my collection. It should be grown as a specimen shrub since it resents pruning. I cherish *Harison's Yellow* for its early Spring bloom and fern-like foliage.

The famous old Climbing Tea *Gloire de Dijon* grows rampantly and produces an enormous crop of large ruffled blooms with "sunset hues in its heart." Other Climbers that I rate highly are *Mermaid, Dr. Nicolas, Thor, Mrs. Pierre S. duPont, City of York, High Noon* and *Paul's Scarlet Climber.*

Some of the old perpetual roses and the Teas are wonderful for gardens. The old *General Jacqueminot* grows so tall that it needs a post to lean on. The giant blooms of *Paul Neyron* are striking against a background of green foliage. *Baronne Henriette Snoy,* one of the new Teas, has well-shaped blooms of peach-pink, that resemble crushed velvet in the center when fully open.

The Moss roses are very beautiful reminiscences of by-gone days.

The intriguing Miniatures are quiet different. *Pixie* is known as the world's tiniest white rose. *Midget* is red. These small roses are hardy and easy to grow.

Single roses, too, are good bloomers and add beauty to the perennial border. *Dainty Bess* is well-known and loved by all flower arrangers. I also enjoy the long, spiral buds of *Lula.*

I can sum up my favorites in this manner: bush roses, pink— *Radiance, Briarcliff, Mrs. Charles Bell, Mme. Butterfly, Editor McFarland, Mrs. John Laing, Stockton's Beauty, John L. Mock, President Macia, Dainty Bess, Picture, San Anita, The Doctor, Showgirls, Dr. Debat, Capistrano, Yours Truly, Chestnut Rose, La France, Contesse Vandal, Mission Bells, Helen Traubel, Good News, Enchantment, Crested Moss, Suzon, Lotthe, William R. Smith, Mme. Henirettia Snoy, Mabelle Sterns, Frolic, Lilibet, Ma Perkins, Pinocchio, The Fairy, Cecile Brunner, Fashion, Rosa rouletti, Sweet Fairy, Columbia, Queen Elizabeth, Dame Edith Helen* and *Ernie Pyle;* red—*Red Radiance, Etoile de Hollande, Charles Mallerin, Ami Quinard, Better Times, American Beauty, Rose of Freedom, Christopher Stone, Charles K. Douglas, Heart's Desire, Crimson Glory, Mirandy, Nocture, New Yorker, Gruss an Teplitz, Red Ripples, Ming Toy, Red Sweetheart, Donald Prior, Floradora, Symphonie, Charlotte Armstrong, Grande Duchesse Charlotte, Chrysler Imperial, Tallyho, Goethe, Paul Neyron, Vogue, Mojave, Rubaiyat, Embers, Valentine, Eutin, Carrousel, Red Pinocchio, Crimson Rosette, Texas Centennial, Poinsettia, Happiness, Frensham, Tom Thumb, Midget, Kriders Thornless Red, General Jacqueminot, Colin Kelly* and *E. G. Hill*; yellow— *Golden Dawn, Mrs. Pierre S. duPont, Mrs. E. P. Thom, Golden Charm, Phyllis Gold, Soeur Therese, Lowell Thomas, Sunburst, Luxemburg, Fred Howard, Eclipse, Peace,*

*Buccaneer, Diamond Jubilee, Chief Seattle, Debonair, Fantasia, Goldilocks, Golden Sceptre, Joanne Hill, Lady Hillingdon, Mrs. Dudley Cross* and *Baby Gold Star;* bi-color blend—*President Herbert Hoover, Forty-niner, Sutter's Gold, Condesa de Sastago Talisman, Taffeta, Lula* and *Horace McFarland;* white—*Frau Karl Druschki, Calodonia, Kaiserin Auguste Viktoria, Mme. Jules Bouche, Neige Parfum, McGredy's Ivory, Snowbird, Konigan Louise, Maman Cochet, Pedralbes, Summer Snow* and *Pixie;* Climbers—red—*Thor, Blaze, Paul's Scarlet Climber, Red Radiance* and *Crimson Glory;* pink—*Dr. Nicholas, Gloire de Dijon, Radiance, Descano Pillar, Cecile Brunner, Kathleen* and *Meda;* white—*City of York* and *Prosperity*; yellow—*Mrs. Pierre S. duPont, High Noon, Mermaid, Gold Rush, Marechal Neil, Paul's Lemon Pillar, Harrison's Yellow* and *Peace.*

Roses should be planted here in January and February, although I have planted them in November and December. It's best to transplant them when they are thoroughly dormant after a good cold spell.

I dig the bed out well below the sub-soil, about 18″ deep, and fill in with good soil. Then I add part sand and from one to five cups of bone meal. Peat moss may be placed in the bed, or on top. It's important to give the roots plenty of room to grow in.

Dust the bed with sulphur to repel insects and diseases. I use Black Leaf 40 and 74% chlordane for insects, and captan and sulphur dust for blackspot with fine results. On our hottest days, I dust around 2 p.m., and then give my roses a good well-water bath the next day about 11 a.m. I do try to pick cloudy days. I have every reason to believe that this 21-hour sulphur treatment is a big help. Besides, the bath helps to acidify the soil around the roots since I use a lot of sulphur. I also treat my azaleas, camellias, amaryllis and begonias the same way, and have luck with all.

I feed my roses at least three times a year. While I have tried a variety of commercial foods, bone meal and super-phosphate seem to do the trick nicely.

Water roses deep once a week in warm, dry weather. Be sure that the roots are thoroughly soaked.

I always used to prune my roses on New Year's Day—until we had a couple of bad storms in late January and March. Now I prune them in early February.

To protect roses from freezes (30° won't hurt them), fasten news-papers around the bushes with clothes pins.

Roses are somewhat like relatives—one has to live with them to really know them! While familiarity may breed contempt among relatives. I can assure anyone that it's impossible to live with roses, care for them and study their personalities without absorbing some of their sweetness.

I have made roses my long suit, and they have done more for me than any of my other hobbies (sewing, all kinds of needle work, bridge and a little charity and community work). I feel so near to God in my rose garden. They are my recreation, health and relaxa-tion. Oh! what a joy it is to take a top-quality *Peace, Charlotte Arm-strong, Chrysler Imperial, Picture, Comtesse Vandal* and *Kaiserin Auguste Viktoria* to hospitals, friends and neighbors. My wonderful husband presented me with an air-conditioned car in 1956 that en-ables me to take roses to friends out of town. Can you rose lovers imagine the scene that I created as I stepped out of my car on one hot Summer day in the heart of a crowded street in Houston? I stopped the pedestrian traffic with big, beautiful, long-stemmed roses of mixed colors wrapped in a cone of Reynold's Wrap. It took 25 minutes to get to the little clerk to whom I was presenting the roses, and I was very pleased when a man reached over my head (I am very short), touched a *Peace* petal, turned to his wife and said, "Yes, they are real." Several people asked to buy them.

I owe a lot of my success to Dr. R. C. Allen. In March 1952, I was in a big rush to return a book that I had purchased and was dissatis-fied with. It was during the noon rush, and the clerks were all busy, so I decided to make a fair exchange. I quickly glanced at the display of books and grabbed the one with the pretty roses on the cover. Who says never judge a book by its cover! I started out with a bang, but' was let down temporarily when I was told by all the good rose dealers that it was too late to plant. So, I took Dr. Allen's advice and joined the American Rose Society, then started out that December.

I am crowding 60, but instead of slowing down, I am automatic-ally speeding up, thanks to the good Lord for my wonderful luck with **roses.**

# Let's Breed
# For Blackspot Resistance

Stephen F. Hamblin
Lexington, Mass.

T HE most discouraging pest of modern roses is a fungus disease
known as blackspot. Its spores fly about on the wind, land on moist
leaf surfaces and enter and kill the leaf cells. You first notice it when
small dark spots appear on the leaves. The spots increase in size, the
diseased leaflets soon fall and the partly-defoliated plants stop growing and blooming and go into a premature winter rest. The severity
of attack varies with local conditions. Faithful spraying with fungicides can largely control this disease for the season, but next year
may be another story.

## ALL EUROPEANS HAVE IT

You can expect blackspot to infest roses which have European an-
cestors. But, some plants are rarely or never attacked. Hybrids show
varying immunity, depending on the combinations of characteristics
that they have inherited from their parents. No one has yet studied
the frequency of infection of all rose varieties, though much thought
has been given to methods of control.

Possibly a more certain (but more slowly-achieved) solution will
come when we breed new roses using parents which are truly-resist-
ant to this disease. Then spores falling on foliage of new naturally-
resistant varieties and their hybrids will have no effect.

We might consider that susceptibility to leaf-spot attack is a character inherited through the genes of the chromosomes, just as other
foliage and flower characteristics are. First of all, we need to study
those wild species roses which never show blackspot under any circumstances. This check-up should be made under the varied condi-

tions of all the regions in our country to see if heat or cold, moisture or dry air, soil, culture or any local factor causes it to appear.

We may group our wild species roses geographically into three classes: European, North American and Asiatic. Those which have been cultivated the longest are the ones from Europe, the so-called "old-fashioned" roses. From these "cottage," "cabbage," Moss, "French," "Scotch" and "Austrian" roses have come our currently-popular Hybrid Perpetuals and Hybrid Teas. As more Hybrid Tea blood goes into Floribundas, leaf troubles may increase. Although they become defoliated early (after the June bloom), blackspot does not seem to harm the health of the plants. It does make them unsightly in mid-Summer, but they come back year after year.

## AMERICANS ARE UNTESTED

The American wild roses (like *Rosa setigera*) have not been used much in creating new garden varieties. We don't know whether blackspot was present here originally, but we do know that it showed up when European wild roses and garden forms were planted in the New World. It would be interesting to discover if any American wild species are naturally immune.

Resistance may be more pronounced in Asiatic wild roses. We should check them to find out. *Rosa hugonis* never shows the least touch of blackspot. Nor do its sisters *Rosa ecae, Rosa primula* and *Rosa xanthina,* all of which produce lovely yellow blooms in June. *Rosa roxburghii* grows into a giant shrub with prickly hips. *Rosa rugosa* bears huge tomato-like hips, but its hybrids are not immune to leaf-spot. *Rosa multiflora* holds its foliage well, as do many of its hybrids (particularly the older Polyantha varieties which are the result of a union with *Rosa chinensis*. Perhaps the most striking "resister" is *Rosa wichuraiana.* Its glossy foliage is never attacked by blackspot. This character goes over into many of the Large-flowered Climbers, in spite of the influence of the other Hybrid Tea parents. Some Polyanthas and Floribundas (like *The Fairy* or *Johanna Tantau*) which have *Rosa wichuraiana* in their ancestry are practically immune to blackspot. Although first generation seedlings of *Rosa wichuraiana* hybrids are robust climbers, they can be reduced in bulk by crossing with a bush species, and could carry immunity into endless generations of bush roses. The two Asiatic bush roses which are much used as parents in our modern roses are *Rosa chinensis* and *Rosa odorata*. The pure form of the former is almost never seen today. Its hybrids are often a combination with European species roses. *Rosa chinensis viridiflora* has clean foliage. So do the modern Miniature roses which are mostly in-bred Chinas. The climax of resistance is found in *Rosa odorata* and its Tea offspring, although the plants are not hardy in 0° weather (and now rarely seen in our gardens). While we find Tea blood in nearly every modern rose, it is usually combined with that of an European rose, and its natural immunity is endangered by the susceptibility of the weaker parent. While some Hybrid Tea forms are nearly or truly immune (as is *Peace*), their seedlings or hybrids may "throw back" to the weakness of an old Hybrid Perpetual or "Peretiana" which fills the other half of their family tree. *Gardenia* and *Sweetheart* (and other rarely-seen varieties), both Ramblers with *Rosa wichuraiana* and *Rosa odorata* in their background, are guaranteed free from blackspot. Several generations of inbreeding might produce bush forms that are hardy and everblooming. Or, we might breed *Rosa wichuraiana* with some of the Miniatures to produce good Floribundas, and with *Rosa odorata* to get the flower size, hardiness and fragrance of our present-day Hybrid Teas. The late Walter Brownell did this when he created *Pink Princess*.

So, the only sure way to be certain of complete blackspot immunity in future rose generations is to breed from parents of certain immunity. This means that we must entirely by-pass the European types and their hybrids (even modern Hybrid Teas, Floribundas and all their kin).

## MIRACLE

We muse on miracles who look
But lightly on a rose!
Who gives it fragrance or the glint
of glory that it shows?

Who holds it here between the sky
and earth's rain-softened sod?
The miracle of one pale rose
is proof enough of God!

Edith Daley

# Good Roses For The Finger Lakes

Clifford N. Strait

Canandaigua, N.Y.

Dᴜʀɪɴɢ ᴛʜᴇ ᴇᴀʀʟʏ Winter of 1952, I decided to move a number of Hybrid Tea bushes into a separate bed and attempt in my humble, clumsy way to keep an accurate record of their performance.

While trying to decide about location, size, etc., I also gave some thought to just what I wanted in a rose. In reverse order, the result seemed to be a prejudice against varieties with low, spreading growth, and single, Polythantha-type bloom. I favor reasonably-long pointed buds that open rather slowly on stems long enough for cutting and use in home bouquets.

I picked a spot 500′ from a building that is exposed to the elements and has a heavy clay soil. I reasoned that the varieties which performed well under my average or below-average care would perform well for the average novice, who is apt to be either neglectful or too careful. I did not specially prepare the bed. Instead, I merely dug a series of holes about 15″ in circumference and 15″ deep during thawing weather in the Winter and early Spring, so that the bushes, when planted, would be about 18″ apart. I left a ridge of soil about 3″ wide between the holes.

I purchased the bushes from various sources. They were quite well divided among Eastern, Pacific, mid-western and Texas growers.

I started moving or planting bushes as early as possible, and continued until mid-May. I planted some more bushes during the next Fall and again during the Spring of 1954. The bed held 80 bushes by the time that I started my first records on June 1, 1954.

In planting the bushes, I mixed part of the clay taken from the holes with good top soil and old rotted manure. When I finished, I put a ½″ layer of mulch composed of mixed sand, peat moss and buckwheat hulls on top of the bed to keep the soil from cracking when the clay baked under the sun. I topped this with straw held down with chunks of clay until growth started.

After uncovering and pruning lightly, I spread 10 pounds of 8-12-6 commercial fertilizer and 25 pounds of dry cow manure as evenly as possible among the bushes. I also gave each bush a 5-milligram tablet of Vitamin B-1. Beginning on June 1, I fed the bushes 6 gallons of Ra-Pid-Gro solution every week from an ordinary sprinkling can, allowing the solution to fall onto the leaves as much as possible. I stopped feeding on August 15.

I have never had more than ordinary trouble with insects or diseases. Consequently, I started the season by dusting and spraying with DuPont Rose Dust once a week and after a heavy shower or prolonged rain. I saw practically no evidence of blackspot or insect damage during all of the June bloom. Rainfall was above normal during the early Spring, but, unfortunately, we had none from mid-June till early August (a total of 53 days), and there was an almost-steady hot, dry wind. The first rains to fall in early August disappeared like magic.

While I am willing to take the word of good pathologists that blackspot needs moisture to germinate and that an early infestation may be caused by water drops splashing spores from the ground onto the leaves, I am convinced that my bushes were "dusted" constantly with spores carried by the wind and that they didn't need water to cause an infection. By late July, my bushes showed the worst blackspot infection that I have ever seen, in spite of the early and regular use of good sprays and dusts. Not a single bush was immune. Naturally, I stepped up the use of Fermate, but new leaves would still show blackspot symptoms in 24-48 hours. Finally, in desperation, I covered the leaves (top and bottom), stems and bed with a heavy Bordeaux mixture. I repeated this dose the next day. On the fourth day, I applied half-strength Bordeaux and half-strength Fermate. During the next 12 days, I applied straight Fermate three times. By then I had some new foliage, thanks to considerable assistance from three good showers. Five days later I began using captan twice a week. Some bushes showed blackspot symptoms throughout the balance of the season, but the bed as a whole showed a reasonable amount of control by September 10. Basically, these bushes must have been strong in order to recover so admirably from such an epidemic of disease and wild dosages of chemicals. Undoubtedly, the practices that I used were wrong, unnecessary or excessive, and probably typical of a bull-headed amateur, but what would you do if your rose bushes were suddenly completely covered with blackspot, then defoliated? Throw them away and start a new bed? No, that's where the bull-headedness comes in.

I didn't prove anything, except, possibly, that a prolonged drought is not good for roses, and that dry wind (either hot or cold) causes much damage to succulent growth. Several of my friends suggested that my careless foliar feeding might have provided enough moisture for a sufficient length of time to permit blackspot to germinate. However, I checked this carefully all through August, and usually all leaves dried completely within 48 minutes. There was little time, if any, when there was no dust or spray on the leaves. Maybe not enough, but certainly as much as I ever used at any time during the last quarter century.

For the sake of my records, I did not disbud. I counted all buds or blooms except a few rare cases of thread-like side shoots bearing buds decidedly below average size for the variety. I paid careful attention to the number or percentage of damaged buds and those tending to ball, blue or burn (and the possible cause of such disfigurement) since they would hardly be used in the average home bouquet.

I paid more attention than usual to color changes through the blooming season. As a final check, I cut one good strong side shoot from each bush after a severe Spring storm had broken several of the bushes. I cut all bloom while in the bud stage with 6-8" stems in order to leave as much foliage on the plant as possible. I allowed an occasional bloom to mature on the plant in order to check the petal count with that given by the grower or in Modern Roses IV. I found practically no deviation from the number of petals that each variety is supposed to have.

The performance results are more interesting and understandable in tabular form, but I cannot resist making a few comments. I noticed a picture of *Girona* in an Armstrong catalog several years ago and wanted one. But, after reading that it did not do well in areas outside of the cool, moist climate of the Pacific coast, I held off until 1953. I almost went on the warpath when the first blooms did not in any way fit the picture or the description. However, I finally decided that since the buds and bloom were very attractive, of good size and on very good cutting stems, I would not complain but would keep the plant. That Fall, I was very explicit when I ordered additional plants. You can well imagine my delight the following year when I picked numerous June buds and flowers exactly like the picture in the catalog. Just to match that picture was well worth the cost and effort devoted to those bushes. In the hot, dry season, the buds and bloom resemble a good *Pilar Lande-cho,* with a little more red on the outside of the bud. This is a beautiful rose in any season, and, contrary to the caution in the catalog, it grows and blooms well for me.

*Debonair* is a dirty white rose all during June. It does not pick up a fair yellow coloring until late July. It is inclined to ball, and is damaged easily in wind and rain. While it produces a better-than-average number of buds, they come on short stems in groups of two or three. Growth is excellent, but with bud stems confined largely to the top of the bush. *Debonair* was defoliated for the longest period of any variety, and thus made the slowest recovery from blackspot.

*Good News* is one of the top performers for bloom. But, like *Debonair,* it is only a dirty pinkish-white during June, with most of the buds in groups of two or three on short cutting stems. It does not show its true color or produce many "usable" blooms before early July.

The same is true to a less degree of *Fanny Blankers-Koen.*

I removed *Orange Ruffles* because it behaves like a Floribunda; blooming heavily during the Spring, with almost no bloom during late July and August. Buds are on short stems and in groups.

I left *Sunburst* and *Lucia Zuloaga* in the bed although they are single, open quickly and last but such a short time that they can seldom be used as cut flowers.

*Saturnia* and *Night* open quickly, and petals begin to fall within 24-72 hours, but they are satisfactory as cut flowers if cut while the bud is still tight. *Saturnia* makes a brilliant show, and *Night* is almost black.

I may discard *Butterscotch* because so few of the buds develop into good bloom.

After admitting that all but from 5-10% of the blooms are usable, I still cannot see any chance of voting for *Peace* in first place. The bloom is large, opens slowly and lasts a long time, but so do *Enchantment, Remembrance* and *Tallyho,* all of which produce more usable blooms after discarding from 10-20% of the buds. I'll vote for *Peace* as an unusual and very fine rose, but for first place I honestly must rank my favorite roses as follows: *Sutter's Gold, Helen Traubel, Nocturne, Tallyho, Fanny Blankers-Koen, Buccaneer, First Love, Show Girl, Girona, Pilar Landecho* and *Sterling*. I admit that another season might easily replace some of these choices in my affections.

Among the best performers, only *Tallyho* is in the very double class. My natural preference is for the *Sutter's Gold, Nocturne* and *Helen Traubel* type, but I must admit that *Tallyho* does perform well. Along with *Peace, Enchantment* and *Remembrance,* it produces large, long-lasting flowers.

Everyone who saw the buds was intrigued by the manner in which *First Love* (and to a lesser degree *Show Girl* and *The Doctor*) "unfurl" rather than open. Undoubtedly, this adds to their charm. *First Love* is smaller than the other two, but produces a surprisingly-large flower in comparison to the size of the early bud.

The bi-colors, like *Boudoir* and *Tango,* are not outstanding performers. But, they add a striking bit of color and change to an assorted variety of roses. I like them.

All of my roses seemed to pick up more color during the bloom period following hot dry weather. This change intensified as cooler Fall weather moved in. The blooms produced during the hot dry period varied less in color than those immediately following. Oranges deepened perceptibly. Those with red veining in the petals changed to more striking markings. The outside of the outer petals was often almost solid scarlet. The light reds changed the least. I had not noticed before that *Chrysler Imperial* has a faint bluish or purplish cast, whereas *Nocturne* stays red or maroon-red.

Hot dry weather also has a greater immediate effect on the size of stems and blooms than on growth or quantity of bloom. Recovery of growth and size of bloom is rapid when sufficient moisture becomes available. It seems quite natural that the ability to produce new growth is in direct proportion to the ability to recover from fungus damage and defoliation.

Neither the table nor my records contain any information on fragrance, so whatever I say is mostly b'guess and b'gosh. An excellent pollen allergy (hay fever to you) compelled me to have my wife and other members of the family do the "sniffing.' Seemingly, the leaders would be *The Doctor, Sutter's Gold, Girona, Nocturne* and *Sterling*.

Perhaps all of my conclusions are hardly fair since the records are for one season only and include several little-known varieties. Individual or test garden records cannot be all-conclusive. You will note somewhat different performance regardless of the varieties that you may use.

In Table 1, the first column states whether the bush was in the bed 1 or 2 years. The second column gives the maximum height attained in 1954. The third and fourth colums refer to susceptibility to, and recovery from blackspot: E (easily susceptible), M (medium), S (slow); R (rapid recovery), M (medium), S (slow). The fifth column gives the date the first bud opened. The sixth, the total bloom for this season. The seventh, the number of burned, balled or damaged blooms. The eighth, the number of blooms in groups or on short stems (4″ or under). The final column lists the total number of usable buds or blooms (according to my own notions) for home bouquets.

## TABLE I

### Hybrid Tea Performance

| Variety | Years | Height in Inches | Disease Susceptibility | Recovery | Date of First Bloom | Total Blooms | Damaged | Multiple or Short Stems | Usable Blooms |
|---|---|---|---|---|---|---|---|---|---|
| *Applause | 1 | 18 | M | S | 7/12 | 21 | 1 | 1 | 19 |
| Autumn | 1 | 18 | E | M | 7/8 | 29 | 2 | 1 | 26 |
| | 1 | 26 | E | S | 6/22 | 31 | 2 | 2 | 27 |
| | 1 | 24 | E | S | 6/17 | 32 | 2 | 3 | 27 |
| | 1 | 26 | E | S | 6/19 | 38 | 4 | 3 | 31 |
| | 1 | 27 | E | M | 6/15 | 44 | 4 | 3 | 37 |
| | 1 | 26 | E | M | 6/28 | 28 | 2 | 3 | 23 |
| Bravo | 2 | 33 | M | M | 6/14 | 42 | 3 | 4 | 35 |
| Buccaneer | 2 | 38 | M | R | 6/11 | 78 | 5 | 18 | 55 |

*In fairness to all, I question my records for *Tango, The Doctor, Applause* and *Heinrich Gaede* because, for reasons not evident to me up to the present time, they started poorly and have not made sufficient growth to give any fair indication of possible performance.

| Butterscotch | 1 | 35 | E | R | 7/2 | 31 | 15 | 4 | 12 |
|---|---|---|---|---|---|---|---|---|---|
| Boudoir | 1 | 19 | M | S | 7/13 | 41 | 2 | 6 | 33 |
| Charles Mallerin | 1 | 37 | M | R | 6/20 | 27 | 1 | 1 | 25 |
| Charlotte Armstrong | 2 | 18 | S | M | 6/19 | 27 | 1 | 2 | 24 |
| Chrysler Imperial | 2 | 32 | S | R | 6/8 | 33 | 2 | 1 | 30 |
| Confidence | 1 | 23 | M | M | 7/2 | 32 | 3 | 2 | 27 |
|  | 1 | 21 | M | M | 7/8 | 29 | 3 | 3 | 23 |
| Crown of Gold | 1 | 32 | R | R | 7/3 | 34 | 1 | 6 | 27 |
| Debonair | 2 | 33 | E | S | 6/15 | 57 | 16 | 15 | 26 |
| Edith Krause | 1 | 40 | S | M | 6/21 | 33 | 2 | 3 | 28 |
| Edith Willkie | 1 | 26 | S | M | 7/5 | 32 | 2 | 1 | 29 |
| Enchantment | 1 | 23 | M | R | 6/20 | 38 | 4 | 2 | 32 |
| Fandango | 2 | 32 | M | M | 6/12 | 59 | 2 | 11 | 46 |
| Fanny Blankers-Koen | 2 | 36 | E | M | 6/15 | 97 | 13 | 24 | 60 |
| First Love | 2 | 34 | S | S | 6/12 | 64 | 3 | 5 | 56 |
| Fred Edmunds | 2 | 22 | M | S | 6/6 | 38 | 2 | 2 | 34 |
| Girona | 1 | 26 | S | M | 6/15 | 40 | 1 | 3 | 36 |
|  | 1 | 25 | E | M | 6/13 | 32 | 1 | 1 | 29 |
|  | 1 | 26 | M | M | 6/16 | 33 | 1 | 2 | 30 |
|  | 2 | 29 | E | R | 6/11 | 46 | 2 | 3 | 41 |
| Good News | 2 | 30 | E | S | 6/14 | 101 | 29 | 33 | 39 |
| Hadley | 1 | 25 | R | R | 7/6 | 56 | 4 | 9 | 43 |
| Hearts Desire | 1 | 27 | E | M | 7/1 | 26 | 2 | 2 | 22 |
| Hedda Hopper | 1 | 29 | R | S | 6/28 | 51 | 2 | 8 | 41 |
| *Heinrich Gaede | 1 | 26 | E | S | 6/17 | 16 | 1 | 4 | 11 |
|  | 1 | 28 | E | S | 6/29 | 24 | 1 | 3 | 20 |
|  | 2 | 29 | E | S | 6/14 | 39 | 3 | 5 | 31 |
| Helen Traubel | 1 | 31 | M | R | 6/21 | 48 | 33 | 5 | 40 |
|  | 1 | 33 | M | R | 6/19 | 47 | 2 | 4 | 41 |
|  | 2 | 38 | M | R | 6/12 | 84 | 4 | 7 | 73 |
| Horace McFarland | 2 | 30 | E | S | 6/6 | 34 | 2 | 4 | 28 |
| Hortulanus Budde | 1 | 23 | E | R | 6/11 | 34 | 3 | 5 | 26 |
| Korovo | 1 | 26 | S | M | 7/5 | 36 | 1 | 0 | 35 |

*In fairness to all I question my records for *Tango, The Doctor, Applause* and *Heinrich Gaede* because, for reasons not evident to me up to the present time, they started poorly and have not made sufficient growth to give any fair indication of possible performance.

| Lucia Zuloaga | 1 | 17 | E | S | 6/14 | 27 | 0 | 3 | 24 |
|---|---|---|---|---|---|---|---|---|---|
| Mark Sullivan | 1 | 30 | E | R | 7/7 | 32 | 2 | 0 | 30 |
| McGredy's Ivory | 1 | 31 | S | M | 7/6 | 34 | 1 | 2 | 31 |
| McGredy's Sunset | 2 | 24 | E | S | 6/10 | 33 | 3 | 5 | 25 |
| Miami | 1 | 16 | E | M | 7/9 | 22 | 1 | 1 | 20 |
| | 1 | 20 | E | M | 7/1 | 27 | 1 | 1 | 25 |
| | 1 | 19 | E | M | 7/7 | 21 | 0 | 2 | 19 |
| Mme. Joseph Perraud | 1 | 29 | M | R | 6/22 | 47 | 1 | 1 | 45 |
| Mojave | 1 | 19 | M | R | 7/11 | 24 | 1 | 1 | 22 |
| Night | 2 | 29 | M | M | 6/8 | 66 | 7 | 19 | 40 |
| Nocturne | 1 | 22 | M | R | 6/30 | 42 | 3 | 7 | 32 |
| | 1 | 28 | E | R | 6/16 | 52 | 3 | 3 | 46 |
| | 1 | 23 | M | R | 6/14 | 44 | 2 | 3 | 39 |
| | 2 | 33 | M | R | 6/6 | 72 | 3 | 7 | 62 |
| Olive Percival | 1 | 19 | M | M | 6/15 | 44 | 3 | 7 | 34 |
| Peace | 1 | 26 | S | R | 7/6 | 23 | 1 | 0 | 22 |
| | 2 | 21 | M | R | 6/23 | 32 | 1 | 0 | 31 |
| Pearl Harbor | 1 | 27 | M | S | 7/11 | 26 | 3 | 2 | 21 |
| Picture | 1 | 22 | S | M | 6/14 | 38 | 1 | 3 | 34 |
| Pilar Landecho | 1 | 45 | S | R | 6/28 | 46 | 2 | 2 | 42 |
| Remembrance | 1 | 26 | E | M | 7/6 | 39 | 4 | 3 | 32 |
| Santa Anita | 1 | 26 | M | M | 7/5 | 46 | 2 | 3 | 41 |
| Saturnia | 1 | 25 | S | R | 6/15 | 53 | 3 | 11 | 39 |
| | 1 | 31 | M | R | 6/28 | 33 | 1 | 3 | 29 |
| Show Girl | 2 | 36 | M | R | 6/14 | 64 | 5 | 7 | 52 |
| Sterling | 1 | 38 | S | R | 6/19 | 59 | 3 | 7 | 49 |
| Sunburst | 1 | 20 | E | S | 7/7 | 31 | 0 | 2 | 29 |
| Sutter's Gold | 2 | 38 | M | R | 6/9 | 69 | 2 | 5 | 62 |
| Tallyho | 1 | 33 | M | R | 7/4 | 38 | 2 | 1 | 35 |
| | 2 | 38 | M | M | 6/13 | 65 | 5 | 3 | 57 |
| *Tango | 1 | 17 | M | S | 7/2 | 18 | 0 | 2 | 16 |
| *The Doctor | 1 | 24 | M | M | 6/15 | 24 | 1 | 2 | 21 |
| Will Rogers | 1 | 21 | M | S | 7/7 | 29 | 2 | 3 | 24 |

*In fairness to all I question my records for *Tango, The Doctor, Applause* and *Heinrich Gaede* because, for reasons not evident to me up to the present time, they started poorly and have not made sufficient growth to give any fair indication of possible performance.

# Jamadar And His Roses

Hazel H. Bruce
Kabul, Afghanistan

Our greatest pride here in Kabul is our rose garden. Though we neither planted, chose, nor originated this show, it gives us a sort of elegant delight when Jamadar, our gateman, opens the door onto the street to let the car in or out, to see a whole wreath of dark faces peering in, their eyes wide with awe and their noses quivering at the odor.

For up here roses have fragrance as well as size and color. When you step into a compound on a June evening, such a breath of rich perfume meets you as you never experienced at home. It may be that for centuries the people who have dwelt within these stony hills have cherished and cultivated all that was soft and gentle and delightful, just by way of contrast. For Afghanistan is a hard country, with steely bones of rock.

## Our Vigilant Watchman

The owner of our garden, a distinguished engineer of European education and continent-wide fame, built it for his pleasure. His instrument was a gnarled old man, the Agha Abdul, formally, but Old Rosy among the Americans. Though the owner no longer lives here, Old Rosy cannot let his charges go and I have wakened startled at night to see a quiet, creeping figure going down the rose garden, stopping to snip off here and mutter a desecration there.

He came to see me one morning, his thin old face wrinkled with distrust. "Memashib," he announced, "someone is stealing the flowers."

Since he no longer lives in our compound, I could not tell whether he was reproaching me for unauthorized cutting or really did believe that someone was helping himself to our flowers.

"You have seen someone?" I asked.

"No . . . no. But . . . I sense. Yesterday there were flowers on the

*Red Glory*. Today are none. Last week, the *Gold Flame* bloomed . . .
this week not even a bud."

I looked around for our current gardener, Jamadar, the gateman.

"Jamadar," I called. He came hurrying. "Agha Abdul says someone is stealing the flowers."

Jamadar's simple face wrinkled with shock. "No . . . oh . . . no,
Memsahib. I am here at all times . . . no one has come."

## WHO WAS THE CULPRIT?

I looked at him doubtfully: Jamadar's little gateman's house by
the door is a comfortable place for an afternoon snooze, and I am
not always sure that he recognizes what constitutes his duty.

"No one has been here," he reiterated. "I have been here, tying
up the fruit."

As so often happens in this country when a delicate subject in-
trudes into the conversation, the wrong person is apt to feel embar-
rassed. I felt my face redden: last year in the Spring, before the great
flights of birds came on their way from Africa to the Russian steppes,
Jamadar had spent days tying up in paper the bunches of newly-
forming grapes which spread over a long trellis.

So, we watched our paper-clad bunches warming in the sun all
Summer long. When we began to open them at last in August,
we were surprised to find that about half of them contained nothing.

When faced with the empties, Jamadar looked at them, incred-
ulous.

"Memsahib," he told me, "from time to time I have tasted, to test
the sugar. But this . . ." He looked at the pile of paper covers with
truly astonished eyes . . . "this I do not understand!"

## THE LIGHT DAWNS

It was Mohammed Ali, our wise and intelligent young driver, who
put us *au courant* with the true situation.

"You must know, Memsahib," he said compassionately, "that
Jamadar has probably never had enough to eat in his life. He comes
from grape country where, when the fruit comes in, everybody eats
and eats and eats . . . as if to store up some warmth for Winter
when they must live on a little tea and bread. I have seen Jamadar

eat grapes till . . . so-o . . ." He made rounded gestures over his own lean middle.

"Well, say no more about it, to anyone," I decided.

But now in the early Spring glory of the garden, we really could not tolerate any misunderstanding about whose roses were whose. I gave Old Rosy a self-righteous stare and decided that whatever measures were taken must be taken privately.

"Thank you, Agha Abdul," I told him with dismissing courtesy. "It is good of you to warn us. We shall be watching to see that no more roses are taken."

For a few days nothing happened. And then I went out one morning to gather some special long-stemmed blooms that I had been saving for a copper bowl in a big window: the roses were copper-colored themselves, with deep splashes of scarlet and yellow. Not one, not even a opening bud, remained on the tall bushes.

## No Other Recourse

There was nothing to do but call Jamadar to account, and that quickly.

"Jamadar," I said sternly, "where did the copper roses go this morning? Yesterday there were plenty . . . today not one bud. What has happened?"

Jamadar's startled eyes searched mine.

"Why, no," he stammered. "Nobody . . . that is . . . nothing."
He stopped.

To my surprise, I saw a foolish look of pride steal over his dark features. Jamadar's tongue came out and touched cautiously at the corners of his mouth, as if he were testing a secret and was doubtful about sharing it with me, facing him with my penalizing eye.

"Well, it may be," he began cautiously. Then, for him, there began to spurt out a great spate of narrative.

"This morning, Memsahib, when I was outside the gate, cleaning the juey (this is the communal water ditch that feeds all our gardens at stated intervals), a gentleman stopped by . . . a sahib," he repeated. "The gate was open, but, Memsahib, I was right there . . . no one could enter past me!" He glanced at me, triumphantly righteous.

"The gentleman stopped . . . he looked to me," added Jamadar dreamily, "like a very great gentleman . . . he wore a fine brown chapan (winter overcoat) stitched with green flowers. He stopped beside me and looked in. I saw no harm in that . . . the gentleman was only looking! Then the turned to me and said, 'Is this the king's garden?' "

## IMAGINE—THE KING!

Jamadar stopped, overcome by the idea. Then a sly smile began to steal across his dark face, as at the simplicity of some people.

"I said, 'No, this garden is not the king's . . . it belongs . . . that is it *now* belongs to the Sahib and Memsahib who are Americans. But it is I who take care of it, who cultivate the blooms and . . .' "

"Well, yes?" I broke in impatiently.

Jamadar went on in his awe-struck tone: "Then the gentleman said, 'Well, I will just step in. Since it is not the king's, I am sure that he would like to hear about it. I doubt if even *he* has such roses!' "

"Did you follow him in?" I broke in sharply.

"Why, no, Memsahib. I thought he would prefer to look quietly, so he might tell the king."

Something in my gaze must have warned him, but he went on bravely, "I did not see him again. I think he must have gone out the back gate."

## JAMADAR TRIUMPHS

Jamadar did not look at me for a minute, but when he turned back I saw that he had accomplished that complete shift of point of view which makes life in these latitudes so confusing.

"If he *had* been going to see the king, Memsahib, you would surely have wished him to take some roses?"

Of course, I nodded.

"And if he wasn't going," went on Jamadar serenely, "Memsahib, you would have wished the gentleman himself to enjoy them?"

"Yes . . . no!" I shouted.

But Jamadar was walking away, without any sign of slyness or triumph: just a man in possession of a tricky question and a perfect solution.

Reprinted with permission from the Christian Science Monitor, May 2, 1958.

# We Grow "Show Me" Roses

## Denfred O. Watskey
## Independence, Mo.

WHEN the 1957 Jackson County Fall rose show in Raytown closed, I found to my amazement that my 42 entries had won 41 ribbons and four trophies. Only one bloom did not win anything. I was very elated, as I had never competed for a challenge trophy before.

Four years ago, I didn't know a Floribunda from a Tea. But, I had an interest in roses, attended a few shows and decided to grow some for myself. At 37, I needed a hobby to occupy the hours that I'm not on the job manufacturing railroad lanterns. This was it!

I entered my first show (the Clay County Rose Society's) two years ago and won Queen of the Show. Needless to say, I was speechless, elated and just couldn't believe it. This encouraged me to enter the Jackson County Fall Rose show one week later with the same result. You can imagine how pleased I felt. Jubilation reigned when I walked off with the top award (the Nicholson Perpetual Challenge Bowl) at last year's national rose show in Kansas City.

My few roses grow along a white fence in front of my home, and a long double row stretches along a 70-foot white fence on the east side of my back lot. A *Gladiator* pillar surrounded by a circle of *Peace* roses flourishes in the center of the yard. There are some beds on the west side, and a half-dozen really fine climbing roses against the end of the house reach for the moon.

There's no secret to our success. You can have the same results. Here's how I grow my roses in answer to a local newspaper reporter's questions:

*How did you learn the rules for good rose growing?*

I belong to the American Rose Society and read its monthly magazine. I also belong to the National Rose Society of Great Britain. This costs me $3.00 a year, but the literature is worth far more. I also read other books on rose growing.

*What about your soil?*

The soil out here is like the prairie soil all along the Blue Ridge area. It's just ordinary soil, mixed liberally with the clay excavated from building our basement. I mix in a couple of shovels of barnyard manure, when available, or peat moss when I plant each bush. The second year, I mulch the roses with 3″ of barnyard manure. Twice a year, in April and July, I feed a cup of commercial fertilizer to each mature plant, and a half-cup to the new plants.

*What commercial fertilizer?*

An all-organic brand with an analysis of 10-6-4. On the newer west bed, I use compost from a mushroom house to help break up the very hard clay so that it can be worked. After each rain, I scratch the soil to produce a dust mulch, which I deem essential. It sends the roots down instead of upward. Before I added something to this clay soil, I could hardly scratch it—even after a rain.

*How do you water your roses?*

Every eight or nine days I string perforated hose along the rows and turn on the water at low pressure. In about four hours the soil is soaked about 4″ down. This does not get water on the foliage.

*Isn't water expensive?*

Yes, but with several hundred dollars invested, and uncounted labor, it wouldn't pay to ruin them for lack of water.

*Where and when do you get your rose plants?*

So far as possible, I buy the best named patent varieties of western roses. Potted roses also do well for me if the roots are cut to fit the pots. I get my roses in the Spring, as Fall planting doesn't work for me.

*What do you do about Winter care?*

Nothing, except when I can get it I may scatter a few inches of barnyard manure and leave it on for the Winter. I do not mound earth around the plants.

*What do you do in the Spring?*

I cut the canes back to 2-3′ high, maybe more. If they need reshaping or thinning, they get it, but in general I work on the theory that the plant's energy has gone into growing these canes, so I will let them produce for me instead of forcing new growth. You can build a large bush with moderate pruning. This also gives me some protection against late Spring freezes, which I've never missed, as the first growth is high and can be pruned if it freezes.

*You have about as sturdy canes as one can find anywhere; what do you do about withered blooms in Summer?*

I trim off withered blooms at the base of the actual flower stem, not down several leaves below it. This latter procedure leaves an open stem into which cane borers enter to do harm unless painted.

*You haven't missed a thing it seems; which is why you're a champion. What about bugs, etc.?*

I use a rose dust unless wind does not die down; then I make a water solution of the dust and spray it on. Red spider became a real pest at one period, so I used malathion several times in succession, then went back to the rose dust and spray. That is standard procedure. Treat a special pest with a special deterrent at the time it's needed. This applies to blackspot, which I do not have, and mildew, which I did have.

*How could you afford all these roses?*

I quit smoking cigarettes and put the money into a special box. In about two-and-a-half years, that fund paid for these roses.

*How many do you have?*

About 75 varieties, including about 100 Hybrid Tea, 10 Floribunda and 10 Climber plants.

It's a family operation. My young daughter won a blue ribbon for her flower arrangement in the Raytown show.

Mrs. Watskey takes over when it comes to getting the flowers ready for the rose show. It's a tremendously important part of the operation. Many a prize-winning rose goes on blushing unseen because nobody gets it ready to be shown.

We start cutting specimen blooms three days before the show. We find that if cut any sooner, they lose their substance and will not hold up well in a show. Each bloom or group of blooms is sealed in Saran Wrap with the base of the stem protruding out. These are all set in water and the whole collection kept in the refrigerator.

We practically fast during this time, getting along without the refrigerator, but many of the flowers are improved by this treatment because it hardens them off and prevents dehydration.

# Observations On The Genetics of Doubleness In Roses

## Dennison Morey*
## Pleasanton, Calif.

F LORAL PARTS of the *Rosaceae* family are arranged in whorls of five. Normally, wild members have only this one set of five petals. There are, however, a number of wild semi-double species. In general, these extra petals (called petaloids) result from the failure of stamen initials to develop properly.

This is also true in cultivated roses. For example, if we select a seedling which has five petals and from 1-10 petaloids, subsequent flowers will generally have anywhere from 5-10 petals, depending upon external conditions (climate, etc.), the plant itself and the position of the flowers on it.

Petaloids vary rather markedly in their degree of perfection. So, it is quite difficult to demonstrate on a morphological basis whether or not one is dealing with true petals, or with very perfect petaloids. This is important, because the concept of "dedoublement" has been a classical hypothesis to explain increases in petal number. Dedoublement means that instead of one whorl of petals being formed, there are two, three or more.

If a Hybrid Tea rose seedling with five petals and one or two petaloids is budded and observed for several years, we see that those flowers with few petaloids have but five perfect petals. However, when seven or eight petaloids are present, several of them may be perfect petals. If enough petaloids are formed, five of them might be perfect. This would create an impression of dedoublement. But, previous observation of the variety has emperically established the fact that there are but five true petals.

Thus, "false" petals in the form of perfect petaloids vary in number. If there are five of these "false" petals, in the absence of prior observation one might conclude that he is dealing with dedoublement rather than petaloidy (also called staminody).

If dedoublement is the basic cause of doubleness in roses, a poly-

---

*Director of research, Jackson & Perkins Co. of California.

modal (or at least a bimodal) frequency curve for petal numbers would be expected in a self-population of a semi-double rose.

We grew the rose *Golden Scepter* and a population of its self-seedlings in order to determine the frequency pattern of petal number segregation. A strongly bimodal curve is evident in the petal frequencies of the seedlings (Figure 1). At first glance, this curve

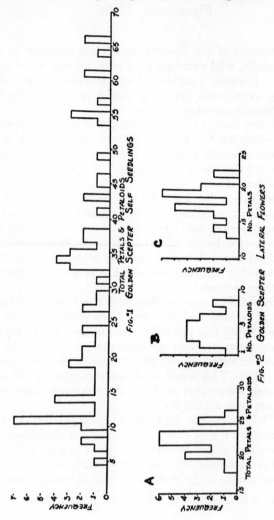

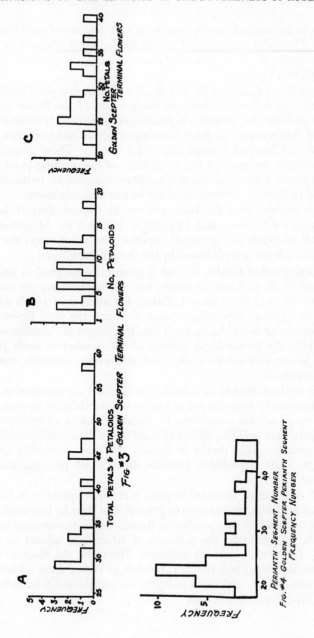

seems to establish dedoublement as a basic feature of doubleness in roses. Thus, the more plausible hypothesis that doubleness in roses is the result of the action of genes causing petaloids must be examined very critically.

From data taken from the parent, it is obvious that petal number is considerably influenced both by the position of the flower on the plant and by the overall environmental situation. Terminal and Spring flowers tend to have both more petals and petaloids than lateral and Summer flowers (Figures 2 and 3). These phenomena undoubtedly account for the bimodality of the seedling petal frequency curve where the distinction between lateral or terminal and Spring or Summer flowers could not be conveniently made.

It is evident that the basic pattern in *Golden Scepter* lateral flowers is for 19 petals and 4 petaloids (Figure 2 B). Moreover, the number of petals and petaloids depends very much upon the total number of floral parts initiated by the floral primordium.

It appears that *Golden Scepter* is genetically designed to have an average of 22 perianth segments, but unless there are an average number of total floral parts initiated, the number of petals will be lesser or greater, depending upon how much the total flower part number varies from the mean. Thus, the degree of "doubleness" is essentially the proportional division of the number of floral promordia initiated in the particular bud into petals, petaloids, stamens and carpels.

It is well-established in hybrid roses that the alteration of vegetative impulses to reproductive is a thing of very delicate balance, and that, under certain conditions, no floral primordia of higher order than petals are possible, so that all parts of the flowers are petalaceous or vegetative. This results in flowers that are excessively double through what is probably heterotically-induced physiological imbalance.

The distribution observed in petal number frequencies in *Golden Scepter* seedlings, and in roses in general, can then be best-explained on the basis of five true petals plus the independently-controlled production of petaloids, the numbers of which are subject to wide limits of externally-induced variation. Moreover, the absolute petal number depends upon the total number of flower parts initiated in any given flower, and upon independently-regulated tendencies toward hypervegetative flowers.

GOVERNOR ROSELLINI GR.
R. V. Lindquist; introduced Howard Rose Co., Hemet, Calif. Described page 246.

ROYAL GOLD CL.
Dennison Morey; introduced Jackson & Perkins, Newark, N.Y. Described
page 256, 1958 American Rose Annual

# The Mighty Rose

Jens Landey

Minneapolis, Minn.

Rose, or rosa, has the same name in dozens of languages around the world; it is truly the universal flower. The Hybrid Tea rose is a product of our time. You have hundreds of different roses to select from. Perhaps a dozen of each color would do for a start.

Plant them in your garden in the early Spring. Soon you will see tender sprouts shooting out in all directions from the upright canes. As you watch them grow, dust them gently to keep them healthy.

In the early days of June, if you live in a Northern clime, you will waken in the morning and find the plants loaded with a beautiful red, pink, yellow and two-toned gorgeous display.

July brings the burning midsummer sun. Partial shade is relished now by the best of roses. Yet through the heat of July and August, they will continue to produce beautiful and fragrant blossoms.

September brings cooling days of early autumn when the mighty rose puts on another gorgeous show of color. Although the late days of September and early days of October bring a touch of frost to lay low the tender geraniums, profusely-blooming petunias and all their tender sister flowers, the rose keeps right on blooming until well into wintry November.

When the ground begins to freeze, take your spade and gently move a portion of Mother Earth around the still-green rose plants. A liberal covering of straw or hay finishes your labor for the year.

While you sleep, the good Lord will place a liberal covering of white snow on top to keep the roses in slumberland in perfect safety till the warm sun of early April brings on another growing season.

Then take your pruning shears and clip the dead, diseased or injured canes. Gather up and burn the clippings to kill the little critters that rode out the Winter in the canes of the roses. As you watch new shoots spring out in all directions, you will wonder why more people do not grow the mighty rose that gives you so much for so little of your time and money.

# Cytology of Two Fertile Triploid Roses

## Dr. H. D. Wulff*

### Saarbrucken, Germany

LIKE OTHER triploid plants, roses which possess three sets of 7 chromosomes each are generally sterile. As early as 1920, Täckholm[4,5] demonstrated how this sterility arises from irregularities of their meiotic divisions.

In 1929 and 1933, Erlanson[1,2], gave further details of the cytology of triploid roses, drawing special attention to the fact that some of them *are* able to set seed. The triploid hybrid *Rosa blanda x Rosa carolina,* for instance, proved to produce "a crop of good hips and achenes."

Dr. Erlanson asked (and so may we) whether the progeny of such a fertile triploid rose would also be triploid, or diploid or tetraploid. In the last cases, propagation of diploid or tetraploid offspring involves certain irregularities in the reduction division, but normal sexual processes still occur. If the progency is triploid like the mother plant, an alternative arises: the mother plant might be apomicotic (and thus represent asexual propagation) or it might behave like *Rosa canina* and produce egg cells and pollen grains with different chromosome numbers (14 and 7, respectively).[7]

In recent years, two other triploid roses of hybrid origin and of rather high fertility were found among the creations of the late nurseryman, Mathias Tantau, Sr. (seedling number 83 and *Schneeschirm*). Dr. H. W. Rehagen and I investigated their cytology at the Botanical Institute of the University of Kiel (Germany), and made the first successful attempt to raise seedlings in order to study their cytology as well.

Seedling numbr 83 [*Rosa multiflora x (Rosa canina x Rosa coriifolia froebelli)*] produced a new fertile triploid rose and 27 diploid sister plants. Morphologically, this triploid plant was highly similar

*Professor, Botanical Institute of the University of Saarbrucken.

118

to the female parent. So, we concluded that it contained two chromosome sets of *Rosa multiflora* (probably from an unreduced egg cell with 14 chromosomes) and one set of 7 chromosomes from the male parent *(Rosa canina x Rosa coriifolia froebelii)*. I then published a description of its reduction division.[6] Here let me point out that: (1) meiotic chromosomes pairing predominantly leads to the formation of 3-4 trivalents, besides 4-3 bivalents and 4-3 univalents; (2) the further course of the reduction division is highly irregular. A pronounced elimination of chromosomes occurs, and the viable pollen grain and eggs cells of this triploid rose evidently received only 7 chromosomes, for its offspring (six plants) were diploid. Five of these six plants very closely resembled *Rosa multiflora*.

The ancestry of *Schneeschirm*, an ornamental rose, is not quite clear. It blooms twice a year. The first flowering period lasts from June to August. The second begins after a short interval, and ends with the first frosts.

It is a very remarkable fact that the flowers of both periods differ in their meiotic behavior; only those produced during the first period are able to produce hips and viable achenes. Their reduction division is characterized by the occurrence of only 0-3 trivalents, with more than 60% of the pollen mother cells showing chromosome pairing to 7 bivalents and 7 univalents or 1 trivalent, 6 bivalents and 6 univalents. This reduction division proceeds rather regularly. The univalents, splitting twice, are mostly taken up into the young tetrad nuclei. Chromosome elimination is low, and so the viable pollen grains and egg cells will contain 14 chromosomes.

The offspring of about 60 plants were tetraploid, each seedling having 28 chromosomes in the root tips.

We also studied the reduction division of these tetraploid seedlings. In most pollen mother cells (63%), 14 bivalents were formed. The remaining pollen mother cells showed 10-13 bivalents and the corresponding numbers of uni-, tri- or quadri-valents.

Growth habit and leaf shape are highly similar in the tetrapolid seedling plants and their triploid mother. Differences chiefly exist in some floral characters. The diameter of the tetraploid flower is smaller (4-9 cm) than that of the triploid (8-12 cm), but the former have a tendency to produce double flowers. The number of anthers and ovaries is lower in the tetraploids, and their pollen grains are larger and show a higher degree of fertility. The production of hips and achenes is far better in the tetraploids than in the triploid mother plant.

Reduction division in the second period *Schneeschirm* flowers shows a remarkable increase of trivalent formation. Here only 5% of the pollen mother cells have 0-1 trivalents. 3-5 trivalents are found in 76% of the pollen mother cells. The general course of meiosis is very irregular, chromosome elimination is high and there is a clear tendency to form pollen grains with 7-9 chromosomes (instead of 14 as in the flowers of the first period).

What we are learning from the differences in the meiotic behavior of the flowers of both periods is that the reduction division of the triploid *Schneeschirm* can be rather easily affected by environmental conditions. It seems reasonable to suppose that the warm temperature from June to the end of August causes the formation of no or few trivalents. This prevents chromosome elimination, and favors the production of hips and achenes. On the other hand, the colder temperatures of September and later months seem to be responsible for the high meiotic irregularities and the failure of fruit-setting.

Answering the above questions, we may now say that fertile triploid roses have a restricted sexual reproduction which depends on the chance-formation of viable egg cells and pollen grains. We can preclude the possibilities of apomixis, or the existence of a *Rosa canina*-like sexuality, unless further studies of other triploid roses would reveal them.

---

1. Erlanson, E. W. Cytological Conditions and Evidences for Hybridity in North American Wild Roses. Bot. Gaz. 87: 443-506 (1929).

2. Erlanson, E. W. Chromosome Pairing, Structural Hybridity and Fragments in *Rosa*. Bot. Gaz. 94: 551-566 (1933).

3. Rehagen, H. W. Zur Zytologie Triploider Rosen. Rosenjahrbuch 16: 177-232 (1957).

4. Tackholm, G. On the Cytology of the Genus Rosa. Svensk Bot. Tidskr. 14: 300-311 (1920).

5. Tackholm, G. Zytologische Studien uber die Gattung *Rosa*. Acta hort. Bergiani 7, no. 3 (1922).

6. Wulff, H. D. Cytologische Untersuchungen an einer Fertilen Triploiden Rose. Planta 44: 472-490 (1954).

7. Wulff, H. D. Are the Dog Roses Apomiotic? American Rose Annual 40: 116-124 (1955).

# Roses In California's San Joaquin Valley

Melva Fitzpatrick
Bakersfield, Calif.

THE GREAT VALLEY of California (San Joaquin to the south, and Sacramento to the north) presents few problems in rose growing. The southern portions of the valley, which is open to the north but ringed with mountains to the east, south and west, is where I grow mine (5 miles south of Bakersfield).

Although the city of Los Angeles is but 100 miles to the south, we are in an entirely different province from the standpoint of geology and weather. Rain is usually stopped from the ocean side by the coastal mountain ranges.

Most California rain comes from the northwest, down the length of the valley, and usually seems to push no further south than Fresno (100 miles to the north). Our normal annual rainfall here is only slightly over 5″. Some seasons produce no more than 3½″.

Consequently, almost all of the valley is under intensive irrigated cultivation. Cotton and alfalfa are the chief crops here. Our underground water supply comes from the Sierra Nevadas to the east, whose entire western slope drains into the valley. As in most of the rest of the United States, this underground water supply is diminishing, and the problem is a source of great concern to farmers and other interested segments of the population.

Our climate is relatively mild, generally dropping to no less than 25° in Winter. However, Summer temperatures climb to 95°-105°, with very low humidity (10-20%). Locally, we have a range of 15°-110°, with a little higher humidity because of the field irrigation all around us.

Since the valley is a great sedimentary basin, the soil is predominantly alkaline in nature and needs much humus, as well as sulphur or gypsum.

My husband and I work away from home, and he also works our 60-acre farm. Since he is too busy to garden, I do it spasmodically and as easily as possible. I grow roses for fun and do not maintain any

semblance of a rigid schedule except to water often and generously and to keep the bloomed-out flowers pruned. A healthy rose bush seems to thrive under these conditions. Plants are apt to grow larger than rose catalogs indicate—perhaps because of the long growing season and heavy irrigation.

I know that many more roses than I have tried will do exceedingly well here. I am a rank amateur and my plantings are really very insignificant (50 plants of 32 varieties). With limited time to care for them, my roses are restricted to the immediate yard.

Although I have no objection to using roses in general border plantings, and have found that they do just as well there as in conventional beds, I find it easier to care for them when they are all grouped together in beds which hold only roses.

Many roses on the higher spots in this area do not become dormant at all, and usually continue to bloom throughout most of the Winter. We rarely have a frost until after Christmas.

## How We Grow Them

We usually buy our bare-root roses in January and February and plant them immediately, using more peat and other humus than is generally recommended in order to conserve moisture and combat the alkali. When we bought our farm in 1948, much old well-rotted manure was available. This, plus loads of oak-leaf mold from the area around our mountain cabin, gave our rose beds a good start. Our manure source is now depleted, so we must depend more on mulching and an occasional application of sulphur.

Because of our extreme heat and low humidity, mulching is almost a must. We haul a load of cotton waste from the gin occasionally to use on all flower beds, not just the roses. This works wonders when the air temperature is over 100° and the ground temperature 10-20° above that in the sun.

All of our beds are depressed or bordered for flood irrigation. During the middle of the Summer, we usually flood them twice a week.

We have no blackspot. Our big disease problem is mildew. Several bushes were completely defoliated last year. We occasionally have an exceptionally cool and humid Spring and can make little progress using sulphur and copper sprays to combat it. This year I intend to try Mildex. Since the sun gets hot here quite early in the year, we have to be careful of sprays which will burn the foliage or blooms. The best plan is to replace mildew-prone plants with more-resistant varieties.

I use malathion for aphids. I think that I would have good results if I could keep a weekly schedule, but as it is, the pests have things pretty much to themselves while the weather is proper for them.

The rose chafer mutilates our early light-colored blooms, but is gone when hot weather arrives. I usually hand-pick this pest when I can find the time.

I use very little commercial fertilizer. A handful per plant once a year is about par.

We prune in late January or early February. We often have to strip off old leaves at that time if the Winter has not been cold enough to defoliate the plants naturally. We prune according to individual plant requirements, and have no over-all set method. Some of the Climbers are too large for me to reach, so they go their merry way, bearing blooms too high for me to pick.

After we finish pruning, we do some basic clean-up work. This includes removing the old mulch and replacing it with well-rotted manure and cotton waste.

At present, we have only *Margo Koster* in the Polyantha class. It has been relatively free of mildew here. Its early Spring and late Fall bloom make up for its lack of mid-Summer color. Foliage is generally good all year.

This area is great for most Floribundas. *Pinkie* needs part shade in Summer because of excessive bloom fading. It is quite prone to mildew in the Spring, but when free of this disease it is a little gem. We abandoned *Goldilocks* because the bushes became rather unsightly, suckered badly and the flowers sun-faded excessively. The plants are hardy and disease-resistant, though. My favorite tall Floribunda is *Betty Prior*. For either a beginner, or a busy gardener, it is tops. Plants grow very tall (well over head height), bloom early and late and are only slightly bothered with mildew. Mine are planted directly beneath tall honey locust trees and get only afternoon sun. They take practically no care. I water them at the same time as the lawn, which seems to be sufficient. *Frensham* is another good rose for trouble-free enjoyment. It flowers continually, with dozens of brilliant red blooms on each stem. Here is a red that really holds up in the heat. It has no disease or insect problems.

*Charlotte Armstrong* and her progeny are high on my list of favorite Hybrid Teas: tall, rangy, strong-growing, disease-resistant. These plants stand quite a bit of neglect and still do a good job. I am replacing a nine-year-old plant this year because my early years of amateurish pruning, etc., cut short its life. It will stand a heap of experimentation by novices before it quits. As a relative of *Charlotte Armstrong*, I expected more from *Chrysler Imperial* than my plant has produced. Perhaps I have a weakling. I intend to try another one before I pass judgment. I want to try *Grande Duchesse Charlotte* and *Audie Murphy* this coming year. My *Forty-niner* had nice, but sparse blooms. The plant was always a weakling, and I finally removed it to make way for something more vigorous. I had much the same problem with *Bravo*. When it did bloom, it was breath-taking, but the blooms were few and far between. *Applause,* though one of my favorites where color is concerned, was never a vigorous grower. It seems to prefer afternoon shade. *Mojave* is quite vigorous and tall-growing. Its bloom and color are good, and it does not seem to be afflicted with mildew or any other disease. *Tallyho* is a beauty—vigorous and healthy. However, it does mildew when the weather is cool. *Lowell Thomas* is very vigorous and free-blooming. I like the bud, but the fast-opening flower sun-fades badly and is gone in a day. *Mirandy* is a good hot-climate rose. In cool weather, the bloom balls because of the many petals. In hot weather, it opens slowly and lasts for days. Its one fault is a weak neck, and the plant itself is a poor grower. *Fred Edmunds* is another rose which has no growing problems. The glossy foliage is always attractive and resistant to mildew and other disease. *Taffeta* is vigorous, tall and has attractive foliage. Blooms are sparse, but beautiful, and usually liked by everyone. It has very few disease problems. *Christopher Stone,* the old standby, is one of my favorite reds. It grows well (a medium-height bush here) and takes very little care. *Peace* is always good, and a great favorite. I have only one now, but want to plant more. *Eclipse* is very vigorous, strong and flowers continuously. It has no disease or pest problems here. The buds are always beautiful, but the flower opens in one day and the sun fades it to almost white. *Snowbird,* a low-growing white, is very satisfactory here. The individual buds are beautiful, and the open flower very pretty and long-lasting. Its only enemy is the rose chafer. It looks well in a foreground planting, as in front of *Frensham.*

My only Grandiflora so far is *Carrousel*. Its blooms are beautiful and hold their color very well. However, the bush is not as vigorous as I thought it would be. It is rather sprawly and does not grow as tall as I had hoped.

*Hansa* is a completely disease and pest-free Hybrid Rugosa. The foliage is very attractive. The bush is tall and sprawly, with the old wood a nice weathered-gray. Its pinkish-violet rumpled blooms are favorites of mine. Very fragrant. *Rosa hugonis* needs more room than I provided. It became so huge and spread so far that I finally had to remove it. It truly needs to be off by itself in a poorer soil than a rose bed offers, and with less water. *Lipstick* is tall and sprawly. The tremendous "heads" of turkey-red blooms are very attractive. It needs half-day shade and much mulch here.

## LAST, BUT NOT LEAST

*Climbing Dainty Bess* is my favorite single. It stands well over the top of the eaves with little support. It is disease and pest-free except for the chafer. *Climbing Etoile de Hollande* blooms all season, and its red fragrant blooms are always welcome. Nothing seems to bother it. *High Noon* is a 15' pillar here. It develops a huge trunk in a very few years. It is the first rose to bloom in the Spring, and about the last in the Fall. Requires very little care. Give this one lots of room. *Bonfire* (a Rambler) is gorgeous in the Spring if mildew, spider mite and something like "fire-blight" can be avoided. I was able to do pretty well with it until a year ago when a combination of all three finished it off. *Climbing Crimson Glory* is so mildew-prone that I would not bother with it, except for its beauty of bloom and its wonderful fragrance. It grows quite large and needs room. *Blaze* is always beautiful in the Spring. Although said to be recurrent, it has never re-bloomed more than once or twice. It has no pests or diseases. I train mine sideways on a chain link fence. It is almost completely shaded by two trees, but seems to do all right. *Climbing Condesa de Sastago* would be worth growing just for the fresh bright green foliage. It blooms off and on all season. It also has no disease or pest problems. *Climbing Texas Centennial* has nice Spring and Fall blossoms, but is very mildew-prone, even in full sun. *Climbing President Herbert Hoover* becomes immense and needs lots of room—too much for a small backyard. It's hardy and disease-resistant.

# Hows and Whys
# of Disbudding

George H. Drinkwater
Syracuse, N. Y.

W E KNOW that words of wisdom are often badly garbled by the time they are reported in the newspapers. Here is an item from a recent issue of the Syracuse Herald-Journal which gave me shudders:—

> *Champaign, Ill. (UP)*—Snap off most of the rose buds on your rose bushes and leave a few individual flowers to become very large if you want big roses, a floriculture specialist suggests.
>
> C. E. Ackerman, University of Illinois floriculturist, says that large exhibition-type roses are produced in this manner. If you leave only three or four buds, the flowers will be larger than if the roses are left to bloom in profusion.
>
> To remove a bud, Ackerman said, hold the main shoot in one hand and grasp the bud stem in the other, then twist the bud stem quickly and snap it off.

True, side buds should be removed for a bigger and better bloom at the terminal of a cane, and must be removed if the bloom is to be exhibited. The earlier the better! But, these side buds and side shoots which come from the axil of the leaf at the cane should be snapped off very gently with a pencil point, wooden match stick or other similar implement when they are not larger than the size of a very small pea. If this growth is not noticed until it is somewhat larger, a careful sidewise pull with the fingers will usually snap it out clearly without leaving a stub or too much of a scar.

I cannot conceive under what conditions one would "hold the main shoot in one hand and grasp the bud stem in the other, then twist the bud stem, etc." I wonder if that is what C. E. Ackerman really said?

When we remove the upper side buds when they are very small, we must watch to see that no unwanted growth develops from the lower eyes on canes bearing blooms which appear to be of exhibition quality. If such growth appears, it too must be removed when small, as any side growth anywhere on the cane is not permitted on the show bench, and evidence of recent removal is penalized by the judges. So much for disbudding for exhibition bloom.

Many growers remove the side buds of Hybrid Tea roses only prior to a show, and allow all growth to develop and bloom during the remaining growing season, thinking that the removal of the side buds means less bloom per plant.

I disagree, and remove the side buds throughout the entire season because the function of a plant is to grow and produce flowers, followed by seed, in order to reproduce itself.

A rose will normally produce flowers at the top of the plant. The growth buds in the leaf axils lower on the canes remain more-or-less dormant until the top growth has completed its function. The growth from the buds lower on the cane will be both vegetative and flowering; that from the three-leaflet axils is only flowering.

When side flower buds directly beneath the terminal bud are removed, the energy which they would have taken from the cane is diverted partly to the terminal bud, and partly to the more-dormant growth buds lower on the cane. The earlier the top buds are removed, the sooner the lower buds will become active.

The terminal flower blooms a few days before the side flower buds open, so if the side buds are left to develop, the terminal as a whole has little value as a cut flower for the house. If the spent terminal is removed when it has passed its peak, the remaining short-stemmed leafless, "candelabra" side buds are far from desirable. Until this growth is removed, the main activity in the entire cane is devoted to seed production. When it is removed and the lower growth buds are forced into greater activity, it takes four to six weeks to get other blooms from that particular cane.

So, we remove the side buds, resulting in bigger and better terminal blooms which can be left on the bush until faded or cut for decorative purposes. By the time that we cut our terminal blooms or faded flowers (back to active eyes or growth which will produce the side canes for following bloom), we find that eyes further down the cane have already become activated and we can expect following bloom within three or four weeks instead of the four to six weeks required when canes are not disbudded.

Thus, instead of a bush producing three or four bursts of bloom per season with definite non-blooming periods, our bushes are forced into bloom every week or 10 days throughout the remainder of the season, after a short lull following the first June bloom.

# Roses Can Last In Florida

## Mrs. G. F. Lampkin
## Bradenton, Fla.

**W**HEN growing roses out-of-doors in colder climates, nature supplies a season of dormancy for the plants. But, here in Florida there is no rest for either the plant or gardener. At least this is true in the central west coast section where my experiments and observations have been made. In return for this year-round care, however, a Florida rose garden gives almost continuous bloom, with quality approaching any obtained in climates reputedly more amenable to rose culture.

Possibly the most important phase of Florida rose culture is disease control. Diseases which most concern us are blackspot and mildew. Mildew is usually troublesome only in Spring and Fall. The fungus that causes it needs high humidity to germinate, but water on the leaf actually retards growth of the spores, thus making it of little concern during the rainy season. When prevalent, it rarely kills the bush, but is very unsightly and can, if severe, slow down growth.

### BLACKSPOT CAUSES MOST DEFOLIATION

Although there are several causes of defoliation, the most usual is blackspot. Repeated loss of foliage from this malady weakens the bush, causing decline and eventual death of the plant. Since blackspot spores are spread by splashing water, and germinate when the leaf is wet for as long as six hours, you can easily see why this disease is epidemic in Summer months. Our Summer rains often come in late afternoon, leaving foliage wet for 14 hours or longer. Beating rains wash fungicides from the foliage so that frequent applications are desirable. Yet, because of wind, spraying or dusting on a set schedule is, at times, impossible. These factors make it mandatory to keep the disease at a minimum in favorable weather so there will not be enough spores present at the start of a wet period to build up to hazardous proportions. We try to have a fungicide on the foliage when it starts to rain, and renew the application as soon as possible after it has been washed away.

A leaf spot known as cercospora gives concern in some sections of the state, but good culture and regular applications of fungicides for other diseases seem to prevent serious infestations.

Cankers occasionally occur, but are seldom severe. Most brown and dead canes are caused by a normally weak fungus called diplodia which enters cut canes or wounds and makes headway only in plants that have been weakened by other causes.

## TAKE YOUR CHOICE

Whether you dust or spray is a personal matter. Dusting is usually easier, and has the advantage of being ready for use on a moment's notice when you have a few minutes of spare time, or during a period of favorable calm. However, there are times when spraying is preferable. Sprays stick better, can be applied when it is too windy for dusting, and do a better job of controlling mildew, spider mites and certain scale insects. Good equipment contributes much toward ease of application and good results. All parts of the plant (including the undersides of the leaves) must be covered with spray or dust, but be careful to keep the deposit uniform and light in order to avoid foliage injury.

Recommendations for specific fungicides or insecticides soon become out of date. These preparations are being constantly superseded by more efficient materials that are safer to both the foliage and user at the same time.

Many older materials cause severe foliage injury under certain conditions. Copper injures foliage in cold damp weather, while sulfur burns in high temperatures. Both are good fungicides when used with care and understanding.

Ferbam (Fermate) is much safer in any weather, and has controlled blackspot satisfactorily when used faithfully. Discoloration of flowers, especially light colors, is its main fault. Sulfur must be added when mildew occurs, and insecticides as needed. Fermate and sulfur are available separately in either dust or spray forms, and are combined in many ready-mixed formulas.

A new product known as captan is showing promise for black-spot and does not stain blooms. It is also on the market as a spray or dust, and is contained in some all-purpose dust mixtures. Sulfur can also be added to control mildew.

Malathion has taken care of all insects invading my garden, and is compatible with the above-named fungicides.

A spreading agent added to sprays will help to give better coverage on young foliage, penetrate mildew spores more thoroughly and control insects more efficiently. One-third teaspoon of a detergent (like Vel or Dreft) to a gallon of spray, or a few drops of commercial spreader-stricker will do the trick. Be sure to follow manufacturer's directions for mixing and applying all sprays and dusts.

Roses enjoy a well-prepared bed which contains a generous amount of organic matter, situated where drainage is good and where they get full sun at least six hours daily with no competition from roots of rank-growing shrubs or trees. If drainage is poor, you must build up your beds several inches above the surrounding ground level. If it is excessive, your bed surface should be lower.

Your soil should be slightly acid, so if beach shell or limestone are present, a soil test should be made. Your local county agricultural agent will do the test for you. The best range of pH value for roses is considered to be from 5.5 to 6.5. It usually takes about 1 pound of sulfur per 100 square feet to lower the pH one unit. If the original reaction of your soil was alkaline (7.0 or above), you will probably have to make similar applications of sulfur each year.

## Before You Plant

Work about 4 pounds per 100 square feet of a complete commercial fertilizer (a formula similar to 4-8-8, 5-10-5 or 4-7-5) into the soil. Then let the bed stand for several weeks. Don't add any more fertilizer when you plant.

Feeding established plants is an individual problem. I have seen rose bushes in my area towering head-high in a year's time with no fertilizer other than that present in the prepared bed. This is not always possible. Some soils leach more readily than others. Some lack, or have an excess of certain minerals or other constituents which affect the availability of nutrients. One learns to correct faults of his own garden. Rare is the naturally-perfect spot for roses in our, or any climate. Normally, applications of all major elements (nitrogen, phosphorus and potassium) are needed three or four times a year. It is easiest to use a complete commercial product (like you added when you prepared your bed) at the rate of 1 heaping tablespoon per bush, or about 3 pounds per 100 square feet. If your soil is very light and you have a leaching problem, you may need to use more nitrogen. Unless you understand the use of inorganic sources, it is advisable to stick to organic forms, such as cottonseed meal or manure for this. You just want to maintain good growth and bloom without forcing.

## Don't Forget To Mulch

Beds should always be heavily-mulched, using any easily-procurable material such as leaves, pine straw, peat moss, grass clippings or sawdust.

Light pruning has proven best for mild climates. In Florida, we do this during the Winter months. It consists mainly of removing dead wood, twiggy stems, crossing or rubbing branches and old canes which have ceased to put out good lateral growth. No more than one-third to one-half of the strong, healthy canes is removed—just enough to make a well-shaped bush. Indiscriminate whacking, regardless of the condition of the canes or consideration of the plant growth habit, is one of the practices which contributes to short life of roses in Florida.

In my own tests, rootstocks have made a decided difference in vigor, productivity and life-span of many varieties. *Rosa multiflora* is the most-commonly-used rootstock, but it has proved inferior in my locality. *Rosa odorata* has been excellent, as expected, since it is so closely-related to many of our old varieties which have come to be known as Florida roses. A newer understock known as *Dr. Huey* (also as Shafter and Shafter Robin) is proving very satisfactory, especially where drainage is good, but I believe that *Rosa odorata* is still superior in wet soil. Most of the popular modern varieties are available on these two understocks from California nurseries.

Growing and studying roses can be a very satisfying hobby. Possibilities for their use are unlimited, and in Florida we are privileged to enjoy, every day in the year, fine specimens of the world's most beautiful and best-loved flower.

# Cold Hardiness of
# Rose Varieties

## Dr. Griffith J. Buck*
## Ames, Iowa

T HE adaptation of plants to a given environment is of interest to all gardeners. The gardener in admittedly-difficult climatic areas is especially concerned with this problem, for it very effectively limits the kinds of plants which he can use in his garden. Two climatic factors (temperature and moisture) are involved in plant adaptation. Of the two, temperature (especially sub-freezing temperature) is the principle limiting one.

The ability of woody plants (including roses) to withstand low Winter temperatures without injury is affected by several factors, including the ability of the tissues to retain moisture against freezing and store carbohydrates, drought (during which the plant evaporates fresh water faster than it can be replaced) and growth stimulation (due to unseasonably-warm temperatures in mid-Winter). Plants which combine these factors at their highest positive values are the most resistant to low-temperature injury.

### You Can Increase Resistance

By utilizing various cultural operations, the gardener may build up a plant's relative resistance to low-temperature injury, but he cannot increase this hardiness beyond the inherited maximum for that particular plant.

Observation of a plant's growth habits in a foreign environment, combined with knowledge of its native habitat, including the length of day (photoperiod), as well as temperature range, provides information which permits us to predict those broad climatic zones in which a given plant may be expected to flourish.

This is the type of information presented by Rehder,[2] and more

*Assistant professor of horticulture, Iowa State College.

Journal Paper No. J-3358 of the Iowa Agricultural and Home Economics Experiment Station, Ames, Iowa. Project No. 1212. Presented at the American Rose Society's annual convention, May 29-31, 1958, Kansas City, Mo.

recently by Wyman.[4,5] Rose growers, including Nicolas[1] and Wright[3], have attempted to provide the same type of information for the various garden rose groups and cultivated species.

This information is too general to be of much value to the home gardener. It deals with a broad range of plant material, whereas the gardener is concerned with asexually-maintained plant varieties (called clones).

## Each Type Differs

There are many clonal selections among the species roses in culti- vation. Each differs from the others in many traits, including that of hardiness, yet maintains a certain family resemblance. In general, those specimens coming from the more temperate portions of their habitat are less resistant to cold injury than those from the colder areas.

This inherent variability in resistance to low-temperature injury found in the species roses is also found in present-day garden roses. Within each rose class, individual clones have markedly-greater hardiness than the average for the group. Others are less resistant. The most casual gardener may observe this for himself. And yet, over a period of years, it has been possible to determine the average winter-hardiness of a given rose clone and to classify those clones into groups having a similar degree of resistance to freeze-injury of mature, well-ripened wood. There is still some variability within the groups, although these differences tend to be small.

Occasionally, an unusual weather occurrence aids in segregating the more-resistant members of each group from the less-resistant. Such an event occurred during the Winter of 1956-57. On the night of January 14, 1957, the temperature dropped to -30° F., then with daylight, rose to -19° F. The average minimum temperature for the period of January 12-20 was 10° F.

Compared with this average minimum temperature, the actual minimum temperatures for the period were as follows:

| Jan. | 12 | 40°F. | | Jan. | 16 | -14°F. |
|------|----|-------|---|------|----|--------|
| "    | 13 | - 7°F. | | "    | 17 | - 2°F. |
| "    | 14 | -30°F. | | "    | 18 | 3°F. |
| "    | 15 | - 4°F. | | "    | 19 | 5°F. |

A 15-20° departure from the average in either direction is not un- usual. The lowest minimum temperature normally expected in this vicinity is -25°F. However, this temperature does not occur every Winter. The rest of this particular Winter, both preceding and following January 14, has been characterized as a "normal" one.

What makes this event of interest is that it occurred during the night, with no appreciable air movement and with the soil bare of snow cover. Thus, such modifying effects as sunshine on frozen canes, wind dessication and the insulation effect of snow cover were absent. Coming as it did in mid-January, there had been no warm periods to incite premature growth and thus increase the plant's susceptibility to winter-injury.

## Now We Can Tell

This combination of circumstances made it possible to assess the resistance of a number of rose clones to injury from temperatures lower than those normally expected here when pruning time arrived in mid-April. The following five classes of hardiness were observed:

**Class 1.** No winter-killing of mature wood; plant resumes normal growth and flower habit with growing temperatures.

*Altalaris* (Shrub)
*Ames 5* (Climber)
*Ames 6* (pillar)
*Berry Bland* (Shrub)
*Felicity* (Shrub)
*Haidee* (Shrub)
*Hansen's Siberian Hedge Rose*
  *(Rosa laxa* sp.)
*Harison's Profuse* (Shrub)
*Little Betty* (Shrub)
*Mossman* (Moss)
*Pink Semi* (Rosa laxa rosea?)

*Rosa beggeriana*
*Rosa fedtschenkoana*
*Rosa laxa* (Morden)
*Rosa laxa* (Fall-blooming form)
*Rosa morica*
*Rosa spinosissima altaica*
*Suzanne* (Shrub)
*Therese Bugnet* (Shrub)
*Victory Year* (Shrub)
*Will Alderman* (Shrub)
*Woodrow* (Shrub)

**Class 2.** One-third or less of each cane killed.

*Agnes* (Shrub)†
*Belle Amour* (Shrub)
*Belle des Jardins* (Gallica)
*Blanchefleur* (Gallica)
*Blanche Moreau* (Moss)
*Blush Hip (Rosa alba* sp.) †
*Carmenetta* (Shrub)
*Charles de Mills* (Gallica)†
*Comtesse de Murinais* (Moss)

*Desiree Parmentier* (Gallica)
*Dr. E. M. Mills* (Shrub)
*Frau Dagmar Hartopp* (Hybrid
  Rugosa)
*Fruhlingsanfang* (Shrub)
*Fruhlingsduft* (Shrub)
*Hansette* (Shrub)†
*Hebe's Lip* (Shrub)
*Karl Forster* (Shrub)

*La Belle Distinguée* (Hybrid
    Eglanteria)†
*Lillian Gibson* (Shrub)†
*Maiden's Blush* (Alba)†
*Marie Louise* (Damask)†
*Mary L. Evans* (Shrub)†
*Mrs. Anthony Waterer* (Shrub)
*Nuits d'Young* (Moss)†
*Pax Apollo* (Shrub)†
*Pikes Peak* (Shrub)†
*Pink Glory* (Shrub)†
*Prairie Youth* (Shrub)†
*River's George IV* (Hybrid China)
*Rosa alba incarnata maxima*†
*Rosa alba suaveloens*†
*Rosa canina* (Senff)

*Rosa canina* (Wadenswiler)
*Rosa corymbifera*†
*Rosa gallica*†
*Rosa gallica complicata*
*Rosa gallica conditorum*
*Rosa multiflora* (Clarke)
*Rosa multiflora* (Welch)
*Rosa nutkana halliana*
*Rosa pomifera*
*Rosa rugosa alba*
*Rosa rugosa magnifica*†
*Rosa virginiana*†
*Rose du Maitre d'Ecole* (Gallica)†
*Salet* (Moss)†
*Sonnenlicht* (Shrub)†
*Variegata di Bologna* (Bourbon)

**Class 3.** More than one-third, and less than two-thirds of each cane
killed.

*Assemblage des Beautes* (Gallica)
*Bonn* (Hybrid Musk)
*Celestial* (Shrub)†
*Celsiana* (Damask)
*Coquette des Alpes* (Noisette)†
*Coquette des Blanches* (Noisette)†
*Cramoise des Alpes* (Gallica)
*Elmshorn* (Hybrid Musk)
*Empress Josephine* (Shrub)
*Eugenie Guinoisseau* (Moss)†
*Eureka* (Hybrid Tea)†
*Fruhlingsmorgen* (Shrub)†
*Golden Moss* (Moss)
*Gros Provins Panache* (Gallica)
*Indian Head Cabbage* (Centifolia)
*James Mitchell* (Moss)
*Konigin von Danemark* (Alba)
*Leda* (Tea)†
*Marigold* (Hybrid Tea)
*Master David* (Hybrid Tea)†
*Maytime*†
*Mme. Hardy* (Damask)†

*Mme. Louis Leveque* (Moss)
*Petite de Hollande* (Centifolia)
*Prairie Moon* (Large-flowered
    Rambler)
*Prince Charlie* (Hybrid Tea)
*Rosa alba maxima*†
*Rosa canina* (Gamon)
*Rosa canina* (Heinsohn)
*Rosa canina* (Pfander)
*Rosa canina* (Pollmeriana)
*Rosa damascena semperflorens*
*Rosa multibracteata*
*Rosa noisettiana manetti*
*Rose due Roi* (Damask)†
*Sophie de Baviere (Rosa alba* sp.)
*Stanwell Perpetual* (Shrub)†
*St. Nicholas* (Damask)†
*The Bishop* (Hybrid Tea)
*Tom Maney* (Large-flowered
    Rambler)†
*Unique Panachee* (Centifolia)

**Class 4.** All canes killed to within 6-12″ of plant base.

*Adam Messerich* (Bourbon)*
*Aglaia* (Rambler)
*Alfred de Dalmas* (Moss)*

*Allen's Fragrant Pillar* (Climbing
    Hybrid Tea)
*Aloha* (Climbing Hybrid Tea)

*Aschermittwoch* (Large-flowered Climber)
*Autumn Bouquet* (Shrub)†
*Baronne Prevost* (Hybrid Perpetual)*
*Black Prince* (Hybrid Perpetual)*
*Buff Beauty* (Hybrid Musk)*
*Celine Forestier* (Noisette)*
*Chloris (Rosa alba* sp.)*
*Commandant Beaurepaire* (Bourbon)*
*D'Aguesseau* (Gallica)
*Danae* (Hybrid Musk)*
*Daphne* (Hybrid Musk)*
*Descanso Pillar* (Shrub)*
*Deuil de Paul Fontaine* (Moss)*
*Dr. Huey* (Rambler)
*Duchesse de Montebello* (Gallica)
*Duchess of Sutherland* (Hybrid Perpetual)*
*Duke of Edinburgh* (Hybrid Perpetual)*
*Etaine* (Rambler)
*Felicite et Perpetue* (Rambler)
*Felicite Parmentier* (Alba)
*Flammentanz* (Rambler)
*Fruhlingschnee* (Shrub)
*Fruhlingstag* (Shrub)
*Gabriel Noyelle* (Moss)*
*General Jacqueminot* (Hybrid Perpetual)
*Gloire de Guilan* (Damask)†
*Gloire des Mosseaux* (Moss)
*Goldbusch* (Shrub)
*Golden Wings* (Hybrid Tea)
*Henry Nevard* (Hybrid Perpetual)*
*Hon. Lady Lindsay* (Shrub)*
*Josef Rothmund* (Shrub)
*Lady Curzon* (Shrub)
*La Perle*
*LaVille de Bruxelles* (Damask)

*Lawrence Johnston*
*Leverkusan* (Kordesii)
*Lullaby* (Floribunda)*
*Master John* (Climbing Hybrid Tea)*
*Max Graf* (Hybrid Rugosa)
*Miss Joan* (Climbing Hybrid Tea)*
*Miss Marion Manifold* (Climbing Hybrid Tea)
*Mme. Ernest Calvat* (Bourbon)†
*Mme. Pierre Oger* (Bourbon)
*Nevada* (Shrub)*
*Nymphenburg* (Shrub)†*
*Oskar Cordel* (Hybrid Tea)*
*Parkjewel* (Shrub)*
*Patricia Macoun* (Rambler)
*Paul's Scarlet Climber* (Large-flowered Rambler)†
*Pax* (Hybrid Musk)*
*Pompon Parfait* (Alba)
*President de Seze* (Gallica)
*Prosperity* (Hybrid Musk)
*Rosa centifolia bullata*
*Rosa centifolia cristata*
*Rosa helenae florepleno*
*Rosa moyesii superba*
*Rosa multiflora grandiflora*
*Rosendorf Ufhoven* (Shrub)
*Skyrocket* (Hybrid Musk)*
*Souvenir d'Alphonse Lavalle* (Shrub)
*Sparrieshoop* (Shrub)†
*Thisbe* (Hybrid Musk)
*Tour de Malakoff* (Centifolia)
*Triomphe de l'Exposition* (Hybrid Perpetual)*
*Tuscany* (Grandiflora)*
*Victor Hugo* (Hybrid Perpetual)*
*Will Scarlet* (Hybrid Musk)*
*Zweibrucken* (Kordesii)

**Class 5.** Plants completely killed.

*Antoine Rivoire* (Hybrid Tea)*
*Bloodstone* (Hybrid Tea)*
*Border Queen* (Floribunda)†*
*Bridal Veil* (Floribunda)†*
*California* (Hybrid Tea)*

*Charles Mallerin* (Hybrid Tea)*
*Courtship* (Hybrid Tea)†*
*Coy Colleen* (Hybrid Tea)†*
*Girona* (Hybrid Tea)*
*Golden Glow* (Hybrid Tea)*

*Golden Revelry* (Hybrid Tea)†*
*Heinrich Munch* (Hybrid Tea)†*
*Ida McCracken* (Hybrid Tea)*
*Jackman's White* (Hybrid Tea)*
*Jaune Deprez* (Moss)*
*Karen Poulsen* (Floribunda)*
*Le Vesuve* (China)*
*Lorraine Lee* (Hybrid Tea)*
*Louisiana Purchase* (Hybrid Tea)†*
*Lowell Thomas* (Hybrid Tea)†*
*Lucia Zuloaga* (Hybrid Tea)†*
*Madcap* (Floribunda)†*
*Misty Gold* (Floribunda)*
*Molly Bishop* (Hybrid Tea)*
*Mrs. Edward Laxton* (Hybrid Tea)*

*Mrs. John Laing* (Hybrid Perpetual)†*
*Mrs. Sam McGredy* (Hybrid Tea)†*
*Narzisse* (Hybrid Tea)*
*Nuria de Recolons* (Hybrid Tea)†*
*Poinsettia* (Hybrid Tea)†*
*Rosa highdowensis*
*Rosa moyesii*
*Rosa pruhoniciana*
*Souvenir de Georges Pernet* (Hybrid Tea)*
*Tzigane* (Hybrid Tea)*
*Ulster Monarch* (Hybrid Tea)*
*Virgo* (Hybrid Tea)†*

† Plants would, in normal Winters, be included in next-hardier class (applies to Hybrid Teas, Floribundas and Grandifloras in general).

* Received winter protection in the form of a 10" cone of soil around the base of the plant.

Classifications indicated according to Modern Roses V.

1. Nicolas, J. H. Arcticness and Mathematics. American Rose Annual 22:166-169 (1937).
2. Rehder, Alfred. Manual of Cultivated Trees and Shrubs, 2nd Edition, 1947.
3. Wright, Percy H. The Arcticness of Various Roses. American Rose Annual 23:71-74 (1938).
4. Wyman, Donald. Shrubs and Vines for American Gardens (1953).

## BREATHE A ROSE'S FRAGRANCE

Feast your eyes upon a rose's hue,
To change your mood from indigo to blue,
And marvel at the miracle you see,
An object born of heaven's own ecstacy.
Observe a rose's texture; lightly touch
A petal with your fingertips. How much
Of heaven's mementos can this earth endure?
For such it is, with touch of earth's allure.
Now note a rose's composition, form,
And marcel that it calms the spirit's storm.
Breathe a rose's fragrance, think of God,
For how has heaven issued from earth's sod?

Frances Marley Bell
Mt. Rainier, Md.

# Roses Down On The Jersey Shore

Clare Campbell

Ocean View, N. J.

**W**E OFTEN read that "roses were first brought" to a certain state or country in the year so-and-so. I often wonder if there really is an area anywhere where roses had to be "brought in." Judging from our own New Jersey shore, roses were always present.

This pleases me no end, and I often permit myself to dream that I was around these beaches and neighboring forests when the good King Nummy and his sister, Princess Snow Flower, sat under our big oaks and beeches. Dreaming, I enjoy watching them point out to me the precious little "rabbit roses" that enhance old trail edges; and lovely *Rosa rugosa* with its sparkling green foliage and oh-so-very rosy-red big single flowers.

### RIGHT ON THE BEACH

Very near the ocean (right in the beach sand, in fact), we spied a gorgeous display of them—the kind that flaunt those handsome "apples" come Fall. These hips are over 1″ across and red enough to make you blink! We brought home about 35 of these plants knowing that if we didn't they would soon pass away since our sand dunes are being leveled to make building lots. Now, after two years, they have grown into a hedge that nearly stops traffic. The rosy-red, tissue-paper flowers begin blooming in May, and never cease till frost calls a halt. There is a period of early Autumn when both the flowers and the hips vie for applause, and, set off by the shining green of those rugged leaves, they both rate it.

These priceless heritages have, miraculously, escaped complete ruin by bulldozers and boobs even today. Of course, they are not as numerous and each year become scarcer. But, if you truly love them and really look for them, they can still be found. I never cease to thank God for men like Richard Thomson who care enough about lovely old roses to study them, save them and speak up and write about them with the hope of converting the unenlightened, and awakening in them the conviction that every rose that God ever made is perfection and beauty that we should adore!

## JUST A LITTLE COMMON SENSE

Now, of course, the Jersey shore is noted for its sandy soil. I am often asked, "How can you grow roses with so little moisture in the soil?" We do it by using a little common sense, that's all.

We plant our roses whenever possible in a spot that gets partial shade (roses do not need boiling hot sun all day long any more than you do!) We found that mixing some clay in the soil, or tossing two or three broken-up old bricks or inverted turf blocks in the bottom of the planting hole helps keep the dampness where it needs to be—around the roots.

Of course, when we speak of these moisture-saving tricks, we are referring to the way we plant "new" roses—the hybrids. The native roses do very well anywhere that they are left in peace, without any of these helpful devices of man.

## WE DO FEED

We do feed these roses once a year (in March), but they could do very well without it.

We never dust or spray, because they never need it.

Our main headache is a spray that the "powers that be" puff out of big trucks all along our street and roads to "control" (ha!) the mosquitoes. All of us have lost valuable plants, especially roses, from this lethal gas. Many of us try to grow roses "out front" so that all who pass may enjoy them. Invariably, we lose many of them from that spray, despite the fact that we plead with the squirters to turn off their streams of poison as they approach our gardens.

However, we do grow roses, and nice ones, down along the Jersey shore.

# Roses Have Satellites, Too

Edward B. Risley*

Durham, N. H.

W HILE the geophysical scientists are launching earth satellites, recent examination of the chromosomes in the cells in rose plants has revealed the presence of satellites there also. This discovery resulted from an attempt to count the chromosomes in the root tips of some of the roses that have resulted from seven years of work at the University of New Hampshire in breeding hardy Ramblers suitable for northern New England.[1]

Chromosomes have a rod-shape only for a short period of time (called the metaphase) when each cell is newly-formed and while the slender threads of genes (the tiny bodies believed to control hereditary characteristics) are tightly wound into a hollow spiral coil (somewhat resembling a screen-door spring) which stains black, and looks like a rod.

Each rose variety has a definite number of chromosomes in all its cells. Seven chromosomes make a set in *Rosa,* and most roses that are fertile have two sets (diploids) or four sets (tetraploids). Those having three sets (triploids) are mostly sterile. Table 1 lists examples of these normal conditions, and also some unusual ones such as fertile triploids, sterile diploids and sterile tetraploids.

Rose chromosomes are very small. Most of the ones illustrated here are two to three microns long, which means that it would take around 1300 of them laid end to end to equal 1″. We hoped to see the shape of each individual chromosome clearly enough to be able to identify it as an individual and trace its appearance in the cells of its "children," "grandchildren," etc., by magnifying it 1250 times under an excellent research microscope. In Table 1, an asterisk

*Assistant horticulturist, University of New Hampshire.

Published with the approval of the director of the New Hampshire Agricultural Experiment Station as scientific contribution number 224.

**Figure 1**
Skinners Rambler

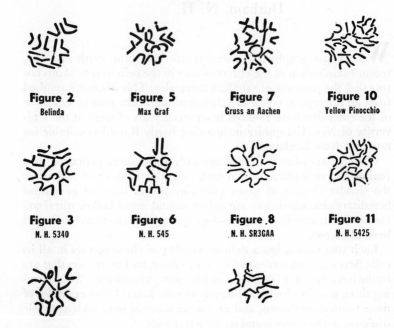

**Figure 2**
Belinda

**Figure 5**
Max Graf

**Figure 7**
Gruss an Aachen

**Figure 10**
Yellow Pinocchio

**Figure 3**
N. H. 5340

**Figure 6**
N. H. 545

**Figure 8**
N. H. SR3GAA

**Figure 11**
N. H. 5425

**Figure 4**
N. H. 535

**Figure 9**
N. H. 551

**Figure 12**
N. H. 500

**Figure 13**
Rosa carolina plena

### Figure 1

*Skinner's Rambler.* The 14 chromosomes in somatic metaphase in this cell appear to be separated into 7 pairs.

### Figure 2

*Belinda.* One of the 14 chromosomes has a satellite.

### Figure 3

*N.H. # 5340 (Skinner's Rambler x Belinda).* The satellite was retained in this hybrid.

### Figure 4

*N.H. #535 (Skinner's Rambler x Belinda).* No satellite appears in this hybrid.

### Figure 5

*Max Graf (Rosa wichuraiana x Rosa rugosa).* One of the 14 chromosomes in this nearly-sterile diploid has a satellite. Note groups of three chromosomes at center and bottom.

### Figure 6

*N.H. #545 (Skinner's Rambler x Max Graf).* The *Max Graf* satellite and two groups of three chromosomes were retained in this hybrid. Note the ring-shaped chromosome held in that position by strands of chromatin material.

### Figure 7

*Gruss an Aachen.* A fertile triploid with one satellited chromosome and a ring or two held in position by a chromatin strand.

### Figure 8

*N.H. SR3GAA (Skinner's Rambler x Gruss an Aachen).* First generation shows 14 chromosomes and a very small satellite.

### Figure 9

*N.H. #551 (Skinner's Rambler x Gruss an Aachen).* Second generation is a fertile diploid with satellited chromosome.

### Figure 10

*Yellow Pinocchio.* A fertile tetraploid with 28 chromosomes.

### Figure 11

*N.H. #5425 (Skinner's Rambler x Yellow Pinocchio).* A sterile triploid with 21 chromosomes. Only 33% of the cells examined had all 21: 4 had 20, 7 had 19, 6 had 18 and 3 had only 17.

### Figure 12

*N.H. #500 (Rosa wichuraiana x Betty Bland).* The nature of sterility in this diploid may be the same as that in *Max Graf.*

### Figure 13

*Rosa carolina plena* (Lynes). A sterile tetraploid with 28 chromosomes.

144                                    AMERICAN ROSE ANNUAL:

TABLE 1.   Some Chromosome Counts in Garden Roses And Their Relation
           to Breeding Behavior

1. Fertile Diploid x Fertile Diploid    →   Fertile Diploid
   *Skinner's Rambler* x *Belinda**      →   N.H. #5340* and N.H. #535

2. Fertile Diploid x Highly Sterile
   Diploid                              →   Fertile Diploid
   *Skinner's Rambler* x *Max Graf**     →   N.H. #545*

3. Fertile Diploid x Fertile Triploid   →   Fertile Diploid
   *Skinner's Rambler* x *Gruss an*      →   N.H. SR3GAA*..F1
        *Aachem**                       →   N.H. #551*        F2

4. Fertile Diploid x Fertile Tetraploid →   Sterile Triploid
   *Skinner's Rambler* x *Yellow*
        *Pinocchio*                     →   N.H. #5425
   *Skinner's Rambler* x *Rosa*
        *virginiana*                    →   N.H. #5314

5. Sterile Diploids
   *Mrs. Anthony Waterer* (?)               (*Rosa rugosa* x *General*
      (*variable)                            *Jacqueminot*)
   N.H. #500                                (*Rosa wichuraiana* x *Betty Bland*)

6. Sterile Tetraploid
   *Rosa carolina plena* (Lynes)[2]

---

*One chromosome has a satellite in these roses.

marks those rose varieties whose root-tip cells have one chromosome bearing a satellite (a short coil of chromatin material attached to the chromosome by a chromatin thread). These "markers" aid greatly in identifying individual chromosomes, and since the chromosome is considered one of the most fundamentally-basic units in a plant, taxonomic studies of the true relationships of the varieties of a species, or species of a genus, are greatly enhanced by chromosome identification. In *Rosa* this would appear to be a most difficult, but not impossible task.

Figures 5 and 6 show the satellited chromosome and two groups of three others connected by "threads" in *Max Graf* and its seedling, *N.H. #545*. Such a relationship is not constant in all cells examined in these roses, and a great amount of observation would be essential before positive identification of any one chromosome could be made in *Rosa*.

Of particular interest is the presence of chromatin threads connecting *Rosa* chromosomes at metaphase in root-tip cells. In Figure 6, a chromosome is bent into a ring and held fast to another chromosome by these threads. In Figure 7, a ring of two chromosomes is held by a thread. In many of the other figures, groups of three or more chromosomes appear to be interconnected. This condition is normally only associated with cell division in the formation of pollen and embryo sacs (in which these connectives are called chiasmata and the resultant chromosome groups are termed bivalents, trivalents, quadrivalents, etc.). Such groupings are associated with malfunction and sterility in varying degrees. What effect these threads have in root-tip cells is unknown.

The number of chromosomes in the cells of one plant are supposed to be constant, and almost always are so. The full compliment of 21 chromosomes of the triploid offspring of *Skinner's Rambler* x *Yellow Pinocchio* are shown in Figure 11. All 21 were not always present in the root-tip cells. Only 33% contained all 21, while the remainder had 20, 19, 18 and 17 chromosomes per cell. This rose should produce an occasional mutation or sport from a bud if this condition of variable chromosomes number exists in all the tissues of the plant.

---

1. Risley, Edward B. Breeding Winter-Hardy Rambler Roses, American Rose Annual 42:57-73 (1957).

2. Lynes, Doris and Wilson. A Rediscovery of the Double Form of Rosa Carolina. American Rose Annual 40:19-24 (1955).

# Roses For Kansas

## Mrs. H. F. Anderson
## Wichita, Kan.

THE HISTORY of the rose is the history of mankind's migrations and colonizations. When covered wagons full of early settlers moved into Kansas, the rose came with them.

Already native to Kansas were the soft pink and rosy-red Prairie Roses *(Rosa setigera* sp.). They are fragrant and very thorny, with the starched, pristine look of a little girl in her first communion dress.

*Harison's Yellow* and *Persian Yellow,* both Shrubs, were two of the first roses widely grown in Kansas. *Harison's Yellow,* the harbinger of Spring, bears its abundant yellow flowers on a branching bush. This sweet-scented rose grows so prolifically that it was found in many an early-day door yard.

The deep gold semi-double bloom with its homemade soap fragrance characterizes *Persian Yellow.* These roses are so easy to transplant that they were given freely to people who wanted roses for their new home.

Next came the old Mosses, Damasks and Centifolias. The Centifolias, better known as the old Cabbage Roses, range in color from deepest red to the purest white, and even to the striped *Variegata di Bologna.* We find Centifolias that are blue-blooded aristocrats. Others are like hard-working peasants. They are believed to be native to Asia Minor. They have a delicious old-time fragrance. Often they carry so many petals that the stems lack the strength to carry the heavy blooms. Most Kansas Centifolias were the old "steeple" type. This means that a hard, green, bud-like growth appeared in the center of each bloom. A deep dark red Centifolia with streaks of white was universally known as the Red Rose from Kansas.

The old Moss roses, ranging from lavender to pink, dark red and maroon, are even beautiful when not in bloom. The mossiness of sepals and calyx and the red color of the canes make this type of rose a much-desired shrub. Many a sunbonnetted child carried bouquets of these roses to her teacher as she trudged down the dusty wagon roads to school.

The Damask rose, with the sweetest perfume of any early or

146

modern rose, was another settler in early Kansas. The foliage is small and light green in color. Its colors range from white to deepest red. It's a flat rose, blooming in clusters, and when it was remontant, it was known as the Rose of Four Seasons.

The roses that I love best are the old Hybrid Perpetuals, the Kings and Queens of Rosedom. Growing too high for a small child to pick, they produce a long stem that is fine for cutting. Some varieties are thornless. Others fairly bristle with thorns. Flowers are either large or exceptionally large, and very fragrant. Hybrid Perpetuals are outstandingly hardy. They were at the top of the popularity poll from 1840 to 1880. An artist's dream of a rose was *La Reine Victoria*. Another outstanding rose of this period was *General Jacqueminot*. Both still retain their popularity in the gardens of old-rose fanciers of today. A light pink Hybrid Perpetual that makes any current All-America Rose Selection winner look to its laurels for form and color is the *Duchess of Sutherland*.

Of the Climbers, *Prairie Queen,* sometimes known as the Cup and Saucer Rose, is a beautiful pink. Seven Sisters Rose *(Rosa multiflora platyphylla)* blooms range from mauve to white in color. *Excelsa* was the favorite rosy-red of a later period. They all bloom in huge clusters.

These varieties all grew around Wichita, and were numerous in the Hayesville community until the march of progress made building sites out of the old homesteads.

The dry years of the '30s took a heavy toll of the old roses. Ofttimes I've been told, "We had a beautiful rose bush like you describe that mother or grandmother brought from Ohio, Pennsylvania or some other state. It grew here for over 60 years until the drought killed it." Old cemeteries used to offer an excellent place to view roses of a bygone era.

When you pick one of these old-fashioned roses, inhale its heady perfume and study its quaint look, your mind pictures the little red schoolhouse and the small white church where people were christened, married and from which they went to their final resting place. It recalls the early frontier that was Kansas; the cowpokes, gunslingers, bustles, the dust of the cowtowns. To me, it's more precious and more individualistic than its proud beautiful sisters of today. These are the roses of a bygone era; roses that bring deep sweet thoughts and stir the imagination.

Fruit-hungry pioneers made jelly and sauce from the hips formed on these old rose bushes. They contain a higher percentage of vitamin C than citrus fruit.

But now, it's time to move on and consider our present-day favorites. So often I have been asked, "What are your favorite roses for Kansas?" This sounds like a simple question to answer, but so many things go in the summing up of a rose. A fellow rosarian will ofttimes disagree with you if your favorite hasn't performed well for him.

Roses today are much hardier and disease-resistant than those of a decade ago. Some varieties are beautiful at any season, and stand heat well. In addition, people are learning to grow roses and do it correctly.

I have grown the following varieties successfully here, and the American Rose Annual's Proof of the Pudding reports from this section verify that they are all fine.

*Mirandy, Chrysler Imperial* and *Crimson Glory* are fine reds for our location. *Mirandy* blues to a degree, but its size, texture and foliage remain good, so I feel that it really belongs here. With these also goes *Bravo*, a bright, cheerful red. It is extremely hardy and persists in blooming even while the other roses rest.

In the lighter shades of red, the husky giant *Tallyho* can't be left out. Neither can the mother and grandmother of so many roses, *Charlotte Armstrong*.

In the yellows, plant *Peace*, the rose that carries the highest American Rose Society rating. *Diamond Jubilee* loves sun, but balls in wet overcast weather. When properly grown, it's a blue-ribbon rose anywhere. *Narzisse*, a pale yellow rose, has good form and texture, and curled-back petals. *Sun Valley* and *Soeur Therese* are egg-yolk yellow with streaks of red. *Mrs. Pierre S. du Pont* is hardy, but loses size, color and texture during our heat. In the cool Fall and Spring weather, it is a lovely thing.

You can see by this time that I prefer roses with heavy petalage that are of rose-show caliber.

In the pinks, I like the newcomer *Tiffany*, which is a beauty. I also like *Korova*, a big lush pink; small *Picture*, with its delicate Dresden appearance; *Capistrano* and *Mission Bells*. These lusty giants grow happily here.

In the orange and blend shades, I like *Mme. Henri Guillot* in raspberry and gold; *Mojave*, with colors of a desert sunset caught in

TORCH SONG HT
Francis Meilland; introduced Conard-Pyle Co., West Grove, Pa. Plant Patent
1760. Described page 258.

GOLD COAST GR.
H. Robinson; introduced Jackson & Perkins, Newark, N.Y. Described page
246.

its petals; *Duquesa de Peneranda,* a fine orange; *Fred Edmunds,* also orange; and the very regal copper and pink *Comtesse Vandal.*

My favorite white is *Mme. Jules Bouche.* I find *Kaiserin Auguste Viktoria* a wonderful big white that gives its best performance in the heat. Wet weather causes it to blast and ball.

The new race of Grandifloras offer much beauty and bloom. They have been wonderful in my garden so far. Among these are *Queen Elizabeth, Montezuma, Carrousel* and *June Bride.* I can't be too specific about *June Bride* as we need more time to become better acquainted.

The Floribundas (*Yellow Pinocchio,* black-red *World's Fair, Red Pinocchio* and white *Glacier)* do well here. Multicolor *Masquerade* really produces bloom. *Spartan* is a honey. Its color is so vibrant that it really shouts for notice. *Ma Perkins,* a camelia-like rose, is very desirable. *Circus,* a *Peace*-type, can't be passed up.

The hardy Brownell roses like us well. They are very disease-resistant, but their blooms get smaller in the heat. Our rapid changes in temperature during the Winter months do not seem to affect them at all, which is an excellent quality in a rose.

There's no reason why Kansas could not easily be referred to as the Rose Bowl, instead of part of the Dust Bowl. Most roses like Kansas, just like you and me.

Summer in Kansas really supplies the real test for a rose. Prolonged periods of 90-100° temperatures with dry heat and hot nights will drain the life from a rose not adapted to the wheat belt. So often we hear people say, "My roses really suffered winter-kill," when Summer has been the real culprit.

Be sure that you buy a No. 1 plant from a good nursery. Then plant your rose correctly, allowing ample root space. Give it all the water that you think it needs, then give it some more. Roses do not require food during the first year; the bone meal that you used when you planted the bush is sufficient. This allows the plant to build an excellent root system which will pay off with larger and more profuse blooms the following year. A mulch is a must for roses in Kansas during the hot Summer months. It acts as a cooling system for your plants.

Beautiful roses can be and are raised in Kansas. Attend a Wichita Spring rose show and you will leave convinced.

# Asia, The Land of Flowers

Wilber Stout

Lancaster, Ohio

Reports by Marco Polo, soldiers, travelers and ship captains in the spice trade about the wealth and beauty of the plant life in Asia led to interest by gardeners and scientists in Europe. Soon, botanists, nurserymen and daring amateurs were attracted to the field. The vast expanse of China and the terrible gorges of the Himalayas afforded a challenge beyond resistance.

Many local areas in Tibet, Nepal, Butan, Assam, northern Burma and the main Himalayan highlands and foothills have been critically examined by such men as Hugh Falconer, George Forest, Joseph D. Hooker, J. F. Rock, David Wallich, J. E. P. Aitchison, T. J. Booth, Reginald Farrer, Albert Regal, F. Kingdon Ward and others. Yet, great areas remain unseen.

In their search, these men brought out great quantities of plants, bulbs, roots and seeds to test for their merits and classification. China, with its wealth of plant life, has added much through the efforts of botanists, nurserymen, churchmen, government officials and plant hunters. Here we revere such names as Robert Fortune, Augustine Henry, Henry E. Wilson, Abbe Armond David, Abbe Delavay, Padre Cyprian, Pere Dejeen, George R. Hall and W. Purdom, to mention only a few.

In Japan, the most prominent collectors were Philip Franz Von Siebold, Max Ernst Wichura and Chenosuke Sugawa. Their names appear often in specie descriptions (as *Rhododendron Fortunei, Iris Delavayi, Lilium Wallichianum,* etc.) Many of the plants that they found have been useful in agriculture, forestry, medicine and many industrial purposes, as well as for garden decoration.

Just what has Asia given the rosarian for his garden? This land has provided most of the useful specie roses known to man. And these, through hybridization, have furnished our modern roses. Roy E. Shepherd states:[1] "The major types of garden roses now grown have been derived from varieties of two or more of the following eight species: *Rosa chinensis, Rosa damascena, Rosa foetida, Rosa moschata, Rosa multiflora, Rosa odorata, Rosa rugosa* and *Rosa wichuraiana*. It is interesting to note that these are all of Asiatic origin, and that the species of other continents have been of little value in creating our modern horticultural varieties. This is due to the fact that Asia is the native habitat of the roses that are freely recurrent in bloom, the only ones that bear yellow flowers and those with a tendency to trailing or climbing habit."

Wilson gives some idea of the abundance of roses there: [2] "Rose bushes abound everywhere, and in April perhaps afford the greatest show of any one kind of flower. *Rosa laevigata* and *Rosa microcarpa* are more common in fully-exposed places. *Rosa multiflora, Rosa moschata* and *Rosa banksiae* are particularly abundant on the cliffs and crags of the glens and gorges, though by no means confined thereto. They often scale tall trees, and a tree thus festooned with its branches laden with flowers is a sight to be remembered. A walk through a glen in the early morning or after a slight shower, when the air is laden with the soft delicious perfume of myriads of rose flowers, is truly a walk through an earthly paradise."

Robert Fortune, the renowned Scotch botanist who learned the Chinese language and even worked as a coolie, gathered the first Tea and yellow-flowering roses for European admiration. Other workers helped to extend the Tea rose collection.

The rugged *Rosa rugosa*, with its beauty of bud and pleasing fragrance, was found growing on the rocky shores of Japan.

The little elfin fairy rose *Rosa rouletti*, or its ancestor, apparently came from the Chinese mainland. We tuck it in our rock garden and admire it for its diminutive bloom and its long flowering period.

Thus, Asia has brought us not only the smallest specie rose *(Rosa chinensis minima)*, but also the largest *(Rosa gigantea)*. Kington Ward in his travels in Manipur states that the latter "grows to 100' or more, and festoons the forest trees with large white blooms."

*Rosa bracteata,* from the interior of China, is a parent of *Mermaid,* a perfect piece of artistry.

*Austrian Copper,* gathered somewhere in southwest Asia, with copper-red on its face and orange-yellow on the back of each petal, is a marvel that only the Creator could fashion.

A bush of *Rosa moyesii*, with its single ruby-red petals, always appeals to the eye.

Even the thrifty *Rosa multiflora,* with its panicle of tiny white flowers, makes an excellent hedge fence and provides nourishing hips for birds in Winter.

Aside from the beauty of the flower, other Asiatic roses are noted for great thorns, red stems, fragrant foliage, shiny leaves, etc. One could go on and on about the charms that nature has here bestowed.

Yes, Asia is truly a land of flowers. In fact, it has given us 60% or more of all the flowers in our gardens. But, the continent contains only 18.1% of the land mass of the world. Why, then, has this continent been such a rich source of flowers and, in fact, of other types of plant life such as fruits, vegetables and trees?

For instance, why did Abies David find over 200 specie rhododendrons in one valley in western Yunnan, now recognized as the rhododendron center of the world? Why did Wilson see tens of thousands of Regal lilies in the headwaters of the Min, a branch of the Yangtze? Why are the most distinctive and useful roses of the Creator gathered on the lowlands and mountain plateaus; some not far below the snow line? Such examples could be repeated over and over.

What are some of the components contributing to the development of such a wealth of plant life? The chief ones, of course, are climate, moisture and soil. To these, however, must be added many modifying factors, such as: age and size of the land mass; its height above the sea; character of the surface (mountain or plain); direction and strength of the winds; type and variability of temperature; amount, kind and constancy of moisture; chemical and physical character of the soil; disturbance by animal life (including man) and exceptional agencies of less frequent occurrence (like continental glaciers, earthquakes and volcanic action). All these agencies are, or have been, contributing factors in the Asiatic area.

The evidence afforded by its rocks and fossil remains indicate that, geologically, Asia is an old land mass. At the surface, it has all types of rocks (from the ingenous granite, gneiss and schist to the sedimentary limestone, dolomite, sandstone, shale, clay and coal to the recent uncompacted loess, silt and sand).

The continent is so old that it has cast its influence on surrounding areas (mainly Europe, Africa, North America and the Pacific Islands) where many plants and animals (including man) are similar to those found in Asia.

Another measure of its age is the plant life still remaining from former geological ages. A good example is *Ginkgo biloba,* the Maidenhair tree, which originated as far back as the Carboniferous (coal formation) age. Numbers of plants now living there are also found in fossils formed millions of years ago. Only extended time can show such results. Most assuredly, Asia is an old land surface.

Our North American mountain ranges, along both the east and west coasts, run in a relatively north-south direction. This allows icy blasts of frigid air from the north to circulate southward through the central plains at unseasonable times. Not so in Asia. The vast Himalayan massive, with its great height, wide expanse and long sweep of over 1,800 miles, extends in a general northwest-southeast direction, and thus obstructs the flow of cold air from the north. This stabilizes the climate (temperature, moisture, etc.) throughout southern Asia, although the climate on a single mountain side can range from mild and temperate to extreme cold.

Aside from the Himalayas, the mountains of central and northern Asia lack both extent and massiveness. Most of them occur in rather short ridges, rather than in cordilleran massives. They lie at various angles to form a more-or-less stirred-up pattern. This arrangement leads to numerous definite pockets or to special habitats for plant growth in varied forms. Here, through the differences in temperature, moisture, soil, sunlight, shade, shelter, air, long ages of growth and self pollenization, plants have altered and developed modified forms. Thus, the plant hunter notes great variation from place to place. Perhaps this shows only as a difference in color of bloom from mountain to mountain or valley to valley. Such special habitats help to account for the vast range of plant life on the Asiatic continent.

Variable soils in the gorgy valleys, massive cliffs, protected shelters, upland meadows and mountains provide a natural habitat for a great variety of plants, ranging in size from those of lofty dignity in the lowlands to the tiny creepers near the line of perpetual snow and glacial ice.

In general, Asia has a varied, but rather wide coastal plain along the three bordering oceans. Then the surface rises rapidly to high mountains and elevated plateaus. In fact, the structural pinnacles in Tibet and Nepal are the most elevated lands in the world. The continent as a whole is well-drained by great rivers with their branching tributaries. Hence, the surface is well-dissected, even through the highly-folded Himalayan mountains where the Indus, Ganges, Brahmaputra, Irrawaddy, Salween and some minor streams cut into or through this massive and empty into the Indian Ocean. In the headwater basins of these streams, precipitation is usually high (commonly above 100″ per year). Three other important rivers (Salween, Mekong and Yangtze) head in Tibet. Part of their upper courses are less than 100 miles apart, yet the Salween flows to the Gulf of Martaban in southeast Burma, the Mekong to the South China Sea in Cochin and the Yangtze to the North China Sea in the northeast China, thousands of miles apart. The Hwangho (Yellow River) and the Siking also help to drain western China and some adjacent areas. The northern Asiatic streams (Amur, Lena and Yenisei) drain into the Arctic Ocean. Since they flow through Russia, they are not so well known, and are of less importance botanically.

All plant life requires water. It must be supplied in sufficient quantities and at seasonable times. The green foliage of smaller types often contains 75-85% water. Asia runs the gamut; from trivial amounts in the dry deserts, to abundant supplies in the rain forests. In fact, this continent contains some of both the driest and the wettest lands on earth. In general, however, the rainfall, amplified by mist, clouds and fog, is sufficient to support hardy plant life. The moisture comes mainly from vapors from the Pacific Ocean, but large supplies are also provided by the monsoons of the Indian Ocean. The Artic Ocean also contributes rain and snow to northern Asia, especially Siberia.

A few specific figures show the pattern of precipitation:

(1) Rainfall is high (usually well over 100″) in the Malay Peninsula of southeast Asia and in Sumatra, Borneo and the adjacent islands. In Burma, the precipitation is some 100″ at Rangoon, but only 33″ at Mandalay. This region contains some of the rainest spots in the world.

(2) Much the same rainfall prevails on the mainland of Asia in Siam, Laos, Annam, Cambodia and Cochin China.

(3) On entering the great Himalayan massive, the moisture increases to rain-forest proportions (230-300″ per year). Here, the vegetation is rank. Many epiphytic plants, including rhododendrons, grow in the upper branches of trees in the Mishmi Hills of Assam, for example. Somewhat similar figures are reported for Butan, Nepal and eastern Tibet.

(4) In general, China is well-watered. The amount varies locally, but is usually between 40-60″.

(5) Japan reports some 60″, Korea approximately 40″ and Siberia a somewhat similar amount.

Thus, *as a continent* this land has plenty of moisture for plant growth. However, Asia is not all so well-provided with water. Rainfall is scarce in much of the high plateaus and steppes of Soviet Russia. The Gobi Desert in Mongolia, an area of some 300,000 square miles, is one of the driest spots in the world. South of the Himalayas in southwest Asia, the land is much-improverished because of a lack of water. The Thar (Indian) desert in western India is a sand waste with few oases. Pakistan and Afghanistan have only about 10″ of precipitation. Iran has 4-26″, Iraq some 7″. Most of Arabia has lacked water for ages. Here archaeologists find civilization after civilization buried one above another by sands containing little traces of human existence. These Asian deserts may be projected westward to the extensive Sahara of northern Africa. Nevertheless, these deserts and dessicated lands of Asia do contain various types of plant life. The kinds vary with the temperature, height above the sea and food content of the soil.

The flood plains of the streams, the higher terraces and even many mountain sides are cultivated or grazed upon throughout most of Asia. Hence, native plant life in these fields is either eliminated or much restricted.

Thus, the chief concentration of virgin plant life is found in the eastern part of the Himalayas, and north throughout the rugged mountainous parts of China which are usually between 5,000 and 10,000 feet in elevation. These lands are highly-dissected. Conditions left by stream erosion in the abrupt, deeply-indented valleys of the mountains and plateaus favor plant growth in several ways. Man has not invaded these areas to establish agricultural or village sites. Mist, clouds, fog and stream evaporation keep the humidity high and relatively constant. This suspended moisture is especially favorable for many types of plants, such as rhododendrons and tiny alpines, which have shallow roots. Various conditions of sunlight and shade are present to attract all types of plants. Special pockets among the upturned rocks provide soil and shelter for plants, and favor their existence for years. No wonder these retreats are special prizes for the plant hunter who is seeking new and unusual finds!

1. History of the Rose, page 5.
2. Wilson, H. E. A Naturalist in Western China. Vol. 1, page 18.

# How To Make Roses Thrive In Southern California

## Fred E. Corfe
## Arcadia, Calif.

**B**EING an amateur, I feel quite complimented upon being asked to write a short article about how I grow my roses in the San Gabriel Valley of southern California.

Frankly, there isn't anything to it, as this locality is almost disease-free. We do have aphids, thrip and mildew, but none of these are prevalent enough to make rose growing discouraging. Blackspot, rust, etc., are unknown here. I have had some crown gall trouble, so now I am extremely cautious about new plants, and I give them a good inspection with my bifocals on before planting.

## Use Standard Controls

I spray for aphids with the old standby Black Leaf 40, and use 50% malathion dust for all the other kind of bugs. Karathane seems best for mildew. I have standardized on these products, and buy a year's supply at a time.

My rose garden is in four sections. The first bed consists of 100 plants, almost all of which are 10 years old. The next bed also has about 100 plants, mostly All-America Rose Selection winners. The third garden contains un-named seedlings—many of my own creation, and some from other hybridizers who have been kind enough to give them to me to test. These seedlings take priority, because nothing would give me more pleasure than to have one of them go on to win the All-America award. I hope that one of mine will someday. My fourth bed of roses consists of my favorite plants which I have budded onto rootstock myself. I always have some *Dr. Huey,*

*I X L* and *Rosa multiflora* rootstock growing somewhere on the back of my place, so that I can multiply anything that I particularly like.

I like to get my new bare-root roses as soon after January 1 as possible. We can get good bare-root plants as late as March 1, but I don't recommend planting much after that date for good first-year performance.

Before planting my new roses, I have my soil tested. I have found that this is the only way to find out what and how much to feed. I just don't believe in, nor can I afford, using an all-purpose food when a soil test reveals that only nitrates are needed. I do not believe in over-feeding or forcing. I see too many gardens with weak, spindly growth and off-color blooms caused by such practices.

For example, if my soil test shows a big deficiency of potash, I get a bag of potassium sulphate. If the test shows a large deficiency of nitrogen, I apply ammonium sulphate. If I am short of phosphorus, I use super-phosphate. In other words, I get the soil as near perfect as possible by applying whatever it needs, then later use an organic fertilizer (I like one derived from city sewage) to maintain the standard, being careful not to overdo it.

I have found that an organic fertilizer also brings out the fragrance in roses. I believe that nearly all roses have some fragrance, but that in many instances it is too weak to be detected.

## Start Pruning Early

I start pruning in January, cutting almost all growth to about 16″. I also prune continuously during the Summer by cutting as long stems as possible on all blooms. I have to prune some of the stronger Hybrid Teas (such as *Fred Howard, Fort Knox, Henry Ford* and *Mojave*) from about 7′ to 3′ in June to keep them in bounds.

Something else that I have learned is not to condemn a rose if you only have one plant, or have not grown it for two years. I consider three plants of each variety grown for two years an absolute minimum before giving any final judgment.

Root stock, in my opinion, is a very important factor affecting the performance of any rose. I like *Dr. Huey* best because I have a difficult time in this mild climate getting my plants to go dormant in Winter, and I don't believe that roses budded on *Dr. Huey* need as long a rest period as those budded on *Rosa multiflora* require.

# City Care of Roses

## A. J. Ryan

## Ft. Wayne, Ind.

There are four things to consider in growing good roses in the city.

First, we must select a location for our beds that has good drainage, is free from tree roots and receives at least six hours of sunlight per day.

Second, we must buy the best No. 1 grade, freshly dug plants from a good reliable nursery.

Third, we should prepare our rose beds in the Fall, designing them to hold two or three rows—fertilize with well-decayed cow manure or compost. Let the soil settle, and when the bushes are planted and firmed in, there will be no danger of heaving by hard freezes during the following Winter. This can damage the plants greatly.

Fourth, try to develop good clay soil. It holds moisture much better than sandy soil.

Now, presuming that you have done these four things before you planted your roses, let me suggest how to take care of them.

First, as soon as the plants show signs of growth, unhill them and give both the plants and soil a good spraying of lime-sulphur before the temperature gets above 70°. Mildew, blackspot and pests from other sources seem to work on rose plants in the city more than out in the open air because the plants do not receive enough wind to keep the pests moving on. They are too protected by buildings, etc.

Second, we must not forget to water the plants at least once a week if the season is dry, and to do no feeding the first year. A good rose grower does not expect too much the first year. He knows what a shock the plant has gone through after being dug from the field. We should cultivate lightly at least once a week to keep the top soil from hardening and to let oxygen into the soil (we call this a dust mulch). This also lets the soil dry under the plants, so that they are less liable to harbor blackspot and mildew spores.

After the first bloom, give your plants a good spraying. Repeat this after each watering during the growing season. The best time to do this is late in the evening, or as early in the morning as possible (never during the day). Otherwise, spray material may burn the foliage.

We are now ready to begin pruning our newly-planted roses. Never let the petals fall from the first bloom. Rather, cut it back to two or three leaf eyes after the flower has been open for two or three days. This will give the plant more strength and encourage root growth. At the same time, you can see if the variety is true to color and name.

Keep a good mulch on your beds. Do not use peat moss, as it absorbs more moisture in dry weather than it holds in the soil for the plants. Good decayed cow manure or compost works better. It can even be cultivated and watered in the soil to help hold the moisture during hot, dry weather. It will also give the plants about the right amount of food for this part of the growing season.

Don't water or feed too late in the Fall or you will promote new growth which will only be frozen during the Winter. Soil that is too wet is hard to hill around the canes and does not filter down around the bud very well. All rose plants in the city should be hilled-up 6-8" just before freezing weather sets in. If they are not planted too close (at least 18" apart), you can use soil in the bed for this. Be sure to use soil as it does not hold moisture next to the plant during Spring thaws. When hilling is finished, fill in the furrows with fresh cow manure or compost. This keeps the hills from washing down during rains and snowstorms. Do not remove this manure or compost in the Spring. Rather, cultivate it into the soil to act as a good fertilizer for the first feeding. If you live where the Winters get colder than 10°, cover everything with good coarse straw or a similar material as an extra precaution. The freezes alone do not hurt roses. Rather, alternating thaws and freezes do the damage.

Only prune long shoots in the Fall that will be whipped around by the wind which will loosen the hills around them.

Remove your covering after the soil has completely thawed out and just before growth starts.

Start pruning after the beds have all been leveled off and bud growth starts. Prune one-year-old plants back to three or four buds on each good healthy stock. Take all weak stocks off at the bud union.

Don't feed until the first bloom is about finished.

If you follow this procedure, you can have the rose from year to year and enjoy one of the best hobbies a citizen can ever hope to have.

# Roses Bring You Nearer To God

Dr. Janie L. Keeter

Ft. Worth, Tex.

WHEN the word rose, or even flowers is mentioned, a feeling springs up in the heart of anyone who loves them that thrills and lifts you to a greater height of thought toward higher ideals and nearer to God. After all, God created the flowers and all other beautiful things. Henry Ward Beecher once said, "Flowers are the sweetest things God ever made and forgot to put a soul into."

Flowers are part of my life. I have always loved all kinds of beautiful plants. Perhaps this attachment was inherited, for childhood memories recall that my mother had flowers all over the place. I can still visualize her milling through Park's, Mill's and Field's catalogs each Spring for plants and seed to order with her butter, egg and chicken money. That was way back during the early 1890's. Well do I recall her taking her large magnifying reading-glass and closely scanning a pot plant to see if some choice geranium or mum was beginning to sprout a new branch or flower bud.

The Rosarian's Creed, by March E. Morse of Portland, Ore., states:
"I.    I will have no other flower before thee, for verily the rose is the queen of all flowers.
II.    I will buy good plants.
III.    Select garden site thoughtfully.
IV.    Prepare ground thoroughly.
V.    Plant carefully.
VI.    Cultivate diligently.
VII.    Fertilize frequently.
VIII.    Water copiously.
IX.    Spray specifically.
X.    Prune intelligently.

And, having done all these things well, my garden shall be of great beauty."

Much has to be taken into consideration in growing good roses. It

160

takes much hard work, persistent care and an abundance of loving patience. If you consider this a drudgery, you have lost that love of expectancy, similar to the patient love that a mother has when she must occasionally rock her baby to sleep in the middle of the night. She looks forward to the future, and to the great things that she hopes are in store for her child when it blooms into womanhood or manhood.

## SCAN CATALOGS FIRST

When I begin to receive my Fall catalogs, I carefully and diligently choose the best and most beautiful varieties that are listed. Often, through force of habit, I decide to buy the current All-America selection. However, there are usually many other fine roses listed that just missed the top rating, but which are worthy of any rosarian's care and admiration. Since most of the best new varieties are pat' ented, all nurseries sell them for the same price.

I always buy from a nursery that I know is reliable so that I can rest assured that my new plants are worthwhile and true to name. If I lost one during the first season, the nursery will replace it (that is, if notified before September 15 of the same year).

I always designate the time for shipment when ordering, therefore know about when the plants will arrive.

As soon as I send in my order (or at least before I expect the roses to arrive) I dig all the holes, have a mound of mulch-fertilizer thoroughly mixed and ready for use and a good supply of well-mixed garden loam and peat moss ready to fill in the holes with.

If my new roses arrive when the weather keeps me from planting them, I dig a trench about 12" deep, remove the wrappers then bury the rose roots carefully, tramping down the soil until only a small cavity a few inches deep remains at ground level. I fill this with medium-warm water and let it stand until the water has completely soaked down. Then I finish covering the roots with loose soil and build a mound around the canes.

When I am ready to plant permanently, I fill a tub or large container about half full with water of medium temperature, then unwrap the bundle, take out one bush at a time (immediately re-covering the others) and go over the canes and roots to see if any have been broken or bruised. If so, I carefully clip them off smoothly with sharp shears. Then I clip the tip of each root before placing the plant deep enough in the tub of water to cover all of the roots for 8-24 hours, according to how fresh the bush is.

I have my rose garden in rows, with each plant set about 18" apart in the row, and about 30-36" between each row, so that I can walk easily between them. Each hole is at least 18" deep and 15" across. I lay aside the top soil to mix with the fill-in soil and discard the clay from the bottom of the hole. Then I throw 2-3" of medium-sized rocks in to make good drainage. Next, I spread a 1-2" layer of well-rotted barnyard fertilizer on top of the stones. Some rosarians turn clods of grass sod upside down on top of the rocks instead. Then I fill about half of the hole with good sandy loam, compost (or leaf-mold) and peat moss (all well mixed). Now I hold the rose bush in place with my left hand over a cone-shaped mound in the center of the hole and pull the fill-in soil up closely under the center of the roots with my right hand, spreading the roots out and downward around the edge of the hole, never allowing any to protrude upward. I check to see that the bud union is not more than 1" below ground - level, then fill the hole until all of the roots are thoroughly covered. Then I tramp the soil down all around the bush with my feet, fill the hole with water, let it stand until the moisture is completely soaked down, then finish filling the hole and building a soil mound around the canes to about 3" above ground level.

When the bushes begin to grow about April 1, I pull the soil down to ground level.

## START PRUNING EARLY

There are always some pretty days about the middle of February when I can prune my roses and other shrubs. I use leather gloves, a good sharp saw and clippers to work over each individual bush from top to bottom. I never prune my roses down to within a few inches of the ground. Too much foliage is lost that way. First, I cut or saw out all dead and near-dead limbs. Then, I remove canes that cross one another, and nearly all lateral or side limbs. I leave all new ones, unless they are ill-shaped, cross or have grown too tall. In any case, I make a clean sloping cut about ¼" above the remaining top bud.

I try to keep each plant as symmetrical as possible throughout the season without cutting away too many leaves, especially during the Summer. When a plant loses its leaves in any way, it is visibly weakened because the foliage manufactures the food that the plant needs in order to survive and grow.

I go over every Hybrid Tea plant each morning during the blooming season and remove the little extra bloom-buds which develop beside the large middle bud by carefully pushing the smaller buds sideways. This gives more strength to the main bud, hence produces a larger blossom.

I never put any fertilizer in the hole around the rose roots. I think that it attracts a fungus or nematodes to them, soon killing the bush. All rosarians do not agree with me on this point. I put all of my fertilizer on top of the ground, and am careful not to let any of it touch a cane.

## COMBINATION MULCH-FERTILIZER

My mulch-fertilizer is a mixture of about equal parts of well-rotted cow manure, good sandy garden loam, compost and peat moss. I carefully place this on top of the soil mound around each newly-set bush, then sprinkle a small handful each of bonemeal, cottonseed meal, lime (or wood ashes) and 8-8-8 Loma on top and mix it all together well.

The surest and easiest way to improve your soil is to use peat moss. It gives your soil new life, opens it up to air and moisture by adding pure weed-free, 97% organic matter that readily mixes in and absorbs 20 times its weight in moisture, prevents surface crusting, gives you healthier soil, more roots, sturdier plants, makes a protective mulch, etc. Remember that your roses or garden can be no better than your soil will let them.

If you are fortunate enough to have a well-rotted compost pile, use this as another organic fertilizer. If you want to make compost, remember to use one-third as much nitrogenous as green matter. For instance, use 2" of fresh animal manure for every 6" of grass clippings, weeds, leaves, kitchen scraps, blood, etc. Add a good sprinkling of bonemeal, lime, etc. Build the pile up to about 4', so that it will generate heat to speed decomposition. If it does not warm up, it either does not contain enough nitrogen or is not built high enough.

I cannot over emphasize the importance of thorough watering during the Summer. Sprinkling is bad for roses, since it brings the little feeder roots to the surface. Then, when our hot sun beats down upon these little roots, they are soon burned, thus injuring the health of the bush. Water roses early in the morning while the ground is cool. I do not water roses on top of the ground. Instead, I use the left corner of a garden hoe (always turning the sharp edge away from the bush in order not to accidentally injure it) to dig a 2-2½″-deep trench from the canes all around each bush. Then I remove the nozzle from my garden hose, lay the open end flat upon the ground and fill each trench in turn. Then I do it all over again. Sometimes, during the very driest and hottest part of the season, I fill the trench a third time. As soon as I finish, I fill in the trench with soil. I repeat this treatment every ten days to two weeks during the hot dry season.

Practically any of the widely-advertised sprays or dusts will provide good pest control if you follow a timely program. Proper timing for diseases such as blackspot, rust or mildew is very essential. Keep the weather in mind, especially rainfall. Make more-frequent applications during rainy periods (within 8-10 hours after each storm). Remember that infestation takes place while the rose leaves are wet. Do not use sulphur dust on roses during the hot Summer months. It can kill foliage.

Lightly cultivate your roses regularly throughout the Summer until September to destroy weeds and aerate the soil. Never allow the soil to bake. Again, your mulch will help to prevent this.

About the middle of November, I pull up all surplus loose soil around each bush with a hoe, then pile 6-8″ of compost or leaf mold (well mixed with peat moss) on top of this and cap it off with 2″ of well-rotted barnyard fertilizer. This will tide your bushes over the cold Winter blasts.

What a difference roses make in our lives! If anyone knows of a better way to bring a little sunshine into a friend's life than by giving him a dozen of your finest blooms and a smile, I have not found it, and would like to know what it is. Growing roses does something to people which makes them better and brings them closer to God.

# Proof of the Pudding

This 33rd nationwide rating of rose varieties now on the market is compiled from reports submitted by the society's affiliated clubs, test gardens and individuals selected by district directors.

Roses are rated for five years, beginning one year after introduction, if at least 20 reports are received on them. The ratings are a valuable guide to you in planning your future rose purchases. Follow those from your area rather than the national rating, however, to find the roses best adapted to your garden.

Key to the listings and abbreviations used to conserve space is as follows: name; type; color, originator, introducer and year of introduction; patent number (if any); year first mentioned in this annual; number of times listed in this feature; number of reports received this year; average height (in inches for bush roses, feet for climbers); and the national rating (based on a scale ranging from 1 to 10). Comments are listed alphabetically by states and societies, gardens or reports. The number preceding the parenthesis in these comments tells how many members' reports were combined in the local rating. Numbers in parenthesis stand for the number of plants, years grown, height and local rating.

Plants ratings between 9 and 10 are considered outstanding; 8 and 9 excellent; 7 and 8 good; 6 and 7 fair; and below 6 generally unsatisfactory.

All classifications correspond with those listed in Modern Roses V. Abbreviations include: Cl (Climber); ClF (Climbing Floribunda); ClHT (Climbing Hybrid Tea); F (Floribunda); Gr. (Grandiflora); HT (Hybrid Tea); Min. (Miniature); and Cl Min. (Climbing Miniature).

## AIDA HT. Rose-red (Mansuino; int. Jackson & Perkins '56) Pat. 1639; ARA '57; PP 2, 73 Rpts.; Av. ht. 33"; NR 7.

ARIZ. *Phoenix R.S.* 4(4-1-36″-7) Very fragrant. Lovely long red bud. CALIF. *Rose Study Club Oakland* 1(4-2-60″-7.9) Good bloomer, vigorous upright plant, disease-resistant, fragrant bloom of rich color. *Pacific R.S.* 1(1-2-29″-7) Moderately fragrant, well-shaped buds, disease-resistant foliage covers the plant well, half-open to full bloom lacks substance. *San Mateo County R.S.* 3(3-2-30″-5) Nice red, fragrant, good substance, not enough bloom, mildews quickly. COLO. *Denver R.S.* 1(1-2-36″-8.5) Does not burn in sun, good mildew-resistant bush does blackspot. D.C. *Potomac R.S.* 3(5-2-36″-7.4) Good color, bud, foliage and form, small thin flower. GA. *Georgia R.S.* 1(1-2-12″-4) Good color.ILL. *Chicago R.S. Reg. 1* 1(2-4-30″-6) Sparse, but colorful bloom. IND. *Indianapolis R.S.* 1(1-1-18″-6.5) Nice, well-formed bud opens to beautiful red. Poor growing plant. *St. Joseph Valley R.S.* 1(2-2-36″-7.8) Good foliage, large blooms, upright plant, sweet fragrance. KAN. *Wichita R.S.* 29(2-1-30″-6.5) Slow grower, holds color, insufficient bloom. KY. *Kentucky R.S.* 1(1-1-18″-3) Exquisite shade of red. *Louisville Chapter ARS* 2(7-2-42″-7) Good disease-resistant foliage. MICH. *Detroit R.S.* 1(1-1-36″-7) Good but small bloom, disease-resistant. *Kalamazoo R.S.* (8-2-33″-7.5) Good growth, foliage and blooms. *West Mighigan Rosarians* 2(2-2-24″-7) Some mildew, nice blooms in cool weather. MINN. *Minnesota R.S.* 2(2-1-29″-6.5) Sturdy, vigorous bush, rich red in cool weather. MO. *R.S. Greater St. Louis* 1(1-2-36″-7) Good medium red. *Sedalia R.S.* 1(1-2-30″-7) Urn-shaped bud, does not hold well. NEV. *Reno R.S.* 3(6-2-24″-6) Excellent red color, fragrant, good substance, poor bloomer, lots of mildew. NEW ENGLAND *New England R.S.* 1(1-2-30″-7.8) Good color and form, poor plant. N.J. *North Jersey R.S.* 2(2-2-36″-7.2) Healthy plant, fairly prolific, good form, color fades. *West Jersey R.S.* 6(8-2-42″-7.6) Good foliage, color fades. *West Jersey R.S.* 6(8-2-42″-7.6) Good foliage and color, large blooms, some fragrance. N.M. *Albuquerque R.S.* 1(1-2-24″-8) Excellent color, good bud. N.Y. *Cornell University T.G.* (4-2-33″-7.5) Fine foliage, vigorous, slight fragrance, poor flower form when open, an ordinary red. *Humboldt Park T.G.* (5-2-18″-9) Healthy dark green foliage, large dark red bud, light red double blooms, fair grower. *Rochester R.S.* 2(2-1-32″-6.5) Fragrant, healthy bush. *Schenectady R.S.* 1(1-1-24″-7.5) Late bloomer. *Syracuse R.S.* 1(2-1-30″-7) Better in Fall than Spring, medium size bloom. OHIO *Greater Cincinnati R.S.* 1(1-1-24″-7). *Stark R.S.* 1(1-1-36″-9) Good mildew-resistant foliage, blooms consistently. OKLA. *Oklahoma R.S.* 2(6-1-36″-8). ORE. *International Rose T.G.* (20-4-36″-6) Good bud form, growth habit not too good, turns magenta. *Medford R.S.* 5(7-1-39″-8.4) Especially nice in bud, good color, disease-resistant foliage, vigorous, compact grower, lots of bloom, burns in extreme heat. PA. *Breeze Hill T.G.* (2-2-28″-6) Nice color and form, large flower, not much bloom. *Philadelphia R.S.* 1(2-2-24″-6) Good color and form, poor plant. TENN. *Nashville R.S.* 1(2-2-45″-7.3) Good foliage, vigorous, medium red. TEX. *Dallas R.S.* 3(5-1-34″-7) Vigorous, good foliage, medium red, little disease. VA. *Eastern Shore R.S.* 3(4-2-50″-7) Disease-resistant, vigorous upright growth, good foliage, too few blooms. VA. *Va. Peninsula R.S.* 1(1-1-48″-6) Very healthy plant, good blooms. WASH. *Seattle R.S.* 2(2-1-33″-6.5) Good red color. *Spokane R.S.* 1(1-2-36″-8) A good red rose. WIS. *Milwaukee R.S.* 1(1-1-24″-5) Nice color, lacks vigor, few blooms, form so-so.

## ALPINE GLOW F. Medium red (Tantau; int. Jackson & Perkins '54) Pat. 1395; ARA '55; PP 4, 30 Rpts.; Av. ht. 28"; NR 7.2.

ARIZ. *Phoenix Rose Society* 2(2-2-30″-7) Brilliant orange-red flower, good foliage, not too prolific. CALIF. *Rose Study Club Oakland* 3(11-3-42″-6.9) Good thick foliage, large blooms, weak stems. GA. *Georgia R.S.* 1(2-3-48″-8.5) Color slightly different than Spartan, otherwise equal. ILL. *Greater Peoria R.S.* 1(1-3-24″-6.9) Good foliage, holds color, sparse bloom. IND. *Vincennes R.S.* 2(2-2-36″-8.5) Seems to like hot weather, no disease. IOWA *Des Moines R.S.* 1(2-2-24″-7) Good color, weak plant. MD. *Maryland R.S.* 1(1-3-30″-7) Very good color, weak stem, slow grower. MICH. *Detroit R.S.* 1(1-1-24″-8) Good color, slow grower. MO. *Rosarians Midland Empire* 1(3-3-24″-7) Good color and substance, disease-resistant. NEW ENGLAND *New England R.S.* 2(4-3-26″-7.5) Brilliant color, not vigorous, blackspots badly. N.J. *North Jersey R.S.* 3(3-2-33″-5.8) Fair to poor bush, sparse bloom, usually good color. N.Y. *Cornell University T.G.* (6-3-18″-6.5) Good bud, flower form and foliage, poor growth habit, not floriferous, blackspots easily, flowers fade and persist. *Humboldt Park T.G.* (19-3-30″-8) Abundant leathery foliage, coppery-red medium-size buds, bright fiery-red semi-double blooms on short stems fade and hang on. *Niagara Frontier R.S.* 1(2-4-30″-7) Glowing color holds well, good in hot weather. *Rochester R.S.* 2(3-3-34″-7.5) Good color, floriferous, long-lasting blooms, weak stems. *Schenectady R.S.*

(24″-8) Very good color and form, blooms too far apart on spray. OHIO *Cleveland R.S.* 1(1-3-24″-7.2) Spreading sturdy growth. *Ohio State University T.G.* (4-3-36″-7.5) Vigorous plant, abundant dark glossy green foliage, free-flowering from June to September, rich red slightly fragrant flower, disease-resistant. PA. *Breeze Hill T.G.* (3-7-26″-7) Brilliant color, nice form, fades. *Pittsburgh R.S.* 1(1-2-18″-7) Good foliage and bloom. UTAH *Utah R.S.* 1(2-1-18″-8) Like the color. W.VA. *Charleston R.S.* 1(1-3-36″-6) Good healthy bloomer, best in cool weather.

## AMY F. Medium pink (Von Abrams; int. Peterson & Dering '54) Pat. 1455 ARA '55; PP 4, 30 Rpts.; Av. ht. 25″; NR 6.7.

ARIZ. *Phoenix R.S.* 2(2-1-24″-7) Dainty pink buds and blooms, good foliage. COLO. *Denver R.S.* 1(9-2-24″-7) Good color, more double and more substance than Fashion, but not enough bloom. GA. *Georgia R.S.* 1(1-2-30″-6) Nice pink, not too different from Fashion, not a strong grower. IND. *Indianapolis R.S.* 1(1-2-24″-6) Good form, nice color, very susceptible to blackspot. IOWA *Des Moines R.S.* 1(1-1-30″-7.5) Beautiful bloom, good foliage. *Linn County R.S.* 2(2-1-14″-6) Good color, form and bloomer. KY. *Kentucky R.S.* 1(1-2-24″-8). *Louisville Chapter ARS* 2(2-2-30″-7.3). MINN. *Minnesota R.S.* 3(3-1-26″-8.3). Excellent form, vigorous, good color and foliage. MO. *Rosarians Midland Empire* 1(1-1-30″-7) Nice flower, shy bloomer. *R.S. Greater St. Louis* 1(1-1-18″-5) Not outstanding. NEW ENGLAND *New England R.S.* 1(3-2-32″-6.5) Poor flower form, blackspots badly. N.J. *North Jersey R.S.* 6(6-1-18″-6.6) Well-shaped buds, nice foliage, variable producer. N.C. *Durham R.S.* 1(2-1-30″-4) Pretty-shaped bloom, color doesn't appeal. OHIO *Akron R.S.* 1(10-1-24″-8.9) A must. *Central Ohio R.S.* 1(1-2-30″-6) Good color, plant not strong, few blooms. *Greater Cincinnati R.S.* 1(3-1-36″-7) Good foliage and grower, beautiful (but too few) blooms. ORE. *International Rose T.G.* (20-4-30″-6) Best in Spring, good sprays and bud form, variable bloom recurrence. *Salem R.S.* 1(20-4-36″-6) Balls early, good in Summer and Fall. PA. *Breeze Hill T.G.* (18-5-24″-7) Lovely color and form, blooms well, nice plant.

## AMY VANDERBILT F. Lavender-lilac (Boerner; int. Jackson & Perkins '56) Pat. 1585; ARA '56; PP 3, 106 Rpts.; Av. ht. 29″; NR 6.7.

ALA. *Twickenham R.S.* 1(1-1-24″-6) A disappointment; sparse bloom, very susceptible to blackspot. ARIZ. *Mesa R.S.* 1(1-1-18″-7) Nice blooms, fair plant. *Phoenix R.S.* 2(2-2-30″-6.8) Persistent bloomer, burns in hot weather (give it afternoon shade). CALIF. *Rose Study Club Oakland* 2(4-1-44″-6.2) Good moderately vigorous disease-resistant plant, attractive true lavender colored bloom fades too rapidly, sparse bloomer. *Peninsula R.S.* 2(2-2-36″-6) Disease-resistant, vigorous, good bloom with poor form fades. *San Diego R.S.* 1(1-1-24″-7.5) Good non-fading color. *San Joaquin Valley R.S.* 1(3-3-30″-6) Good color and foliage, weak stems. *San Mateo County R.S.* 1(2-3-30″-5) Poor color, needs too much attention. D.C. *Potomac R.S.* 2(2-1-30″-5.8) Little to recommend it. ILL. *Tri-City Men's Rose and Garden Club* 2(4-3-42″-8). IND. *Indianapolis R.S.* 1(1-3-29″-5.5) Fair grower and bloomer. *St. Joseph Valley R.S.* 2(2-5-24″-6.9) Good disease-resistant foliage, plenty of flowers this year, petals fade when old and don't come off easily. IOWA *Des Moines R.S.* 3(3-3-18″-6) Good color, bloom holds quite well. *Iowa R.S.* 1(1-3-24″-5) Long-lasting bloom. *Linn County R.S.* 2(4-2-22″-7) Weak neck, bloom fades, unusual color. KAN. *Wichita R.S.* 1(3-3-36″-8) Fair bloomer, good foliage. KY. *Louisville Chapter ARS* 5(16-2-30″-6.9). MD. *Maryland R.S.* 2(2-2-30″-7) Worth growing for color, ordinary form, not too vigorous. MICH. *Detroit R.S.* 6(8-2-30″-7) Good foliage, holds color. *Kalamazoo R.S.* (3-2-36″-7) Good blooms, disease-resistant. *Michigan State University T.G.* (6-2-23″-5) Unusual color, weak necks, blooms look old before open, objectionable old rose fragrance. MINN. *Lindale Park T.G.* (20-3-24″-7) Hardy, unusual color. *Minnesota R.S.* 4(13-3-24″-7.4) Disease-resistant, repeat-bloomer, fades to dirty grey, poor form. MO. *R.S. Greater St. Louis* 3(3-2-30″-6) Not outstanding, blackspots, weak growth. NEW ENGLAND *New England R.S.* 2(4-3-30″-7.3) Interesting color, very fragrant, vigorous, clean, not much late bloom. N.J. *North Jersey R.S.* 6(6-2-28″-7.1) Color good in Spring and Fall, spreading habit, blooms well. *West Jersey R.S.* 3(4-2-30″-7.5) Holds color very well, fairly resistant to blackspot, sprawls. N.M. *Albuquerque R.S.* 1(2-2-30″-7.9) Fragrant long-lasting blooms on healthy sprawling plants, dark green foliage. N.Y. *Cornell University T.G.* (1-2-18″-6) Unusual color, acceptable only on opening, weak plants, poor growth, not winter-hardy. *Niagara Frontier R.S.* 1(1-2-24″-6.5) Shy bloomer. *Rochester R.S.* 2(4-2-24″-6.5) Good pink-lavender color, excellent foliage, slow grower, blackspots. *Schenectady R.S.* 1(1-2-15″-6.8) No outstanding qualities; few flowers, slow growth. *Syracuse R.S.* 1(1-2-18"-6) Unusual color, sparse bloomer, fades, discolors when open, subject to blackspot. N.C. *Charlotte R.S.* 4(3-2-30"-6) Does well in Spring and late Fall, susceptible to blackspot. *Durham R.S.* 2(6-1-33"-8) Non-fading even in hottest weather, constantly in bloom, disease and insect-resistant. *Randolph R.S.* 1(1-2-48"-7) Disease-resistant, blooms fade, not too many flowers. OHIO *Central Ohio R.S.* 2(2-3-24"-6) Good bloom in Spring, poor in Fall, blackspots. *Cleveland R.S.* 3(13-2-24"-6.6) Good durable form and color, weak necks. *Columbus R.C.* 1(1-1-15"-5) Bloomed once, then died. *Greater Cincinnati R.S.* 2(2-1-24"-7) Bushy plant, looks faded after opening, blackspots. *Miami Valley R.S.* 3(3-3-30"-7.5) Good interesting color fades. *Ohio State University T.G.* (4-3-24"-7) Fairly abundant flowering, good foliage, bushy plant, flowers have a rich fragrance, disease-resistant, rich lavender color, leaves tend to turn yellow early. OKLA. *Norman R.S.* 3(5-3-15"-6). ORE. *Lewis & Clark College T.G.* (10-1-24"-5) No outstanding qualities. *Medford R.S.* 1(1-1-30"-7.5) Fragrant, continuous bloom, poor for exhibition. *Salem R.S.* 1(1-3-27"-3) Hot weather rose, poor flower, balls. PA. *Breeze Hill T.G.* (1-4-28"-7) Blooms well, nice plant, good form, dull color at times. *Harrisburg R.S.* 2(7-2-33"-7) Good color in early Spring and Fall, fades in heat, blooms freely, plant not too sturdy, sprawly habit. *Pittsburgh R.S.* 1(1-2-18"-7) Free-blooming good plant. *Philadelphia R.S.* 1(1-2-36"-7) Good color and plant, blooms age badly. TEX. *Corpus Christi R.S.* 1(1-2-36"-9) Prolific blooms, long-lasting, fades to lovely lavender shade, good foliage. *El Paso R.S.* 2(2-2-36"-9) Grows vigorously, blooms well, good shade of lavender, healthy foliage, good substance. WASH. *Spokane R.S.* 2(5-4-24"-5) Old-fashioned rose appearance, not doing very well. *Walla Walla R.S.* 1(3-2-36"-6) Disease-resistant foliage, flowers not appealing. W.VA. *Wyo-Mac R.S.* 3(5-2-24"-6.5) Beautiful bud and bloom, short strong stems, good bloomer, no good for cutting, blackspots and mildews. WIS. *Milwaukee R.S.* 1(1-1-12"-7) Nice but few blooms, does not fade or grow well.

## ARDELLE HT. White. (Eddie; int. Wyant '54) Pat. 1283; ARA '55; PP 3, 157 Rpts.; Av. ht. 36"; NR 6.6.

ARIZ. *Mesa R.S.* 1(1-1-24"-7) Good bushy plant, stands heat well, fine blooms. CALIF. *Rose Study Club Oakland* 2(4-1-54"-7) Disease-resistant foliage, moderate vigor, buds ball and open poorly, many split-center flowers. *Pacific R.S.* 1(1-2-35"-5) Disease-resistant foliage, bloom has beautiful re-curved petals when it opens properly, buds blast very easily, majority are split-centered or quartered, not enough bloom to keep. *Peninsula R.S.* 2(2-2-24"-1) Mildews, balls, very poor grower. *San Diego R.S.* 1(1-1-30"-6). D.C. *Potomac R.S.* 3(4-2-28"-7.1) Good substance, long-lasting well-formed white to cream exhibit bloom, split centers in wet seasons, few flowers. GA. *Georgia R.S.* 2(2-1-36"-4.5) Fair bush, clear clean white, bloom quarters, too few manage to open. ILL. *Chicago R.S. Reg. 1* 2(4-2-30"-4.5) Strong plant, sparse blooms ball or split. *Greater Peoria R.S.* 2(2-1-33"-6.9) Large but sparse blooms, some blackspot, balls. *Morgan Park R.S.* 2(7-1-18"-8). *Tri-City Men's Rose and Garden Club* 1(6-3-48"-6). IND. *Indianapolis R.S.* 2(4-2-34"-7) Good flower and bloomer, balls or is otherwise imperfect in cool weather, plants seem to deteriorate after first season. *St. Joseph Valley R.S.* 1(2-2-30"-7) Good foliage, many petals, balls. *Vincennes R.S.* 2(3-2-30"-8) Beautiful bloom when conditions are right, very prolific. IOWA *Des Moines R.S.* 3(3-2-30"-8) Good bloom, some double centers. *Iowa R.S.* 2(2-2-24"-7) Big bloom. *Linn County R.S.* 1(3-2-36"-7) Good form and color, split centers. KAN. *Wichita R.S.* 3(4-2-42"-7) Prolific bloomer. KY. *Louisville Chapter ARS* 2(2-1-25"-5.5) Good blooms, slow grower, balls. LA. *New Orleans R.S.* 1(1-3-42"-7) Lovely blooms in Fall and Winter, upright grower, candelabras too much, blooms supposed to be of solid color have a dash of pink in them at times. MD. *Maryland R.S.* 2(2-2-48"-8) Very full blooms on long stems, can't take wet weather, at its best in hot weather. MICH. *Detroit R.S.* 7(8-2-30"-5) Sparse bloom, balls, split centers. *Greater Lansing R.S.* 1(1-1-30"-6.7) Not a pure white, plump bud slow to open, very fragrant, little or no blackspot on foliage, best in early Fall. *Kalamazoo R.S.* (4-2-48"-7) Not exhibition type, blooms ball, double clusters. MINN. *Lyndale Park T.G.* (35-3-48"-7.2) Consistent bloomer, balls, blackspots. *Minnesota R.S.* 7(12-2-36"-7.2) Tendency to ball in wet weather. MO. *Rosarians of Midland Empire* 1(2-2-24"-7) Good white bloomer, some exhibition flowers but too many split, sprawling growth. NEW ENGLAND *New England R.S.* 3(10-2-44"-6) Fair plants, clumsy blossoms, good only in cool dry weather, blackspots easily. N.J. *North Jersey R.S.* 7(13-2-35"-5.8) Excellent plant and foliage, splits more often than not, variable color. N.M. *Albuquerque R.S.* 2(2-2-30"-6.7) Good substance, plentiful bloom, likes hot weather, balls and quarters in cool weather, N.Y. *Greater Buffalo R.S.* 2(5-1-48"-8.5) Half of the full, high-centered blooms have split centers, long stem, a good white. *Humboldt Park T.G.* (5-2-30"-6) Light green healthy foliage, upright vigorous grower, large very double creamy white bloom, continuous split blooms ball and hang on, no blackspot. *Long Island R.S.* 2(2-2-42″-5.6) Vigorous grower, branching habit, good glossy foliage resists disease, poor white double-centered blooms ball and have split centers. *Niagara Frontier R.S.* 1(1-2-36″-6.5) Large many-petalled fragrant blooms have split centers, shy bloomer. *Rochester R.S.* 2(2-3-48″-6.8) Vigorous grower, strong canes, not true white, split centers. *Schenectady R.S.* 1(1-1-36″-7.5) Large fragrant flowers, no blackspot or mildew. *Syracuse R.S.* 2(2-2-30″-6.5) Balls badly, vigorous grower, resistant to mildew. N.C. *Durham R.S.* 1(1-2-60″-8.5) Multi-petalled high-centered bloom changes to blush pink in Fall, good grower, unattractive buds in Spring. *Randolph R.S.* 2(2-2-48″-7) Long-lasting blooms waterspot. OHIO *Akron R.S.* 4(15-2-48″-7.2) Second-year bloom large, good foliage, split centers, balls. *Central Ohio R.S.* 4(4-2-30″-6) Strong vigorous bush, shy bloomer, blooms open poorly with split centers, ball easily, some blackspot. *Cincinnati R.S.* 2(6-2-36″-7) Balls frequently, good foliage. *Cleveland R.S.* 4(21-3-42″-7.7) Good white, opens well, high-centered blooms often of exhibition quality, disease-resistant, balls in wet weather. *Columbus R.C.* 3(5-2-60″-7) Good grower, balls, splits. *Euclid R.S.* 3(3-2-24″-6.5) Good foliage, poor bloom, split centers. *Forest City R.S.* 4(9-2-30″-7.5) Strong grower, good foliage, free-bloomer, considerable split centers, exhibition type when right. *Greater Cincinnati R.S.* 2(2-3-28″-7). *Lima R.S.* 4(7-2-36″-7.5) Beautiful blooms, many split centers, not a sturdy disease-resistant plant. *Medina County R.S.* 2(2-2-29″-6.5) Few good blooms, most ball. *Miami Valley R.S.* 3(4-2-12″-5) Rain-spots, balls, double centers. *Ohio State University T.G.* (4-4-33″-7) Blooms well until August, disease-resistant sparse dull green foliage, plants lack vigor. *Park of Roses T.G.* (25-2-42″-7) Good growth, sturdy plant, double buds and split centers, some blackspot. *Stark R.S.* 2(2-2-28″-6) Good growing, blooms ruined by wet weather. OKLA. *Norman R.S.* 2(8-3-24″-6) Big long buds subject to split centers and balling. ORE. *International Rose T.G.* (40-6-84″-7) Lots of bloom, strong grower, most blooms split, ball in wet weather. *Salem R.S.* 2(2-3-42″-7) Some blooms have split centers, good foliage. PA. *Breeze Hill T.G.* (2-3-28″-7) Long stems, good bud form, nice foliage, not profuse bloomer, flower quarters sometimes. *Harrisburg R.S.* 2(8-2-30″-7) Excellent hot weather rose, large full (but not many) blooms ball sometimes, slow grower. *Pittsburgh R.S.* 1(1-2-48″-8) Stems too short. *Philadelphia R.S.* 7(10-2-40″-6) Good foliage color, sprawling canes, quarters, few blooms. TENN. *Nashville R.S.* 2(3-2-30″-7.3) Healthy, resistant, some bloom of excellent form, some malformation of centers, shy bloomer. TEX. *Amarillo R.S.* 2(2-1-24″-7) Blooms near perfect, color interesting, good substance and foliage. *Dallas R.S.* 2(3-4-41″-6.3) Full-petalled bloom lasts well, some balling. *El Paso R.S.* 2(2-2-38″-8) Vigorous growth, healthy foliage, large buds, long-lasting heavy bloom as the weather cools, many split centers, balls in warm weather, not a true white (pink centers). VA. *Va. Peninsula R.S.* 1(1-2-67″-7) Vigorous growth, good foliage, slight pink-white. WASH. *Seattle R.S.* 3(4-2-30″-6.8) Not good in our climate, split centers, balls. *Spokane R.S.* 1(1-2-48″-5) Bloom rain-spots badly, not enough flowers. W.VA. *Charleston R.S.* 1(1-2-6). WIS. *Madison R.S.* 2(1-1-46″-7.3) Nice white, good disease-free foliage, hardy, split centers and balls in wet weather, sparse bloomer. CANADA (British Columbia) *Vancouver R.S.* 4(13-4-60″-6.5) Vigorous upright bush, large exhibition blooms, tends to split centers, balls in damp weather, stingy bloomer.

## ARLENE FRANCIS HT. Yellow. (Boerner; int. Jackson & Perkins '57) Pat. 1684, ARA '58; PP 1, 138 Rpts.; Av. ht. 31″; NR 7.1.

ARIZ. *Mesa R.S.* 4(5-36″-7.7) Good non-fading yellow buds and flowers, bud opens too quickly. *Phoenix R.S.* 6(7-1-30″-8) Good yellow, excellent bud, holds color. CALIF. *Memorial Rose Garden* (10-2-36″-8) Deep yellow, good cutter vigorous, very fragrant, slight mildew. *Rose Study Club Oakland* 2(11-2-44″-7.6) Golden yellow holds well, vigorous grower, prolific bloomer, fragrant. *Pacific R.S.* 1(1-1-25″-7) Mildews, some blooms seem promising. *San Diego R.S.* 2(3-2-29″-6.2). *San Joaquin Valley R.S.* 4(7-1-36″-7) Slow-growing, exhibition quality, excellent color and fragrance. COLO. *Denver R.S.* 2(19-2-36″-7.2) Rich yellow, good clean color and foliage, opens too fast, flower too loose, rounded center, not enough bloom. CONN. *Elizabeth Park T.G.* (17-2-18″-8) Excellent plant, blooms fade to white. D.C. *Potomac R.S.* 3(6-2-30″-7.4) Well-formed bud, soft deep yellow color holds well, dark glossy foliage, blooms only in the Spring and Fall. GA. *Georgia R.S.* 4(6-1-40″-6.2) Good color, poor bush, no vigor, too few blooms. ILL. *Tri-City Men's Rose and Garden Club* 1(12-2-24″-7). IND. *Indianapolis R.S.* 2(3-2-24″-6.7) Nice golden-yellow fragrant blooms, weak grower. *St. Joseph Valley R.S.* 1(2-2-30″-8.5) One of the best yellows, sweet fragrance, sparse blooms. IOWA *Linn County R.S.* 7(11-2-28″-6) Nice yellow, petals do not hold on, blackspots. KAN. *Wichita R.S.* 1(1-1-24″-7) Blooms with no care, fades badly. KY. *Kentucky R.S.* 2(3-1-36″-8) Good foliage and color, too few blooms. *Lexington R.S.* 1(1-1-24″-6.7) Flowers too small, doesn't bloom enough, blackspots badly. *Louisville Chapter ARS* 3(5-1-34"-7.6) Good yellow, susceptible to disease. LA. *New Orleans R.S.* 1(1-2-36"-7) Upright grower, medium green foliage, fades in Summer. MICH. *Detroit R.S.* 2(4-2-24"-7) Wanting in all departments. *Michigan State University T.G.* (6-2-32"-7.5) Good color holds well, vigorous, very fragrant (tea), shy Fall bloomer, slightly susceptible to blackspot, petals have an objectionable indentation at times. MINN. *Minnesota R.S.* 1(2-1-30"-7.5) Good non-fading yellow. MO. *Jewel Park T.G.* (10) Very outstanding. *R.S. Greater St. Louis* 1(2-2-30"-7) Fair yellow. MONT. *Sunset Park T.G.* (10-2-24"-6) Clear yellow holds well, good glossy foliage, could bloom more. NEW ENGLAND *New England R.S.* 3(4-1-30"-4) Vt.—attractive blooms, fragrant, sickly; N.H.—few blooms, no vigor; Me.—useless; Mass.—few blooms, bad blackspot and mildew. N.J. *North Jersey R.S.* 7(16-1-28"-7.1) Excellent color, can be show rose, fine open bloom, plant generally good, promising new yellow. *West Jersey R.S.* 5(15-1-36"-7.6) Good foliage, nice buds, wonderful bloom, attractive flowers do not last. N.Y. *Cornell University T.G.* (48-2-30"-7) Nice V-shaped plants, excellent opening flowers hang on and turn dirty white, not too vigorous, few petals in mid-Summer, shy bloomer late in season. *Greater Buffalo R.S.* 2(3-1-24"-7.5) Brightest yellow yet, not too vigorous, small bloom, good form, blackspots rather badly. *Humboldt Park T.G.* (12-2-15"-7) Upright growth, medium-size sparse foliage, ovoid deep yellow bud, double canary-yellow bloom, globular medium-size blooms hang on and fade quickly, intermittent bloomer, freezes to ground level. *Niagara Frontier R.S.* 1(2-2-18"-7) Large blooms with fair fragrance, color fades, opens flat, not impressive. *Rochester R.S.* 3(28-3-32"-7.3) Good long pointed bud, nice fragrance, weak plant. *Schenectady R.S.* 1(2-1-14"-7) Good deep gold-yellow show bloom, not tall enough. *Syracuse R.S.* 3(4-2-30"-7) Good yellow blooms last well, fragrant, could stand more flowers. N.C. *Durham R.S.* 3(6-1-24"-6) Good color and form, sparse bloomer. *Randolph R.S.* 1(2-2-36"8) Beautiful flowers, good bloomer. OHIO *Akron R.S.* 3(24-2-30"-6.8) Free-bloomer, brilliant non-fading color, blackspots. *Cincinnati R.S.* 2(4-2-24"-6) Attractive blooms, flop and fade when open. *Cleveland R.S.* 3(10-2-24"-6.5) Good yellow blooms, bush grows too slowly, roses open fast. *Forest City R.S.* 5(7-1-30"-7) Good color and foliage, reasonable amount of bloom, will blackspot. *Lancaster R.C.* 3(5-1-38"-7.4) Good upright bush, disease-resistant glossy foliage, blooms fade. *Ohio State University T.G.* (4-2-28"-7) Large dark green foliage, vigorous fairly bushy plant, fairly abundant flowers, plant grows more narrow and upright than most bushes. *Park of Roses T.G.* (35-2-40"-7) Resistant to blackspot, good growth habit, no lasting quality, fades badly. OKLA. *Norman R.S.* 2(10-2-28"-7) Blooms freely, nice buds, blackspots easily. *Oklahoma R.S.* 1(3-2-36"-8) Holds color well. ORE. *International Rose T.G.* (20-3-36"-6) Long bud form, large open flowers, stamens show nicely. *Salem R.S.* 1(2-2-24"-7) Medium stocky plant, good but stingy blooms. PA. *Breeze Hill T.G.* (3-3-28"-8) Gorgeous color and form, good foliage, profuse bloom fades. *Harrisburg R.S.* 1(300-1-48"-8.5) Upright, good foliage, abundant bloom excellent for cutting, mildew and blackspot-resistant. *Pittsburgh R.S.* 3(15-2-24"-7.9) Healthy, good blooms, lovely color, bad foliage color, opens too quickly, fades. S.C. *Edisto Gardens T.G.* (6-2-42"-7) Good color and form, fairly vigorous grower, very susceptible to blackspot. TENN. *Nashville R.S.* 1(2-2-30"-7.4) Good plant, medium yellow color, not too vigorous. TEX. *Corpus Christi R.S.* 1(1-1-36"-7.5) Non-fading strong stems, well-shaped bud, scarce bloomer, too few petals. *Dallas R.S.* 1(1-1-36"-8.5) Lovely pure yellow, excellent foliage, fades slightly. UTAH *Utah R.S.* 2(22-2-30"-6.8) Holds color well, sparse bloomer, disease-resistant, some winter-kill. VA. *Va. Peninsula R.S.* 1(1-1-48"-7) Free-blooming good color. WASH. *Spokane R.S.* 2(9-2-24"-8) Excellent yellow, old-rose fragrance. WIS. *Madison R.S.* 1(1-1-60"-8) Medium growth, disease-resistant foliage, strong stem, exhibition rose, excellent form, sparse bloomer. *Milwaukee R.S.* 1(1-1-26"-6) Beautiful color, poor form (as most other yellows). CANADA (British Columbia) *University of B.C. T.G.* (4-2-32"-6) Pale yellow flowers fade to white, medium fragrance, no mildew resistance.

## AUDIE MURPHY HT. Currant to cherry-red. (Lammerts; int. Roseway '56) Pat. 1558; ARA '57; PP 2, 136 Rpts; Av. ht. 46"; NR 7.8.

ALA. *Twickenham R.S.* 2(3-2-42"-8.1) Blooms freely. CALIF. *Rose Study Club Oakland* 2(5-3-78"-8.2) Tall vigorous plant, leathery disease-resistant foliage, beautiful buds open fast, rather poor open form. *Pacific R.S.* 3(4-1-46"-9.2) Vigorous, disease-resistant foliage, long tapering perfect buds on long straight stems open fast. *Peninsula R.S.* 1(1-2-72"-6) Vigorous, good bloomer, disease-resistant, needs cool climate for bloom to hold. *San Diego R.S.* 3(3-1-46"-7.1) Long slim buds of Grande Duchesse Charlotte color. *San Joaquin Valley R.S.* 2(2-1-53″-8) Beautiful bud, floriferous, bright color, an all-around good performer (even in hot weather). D.C. *Potomac R.S.* 2(3-2-48″-8.2) Excellent garden rose, good long stem, brilliant red flowers for arranging, long small buds like Eclipse, good grower, fine foliage. GA. *Georgia R.S.* 4(10-2-60″-6.1) Beautiful cherry-red color, blackspot-resistant, too few petals open too quickly. ILL. *Chicago R.S. Reg. 1* 4(4-2-36″-8.5) Long pointed buds, unusual red, clean disease-free foliage, sparse bloom. *Greater Peoria R.S.* 2(2-1-37″-7.2) Good color and form, long tapered buds, strong canes, disease-resistant, weak necks, bloom doesn't last long. *Tri-City Men's Rose and Garden Club* 1(1-2-7.5). IND. *Indianapolis R.S.* 1(3-1-60″-9) Disease-resistant, repeats well, not enough petals. *St. Joseph Valley R.S.* 1(1-2-36″-8) Tall spreading bush, good color, 4″ flower. IOWA *Linn County R.S.* 4(2-2-27″-6.4) Nice color, opens too quickly. KAN. *Wichita R.S.* 3(6-2-48″-7) Profuse bloom, disease-resistant, good color, few petals. KY. *Louisville Chapter ARS* 2(2-1-42″-7.5) Brilliant red color, cool weather rose. MD. *Maryland R.S.* 3(7-2-54″-9) Wonderful bud, decorative bloom, many canes, very healthy foliage. MICH. *Detroit R.S.* 5(7-2-42″-7.5) Too few petals, opens quickly, does not last. *Greater Lansing R.S.* 2(3-1-54″-7.5) Not too full, wavy petals like Charlotte Armstrong, good when half-open, unique rich red color, very fragrant, upright plant, good canes, floppy when fully open, mildews and blackspots. *Kalamazoo R.S.* (1-2-60″-8) Good color, long bud, loose beautiful bloom. *West Michigan Rosarians* 1(2-1-36″-7.5) Nice bud, floppy blooms. MINN. *Minnesota R.S.* 8(9-1-35″-7.2) Good color and bud form, flowers borne singly, opens too fast. MO. *Rosarians Midland Empire* 3(7-2-48″-7.5) Vigorous bloomer, disease-resistant, good color, not enough petals. *R.S. Greater St. Louis* 2(2-2-48″-7) Beautiful cherry-red color, leggy plant, blooms don't last. *Sedalia R.S.* 1(1-2-50″-8.4) Beautiful long-pointed buds, lots of bloom, good plant, color fades. NEW ENGLAND *New England R.S.* 1(3-2-48″-8) Healthy, fairly hardy, good bud and flower, sparse bloomer. N.J. *North Jersey R.S.* 4(5-1-30″-7.7) Vigorous plant, vibrant red, excellent producer, not for exhibition. N.M. *Albuquerque R.S.* 4(5-1-33″-8.2) Love the color, strong healthy plant with disease-resistant foliage, shows promise of being a good show rose, good bloomer, some weak stems, opens too quickly. N.Y. *Greater Buffalo R.S.* 5(10-2-48″-8) Clusters, intense coloring, not exhibition type, large floppy petals. *Humboldt Park T.G.* (5-2-24″-9.9) Upright, very vigorous, abundant glossy large very disease-resistant foliage deep dark red buds, open globular currant-red blooms with yellow stamens showing when fully open, no faults. *Long Island R.S.* 1(2-2-72″-8.5) Constant blooming, exceptionally vigorous, disease-resistant, hardy, exquisite bud and long stems, holds color. *Niagara Frontier R.S.* 3(5-1-46″-8.5) Tops in bloom production, healthy vigorous plant, wonderful velvety petal texture, blooms rather short-lived. *Schenectady R.S.* 1(3-1-24″-8) Luminous coloring, large loose flowers, healthy plant, not many blooms. *Syracuse R.S.* 2(3-2-48″-7) Blooms open too fast, poor lasting quality, vigorous growth, winters well, good bloomer. OHIO *Central Ohio R.S.* 1(5-1-36″-7.2) Prolific bloomer, beautiful color, long buds, vigorous disease-resistant plant, bloom not for exhibition, opens very fast. *Cincinnati R.S.* 3(9-2-48″-7) Wonderful plant resists diseases but opens too rapidly. *Lancaster R.S.* 3(5-3-72″-8) Good garden decorative, upright, bushy, disease-resistant, good bloomer. *Medina County R.S.* 1(1-2-72″-8.9). *Ohio State University T.G.* (4-1-48″-8) Excellent foliage, very vigorous and bushy, abundant fragrant flowers until October, holds leaves at base of plant. *Park of Roses T.G.* (50-2-64″-9) Nice bud, good vigorous growth, blackspot-resistant. OKLA. *Norman R.S.* 2(3-1-30″-6) Good color, opens rapidly. ORE. *Eugene R.S.* 6(5-1-48″-9) Good bedding plant and cut flower, strong grower, constant bloomer, perfect buds, clean foliage, appealing red color, bush too spreading, petalage too loose for show. *International Rose T.G.* (40-6-72″-8) Very good recurrence and disease resistance, lots of cutting roses, long stems ,fine tapered bud, flat open flower, loses color. *Lewis & Clark College T.G.* (12-1-42″-8) Excellent color, many buds, some mildew. *Medford R.S.* 7(7-2-49″-7.6) Beautiful red, long-pointed buds, extremely floriferous, disease-resistant foliage, tall vigorous bushy plant, blooms open too rapidly, floppy like Eclipse. *Rogue Valley R.S.* 3(5-3-54″-8) Excellent color, best in bud disease-resistant, vigorous grower and bloomer. *Roseburg R.S.* 2(2-1-48″-9) Excellent form, good color, good foliage. *Salem R.S.* 5(6-2-42″) Vigorous grower, good foliage, single stems, showy decorative, opens fast. PA. *Breeze Hill T.G.* (3-6-40″-8) Pleasing color ,fragrant, good growth and foliage, loose form. *Philadelphia R.S.* 1(2-2-48″-8.5) Good bloom on strong plant with excellent foliage, opens too fast in heat. TENN. *Nashville R.S.* 1(1-2-30″-7) Good bud and color, sparse blooms. TEX. *Corpus Christi R.S.* 1(1-2-48″-8.5) Prolific bright red long-lasting bloom and bud, too tall, hard to control, new buds form before old ones mature. *Dallas R.S.* 1(2-1-48″-9) Vigorous ,healthy, free-blooming, good color, pointed buds. *El Paso R.S.* 1(1-1-32″-6) Lovely red color, long well-formed buds, too few petals, opens quickly, weak stems. WASH. *Spokane R.S.* 5(39-2-36″-8) Brilliant color, lovely buds, a lot like Charlotte Armstrong. W.VA. *Wyo-Mac R.S.* 1(1-2-10) Outperforms everything in garden, always in bloom from May until November, beautiful on bush (in bud and full bloom) and in arrangements. CANADA

(Brtiish Columbia) *Vancouver R.S.* 4(14-3-60″-8) Excellent garden rose, good color, long bud and stem, no flower form, disease-free, too few petals, prolific bloomer.


**BABY BLAZE F.** Medium red. (Kordes; int. Jackson & Perkins '54) Pat. 1362; ARA '55; PP 4, 93 Rpts.; Av. ht. 37″; **NR 7.6.**

ARIZ. *Mesa R.S.* 1(1-2-36″-6) Weak growth, chlorotic, good color, no outstanding feature. *Phoenix R.S.* 2(2-2-36″-7.8) Constant bright red blooms hold color, vigorous plants, could have more petals. CALIF. *Rose Study Club Oakland* 2(10-3-42″-8.1) Blooms in large trusses, good for mass planting, non-fading red, good disease-resistant foliage and bloomer, open flower does not last long. *San Joaquin Valley R.S.* 1(1-2-28″-6) Plant not vigorous, flowers do not stand heat. COLO. *Denver R.S.* 2(31-5-27″-7) Profuse bloom for long period, showy red, dull foliage, plant not especially attractive. GA. *Georgia R.S.* 2(9-3-72″-8.8) Excellent vigor, good color, blooms freely, flowers have the same color and form as the Climber. IND. *Indianapolis R.S.* 2(7-2-33″-9) Constantly in bloom from June to frost, no faults. *St. Joseph Valley R.S.* 1(2-3-30″-7.8) Prolific blooms in clusters, a fine border rose. IOWA *Iowa R.S.* 1(1-3-24″-3) Opens too fast. *Linn County R.S.* 2(2-2-26″-6.5) Holds color, blooms frequently. KY. *Louisville Chapter ARS* 1(3-2-48″-7.5) Good foliage and bloomer, disease-resistant, weak necks. MICH. *Detroit R.S.* 2(4-1-36″-7.5) Good color, petals fall too soon, blackspots. *Kalamazoo R.S.* (2-2-30″-8) Prolific, disease-resistant. *Michigan State University T.G.* (6-4-24″-7.7) Excellent color, resistant to disease, semi-weak necks, no fragrance. MINN. *Lyndale Park T.G.* (70-5-48″-8.6) Consistent bloomer, very hard, disease-resistant. *Minnesota R.S.* 8(33-2-32″-8.3) Floriferous cerise-red blooms, vigorous and hardy. MO. *Rosarians Midland Empire* 1(3-3-60″-7) Good color and bloomer, too few petals. *R.S. Greater St. Louis* 1(2-4-60″-7) Good tall Floribunda. MONT. *Sunset Park T.G.* (20-3-24″-7) Tough rollicking freebloomer that is good all season, color and shape of blooms not appealing. NEW ENGLAND *New England R.S.* 3(6-2-30″-6.6) Lacks character and class. N.J. *North Jersey R.S.* 3(6-2-25″-6.7) A bedding rose. *West Jersey R.S.* 2(8-3-24″-7.5) Good bloom, nice color, plants don't seem to bush out enough. N.M. *Albuquerque R.S.* 1(1-3-30″-7) Good color doesn't fade, not a profuse enough bloomer. N.Y. *Conrell University T.G.* (12-5-25″-8) Good color, floriferous until mid-August, petals drop before they become discolored, shy of bloom in late August, poor flower form, too much foliage for amount of bloom, not a specimen plant (but good as a hedge). *Humboldt Park T.G.* (23-4-36″-9.9) Always one mass of bloom, healthy, vigorous, very disease-resistant, blooms borne on long strong stems, no faults. *Rochester R.S.* 2(66-3-30″-8) Free-bloomer, color holds well. *Schenectady R.S.* (30″-8.5) Very good color and form. *Syracuse R.S.* 5(9-3-36″-7.5) Nice color, plenty of bloom in large clusters, healtyh plant, nice blend of color between foliage and plant, some weak necks. N.C. *Randolph R.S.* 2(9-4-60″-8) Good grower, always in bloom. OHIO *Akron R.S.* 2(7-3-36″-7.7) Continuous bloom, good foliage, has hedge or mass-planting qualities, not distinctive, same as the Climber. *Cincinnati R.S.* 7(10-3-48″-7.5) Tall, vigorous, bloom quality like the Climber. *Cleveland R.S.* 2(7-3-48″-7.9) Always in bloom, long-lasting clusters, plenty of canes, good color. *Forest City R.S.* 3(7-3-36″-8) Wonderful bloomer, hardy, good color, weak stems. *Lima R.S.* 1(1-2-30″-7) Good bloomer, lovely color. *Ohio State University T.G.* Abundant flowers in Spring, Summer and Fall, vigorous bushy plant, dark glossy leaves, abundant disease-resistant foliage. *Park of Roses T.G.* (100-4-52″-9) In constant bloom all Summer, foliage resistant to blackspot, a little tall for a Floribunda. *Stark R.S.* 1(1-3-48″-8.5) Continuous bloom, good color, lasts well, weak stems. OKLA. *Oklahoma R.S.* 1(3-3-54″-7) Husky grower. ORE. *International Rose T.G.* (20-5-36″-7) Continual bloom on good trusses, color holds to finish, best for mass plantings, susceptible to blackspot. *Lewis & Clark T.G.* (1-1-36″-8) Good color, excellent foliage, full bush. *Medford R.S.* 1(1-2-43″-8) A good Floribunda, nice color, blooms continuously, no disease, vigorous. *Salem R.S.* 2(3-5-32″-7) Tough plant, color a bit dull, intermittent bloomer. PA. *Breeze Hill T.G.* (3-5-40″-8) A good tall Floribunda, blooms well. *Philadelphia R.S.* 1(2-3-27″-8) Good repeat in heat, good foliage, narrow plant. *Pittsburgh R.S.* 2(4-2-30″-9) Good constant blooms hold their color, good foliage. TENN. *Nashville R.S.* 1(1-3-48″-7.5) Healthy vigorous plant all Summer. TEX. *El Paso R.S.* 1(1-1-36″-7) Good foliage, ordinary single blooms, good landscape rose. UTAH *Utah R.S.* 2(4-4-34″-7.7) Color not deep enough, fades. WASH. *Spokane R.S.* 1(1-2-18″-10) Brilliant color. W.VA. *Charleston R.S.* 1(3-3-36″-4) Good bloomer. WIS. *Madison R.S.* 1(1-1-20″-8) Nice color, long-lasting small bush, not a prolific bloomer. *Milwaukee R.S.* 2(3-2-34″-7.5) Good healthy bush, constant bloom, lovely color, not as good as Frensham, does not hold color. CANADA (British Columbia) *Vancouver R.S.* 2(12-3-36″-7) Good foliage, flower form not attractive, good bloomer, there are better Floribundas with a similar color.

## BABY MASQUERADE. Min. Red blend. (Tantau; int. Jackson & Perkins '56) Pat. 1589; ARA '56; PP 3, 54 Rpts.; Av. ht. 15"; NR 8.1.

ARIZ. *Phoenix R.S.* 2(2-2-24"-7.8) Vigorous, prolific, nice border plant. CALIF. *Peninsula R.S.* 1(1-1-10"-7) Beautiful bud, exciting color, vigorous, some rust in Spring. *San Joaquin Valley R.S.* 2(2-2-24"-7) Good grower, healthy plant, striking color. D.C. *Potomac R.S.* 1(1-2-12"-7.9) Compact plant, excellent growth, nice star-shaped blooms of unusual coloring, some mildew. GA. *Georgia R.S.* 1(1-3-28"-10) The most satisfactory Miniature, outstanding color, likes heat, not faults. IOWA *Linn County R.S.* 1(1-2-12"-8) Grows well, attractive blooms. KAN. *Wichita R.S.* 2(4-2-18"-9) Well-shaped bush, constant bloomer. KY. *Louisville Chapter ARS* 3(4-1-11"-7.5) Good color, prolific grower. LA. *New Orleans R.S.* 1(12-1-15"-9) A very good bi-color, good for hedges, no faults. MICH. *Detroit R.S.* 3(4-2-18"-7.5) Vigorous plant, color fades fast. N.J. *North Jersey R.S.* 7(20-3-17"-8.7) Highly recommended, may grow too tall and vigorously for a Miniature, always in bloom. N.M. *Albuquerque R.S.* 1(1-2-15"-9.5) Lovely color, good growth for tall Miniature, fine bloom quality. N.Y. *Niagara Frontier R.S.* 1(1-2-17"-8) Healthy vigorous plant, profuse bloomer, blooms seem too large for the type. *Schenectady R.S.* 3(7-2-13"-8.4) Prolific bloomer, needs blackspot and mildew protection. *Syracuse R.S.* 1(5-2-8"-9) Good profuse bloomer, vigorous, disease-resistant foliage, winter-hardy. OHIO *Akron R.S.* 2(2-1-10"-8) Good foliage, average to fair bloom. *Central Ohio R.S.* 1(1-1-10"-7.8) Blooms well, nice color change, good addition to its class, mid-Summer lull, some blackspot. *Cleveland R.S.* (12"-8) Constant colorful bloom, very hardy. *Miami Valley R.S.* 3(5-2-12"-8) Very good color, prolific bloomer, blackspots. ORE. *Medford R.S.* 6(11-2-16"-7.5) Outstanding color, miniature form of Masquerade, good foliage, vigorous, could bloom more, some blackspot. *Salem R.S.* 2(2-2-14"-8.7) Striking color for a Miniature, clean foliage, good bloomer. PA. *Pittsburgh R.S.* 1(2-2-18"-5) Free-blooming. TENN. *Nashville R.S.* 1(1-1-10"-7.9) Lots of good showy blooms, loses foliage in hot weather. TEX. *El Paso R.S.* 2(1-2-18"-9) Blue ribbon winner, strong healthy foliage and stems, large flower clusters, disease-resistant, beautiful blend of rich colors, sparse blooms in Summer. WASH. *Seattle R.S.* 2(2-1-15"-8.7) Colors like the Floribunda, strong grower for a Miniature, lots of bloom. *Spokane R.S.* 2(2-2-9"-8) Very good plant, unusual color combination. WIS. *Milwaukee R.S.* 1(2-1-6"-9) Bright blossoms, constant bloom, healthy bush, an attention-getter.

## BETSY McCALL F. Coral pink. (Boerner; int. Jackson & Perkins '56) Pat. 1603; ARA '57; PP 2, 126 Rpts.; Av. ht. 28"; NR 7.4.

ARIZ. *Phoenix R.S.* 3(3-1-24"-7) Long buds, dainty pink blooms. CALIF. *Memorial Rose T.G.* (12-3-24"-4) Pleasing coral color, very fragrant, dies back, not vigorous. *Rose Study Club Oakland* 3(6-2-34"-7.3) Beautiful coral-pink buds, rather sparse flowers, blooms best in mild weather, plants lack vigor, some rust and mildew. *San Diego R.S.* 1(1-1-41"-8) Prolific bloomer, good foliage. COLO. *Denver R.S.* 1(9-3-38"-8) Attractive shell-pink, has substance, profuse bloom, vigorous, good foliage. CONN. *Elizaebth Park T.G.* (6-3-18"-7) Rather open plant, weak necks. D.C. *Potomac R.S.* 4(8-3-24"-7.6) Light pastel-pink colored bud with good form, makes good spray when center bud is removed. GA. *Georgia R.S.* 3(5-2-42"-7.5) Good new color, light pink, good foliage, high-centered long-lasting flowers, could bloom more often. ILL. *Tri-City Men's Rose and Garden Club* 2(7-2-30"-8.3). IND. *Indianapolis R.S.* 1(1-1-30"-8) Nice delicate peach bloom, weak grower. IOWA *Des Moines R.S.* 2(2-2-24"-7) Good clear pink, not too many blooms. *Iowa R.S.* 1(1-2-24"-7) Nice little buds. *Linn County R.S.* (30"-7.4) Good form and color, continuous bloom, blackspots. KAN. *Wichita R.S.* 3(3-1-30"-7) Vigorous, there are better light pinks. KY. *Lexington R.S.* 1(1-1-28"-8.5) Nice buds, ocntinuous blooms, beautiful clear color, could be more vigorous. *Louisville Chapter ARS* 6(12-2-28"-7.7) Good color and substance, weak plants, tender foliage. LA. *New Orleans R.S.* 1(2-2-48"-9) Upright grower, good foliage, beautiful pink flowers. MICH. *Detroit R.S.* 5(9-2-30"-7.5) Nice color, good bloomer, too much lapse between bloom. *Greater Lansing R.S.* 1(1-1-24"-7.6) Small flower, color finishes salmon-pink, round bud, slight fragrance, good foliage with no blackspot, continuous bloom throughout Summer. *Kalamazoo R.S.* (2-2-33"-7.5) Nice buds, disease-resistant, good bloomer. *Michigan State University T.G.* (6-2-22"-7.) Excellent color and form, moedrate apple-blossom fragrance. MINN. *Lyndale Park T.G.* (20-3-24"-6) Sparse bloomer. *Minnesota R.S.* 5(17-2-25"-7.6) Hardy bush, not enough blooms, good color doesn't fade. MO. *Jewel Park T.G.* (7) Slow bloomer. NEW ENGLAND *New England R.S.* 4(6-2-20"-7) Good color, fair vigor, not outstanding. N.J. *North Jersey R.S.* 2(5-2-19"-6.2) Good color and form, blooms only twice. *West Jersey R.S.* 6(10-2-30″-8) Good foliage, strong spreading plant, very nice pink bloom all Summer, very fragrant. N.M. *Aubuquerque R.S.* 2(3-2-27″-7.5) Nice color, plentiful blooms, good stems, nice for corsages, sunburns and mildews, plant not robust. N.Y. *Cornell University T.G.* (4-2-21″-7) Excellent delicate opening color, good bud form, good but sparse foliage, good early and late flower form deteriorates in mid-Summer, sparse foliage, plants not too vigorous. *Humboldt Park T.G.* (12-2-24″-8) Branching, vigorous, open globular coral-pink blooms, very good lasting quality, moderate fruity fragrance, foliage in late Summer does not have the best appearance (rusty looking). *Niagara Frontier R.S.* 1(1-3-16″-6) Poor plant, subject to all the ills. *Rochester R.S.* 2(28-3-33″-6.2) Good color, holds bloom well, sparse bloomer. *Schenectady R.S.* 1(5-2-42″-8.8) Good color and form, very good clusters. *Syracuse R.S.* 5(7-2-36″-6.8) Attractive color, good bloomer, disease-resistant, nice form, weak necks at times. N.C. *Durham R.S.* 1(2-2-36″-7) Bushy growth habit, profuse bloomer, lacks substance and cankers. *Randolph R.S.* 1(2-2-48″-8) Beautiful soft pink flower, good bloomer, nice foliage. OHIO *Akron R.S.* 6(15-2-26″-7.4) Good color, growth and bloomer, dark leaves, some blackspot. *Cleveland R.S.* 2(12-3-24″-5.2) Blooms well, good color and form, blackspots badly. *Greater Cincinnati R.S.* 2(2-1-20″-8) Good bloomer, blackspots badly. *Lancaster R.C.* 1(1-3-24″-6.5) Poor vigor, bloom fades, blackspots. *Miami Valley R.S.* 2(4-2-24″-7.5) Good clear, pink, blooms all season, some blackspot and mildew. *Ohio State University T.G.* (4-3-24″-7) Abundant flowering most of the year, good dark green glossy foliage, bushy vigorous disease-resistant plant, old flowers look poor if allowed to remain on plants. *Park of Roses T.G.* (25-2-24″-6) Fair quality bloom, blackspots badly, not too vigorous, poor foliage. *Stark R.S.* 2(2-2-21″-6.5) Low grower. OKLA. *Norman R.S.* 1(5-2-15″-7.6). *Oklahoma R.S.* 2(6-2-30″-8) Good bloomer. ORE. *International Rose T.G.* (20-4-48″-7) Huge sprays of clean color, well-formed buds, good for arrangements, spreading habit. *Medford R.S.* 3(3-1-31″-8.3) Good pink Floribunda, well-shaped bud and blossom, slight perfume, does not fade, compact grower, could bloom more, some mildew. *Salem R.S.* 1(2-3-24″-7.5) Good clear pink buds on a low bush. PA. *Breeze Hill T.G.* (6-5-27″-8) Exquisite color and form, profuse blooms. *Harrisburg R.S.* 1(500-1-42″-8.9) Free-blooming all Summer, good color, leathery foliage. *Pittsburgh R.S.* 4(16-4-24″-8) Good foliage and very fine flowers, many constant blooms hold their color. S.C. *Edisto Garden T.G.* 6(4-3-18″-6) Good form and color of bud and flower, plants lack vigor, too few flowers. TENN. *Nashville R.S.* 1(2-3-38″-7.4) Good color and quality of bloom, not too vigorous. TEX. *Dallas R.S.* 2(2-1-31″-6.6) Blooms outstanding in shape and color, good foliage, shy bloomer. UTAH *Utah R.S.* 6(20-3-26″-8.2) Lovely pink, holds color and form, vigorous foliage, but weak necks. VA. *Eastern Shore R.S.* 1(1-3-18″-5) Beautifully-formed small rose, slow-grower, does not bloom as fully as most Floribundas. WASH. *Spokane R.S.* 1(10-2-24″-5). *Walla Walla R.S.* 1(5-2-36″-8) Very outstanding mass bloomer, shell-pink blooms. W.VA. *Wyo-Mac R.S.* 1(1-2-26″-7) Beautiful blooms, strong canes, ever-bloomer, blackspots. WIS. *Madison R.S.* 1(1-1-30″-8.5) Medium growth, disease-resistant foliage, excellent form, good substance, intermittent bloomer. *Milwaukee R.S.* 1(3-3-28″-10).

## BETZEL'S PINK HT. Pink blend. (Edmunds '55) ARA '56; PP 3, 33 Rpts.; Av. ht. 38″; NR 8.2.

ARIZ. *Mesa R.S.* 1(1-1-54″-8.5) Good. CALIF. *Peninsula R.S.* 1(2-2-24″-6) Exhibition form, shy bloom, plant not too vigorous. *San Mateo County R.S.* 1(2-2-36″-9) Lovely spiraled pink exhibition-type fragrant bloom, good stems and foliage, some blooms not true to form. IND. *Indianapolis R.S.* 1(2-1-30″-8) Disease-resistant, repeats very well, does not open well in changeable or damp weather. MD. *Maryland R.S.* 2(3-2-42″-8) Large bloom with little substance, good in dry weather. MICH. *Detroit R.S.* 4(7-1-36″-7.8) Exhibition-type, good color. *West Michigan Rosarians* 1(4-2-42″-8.5) Excellent plant, upright, very good repeat bloom. MO. *Rosarians Midland Empire* 1(2-2-30″-8) Good exhibition pink, profuse bloom, disease-resistant. NEV. *Reno R.S.* 5(7-2-36″-8) Nice spiral pink fragrant show rose, large stem and foliage. N.M. *Albuquerque R.S.* 1(3-2-36″-8.3) Large well-formed blooms with exquisite coloring. N.Y. *Greater Buffalo R.S.* 1(1-1-18″-7) Exhibition form, vigorous grower, disease-resistant, lacks in size and color. OHIO *Cleveland R.S.* 1(1-1-46″-9) Colorful blooms on long stems, reblooms quickly. *Lancaster R.C.* 3(6-2-42″-7) Dark green foliage, good exhibition rose under good weather conditions. ORE. *Eugene R.S.* 3(4-2-48″-9) High-centered bloom holds its form, vigorous grower, fine foliage. *International Rose T.G.* (10-1-36″-8) Exhibition-type bloom, good foliage, huge pink flowers. *Medford R.S.* 2(2-2-41″-8.9) Very floriferous, vigorous, disease-resistant foliage, long bud, coral-pink blooms with satiny petals. *Salem R.S.* 1(2-1-34″-9) Beautiful pink-salmon undertone, large flowers, excellent plant and foliage.

WASH. *Spokane R.S.* 2(2-3-36″-10) Very good foliage, beautiful bloom. W.VA. *Charleston R.S.* 1(1-1-24″-7) Good blooms and foliage.

## BINGO HT. Cardinal red. (Robichon; int. Ilgenfritz '55) Pat. 1392; ARA '56; PP 3, 47 Rpts.; Av. ht. 42″; NR 7.5.

CALIF. *Pacific R.S.* 1(1-1-60″-7.5) Good color, prolific flowers. *San Diego R.S.* 1(1-1-27″-7.5) Good buds, shy bloomer. *San Joaquin Valley R.S.* 1(1-1-48″-7) Vigorous grower, continuous bloom. CONN. *Elizabeth Park T.G.* (4-4-30″-8) Good plant, strong stems support large blooms. GA. *Georgia R.S.* 2(3-2-48″-7.5) Big strong plant, long stems, dark-red color similar to Crimson Glory, not high-centered, good cut flower, bloom burns in heat, foliage easily spray-burned. IND. *Vincennes R.S.* 2(2-2-48″-9) Fine bloom, very profuse, hardy, no faults. IOWA *Linn County R.S.* 2(6-2-30″-7) Good color and form, disease-resistant, sparse bloomer. KAN. *Wichita R.S.* 1(2-2-60″-8) Good grower, beautiful bloom. MD. *Maryland R.S.* 2(3-3-72″-8.5) A dark crimson for cutting, very healthy plant. MICH. *Detroit R.S.* 2(2-1-30″-7) Good color, sparse bloom. *Michigan State University T.G.* (6-1-39″-3.5) Good color, strong old-rose fragrance, shy bloomer, slightly resistant to blackspot. *West Michigan Rosarians* 1(1-1-42″-7.5) Nice blooms, very dark red, sparse bloom. MINN. *Minnesota R.S.* 6(8-2-32″-8.3) Vigorous, free-blooming, outstanding color, good form. MO. *Rosarians Midland Empire* 1(1-1-60″-7.4) Nice large blooms, good red, very uneven growth. *R.S. Greater St. Louis* 1(3-1-84″-8) Never without bloom, large flower holds color on strong bush. NEW ENGLAND *New England R.S.* 3(6-4-60″-8.3) Too few large fragrant blooms, vigorous plant. N.J. *North Jersey R.S.* 1(1-3-50″-5) Fine plant, fair color, formless. *West Jersey R.S.* 1(1-1-66″-7.8) Healthy strong plant, blooms blue with age. N.Y. *Humboldt Park T.G.* (5-2-36″-8) Large leathery green foliage, no blackspot, large deep red buds, full globular cherry-red blooms hang on and blue when finishing. OHIO *Cleveland R.S.* 1(1-1-46″-7.5) Very fragrant, strong grower, healthy, balls and splits in cool wet weather. *Euclid R.S.* 1(1-2-40″-7) Nice foliage, good bloom, too few blooms, mildews. *Forest City R.S.* 3(1-5-30″-7) Large rose, good form, color and foliage, better bloom in Fall. *Lima R.S.* 1(2-2-60″-8.5) Large bud and double bloom, blooms well, big plant, no blackspot. ORE. *International Rose T.G.* (20-1-48″-7) Large bud, fragrant, strong stems and necks, open habit, burns in temperature extremes. PA. *Breeze Hill T.G.* (2-4-27″-7) Well-formed velvety red flowers, delightful fragrance, not profuse. TEX. *Dallas R.S.* 3(5-2-36″-7.9) Big fine dark red blooms, no bluing, good stem and foliage. UTAH *Utah R.S.* 1(5-2-20″-2) Not enough blooms, balls. WASH. *Spokane R.S.* 1(2-1-24″-5) Fragrant, color like New Yorker with black shadings. W.VA. *Charleston R.S.* 1(2-3-72″-9) Vigorous healthy plant with many fine blooms, dark red, old-rose fragrance. WIS. *Madison R.S.* 1(1-1-50″-8.5) Beautiful large red flower, strong vigorous plant, not enough bloom. *Milwaukee R.S.* Beautiful dark red, lovely form, bush not symmetrical.

## BIT O' SUNSHINE. Min. Yellow. (Moore; int. Sequoia '56) Pat. 1631; ARA '57; PP 2, 23 Rpts.; Av. ht. 13″; NR 7.0.

CALIF. *Peninsula R.S.* 2(3-2-10″-8) Excellent color, good plant, generally disease-resistant. *San Diego R.S.* 1(1-1-8″-6) Prone to mildew. GA. *Georgia R.S.* 1(1-2-16″-8) Clear clean yellow, good bush, blooms hold well, subject to blackspot. KAN. *Wichita R.S.* 1(1-2-12″-6.5) Weak bush, poor color. KY. *Louisville Chapter ARS* 1(2-1-18″-8.5) Best yellow Miniature. MICH. *Detroit R.S.* 1(2-1-12″-7.5) Too few blooms, too large for a Miniature. N.J. *North Jersey R.S.* 3(3-2-14″-6.8) Good growth, nice bud, fades, shapeless. N.M. *Albuquerque R.S.* 2(9-2-10″-6.2) Good bloomer and growth on strong compact plant, nice foliage, few blooms, weak color, opens too fast, fades. N.Y. *Schenectady R.S.* 1(1-2-12″-5) Trashy little blackspotter, bushy and vigorous, many bright yellow buds and stringy straw-colored flowers. OHIO *Miami Valley R.S.* 1(1-2-18″-8) Very good yellow color, gets a little tall for a Miniature. ORE. *International Rose T.G.* (18-3-24″-6) Plenty of bloom and plant, not resistant to foliar diseases. *Medford R.S.* 1)1-2-12″-8) Compact plant with excellent foliage, bright yellow buds, blooms fade, some blackspot. TEX. *El Paso R.S.* 3(3-1-18″-8.5) Strong healthy foliage and stems, blooms well during the Summer months, disease-resistant, opens quickly into a colorless bloom. W.VA. *Charleston R.S.* 1(1-1-12″-8) Beautiful fragrant yellow on a strong plant. WASH. *Spokane R.S.* (3-6-1-10″-5) A good Miniature.

## BURNABY HT. White with primrose center. (Eddie; int. Eddie '52) Pat. 1314; ARA '54; PP 5, 1959, 345 Rpts.; Av. ht. 35″; NR 7.9. Total reports 5 years 894; Av. NR 8.1.

## CARELESS LOVE HT. Red blend. (Conklin; int. Golden State '55) Pat. 1582; ARA '56; PP 3, 72 Rpts.; Av. ht. 34"; NR 6.7.

ARIZ. *Mesa R.S.* 1(1-2-42"-7.5) Mildew-free good green foliage, blooms steadily. *Phoenix R.S.* 3(4-2-30"-6.8) Novelty stripe, good growth, blooms repeatedly, not exhibition form. CALIF. *Rose Study Club Oakland* 1(11-2-45"-5.8) Good grower, crazy uncertain coloring, poor form. *Pacific R.S.* 2(2-2-36"-8.5) Unusually-bright contrasting striped rose, easy to grow, attractive average number of blooms, little mildew. *Riverside R.S.* 11(14-6-24"-7.8) Seems to love hot weather and lots of water, good strong plant, lovely buds. *San Diego R.S.* 1(1-1-30"-6) Interesting color variations, poor form and substance. *San Joaquin Valley R.S.* (30"-6) Good novelty, interesting color, good foliage. *San Mateo County R.S.* 2(2-1-36"-8) Too few blooms. CONN. *Elizabeth Park T.G.* (8-5-24"-5) Interesting color blend. D.C. *Potomac R.S.* 1(1-2-36"-6.7) Vigorous plant, unattractive bloom, unstable color, just fair as a novelty. GA. *Georgia R.S.* 8(12-2-48"-7.1) Good vigor, novelty value only, not exhibition type, good for public planting, poor form, lots of clear color, blooms not variegated. ILL. *Greater Peoria R.S.* 1(1-1-20"-7) Novel addition to garden, fragrant, sparse bloom, blackspots easily. *Tri-City Men's Rose and Garden Club* 1(1-2-24"-6.9). IOWA *Des Moines R.S.* 1(3-3-24"-5) Striking color, balls. *Iowa R.S.* 1(3-3-24"-5) Good color, balls. KAN. *Wichita R.S.* 1(1-1-6). KY. *Louisville Chapter ARS* 1(2-2-42"-1) MICH. *Detroit R.S.* 1(1-1-36"-6.7) Strong grower, good bloomer. MINN. *Minnesota R.S.* 4(4-2-35"-6.3) Novel vigorous bush, loose flower. MO. *Rosarians Midland Empire* 1(1-2-60"-5). NEV. *Reno R.S.* 3(4-2-36"-7) Poor bloomer, fades quickly, mildews badly. NEW ENGLAND *New England R.S.* 2(2-1-30"-6.3) Fairly vigorous, scattered bloom opens and drops quickly. N.J. *West Jersey R.S.* 3(5-1-30"-5) Just a novelty, healthy plant, bloom does not last, some are a solid color. N.Y. *Humboldt Park T.G.* (5-2-30"-9.9) Healthy foliage, very interesting white streaked pink-red blooms, no faults. *Rochester R.S.* 3(3-2-30"-6.8) Interesting novelty, poor in hot weather. *Syracuse R.S.* 1(1-1-48"-6) Unusual color, disease-resistant, a novelty—not an exhibition rose. OHIO *Akron R.S.* 1(1-3-48"-7.5) Good bloomer, plant similar to Radiance, a novelty, no form, weak neck. *Cleveland R.S.* 1(2-1-24"-4) Nice clusters of very double and clean bloom, disease-resistant. OKLA. *Norman R.S.* 1(1-1-24"-7). ORE. *International Rose T.G.* (8-2-48"-5) A novelty with unique and distinct striped petals, fragrant, no form, round center. *Medford R.S.* 1(1-2-51"-8) Very unusual color, at least half of the blooms are pale pink. PA. *Philadelphia R.S.* 2(4-2-30"-7.7) Good color combination, some blooms only pink, never prolific, not bad in heat, good novelty. TEX. *Corpus Christi R.S.* 1(1-1-24"-6) Beautiful bud, long-lasting in cool weather, fades in hot sun. *El Paso R.S.* 2(2-2-36"-6) Good color, never any two the same shade, strong healthy foliage and stem, disease-resistant, opens too quickly, does not hold well as a cut flower, strictly a novelty rose. VA. *Va. Peninsula R.S.* 1(1-1-30"-6) Good plant, well-formed bloom does not last very long. W.VA. *Charleston R.S.* 1(3-2-5) Not true to any color, hard to control. WIS. *Madison R.S.* 1(1-1-40"-10) Large blooms, long stems, healthy foliage, interesting color effect. *Milwaukee R.S.* 2(2-2-7) Interesting novelty color, poor form, good foliage, small plant, bloom opens shapeless.

## CENTENNIAL HT. Orange-apricot and light gold. (Mallerin; int. Jackson & Perkins '54); Pat. 1384; ARA '54; PP 5, 1959, 38 Rpts.; Av. ht. 28"; NR 6.4. Total reports 5 years 156: Av. NR 6.1.

## CHARLIE McCARTHY F. White. (Wiseman; int. Howard & Smith '55); ARA '55; PP 4, 25 Rpts.; Av. ht. 21"; NR 6.5.

CALIF. *San Diego R.S.* 2(3-3-39"-8.5) Prolific, good foliage, petals fall cleanly. *San Mateo County R.S.* 2(2-3-18"-5) Foliage free of disease, too few blooms, old blooms hang on too long, unattractive. ILL. *Tri-City Men's Rose and Garden Club* 1(1-3-36"-6.5). MICH. *Detroit R.S.* 1(302018"-5) No substance to petals, poor for cutting. MO. *R.S. Greater St. Louis* 1(4-5-24"-6) Good low-growing white if it would drop petals which give it a dirty look. NEV. *Reno R.S.* 1(2-2-20"-5) Poor bloomer, very few good blooms, color fades, nice foliage. NEW ENGLAND *New England R.S.* 1(2-4-10"-5) Weak and sickly. N.J. *North Jersey R.S.* 3(8-3-19"-6.3) Healthy bedder. *West Jersey R.S.* 4(9-4-18"-8) Completely disease-free, almost an evergreen shrub, small compact bush, many small cream flowers, does not shed old petals well. N.M. *Albuquerque R.S.* 1(1-2-24"-7.5) Good blooms in Spring and Fall, sparse bloom in our Summer heat. N.Y. *Humboldt Park T.G.* (6-3-12"-9) Clean healthy foliage all Summer, one mass of bloom in

September, doesn't like hot weather (foliage turned rusty-looking in heat). *Long Island R.S.* 1(1-1-12"-4) Excellent disease-resistant foliage, nice blooms when they come, weak stems. OHIO *Central Ohio R.S.* 1(1-1-24"-5) Weak slow-growing plant with an insignificant small white flower. *Cincinnati R.S.* 3(6-1-6) Blackspots. *Greater Cincinnati R.S.* 1(1-3-12"-7) Lots of small white flowers, not too good in shape or stamina, blackspots. PA. *Philadelphia R.S.* 1(2-4-20"-5.5) Prolific bloom of almost Miniature size on sprawly poor plants.

## CHIC F. Light coral-peach. (Boerner; int. Jackson & Perkins '53) Pat. 1286; ARA '54; PP 4, 41 Rpts.; Av. ht. 32"; NR 7.7.

CONN. *Elizabeth Park T.G.* (17-4-15"-8) Good plant, different stem heights. GA. *Georgia R.S.* 6(24-3-42"-8) Clean pink, vigorous plant, disease-resistant, constant bloomer, holds up well in heat. KAN. *Wichita R.S.* 1(1-4-36"-8.6) Fine color and foliage. KY. *Louisville Chapter ARS* 6(29-2-38"-7.8) Hardy, good color bloom, disease-resistant, does not blackspot. MICH. *Detroit R.S.* 3(4-2-36"-8) Profuse bloom, not too vigorous, winter-kills. *West Michigan Rosarians* 1(2-1-18"-7) Beautiful blooms. MONT. *Sunset Park T.G.* (10-3-7) As good as Spartan in many ways, could have more vigor. NEW ENGLAND *New England R.S.* 1(2-4-14"-6). N.Y. *Cornell University T.G.* (25-3-22"-7) Good foliage and growth habit, floriferous, good bud, poor flower form when open, flowers persist and fade to a dirty whitish-pink, not very effective in the garden. *Humboldt Park T.G.* (25-3-18"-8) Abundant bloom, good lasting quality, intermittent bloom clusters of medium full globular form coral-peach color hang on, not enough foliage. *Rochester R.S.* 1(10-3-28"-6) Flower blotches in sun, weak color. N.C. *Durham R.S.* 1(2-3-36"-8) Uniform growth habit, profuse bloomer, good color, vigorous, should have a little more substance. *Cincinnati R.S.* 1(1-1-30"-8) Good bloomer and foliage, slow in building up new wood. *Cleveland R.S.* 2(5-3-30"-8.7) Good color, very double, disease-resistant. *Ohio State University T.G.* (4-4-27"-8) Abundant bloom all season, vigorous plant, abundant good disease-resistant small to medium foliage. *Park of Roses T.G.* (35-4-42"-7.5) Good growth habit and foliage, resistant to blackspot, bloom could have better color and quality. OKLA. *Oklahoma R.S.* 2(5-3-42"-9) Free-bloomer. ORE. *International Rose T.G.* (20-4-30"-6) Attractive opening color and ¾ bloom, petals shatter easily. *Salem R.S.* 1(2-3-18"-7) Odd color, good buds, intermittent bloom, fades in hot sun. PA. *Breeze Hill T.G.* (6-4-24"-7) Blooms well, good plants, foliage and color, fades much. UTAH *Utah R.S.* 2(4-4-28"-8) Hardy, compact flower, disease-resistant plant, blooms fade some. WASH. *Spokane R.S.* 1(6-3-24"-8) Always in bloom. WIS. *Milwaukee R.S.* 2(4-2-22"-7.7) Beautiful open flower, good color, does not bloom enough. CANADA (British Columbia) *Vancouver R.S.* 2(3-2-30"-6.5) Blooms well, good color and form, bleaches in hot sun, fades unattractively.

## CIRCUS F. Yellow blend. (Swim; int. Armstrong '56) Pat. 1382, ARA '56; PP 3, 449 Rpts.; Av. ht. 29"; NR 7.9.

ALA. *Twickenham R.S.* 2(2-3-27"-6.8) Good bloomer. ARIZ. *Mesa R.S.* 1(2-2½-42"-8.4) Good in every respect; healthy bush, good foliage, bud and open flower. *Phoenix R.S.* 4(9-2-36"-8.3) Constant bloomer, good compact growth, healthy foliage, very colorful. CALIF. *Memorial T.G.* (20-4-40"-9) Vigorous, free-bloomer, marvelous color changes, slight fragrance. *Rose Study Club Oakland* 6(21-3-37"-7.8) Good grower, free-bloomer, fragrant, practically no mildew, cleans itself well, best for mass planting. *Pacific R.S.* 6(8-2-38"-8.5) Heavy bloomer, vigorous plant, disease-resistant, bloom has good form, good as a hedge. *Peninsula R.S.* 4(5-3-36"-8) Prolific bloom, vigorous grower, disease-resistant, lasts well as a cut flower. *Riverside R.S.* 12(40-2-24"-6.7) Hardy, fast-growing, flower clusters don't drop dead and faded petals. *San Diego R.S.* 3(4-2-35"-8). *San Joaquin Valley R.S.* 7(15-3-33"-8.5) Constant bloom does not fade in warm weather, excellent foliage, good show rose. *San Mateo County R.S.* 11(26-3-36"-9.5) Beautiful plant, compact, sturdy grower, trouble-free foliage, free-flowering, only possible fault is spotty red on old blooms. COLO. *Colorado Springs R.S.* 1(2-2-24"-6) Infrequent small blossoms. *Denver R.S.* 3(37-4-26"-8) Good bloomer, showy large double profuse flowers, compact growth, colors are not pleasing. CONN. *Elizabeth Park T.G.* (4 yr. 30"-10) Very good appearance, slight tendency to legginess. D.C. *Potomac R.S.* 5(10-2-36"-8.2) One of the best new Floribundas, attractive coloring, individual bud, well-formed foliage, some mildew. GA. *Georgia R.S.* 8(18-2-40"-7.5) Waxy foliage, beautiful bloom, likes hot weather, some mildew and black-spot, too few basal breaks. ILL. *Chicago R.S. Reg. 1* 2(5-2-30"-8) Good healthy bush with colorful attractive blooms. *Greater Peoria R.S.* 5(7-2-34"-7.7) Excellent coloring, good growth, some blackspot. *Morgan Park R.S.* 1(1-1-24"-9) Prolific, hardy. *Tri-*

*City Men's Rose and Garden Club* 4(33-3-36"-7.8) Drops petals too quickly, does not like hot weather. IND. *Indianapolis R.S.* 8(14-3-29"-7.7) Good bloom, unusual color blend, some blackspot. *St. Joseph Valley R.S.* 3(9-7-30"-8) Free-bloomer, good foliage, fine for border. *Vincennes R.S.* 6(32-3-26"-9.5) Very profuse bloomer in all weather, no disease. IOWA *Des Moines R.S.* 8(16-3-24"-8) Good color, prolific bloomer. *Iowa R.S.* 4(15-2-24"-7.8) Lacks vigor, good bloom, interesting color. *Linn County R.S.* 4(11-3-26"-7.3) Nice glossy-leaf, unusual coloring, not too hardy. KAN. *Wichita R.S.* 1(1-1-24"-7.2) Good bloomer and foliage. KY. *Kentucky R.S.* 2(3-2-30"-5) Needs a warm climate. *Lexington R.S.* 2(6-4-24"-7.4) Good foliage, very colorful bloom. *Louisville Chapter ARS* 10(14-2-32"-7.6) Lovely color, holds bloom well, good foliage, slow producer, tends to blackspot. LA. *New Orleans R.S.* 4(6-2-36"-8) Good growth, profuse bloom, good foliage. MD. *Maryland R.S.* 5(8-2-42"-7.5) Attractive blooms on a good plant. MICH. *Detroit R.S.* 5(8-2-24"-8.2) Good grower, nice bloom, good foliage. *Greater Lansing R.S.* 1(5-2-30"-7.8) Medium fragrance, good shape and form, glossy disease-resistant foliage. *Kalamazoo R.S.* 7(14-2-33"-8) Good bloomer, disease-resistant, novelty rose. *Michigan State University T.G.* (6-4-21"-7.7) Interesting color, vigorous, short, not very disease-resistant. *West Michigan Rosarians* 2(4-3-24"-8.5). MINN. *Lyndale Park T.G.* (30-4-18"-7) Blooms in spurts. *Minnesota R.S.* 15(32-2-25"-7.7) Cheerful changeable color, does best in some shade. MO. *Rosarians Midland Empire* 2(13-3-30"-7.6) Nice foliage, good color, sparse bloomer. *R.S. Greater St. Louis* 4(5-3-36"-8) Fine novelty, not enough bloom. *Sedalia R.S.* 4(6-2-26"-7.5) Good form, unusual color, plant not vigorous enough for a Floribunda, blooming periods too far between. MONT. *Sunset Park T.G.* (12-3-20"-9) Consistently good even in the hottest weather, daily change of colors a delight to watch. NEV. *Reno R.S.* 27(35-3-24"-9) Beautiful buds, fine for boutonnieres, sturdy grower, no mildew, fine for cutting, foliage free of trouble, blooms well. NEW ENGLAND *New England R.S.* 8(37-3-30"-8) N.H.—vigorous, productive and clean; R.I.—fairly clean, interesting; Conn.—good growth, attractive blooms. N.J. *North Jersey R.S.* 18(27-2-23"-7.5) Refreshing color in Spring and Fall, beautiful glossy foliage. *West Jersey R.S.* 5(12-2-30"-8) Very nice bi-color, good bloomer, long-lasting flower, some mildew. N.M. *Albuquerque R.S.* 6(14-2-26"-8.1) Good form, striking color, constant-bloomer, strong straight stems, not hardy in extreme temperature changes, dislikes reflected heat. N.Y. *Greater Buffalo R.S.* 7(12-3-24"-8) Unusual color, good thrifty bush, many blooms in cluster, nice border plant. *Humboldt Park T.G.* (19-3-24"-7) Full globular profuse continuous double blooms, lemon fragrance, medium size cluster, great deal of die-back blooms hang on short stems. *Long Island R.S.* 4(4-2-26"-7) Blackspots, has only two or three blooming periods. *Niagara Frontier R.S.* 6(12-3-32"-7.8) Sturdy disease-resistant plant, produces a generous amount of nicely-formed blooms, color fades at end. *Rochester R.S.* 4(36-3-26"-7.8) Outstanding color, lasts well, good for mass planting. *Schenectady R.S.* 5(8-2-21"-6.8) Nice novelty rose, bushes not too vigorous, fair blooms don't last long. *Syracuse R.S.* 5(11-2-28"-8.2) Profuse-bloomer, healthy foliage, upright, hardy plant, pleasant color, a little short on substance. N.C. *Durham R.S.* 6(25-2-48"-8.5) Good range of color and vigor, nice form, needs more substance. OHIO *Akron R.S.* 5(29-2-30"-8) Good color, foliage and bloomer, fair grower. *Central Ohio R.S.* 5(7-2-24"-7) Lovely long-lasting bloom, not a strong grower, subject to blackspot, not a free-bloomer. *Cincinnati R.S.* 8(15-2-30"-8) Good color, excellent form, drops petals too soon. *Cleveland R.S.* 3(13-3-30"-8) Heavy bloomer, bushy plant, no disease, great color. *Columbus R.C.* 4(10-3-24"-6.5) Shy double bloom, not too healthy. *Euclid R.S.* 3(3-3-30"-7.2) Very good color, nice foliage, could bloom a little more. *Forest City R.S.* 5(8-3-24"-8) Interesting color, sparse bloomer, good bush, satisfactory foliage. *Greater Cincinnati R.S.* 2(2-2-24"-7) Fair bloomer, no blackspot or mildew. *Lancaster R.C.* 5(8-3-27"-7) Large leathery foliage, good bloomer, black-spots. *Lima R.S.* 7(16-2-36"-8.8) Beautiful long-lasting bloom, good foliage and bloomer. *Medina County R.S.* 2(3-3-30"-7.5) Blooms scarce during Summer but wonderful during Spring and Fall. *Miami Valley R.S.* 4(6-2-24"-8) Beautiful color, good foliage, profuse bloomer, a real eye-catcher, short stems. *Ohio State University T.G.* (4-4-24"-7) Excellent abundant foliage, vigorous plant, abundant bloom until September, disease-resistant. *Park or Roses T.G.* (50-2-30"-8) Glossy foliage, fairly resistant to blackspot, not vigorous-growing. *Stark R.S.* 1(1-2-18"-7). OKLA. *Oklahoma R.S.* 3(7-2-24"-7) Poor plant, very ordinary bloom. ORE. *International Rose T.G.* (40-5-36"-7) Color, bud and flower form outstanding, loses color in too much sun. *Lewis & Clark T.G.* (10-2-24"-7) Excellent performer. *Medford R.S.* 9(19-2-28"-8.2) Constant blooms all season with clusters of nicely-formed buds change color as they open, bushy compact growth with very healthy foliage. *Rogue Valley R.S.* 4(24-3-30"-8) A riot of color, good bloomer, disease-resistant, very attractive. *Roseburg R.S.* 5(9-3-36"-7) Nice blooms, disease-resistant. *Salem R.S.* 3(4-3-25"-8.5) Low compact bush, striking color, good for mass planting. PA. *Breeze Hill T.G.* (3-6-22"-8). *Harrisburg R.S.* 3(506-2-30"-8) Unique color, blooms all Summer, burns in hot sun, blackspots, good for foundation planting. *Philadelphia R.S.* 5(9-3-34"-8) Heavy canes, pleasing bloom, opens fast in Summer, better in groups. *Pittsburgh R.S.*

4(16-4-18″-7.5) Good healthy plant, flowers and foliage, profuse bloomer, fades, blackspots easily. S.C. *Edisto T.G.* (20-4-24″-7) Fascinating colors, lacks vigor. TENN. *Nashville R.S.* 4(11-3-26″-7.9) Sturdy plant, good bloom quality and form, rests between bloom cycles. TEX. *Amarillo R.S.* 2(2-2-30″-8.9) Good substance, withstands sun well. *Corpus Christi R.S.* 1(2-3-36″-9) Lots of colorful bloom, large for a Floribunda, good foliage. *Dallas R.S.* 2(6-3-27″-8.5) Disease-resistant, very prolific, good color and form, long-lasting. *El Paso R.S.* 8(8-2-24″-8.5) Healthy foliage, strong stems, good color blend, blooms fairly well in hot months, some mildew and balling in Summer. UTAH *Utah R.S.* 7(31-3-29″-7.3) Good plant, compact growth, beautiful buds, fine foliage, free-bloomer. VA. *Va. Peninsula R.S.* 3(4-6-35″-6.3) Interesting variety of color, constant bloomer, subject to blackspot. WASH. *Seattle R.S.* 5(8-3-30″-7.9) Good color and bedding plant. *Spokane R.S.* 10(24-3-30″-8) Very pleasing clusters of consistent blooms, wonderful for arrangements. *Walla Walla R.S.* 2(4-3-30″-10) Very vigorous, fine foliage and colorful buds. W.VA. *Wyo-Mac R.S.* 1(1-3-42″-10) Beautiful bloomer, good show rose. WIS. *Madison R.S.* 2(2-2-30″-7.8) Nice foliage, interesting color, good form, not as good a bloomer as Masquerade. *Milwaukee R.S.* 3(6-2-27″-7.8) Outstanding color, profuse-blooming, buds ball before opening. *Charleston R.S.* 3(103-2-27″-8) Appealing, consistent, heavy bloomer, best Floribunda produced. CANADA (British Columbia) *Vancouver R.S.* 10(30-3-36″-8) Long interval between blooming periods after great splash in June, bright varied attractive colors. (Nova Scotia) *Buchanan* (3-3-22″-4) Not hardy, nice color.

## C1. CHRYSLER IMPERIAL ClHT. Chrysanthemum-crimson. (Begonia; int. Germain's '56) Pat. 1528; ARA '58; PP 2, 48 Rpts.; Av. ht. 8'; NR 7.6.

ARIZ. *Mesa R.S.* 1(1-1-8″-7.9) Good Climber, nice buds and blooms. *Phoenix R.S.* 2(2-2-6′-7.5) Slow starter, beautiful fragrant blooms. CALIF. *Pacific R.S.* 1(1-1-3′-7) Good foliage, not sufficient bloom, does not climb. *Peninsula R.S.* 3(3-2-10′-7) Slow to start but generally vigorous, blooms well, some mildew. *San Diego R.S.* 1(1-2-15′-9) Superior to bush variety. *San Joaquin Valley R.S.* 1(1-2-12′-9) Perfect single buds, excellent foliage, healthy and vigorous. *San Mateo County R.S.* 4(5-2-7′-9) Blooms better than bush, could have more flowers on the lush canes. COLO. *Colorado Springs R.S.* 2(9-3-3½'-8) Exquisite unfading red, prefer it to Blaze for vigor and color. D.C. *Potomac R.S.* 1(1-2-10′-8) Similar to bush, good long-stemmed blooms. IND. *St. Joseph Valley R.S.* 1(1-1-8′-7). *Vincennes R.S.* 1(1-2-6′-7) Some bloom, lost some wood in Spring freeze, no disease. IOWA *Des Moines R.S.* 2(5-2-5′-7.5) Fragrant, more like a Pillar, not enough bloom. *Linn County R.S.* 1(1-2-7′-6) Good bloom but shy. KAN. *Wichita R.S.* 2(6-2-10′-7.3) Excellent bush, good color and bloom. MICH. *Kalamazoo R.S.* 2(2-2-7′-7.5) Good grower, does not bloom enough. NEV. *Reno R.S.* 3(5-4-9′-9). Beautiful bud blooms steadily all Summer, color does not fade, does not mildew, finest cane growth of all the Climbers. N.J. *West Jersey R.S.* 1(1-2-15′-8) Very strong grower, beautiful fragrant flowers, sparse repeat bloom. N.M. *Albuquerque R.S.* 2(2-2-8′-7.3) Lusty grower, one of the best Climbing Hybrid Teas, poor foliage. N.Y. *Greater Buffalo R.S.* 2(3-2-8′-7) Not enough bloom, disease-resistant. *Long Island R.S.* 2(3-1-6′-8.8) Consistent shape, size and abundance of bloom, rich long-lasting color, fragrant, disease-resistant. N.C. *Durham R.S.* 2(2-1-9′-5) Good foliage, grows well, no bloom. OHIO *Cleveland R.S.* 1(2-2-7′-5) Large blooms, but too few. *Lima R.S.* 1(1-1-10′-8) Good growing plant, no bloom. *Stark R.S.* 1(2-2-2′-7) Dies back in Winter. PA. *Harrisburg R.S.* 1(300-2-10′-8.3) Large blooms of good color, will repeat, should be planted in sheltered spots. *Philadelphia R.S.* 1(1-2-12′-7) Fast grower, good June bloom, fair repeat, mildews. TEX. *Corpus Christi R.S.* 1(1-1-3′-8.6) Hardy plant, wonderful fragrance, lovely cut flowers, slow Climber, blues as its ages. *El Paso R.S.* 1(1-1-6′-6) Slow grower, very little bloom. UTAH *Uath R.S.* 1(1-1-6′-8) Vigorous growth, good foliage, blooms have good form and pleasing fragrance. W.VA. *Wyo-Mac R.S.* 2(2-2-6′-7.5) Beautiful blooms, long strong wild-looking canes, everblooming.

## C1. SUTTER'S GOLD ClHT. Yellow blend. (Weeks; int. Armstrong '54); Pat. 1185; ARA '54; PP 5, 1959, 32 Rpts.; Av. ht. 10'; NR 8.3. Total report 5 years 85; Av. NR 7.5.

## C1. YELLOW SWEETHEART ClF. Yellow. (Moore; int. Marsh '52) Pat. 1235, ARA '52; PP 5, 1959, 3 Rpts.; Av. ht. 6'; NR 5.3. Total reports 5 years 61; Av. NR 7.4.

**COCORICO F.** Geranium-red. (Meilland; int. Conard-Pyle '54) Pat. 1193; ARA '54; PP 5, 1959, 133 Rpts.; Av. ht. 40''; **NR 8.2.** Total reports 5 years 518; **Av. NR 8.4.**

**CONTENTMENT HT.** Delicate pink suffused with yellow. (Boerner; int. Jackson & Perkins '56) Pat. 1644; ARA '57; PP 2, 78 Rpts.; Av. ht. 29''; **NR 6.8.**

ALA. *Twickenham R.S.* 1(1-1-24''-7) Beautiful blooms, hasn't grown very fast. ARIZ. *Mesa R.S.* 1(1-2-8) Vigorous bush, lovely light pink flowers. *Phoenix R.S.* 2(3-3-45''-7.8) Enormous blooms, good growth, long stems, not enough blooms. CALIF. *San Joaquin Valley R.S.* (1-2-36''-8) Vigorous, disease-resistant, very fragrant, full flowers, good form, bloom sometimes too heavy for stem. GA. *Georgia R.S.* 4(9-2-50''-6.8) Large blooms, fair form, vigorous, spreading plant, disease-resistant, too-few blooms lack substance in heat. ILL. *Chicago R.S. Reg. 1* 1(1-3-30''-7) Insufficient bloom. *Greater Peoria R.S.* 2(2-1-30''-7.7) Large bloom, good color, disease-resistant, some blackspot. *Tri-City Men's Rose and Garden Club* 1(2-44-42''-8.5). IND. *Indianapolis R.S.* 1(1-2-30''-6.5) Nice color, not exhibition form, will blackspot. IOWA *Linn County R.S.* 2(3-1-29''-7.3) Exhibition rose, good size, form and color. KY. *Kentucky R.S.* 1(2-1-24''-7) Good blooms, but not many. *Louisville Chapter ARS* 4(11-1-23''-5.1) Weak plant, slow growing, weak necks. MD. *Maryland R.S.* 1(1-1-30''-7.5) Fine form and color, but too large, fair bush. MICH. *Detroit R.S.* 1(2-3-18''-6) Blackspots. *Kalamazoo R.S.* 3(6-1-30''-6) Poor plant, does not bloom enough. MINN. *Minnesota R.S.* 3(3-1-22''-7.2) Not outstanding, large bloom, many petals, bush too small. NEW ENGLAND *New England R.S.* 3(9-2-30''-7.5) Vt.—fragrant, too heavy blooms, good plant; N.H.—excellent bud and bloom, but too few; Conn.—sparse bloomer. N.J. *North Jersey R.S.* 3(4-2-24''-6.7) Large round flower on an unsteady plant. *West Jersey R.S.* 3(5-2-28''-7.5) Exceptionally large good medium pink bloom, well-formed buds, plant slow getting started. N.M. *Albuquerque R.S.* 1(1-2-36''-7.5) Large flowers, lovely color, fragrant, awkward growth, balls, weak stems. N.Y. *Greater Buffalo R.S.* 2(3-1-18''-7) Some split centers, large beautiful high-centered bloom, canes not large enough for bloom. *Humboldt Park T.G.* (3-2-18''-8) Large dark glossy foliage, beautiful full high-centered blooms, strong delectable fragrance, continuous bloom, no diseases, healthy plants, not enough vigor. *Long Island R.S.* 1(1-1-16''-6) Slow grower, weak stems. *Rochester R.S.* 3(4-2-24''-6) Good healthy bush with large blooms. *Schenectady R.S.* 1(1-1-19''-6.5) Good foliage, well-shaped blooms, strong stems, did not bloom until late Spring, slow grower. *Syracuse R.S.* 4(7-2-32''-7.4) Consistent color, exhibition rose, not too heavy a bloomer, big healthy plant, vigorous. N.C. *Randolph R.S.* 1(2-3-48''-7) Scarce bloom, buds not pretty, good foliage. OHIO *Akron R.S.* 2(3-2-27''-8) Good form and color, fragrant, medium bloom. *Central Ohio R.S.* 1(1-1-18''-5.8) Just an average plant and flower, very sparse yield. *Euclid R.S.* 1(1-2-42''-7) Very nice blooms when they come, little blackspot, slow grower. *Lancaster R.S.* 1(1-3-36''-6.5) Bushy plant, large glossy foliage, blackspots. *Lima R.S.* 2(2-2-28''-7) Beautiful bloom, weak stem, sparse bloomer. *Miami Valley R.S.* 2(4-2-24''-7.5) Good clear pink, nice glossy foliage, sturdy stems, blackspots, split centers. *Ohio State University T.G.* (4-1-15''-4) Fragrant flowers, disease-resistant, plant not bushy and lacks vigor, sparse bloom and foliage. *Stark R.S.* 1(1-1-18''-6). ORE. *Medford R.S.* 1(1-2-23''-6.5) Very double sparse pink bloom, not vigorous. PA. *Breeze Hill T.G.* (1-2-26''-6) Large flowers of nice color and form, good foliage, could bloom more. *Philadelphia R.S.* 1(1-2-12''-4) Weak growth, won't hold heavy dull pink bloom. *Pittsburgh R.S.* 1(1-3-36''-6.5) Nice blooms, but not enough. S.C. *Edisto T.G.* (6-3-24''-5) Flowers have good form and color, poor grower, few flowers. TENN. *Nashville R.S.* 2(5-3-34''-8) Healthy, vigorous plant, medium pink exhibition bloomer. TEX. *Corpus Christi R.S.* 1(1-1-24''-7) Gorgeous buds and blooms, slow to grow, blooms too scarce. *Dallas R.S.* 2(4-1-27''-6.8) Good color and form, not prolific, good foliage. WASH. *Spokane R.S.* 3(7-3-24''-8) Good foliage, show rose. *Walla Walla R.S.* 1(2-2-36''-7) Delicate pink high-centered flowers. W.VA. *Charleston R.S.* 1(1-3-24''-2).

**CORAL DAWN Cl.** Medium pink. (Boerner; int. Jackson & Perkins '52) Pat. 1117; ARA '52; PP 4, 64 Rpts.; Av. ht. 8'; **NR 7.8.**

ALA. *Twickenham R.S.* 1(1-1-1'-6) Not a free-bloomer; New Dawn is much better. ARIZ. *Phoenix R.S.* 2(2-2-6'-7.8) Blooms freely, dainty bud, excellent Pillar plant. COLO. *Denver R.S.* 1(2-2-5'-6) Good coral, no fading, lasts well. ILL. *Tri City Men's Rose and Garden Club* 1(1-5-8'-8) Requires protection, good grower. IND. *Indianapolis R.S.* 4(4-3-7'-8.3) Blooms all season, beautiful color, well-formed bud and flower, weak necks,

KORDES' PERFECTA HT
Wilhelm Kordes; introduced Jackson & Perkins, Newark, N.Y. Plant patent
1604. Described page 249.

BELLINA F
G. J. Von Abrams; introduced Peterson & Dering, Scappoose, Ore. Plant
patent applied for. Described page 240.

good foliage. *St. Joseph Valley R.S.* 1(1-2-6'-8.5) One of the few very prolific Climbers. *Vincennes R.S.* 1(1-1-6'-7) Nice bloom, slow-growing. IOWA *Linn County R.S.* 1(1-2-8'-7). KAN. *Wichita R.S.* 3(3-6-7.5) Repeats well, good bloom, good foliage. KY. *Kentucky R.S.* 2(2-2-10'-8.5) Good growth, nice shape and color. *Louisville Chapter ARS* 4(4-2-68"-6.3) Good color and form, fragrant, few blooms. MD. *Maryland R.S.* 2(2-2-10'-8) Good pink, blooms regularly. MICH. *Detroit R.S.* 1(2-2-12'-7.5). *West Michigan Rosarians* 1(1-2-5'-7.5) Nice foliage and bloom. MINN. *Minnesota R.S.* 1(1-1-48"-7.5) Sturdy bush, fine flower, good color but not enough bloom. MO. *Rosarians Midland Empire* 1(3-1-8'-8.5) Very good bloomer, repeats, fine color, disease-resistant. *R.S. Greater St. Louis* 2(2-2-7.5) Good grower and bloomer, poor bloom in Fall, blackspots. NEW ENGLAND *New England R.S.* 3(4-3-7.5) N.H. medium 7' Climber, repeats, clean; R.I.—15' Climber, resists mildew but not blackspot. N.J. *North Jersey R.S.* 3(3-3-4'-7.1) Spindly growth, variable form, good color. *West Jersey R.S.* 1(1-1-5'-6.9) Slow starter. N.Y. *Long Island R.S.* 1(1-2-7'-10) Most everblooming Climber, beautiful pink flowers. *Rochester R.S.* 1(1-4-7'-8) Free-bloomer, vigorous grower. *Schenectady R.S.* 1(3-3-8'-8.5) Prolific bloomer. *Syracuse R.S.* 4(4-4-10'-8.5) Perfect form and color, everblooming, disease-resistant, not hardy in cold climate, glossy foliage. OHIO *Akron R.S.* 1(3-2-7'-9) Very good Climber, generous bloom and foliage, fragrant. *Cincinnati R.S.* 2(3-3-8'-7.5) Good Pillar, will blackspot. *Greater Cincinnati R.S.* 2(3-3-7'-8) Lovely coral color, blooms all Summer. *Lima R.S.* 1(1-2-5'-8) Good color, lovely blooms, slow getting started. OKLA. *Norman R.S.* 2(6-5-10'-8). ORE. *Medford R.S.* 1(1-1-4½'-8) Promising coral-pink Climber, hasn't shown much vigor. PA. *Breeze Hill T.G.* (1-5-10'-7) Beautiful color, nice form, fairly profuse. *Harrisburg R.S.* 1(300-1-10'-9) Rich unfading color, large flowers, good bloomer, very hardy. *Pittsburgh R.S.* 2(2-2-6'-7.5) Very good color and fragrance, not a strong bush or a profuse bloomer. TEX. *Dallas R.S.* 1(1-1-4'-8.5) Prolific. UTAH *Utah R.S.* 1(1-6-25'-8) Climbs and blooms freely, lovely color. WIS. *Madison R.S.* 1(1-1-7'-9.3) Good growth, disease-resistant, good foliage and bloomer, excellent form, substance and lasting quality of blooms. *Milwaukee R.S.* 2(3-3-6'-7.5) Fine color and form, bloom is pretty when there is any, slow grower, lacks vigor. CANADA (British Columbia) *Vancouver R.S.* 3(12-4-10'-8) Very good color and foliage, no disease, continuous bloom this season.

## COURTSHIP HT. Medium pink. (Shepherd; int. Bosley '55) Pat. 1511; ARA '55, PP 4, 59 Rpts.; Av. ht. 37" NR 7.5.

COLO. *Colorado Springs R.S.* 2(6-2-30"-6.5) Winter-hardy, could bloom more, lacks vigor, weak coloring. IND. *Indianapolis R.S.* 1(3-5-30"-7.8) Good substance and color, but could bloom more, disease-resistant. *St. Joseph Valley R.S.* 1(3-3-42"-7.8) Beautiful 6" blooms, needs protection against blackspot. *Vincennes R.S.* 1(1-2-36"-7.5) Sufficient bloom, no disease, lacks substance in full sun. KY. *Louisville Chapter ARS* 1(1-3-36"-6) Vigorous, bright color, good substance, not enough bloom or new canes, subject to winter injury, poor bud and flower form, fades. MICH. *Detroit R.S.* 3(5-3-36"-7.5) Good color, too few blooms, good foliage. *Kalamazoo R.S.* 1(2-3-48"-7.8) Could bloom more, exhibition rose, foliage same as Peace. MINN. *Minnesota R.S.* 1(1-2-30"-8.2) Beautiful color, long-lasting, attractive foliage, many basal breaks. NEW ENGLAND *New England R.S.* 3(16-3-60"-8) N.H.—very vigorous, clean, constant bloomer; Me.—good bush, poor flowers; R.I.—Excellent except for some mildew. N.J. *North Jersey R.S.* 4(4-2-34"-7) Good plant, good color, lacks form and substance. *West Jersey R.S.* 1(1-1-24"-7) Good bloom, slight fragrance, plants not tall enough, stems too weak, too few buds set. N.Y. *Long Island R.S.* 1(1-3-48"-7.5) Nice bush, good exhibition rose, does not bloom enough. *Niagara Frontier R.S.* 1(1-3-42"-8.5) Big husky plant, short stems. OHIO *Akron R.S.* 4(8-3-36"-7.3) Good color, vigorous grower, clean foliage, not for exhibition, blooms off-center and open fast. *Central Ohio R.S.* 3(3-2-36"-7) Strong plant, excellent foliage, good color, lovely full blooms, opens too fast, not exhibition form, will blackspot. *Cincinnati R.S.* 8(14-3-39"-8). *Cleveland R.S.* 1(2-3-36"-4) Fades badly. *Columbus R.C.* 3(3-2-48"-7.8) Good color on first day then fades, opens too fast. *Euclid R.S.* 1(1-1-40"-6.5) Beautiful foliage and buds, fair bloom, opens too quickly, not many canes. *Forest City R.S.* 6(7-3-30"-8) Good foliage, color and form, opens fast, not a prolific bloomer. *Greater Cincinnati R.S.* 1(1-3-30"-8) Exquisite buds, pleasing open flower fades, nice foliage. *Lancaster R.C.* 1(1-3-42"-6.5) Upright bushy plant, large foliage, blackspots. *Lima R.S.* 1(1-1). *Medina County R.S.* 3(3-2-30"-8.6) Tendency to blackspot, otherwise it's tops. *Stark R.S.* 1(1-2-30"-8) Lovely bloom, first to show blackspot. PA. *Pittsburgh R.S.* 2(2-2-24"-6.5) Nice large pink, some fragrance, doesn't bloom profusely, winter-killed. TEX. *Dallas R.S.* 2(1-2-37"-6.5) Good growth, free continuous blooms, good color, healthy. WIS. *Madison R.S.* 1(1-1-36"-8) Good growth, disease-resistant, good foliage, sparse blooms. *Milwaukee R.S.* 1(1-1-26"-7) Nice color, occasional beautiful bud, does not grow enough.

## DAY OF TRIUMPH HT. Medium pink. (Meilland; int. Breedlove '55) Pat. 1358; ARA '56; PP 3, 34 Rpts.; Av. ht. 40''; NR 7.2.

CALIF. *Rose Study Club Oakland* 1(2-2-48''-6.9) Fine clear pink blooms of exhibition form and quality, upright grower, disease-resistant foliage, moderate fragrance. D.C. *Potomac R.S.* 2(2-3-48''-8.9) Good stable pink, shapely bud, good bush and foliage, stems a little short. GA. *Georgia R.S.* 2(3-3-52''-7) Good disease-resistant bush, outstanding color, too few blooms, some irregular. ILL. *Tri City Men's Rose and Garden Club* 2(4-2-48''-6) Winterkills, lacks vigor, good color. IND. *Indianapolis R.S.* 1(4-1-36''-8) Good color and form, some blackspot. IOWA *Linn County R.S.* Good form, sparse bloomer. LA. *New Orleans R.S.* 1(1-2-36''-4). MD. *Maryland R.S.* 1(1-3-52''-9) Blooms of perfect form with good substance, no blackspot or mildew. MICH. *Detroit R.S.* 2(3-3-36''-7) Good clean bush, Spring and Fall bloomer. MINN. *Minnesota R.S.* 6(11-2-33''-7.5) Susceptible to mildew and blackspot, good color in bud and flower. NEW ENGLAND *New England R.S.* 1(1-3-42''-8.5) Huge well-formed blooms, not prolific. N.Y. *Humboldt Park T.G.* (5-3-24''-7) Upright plants, medium size foliage, deep pink ovoid buds, large full high-centered blooms drop petals cleanly, free flowering, disease-resistant, short-stemmed, only moderate vigor. *Syracuse R.S.* 1(1-3-48''-7.8) Large plant and exhibition-type blooms, disease-resistant. OHIO *Cleveland R.S.* 1(1-2-44''-7.5) Good exhibition rose, different shade of pink, upright grower, good stems. *Lancaster R.C.* 3(13-2-53''-8) Vigorous, upright, bushy, large foliage, non-fading pink exhibition bloom. ORE. *Salem R.S.* 1(1-3-36''-7.5) Large clear pink flower of good form, healthy plant, sparse bloom. PA. *Breeze Hill T.G.* (2-3-28''-7) Large flowers of nice color and form. *Philadelphia R.S.* 1(2-3-36''-6). *Pittsburgh R.S.* 1(2-2-30''-7.5) Fair number of red blooms, mildews. TEX. *Dallas R.S.* 2(6-4-40''-7.5) Good color and bud form, fine for exhibition, sparse bloom. UTAH *Utah R.S.* 2(4-3-27''-6) Defoliates badly in hot weather.

## DEAN COLLINS Gr. Light red. (Lammerts; int. Roseway '53) Pat. 1279; ARA '54; PP 5, 1959, 141 Rpts.; Av. ht. 44''; NR 7.4. Total reports 5 years 514; Av. NR 6.9.

## DWARFKING Min. Blood-red. (Kordes; int. Jackson & Perkins '57) Pat. 1577; ARA '57; PP 2, 25 Rpts.; Av. ht. 10''; NR 8.4.

GA. *Georgia R.S.* 1(1-2-18''-7). IND. *Vincennes R.S.* 1(1-1-6''-3) Nice bloom. IOWA *Des Moines R.S.* 1(2-1-7''-7) Good bloomer. *Iowa R.S.* 1(2-1-7''-7) Good bloomer. *Linn County R.S.* 1(2-2-10''-8) Good bloomer, vigorous bush, dark red, blackspots. KY. *Louisville Chapter ARS* 2(4-1-10''-8) Good color and vigor, lasts well, no faults. MINN. *Minnesota R.S.* 1(1-2-14''-9) Profuse bloomer, disease-resistant, winters well. MO. *R.S. Greater St. Louis* 2(3-1-9''-8) Good dark red. NEW ENGLAND *New England R.S.* 2(4-2-15''-8.5) Better form and color, slightly larger than most Miniatures. N.J. *North Jersey R.S.* 3(5-1-10''-9.1) Substantial plant, generous deep flaming red blooms. N.M. *Albuquerque R.S.* 1(1-1-9''-10) Good growth, blooms well, beautiful dark red color, Hybrid Tea form. N.Y. *Greater Buffalo R.S.* 1(6-1-10''-9) Beautiful form for a Miniature, disease-resistant, clear color, well-formed plant. *Syracuse R.S.* 1(1-1-10''-8.7) Fine form, attractive dark red color. OHIO *Akron R.S.* 1(3-1-8''-8.5) Excellent bloomer, one of the best Miniatures, some blackspot. *Central Ohio R.S.* 1(1-1-14''-9.2) Taller than most Miniatures, lovely continuous bloom. TEX. *El Paso R.S.* (12''-9) Good growth and color, blooms constantly, full double rich garnet-red blooms. UTAH *Utah R.S.* 1(2-2-8''-9) Very nice red Miniature, better than Robin. WASH. *Spokane R.S.* 2(2-1-11''-10). WIS. *Milwaukee R.S.* 1(1-1-4''-10) The most perfect buds and blooms imaginable, healthy bush, long-pointed buds, no faults.

## ENCORE F. Deep rose-pink to cameo-pink. (Von Abrams; int. Peterson & Dering '57) Pat. 1662; ARA '58; PP 1, 23 Rpts.; Av. ht. 30''; NR 6.9.

COLO. *Denver R.S.* 1(7-2-24''-7) Delicate semi-double pink, good bloomer, nice foliage, a little leggy. IND. *Indianapolis R.S.* 1(1-1-12''-3) All blind wood. KY. *Lexington R.S.* 1(1-1-28''-8.7) Green glossy foliage, vigorous bush holds color even in heat, no real faults. MINN. *Minnesota R.S.* 1(1-1-30''-9) Sprays of delicate color, good bloomer, bush form could be better. MO. *R.S. Greater St. Louis* 1(1-1-30''-7). MONT. *Sunset Park T.G.* (20-1-24''-8) Attractive blend of colors, good bloomer, compact healthy plant. N.J. *North Jersey R.S.* 3(3-1-24''-6.9) Good growth. N.C. *Durham R.S.* 1(1-1-66''-

9.2) Delicate coloring, vigorous, lovely. OHIO *Akron R.S.* 1(12-1-18″-8). *Greater Cincinnati R.S.* 2(4-1-30″-7.5) Nice bushy plant, good foliage, does not blackspot, blooms shatter too quickly, not many petals. *Lancaster R.C.* 1(2-1-39″-8.6) Upright, well-foliaged, large clusters of long-lasting non-fading blooms. *Medina County R.S.* 1(1-1-36″-8.8) Very attractive. *Ohio State University T.G.* (4-2-27″-7) Very vigorous plant, abundant bloom until October, disease-resistant, good abundant foliage. ORE. *International Rose T.G.* (20-3-48″-7.7) Cupped water-lily-like singular flowers are attractive in sprays, fade rather fast. *Lewis & Clark T.G.* (9-1-34″-5) Good color, not sufficient bloom or vigor. *Medford R.S.* 1(1-1124″-7) Dainty clusters of blossoms repeat quite freely. *Salem R.S.* 2(25-1-28″-3) Fades quickly, sparse bloomer. PA. *Breeze Hill T.G.* (2-4-26″-7) Attractive profuse flowers. CANADA (British Columbia) *Vancouver R.S.* 1(3-3-42″-6) Good foliage, semi-double blooms are too light and washed out.

## FANFARE F. Pink blend. (Swim; int. Armstrong '56) Pat. 1385, ARA '56; PP 3, 104 Rpts.; Av. ht. 36″; NR 7.7.

ARIZ. *Phoenix R.S.* 2(2-2-30″-7.5) Lots of bloom, delicate colors, good growth and foliage. CALIF. *Memorial T.G.* (20-3-30″-7) Vigorous, free-bloomer, apricot color fades to light purple. *Rose Study Club Oakland* 2(5-3-48″-7.8) Vigorous plant, disease-resistant, good live color. *Pacific R.S.* 3(3-2-50″-9) Consistent bloomer with interesting changes in color, drops petals cleanly, vigorous growth, occasional mildew. *Peninsula R.S.* 1(1-1-30″-7) Very floriferous, good growth habit and color, flower opens fast and fades. *San Joaquin Valley R.S.* 5(12-2-36″-7) Beautiful foliage, flowers open and fade fast, outstanding color. COLO. *Colorado Springs R.S.* 1(18-3-36″-9) Lots of blooms, hardy. *Denver R.S.* 1(30-3-30″-9) Interesting colors, good bloomer, excellent foliage, disease-resistant, vigorous. CONN. *Elizabeth Park T.G.* (27-3-8) Good plant, weak neck and stems. D.C. *Potomac R.S.* 2(2-2-7) Mass of orange-yellow and red semi-double blooms, good grower, not enough repeat blooms, good for landscape effect. GA. *Georgia R.S.* 4(14-3-48″-7.3) Unusual pleasing color, constant bloomer, disease-resistant, vigorous plant, flat short-lasting fading bloom. ILL. *Greater Peoria R.S.* 1(1-1-48″-7.5) Vigorous growth, good bloomer and color, blackspots. *Tri-City Men's Rose and Garden Club* 2(15-5-30″-7.6). IND. *Indianapolis R.S.* 1(2-2-24″-7) Repeats well, good color, lacks vigor, fades badly, disease-resistant. *St. Joseph Valley R.S.* 1(1-2-36″-7) Tall, spreads, prolific bloomer. IOWA *Des Moines R.S.* 4(4-3-30″-7.5) Plenty of bloom opens too fast. *Linn County R.S.* 1(2-3-24″-7.8) Blooms in sprays, nice color, fades rapidly. KY. *Louisville Chapter ARS* 2(3-3-30″-6.5) Good producer, novel color, disease-resistant, fades in full sun, short-lived bloom. MICH. *Detroit R.S.* 4(7-3-30″-7.4) Free-flowering, good color and foliage. *Kalamazoo R.S.* 1(2-3-42″-7) Fades, blooms do not hold on bush, blackspots. MINN. *Lyndale Park T.G.* (25-3-30″-6.7) Early and constant blooms fade out fast. *Minnesota R.S.* 5(11-2-33″-8.6) Profusion of showy blooms all season. MO. *Jewel Park T.G.* (10) One of the best bloomers. *Rosarians Midland Empire* 3(10-2-30″-6.5) Unusual color, opens too fast, too few petals. *R.S. Greater St. Louis* 1(1-1-36″-7) Lots of bloom, color fades. NEW ENGLAND *New England R.S.* 1(3-3-45″-8.5) Vigorous bush, prolific all season. N.J. *North Jersey R.S.* 7(15-2-48″-8.5) Big sprays. *West Jersey R.S.* 1(1-3-36″-7.8) Continuous bloom in clusters, good upright growth, subject to blackspot. N.M. *Albuquerque R.S.* 1(3-1-36″-8.9) Good color, terrific bloomer, nice plant. N.Y. *Cornell University T.G.* (3-4-22″-7) Good color on opening especially in cool weather, not too vigorous, flowers finish badly, fade. *Humboldt Park T.G.* (9-2-36″-9.9) Very healthy, vigorous plants, abundant large dark foliage, very disease-resistant, deep coral-pink buds in clusters, always in bloom, moderate fragrant, no faults. *Niagara Frontier R.S.* 1(1-3-38″-8.5). *Rochester R.S.* (2-21-2136″-8) Vigorous grower, abundance of bloom. *Schenectady R.S.* 1(3-1-24″-7.9). No real faults. *Syracuse R.S.* 2(4-2-40″-7.5) Very fine for bedding, lots of color, bloom fades too quickly. N.C. *Durham R.S.* 3(12-3-48″-8) Good color, constant bloomer, nice foliage, does not last long when cut. *Randolph R.S.* 2(2-3-36″-7) Rich color in early stage of bloom, short bloom life, fades quickly. OHIO *Akron R.S.* 2(3-2-28″-7) Opens fast, not exhibition form, good foliage, fair bloomer, some blackspot. *Central Ohio R.S.* 1(3-2-30″-7) Continuous bloom, nice color, healthy plant, flowers lack substance and are short-lived. *Miami Valley R.S.* 3(3-2-24″-7) Interesting different color, blackspots. *Ohio State University T.G.* (4-4-36″-8) Excellent foliage, vigorous bushy plant, holds foliage to base of plant, disease-resistant, abundant bloom. *Park of Roses T.G.* (25-2-33″-8) Good foliage fairly resistant to blackspot, vigorous plant, bloom tends to fade quickly. OKLA. *Norman R.S.* 2(6-3-28″-7.6). ORE. *International Rose T.G.* (18-4-48″-6) Attractive semi-double flowers in large clusters fade, blackspots. *Lewis & Clark T.G.* (10-1-36″-8) Color and bloom backed with good foliage, weak growth. *Rogue Valley R.S.* 3(5-3-36″-8) Good color, attractive bloom, vigorous bloomer, disease-resistant. *Salem R.S.* 2(22-3-38″-8) Good performer, excellent bush and foliage. PA. *Breeze Hill T.G.* (3-6-36″-5) Early, vigorous, good foliage, nice color as it opens, fades. *Harrisburg R.S.* 1(400-2-42″-8.9) Very profuse, vigorous, hardy, dark green waxy foliage, a different blend of colors, disease-resistant. *Philadelphia R.S.* 1(2-3-42″-9) Constant bloom, strong canes, good foliage. *Pittsburgh R.S.* 1(12-2-8) Strong and healthy. S.C. *Edisto T.G.* (15-3-36″-7) Good color, vigorous plant, ample bloom, lacks substance. TEX. *Amarillo R.S.* 2(5-3-36″-7.5) Constant bloomer, bright color when fresh, fades. *Dallas R.S.* 1(1-2-30″-7.8) Excellent flower, unusual color. UTAH *Utah R.S.* 3(24-3-36″-6.2) Lots of blooms fade, hugs the ground. CANADA (British Columbia) *Vancouver R.S.* 2(8-3-42″-9) Huge clusters of large flowers, strong plant with fine foliage, no serious faults.

## FLIRTATION HT. Pink, reverse gold. (Shepherd; int. Bosley '54) Pat. 1373; ARA '54; PP 5, 1959, 44 Rpts.; Av. ht. 38″; NR 7.4. Total reports 5 years 183; Av. NR 7.3.

## FORT VANCOUVER HT. Medium pink. (Swim; int. Peterson & Dering '56) Pat. 994; ARA '57; PP 3, 29 Rpts.; Av. ht. 46″; NR 7.2.

CALIF. *Pacific R.S.* 1(1-1-50″-8) Disease-resistant foliage, strong upright plant, large buds, exceptionally good form, fragrant, good bloomer, won't open if cut too soon. D.C. *Potomac R.S.* 1(2-2-72″-7.3) Good grower, long-stemmed blooms, color fades, balls when wet. ILL. *Chicago R.S. Reg. 1* 2(2-2-60″) Large, vigorous, disease-free bush with large fragrant blooms which ball badly in the Spring. KY. *Kentucky R.S.* 1(3-3-48″-7) Good foliage, lovely color, sparse bloom. MICH. *Detroit R.S.* 1(1-3-42″-8) Good color and form, long-lasting, not enough bloom. *Kalamazoo R.S.* 1(1-2-30″-7.9) Good bush. MO. *Rosarians Midland Empire* 2(4-2-36″-7.5) Vigorous plant, large but too few blooms. N.J. *North Jersey R.S.* 6(8-2-31″-7.1) Very fragrant, vigorous plant, large exhibtiion flower, not prolific. N.Y. *Long Island R.S.* 1(1-2-7.1) Huge exhibition-type bloom of good form, some blackspot, lacks continuity of bloom. *Syracuse R.S.* 2(2-2-40″-7.1) Large exhibition bloom, good color, disease-resistant, could bloom more. OHIO *Cleveland R.S.* 1(2-1-48″-7) Vigorous, large flowers. *Lancaster R.C.* 3(7-2-66″-7.3) Vigorous, upright grower, disease-resistant, blooms burn in hot weather. *Miami Valley R.S.* 2(4-1-30″-7.5) Large exhibition-size blooms, substance won't hold up in hot weather. ORE. *International Rose T.G.* (18-8-84″-6) Fragrance, size of bud and flower good in warm weather, not too good in cool weather, color not sharp. *Medford R.S.* 2(2-2-59″-7.9) Continuous bloom, large robust plant. *Rogue Valley R.S.* 1(1-2-54″-7) Beautiful color and form. *Salem R.S.* 1(1-3-40″-7) Large flower, often exhibition quality, necks a bit weak, vigorous plant. TEX. *Dallas R.S.* 1(1-4-24″-5) Good color and form, not vigorous. VA. *Va. Peninsula R.S.* 1(1-2-45″-7) Fast grower, large exhibition-type blooms, good color, too few blooms, subject to blackspot.

## FROLIC F. Pink. (Swim, int. Armstrong '53) Pat. 1179, ARA '53; PP 5, 1959, 108 Rpts.; Av. ht. 31″; NR 7.8. Total reports 5 years 446; Av. NR 7.9.

## FROSTY Min. Clear frosty white. (Moore; int. Sequoia '53) Pat. 1412; ARA '56; PP 5, 1959, 20 Rpts.; Av. ht. 10″; NR 7.4. Total reports 5 years 57; Av. NR 7.1.

## FUSILIER F. Luminiscent red. (Morey; int. Jackson & Perkins '58) Pat. 1709; ARA '58; PP 1, 213 Rpts.; Av. ht. 29″; NR 7.8.

ALA. *Twickenham R.S.* 1(1-1-24″-6) Bright luminous color, does not bloom nearly enough. ARIZ. *Mesa R.S.* 3(9-1-36″-8.6) Best in my garden, wonderful bloomer even in hot Summer, thoroughly good. *Phoenix R.S.* 4(7-1-24″-7.5) Brilliant scarlet blooms, sturdy plant. CALIF. *Memorial T.G.* (10-2-30″-8) Deep red 3″ blooms, free-flowering, very fragrant, no faults. *Rose Study Club Oakland* 2(9-2-42″-8.5) Dark red bud opens to a new color of flaming orange-scarlet, vigorous free-blooming plant, mildews slightly, beautiful in mass planting. *Pacific R.S.* 1(1-1-30"-7.5) Vigorous growth and good color, moderate bloomer. *Peninsula R.S.* 2(2-1-24"-6) Prolific bloomer, slow to start, rusts, mildews, needs heat for good color. *San Diego R.S.* 2(2-2-30"-7.9) Good color and bush. *San Joaquin Valley R.S.* 8(15-1-30"-8) Healthy, vigorous plant, lots of bright lasting bloom, outstanding color. COLO. *Denver R.S.* 5(14-1-24"-8) Excellent plant, long-lasting blooms, does not repeat often. CONN. *Elizabeth Park T.G.* (30-2-15"-5) Bud and bloom good, fading bloom darkens, too much blackspot, not enough bud or bloom, poor weak growth. D.C. *Potomac R.S.* 5(7-2-24"-7.8) Bright orange-red semi-double blooms come in large sprays that last well and petal-spot with age, some blackspot. GA. *Georgia R.S.* 4(6-1-40"-7.9) Striking brilliant color, profusion of bloom, vigorous bush, blooms stand up well in heat, some mildew. ILL. *Greater Peoria R.S.* 1(1-2-26"-8) Eye-catching color, lot of blooms, blackspots. IND. *Indianapolis R.S.* 3(1-3-36"-6.7) Good grower and bloomer, subject to disease, blooms hang on and become unsightly. *St. Joseph Valley R.S.* 3(5-3-36"-8.8) Disease-resistant beautiful foliage, long-lasting flowers. *Vincennes R.S.* 1(3-1-36"-8) Profuse, free of disease, likes the hot sun. IOWA *Des Moines R.S.* 2(3-1-24"-8) Good color holds well. *Iowa R.S.* 3(7-1-30"-7.5) Abundant bloom, sparse foliage. *Linn County R.S.* 5(7-2-24"-6.6) Beautiful color, bushy plant, blackspots and mildews. KAN. *Wichita R.S.* 3(3-1-30"-8) Brilliant blooms, good foliage, holds color. KY. *Kentucky R.S.* 1(1-1-30"-8) Nice color, not enough blooms. *Lexington R.S.* 2(6-1-24"-8) Very colorful bloom lasts long and doesn't lose petals, not enough bloom, mildews badly. *Louisville Chapter ARS* 6(9-1-27"-8) Unusual red, good growth, blooms well, subject to mildew. LA. *New Orleans R.S.* 2(3-2-36"-7.5) Strong, prolific, good color, blooms open quickly. MD. *Maryland R.S.* 2(2-1-24"-8) Color brilliant when fresh, blooms last, not a free-bloomer, blackspots. MICH. *Detroit R.S.* 5(8-1-24"-7.8) Good color, does not blue, good foliage, blackspots. *Greater Lansing R.S.* 3(3-1-36"-7.3) Appealing flower with an irridescent quality, thick short pointed bud, large foliage, mildew and blackspot-resistant, very satisfactory. MICH. *Michigan State University T.G.* (6-2-22"-8) Brilliant non-fading color, slight tea fragrance, petal edges blacken in hot weather, slight resistance to blackspot. MINN. *Minnesota R.S.* 14(20-1-26"-8.5) Brilliant color, blooms repeat often, long-lasting, sturdy bush. MO. *Rosarians Midland Empire* 2(5-1-30"-8) Good color does not fade, disease-resistant. *R.S. Greater St. Louis* 3(4-1-30"-7) Nice color flowers hang on, disease-resistant. *Sedalia R.S.* 2(2-1-18"-7) Good color, plant does not grow or bloom well. MICH. *Kalamazoo R.S.* 1(1-1-24"-7.7). MONT. *Sunset Park T.G.* (10-2-8) Very striking color, moderate vigor, fair amount of bloom. NEW ENGLAND *New England R.S.* 2(4-2-20"-7) Poor grower, few blooms. N.J. *North Jersey R.S.* 10(18-1-28"-8) Sturdy plant, admirable color, large sprays. *West Jersey R.S.* 5(10-1-30"-7.5) Good long-lasting bloom holds color well, healthy foliage, too few blooms. N.Y. *Cornell University T.G.* (8-2-28"-8) Superb color holds well, good flower form, not as vigorous as expected, poor growth habit. *Greater Buffalo R.S.* 2(5-1-24"-8.5) Long-lasting flower, disease-resistant foliage, clear color, some mildew. *Humboldt Park T.G.* (3-2-24"-8) Very upright growth, abundant dark green foliage, brilliant scarlet-red color, very-double globular continuous clustered blooms with very good-lasting quality, blackspots. *Long Island R.S.* 2(3-1-42"-8) Sturdy bush, repeat long-lasting blooms hold color very well. *Rochester R.S.* 4(24-2-24"-7) Good color and foliage, long-lasting. *Schenectady R.S.* 3(5-1-31"-7) Good foliage, vigorous bush, good color, large-sized clusters, not many blooms. *Syracuse R.S.* 5(8-1-30"-7.8) Beautiful color lasts well, disease-resistant, plenty of bloom. N.C. *Charlotte R.S.* 2(2-1-30"-8) Good rose, mildews some. *Durham R.S.* 1(9-1-48"-9.5) Generous bloomer, disease-resistant, good non-fading color and foliage. *Randolph R.S.* 1(1-1-48"-8) Lasting bloom, exceptionally strong upright growth, beautiful dark green foliage. OHIO *Akron R.S.* 4(27-2-30"-8) Disease-resistant dark green foliage, good bloomer, holds bloom long, some blackspot. *Central Ohio R.S.* 4(6-1-24"-8) Healthy plant, blooms have outstanding color, mostly single, some mildew. *Cleveland R.S.* 4(7-2-15"-5.6) Good color, few blooms, sparse foliage. *Columbus R.C.* 1(1-1-30"-8) Healthy plants, outstanding color, mostly single bloom. *Lancaster R.C.* 2(2-1-39"-8.2) Bushy, upright, large disease-resistant foliage, fair bloomer. *Lima R.S.* 4(9-1-36"-8) Long-lasting blooms, unique color, no blackspot. *Miami Valley R.S.* 3(4-1-28"-9) Unusual color, strong sturdy plant, nice bloomer. *Ohio State University T.G.* (4-2-27"-7) Excellent foliage, vigorous plant, disease-resistant, sparse bloom after September. *Park of Roses T.G.* (50-2-24"-7.5) Striking color, good glossy foliage, slight tendency to blackspot. OKLA. *Norman R.S.* 1(9-2-18"-7). ORE. *Eugene R.S.* 3(3-1-24"-8) Long-lasting bloom holds color, good bush. *International Rose T.G.* (20-4-48"-7) Irridescent color, strong canes and sprays, fades somewhat, tends to mildew under the necks. *Medford R.S.* 2(2-1-29"-7.8) Beautiful color, similar to Embers but smaller, spasmodic blooming. *Rogue Valley R.S.* 5(10-1-30"-7.8) Attractive color, nice form, prolific bloomer. *Salem R.S.* 1(2-2-36"-7.5) Good bush, large clusters of scarlet flowers, does not clean. PA. *Breeze Hill T.G.* (2-4-28"-9) Profuse, brilliant color. *Harrisburg R.S.* 3(6-1-33"-8) Nice unfading color, continuous bloom, good form, nice disease-resistant foliage. *Pittsburgh R.S.* 2(15-1-30″-6) Very poor bloomer, blackspots and mildews. S.C. *Edisto T.G.* (12-2-48″-9) Vigorous, floriferous, attractive color, black-spot-resistant. TENN. *Nashville R.S.* 2(4-2-30″-7.9) Vigorous plant, brilliant color, light fragrance, mildews. TEX. *Amarillo R.S.* 1(3-2-36″-7.5) Good color and foliage, should bloom more. *Corpus Christi R.S.* 1(1-1-30″-8.5) Really different color, very showy, sturdy plant, scarce blooms. *Dallas R.S.* 2(3-2-28″-7.6) Bright orange-red color, prolific, very hardy, bloom form not so good, some mildew. *El Paso R.S.* 3(3-1-38″-9) Healthy foliage and stems, full clusters of rich red blooms do not fade in sun, constant bloomer during the year, picks up mildew easy. UTAH *Utah R.S.* 5(13-2-31″-7.5) Good bloomer, vigorous growth, clean foliage, striking color, fights anything. VA. *Eastern Shore R.S.* 1(1-1-36″-9) Unusual orange flower with frilled edge, hardy, disease-resistant, constantly in bloom. WASH. *Spokane R.S.* 4(16-2-24″-8) Good bedding rose, brightest color imaginable. *Walla Walla R.S.* 1(2-1-30″-8) Vigorous growth, size and color of bloom outstanding. WIS. *Madison R.S.* 4(9-1-33″-7.7) Good growth, blooms quite freely, fair foliage, nice color, disease-resistant. CANADA (British Columbia) *Vancouver R.S.* 2(1-2-42″-8) Good color holds well, good bush and foliage.

## GAIL BORDEN HT. Pink interior, apricot-yellow outside. (Kordes; int. Jackson & Perkins '57) Pat. 1618; ARA '58; PP 1, 123 Rpts.; Av. ht. 33″; NR 7.7.

ALA. *Twickenham R.S.* 2(2-1-30″-7.3) Beautiful bloom has good form, could bloom more freely. ARIZ. *Mesa R.S.* 2(3-1-24″-7.2) Beautiful bud and flower, poor bloomer and bush. *Phoenix R.S.* 3(3-1-36″-7) Rugged glossy foliage, gorgeous blooms. CALIF. *Rose Study Club Oakland* 3(8-1-42″-7.4) Perfect open form, interesting bud, dark shiny disease-resistant foliage, no faults. *Peninsula R.S.* (4(5-1-36″-7) Weak plant, good color and form, poor stems, shy bloomer. *San Diego R.S.* 1(1-1-28″-6.2). *San Joaquin Valley R.S.* 1(1-2-72″-7.5) Continuous bloom, grows like a Pillar. *San Mateo County R.S* 1(1-1-36″-9) Outstanding pink combination, beautiful buds, blooms last well, good disease-resistant foliage. CONN. *Elizabeth Park T.G.* (5-6-30″-8) Strong stems, good foliage and color. D.C. *Potomac R.S.* 1(1-1-36″-6.5) Large bloom, nice bud, poor flower form, could bloom more. GA. *Georgia R.S.* 3(5-2-55″-8) Beautiful new color, good form, vigorous bush, rather leggy, some split centers and heavy bloom heads. ILL. *Tri-City Men's Rose and Garden Club* 1(12-2-3″-8) Good bloom and foliage. IND. *Indianapolis R.S.* 3(3-1-29″-7.7) Beautiful large buds and open blooms, soft colors, does not bloom enough, some blackspot. *St. Joseph Valley R.S.* 2(2-2-42″-7.8) Beautiful large blooms, good color, tall bush, sparse blooms. IOWA *Linn County R.S.* 2(2-1-30″-8) Vigorous, long bud, repeats. KAN. *Wichita R.S.* 2(2-2-24″-8.5) Lovely color, few blooms. KY. *Kentucky R.S.* 2(3-1-36″-6) Disease-resistant, too-few blooms. *Lexington R.S.* 1(1-1-24″-6.3) Weak color. *Louisville Chapter ARS* 2(2-2-60″-8.5) Profuse blooms, good foliage. MICH. *Detroit R.S.* 2(3-1-24″-7) Nice foliage, lasts, not exhibition type, very showy. *Kalamazoo R.S.* 3(6-1-30″-8) Good blooms and foliage. MINN. *Minnesota R.S.* 6(7-1-28″-7.8) Bloom and foliage similar to Peace, could bloom more. MO. *Rosarians Midland Empire* 1(2-1-42″-8) Nice plants, clean flowers. *R.S. Greater St. Louis* 1(1-1-24″-7). *Sedalia R.S.* 1(1-1-49″-8) Heavy dark green foliage, large blooms hold well, slight fragrance. NEW ENGLAND *New England R.S.* 4(5-1-30″-6.5) Few large well-shaped blooms on weak plants, blackspots easily. N.J. *North Jersey R.S.* 5(8-1-28″-7.4) Fine large bi-color with substance, erratic growth. *West Jersey R.S.* 5(8-1-42″-8) Exceptionally large well-shaped bloom of good color, shiny foliage, fairly disease-resistant, not enough bloom. N.M. *Albuquerque R.S.* 1(1-1-14″-6.5) Slow to start, good foliage, good colors but not much contrast, full-petalled bloom could have more form. N.Y. *Greater Buffalo R.S.* 3(4-1-24″-8.9) Clear bi-color, long stem, single bloom, excellent foliage, exhibition form. *Rochester R.S.* 2(4-2-30″-8.1) Lovely buds of excellent color, constant bloomer. *Schenectady R.S.* 1(5-2-30″-8.7) Very good bloom opens slowly, very disease-resistant foliage. *Syracuse R.S.* 6(9-2-29″-7.7) Good form, long-lasting bloom, very nice disease-resistant foliage, good bloomer, firm substance. N.C. *Randolph R.S.* 1(1-1-48″-8) Big beautiful bloom, nice dark glossy green foliage, pretty buds. OHIO *Akron R.S.* 4(4-1-30″-7.5) Good color, foliage, form and grower, stingy on bloom. *Cleveland R.S.* 3(10-2-40″-8) Larger than Peace, sturdy stem, lasts well, grows very tall. *Forest City R.S.* 3(3-1-30″-8) Large full blooms, excellent foliage, sturdy, bushy plant. *Lancaster R.C.* 1(1-3-48c-7) Upright, bushy, large glossy foliage, non-fading blooms, blackspots. *Lima R.S.* 3(7-1-30″-8) Beautiful foliage and large bloom, often split centers. *Medina County R.S.* 1(1-1-48″-9) Excellent but sparse bloom. *Miami Valley R.S.* 2(4-1-48″-8) Good color and blooms, disease-resistant, balls in center. *Ohio State University T.G.* (4-2-24″-7) Excellent disease-resistant foliage, blooms well until September, igorous, bushy plant. *Park of Roses T.G.* (100-2-48″-8) Dark leathery foliage, vigorous growth habit, bloom could hold up better. *Stark R.S.* 1(1-1-20″-9) Small plant, uge flower. **OKLA.** *Oklahoma R.S.* 1(3-1-36″-8). **ORE.** *International Rose T.G.* 20-3-36″-7) Form of bud and flower have exhibition possibilities, open habit, heavy loom tips. *Medford R.S.* 3(3-1-34″-8) Beautiful color and form, large many-petalled looms, glossy healthy foliage, vigorous, spreading growth, does not bloom enough. **PA.** *reeze Hill T.G.* (2-4-28″-8) Lovely color and form, fine foliage. *Pittsburgh R.S.* (3-1-24″-7) Good foliage resists blackspot, sparse bloomer. **S.C.** *Edisto T.G.* (6-3-18″-5) Too-few attractive flowers with good color, form and substance, plant lacks vigor. **TENN.** *Nashville R.S.* (33″-7.5) Healthy, vigorous, good size, color and number of blooms, blackspots easily. **TEX.** *Corpus Christi R.S.* 1(1-1-24″-8.2) One of the most showy blooms in cool weather, good color and fragrance, doesn't like hot sun. *Dallas R.S.* (1-1-36″-7.6) Lovely flower, good foliage, husky bush, resistant. *El Paso R.S.* 1(2-1-48″-8.5) Waxy healthy disease-resistant foliage, large fragrant blooms with good coloring, preading bush, strong stems. **VA.** *Va. Peninsula R.S.* 1(1-1-36″-6.5) Average growth, not a free-bloomer. **WASH.** *Spokane R.S.* 6(10-1-36″-10) Glossy foliage, large flowers, esembles Love Song. *Walla Walla R.S.* 1(1-1-36″-9) Very large fine-proportioned blooms. **WIS.** *Madison R.S.* 1(1-1-27″-9.5) Gorgeous color similar to Peace but darker, shiny green foliage, large flowers, big fat buds. *Milwaukee R.S.* 1(2-1-26″-6) Nice color, ordinary form. **CANADA** (British Columbia) *Vancouver R.S.* 1(3-2-36″-7) Good foliage nd color, not enough petals or bloom, does not last, some fragrance. (Nova Scotia) *Buchanan* (1-11-18″-6) Slow to start, good bi-color, fine form.

## GLADIATOR C1. Medium red. (Malandrone; int. Jackson & Perkins '55) Pat. 1524, ARA '56; PP 3, 87 Rpts.; Av. ht. 8′; NR 8.2.

**ALA.** *Twickenham R.S.* 1(1-3-10′-7) Sturdy strong canes, does not bloom very freely. **ARIZ.** *Phoenix R.S.* 3(3-2-6′-8.3) Good sturdy growth, constant bloom, excellent form nd color, no faults. **CALIF.** *Memorial T.G.* (2-4-11′-7) Vigorous 4″ lovely blooms, not a free-bloomer. **COLO.** *Colorado Springs R.S.* 1(1-2-5′-8) Nice plant, well-formed loom, could bloom more. **D.C.** *Potomac R.S.* 2(4-3-10′-9) Best light-red Climber, beautifully-formed buds on long stems, repeats all Summer, does not fade in sun, good oliage, winter-hardy. **GA.** *Georgia R.S.* 1(2-2-6′-9) Continuous good blooms, vigorous, disease-resistant, hardy. **ILL.** *Chicago R.S. Reg. 1* 1(1-1-6′-9 Constant long-lasting bloom of good form, healthy bush. *Greater Peoria R.S.* 1(1-3-9′-9) Blooms well, good as cut lower, disease-resistant. **IND.** *Indianapolis R.S.* 2(2-4-7′-7.8) Beautiful form and color, parse bloomer, lacks vigor, refuses to throw new basal canes. *St. Joseph Valley R.S.* (2-2-6′-7.8) Beautifully-shaped prolific blooms, long stems. *Vincennes R.S.* 5(27-2-8′-9) Profuse, hardy, no disease, best big red Climber. **IOWA** *Linn County R.S.* 1(3-2-10′-8) Best ver-blooming Climber. **KAN.** Wichita R.S. 1(1-1-8) Good grower, foliage and bloomer. *K.Y.* *Louisville Chapter ARS* 2(2-2-5½′-7.8) Good foliage, hardy, long stems, beautiful looms. **MD.** *Maryland R.S.* 2(3-3-9′-8) Very full exhibition-form blooms, repeats. **MICH.** *Detroit R.S.* 2(2-2-6′-7.5) Large blooms all season, disease-resistant. *Kalamazoo R.S.* (2-2-7.9) Disease-resistant, could bloom more, nice long stems, good color. *West Michigan Rosarians* 1(2-1-6′-7.5) Nice repeat bloom. **MINN.** *Minnesota R.S.* 2(3-2-6′-7.8) Grows well, good constant bloom. **MO.** *Rosarians Midland Empire* 2(7-2-7′-7) Good color, disease-resistant, not hardy. *R.S. Greater St. Louis* 2(3-4-12′-7) Good recurrent-bloomer, wish for more flowers at a time. **NEW ENGLAND** *New England R.S.* 2(3-2-6′-8) Vigorous, clean foliage, large fragrant flowers. **N.J.** *North Jersey R.S.* 8(10-2-8′-8.4) Well received, Hybrid Tea-type continuous bloom, best Climber to come along for ears. *West Jersey R.S.* 3(3-2-7′-8) A good Pillar rose, vigorous grower, good long-lasting buds, and flowers on long stems make excellent cut flowers. **N.Y.** *Humboldt Park T.G.* (4-3-7′-9.9) Strong canes, very heathy foliage, large continuous blooms with moderate fruity fragrance, no faults. *Rochester R.S.* 2(8-2-10′- 7.5) Beautiful non-ading blooms, slow to get established. *Schenectady R.S.* 1(2-2-7′-8.8) One of the best red Climbers, beautiful Hybrid Tea-like flowers, some on single stems, continuous bloomer, tands Winters better than Climbing Hybrid Teas, but not as rugged as Blaze. *Syracuse R.S.* Very vigorous healthy, free-bloomer in large clusters with good color, winters well, no faults. **OHIO** *Akron R.S.* 1(3-2-9′-8.5) Good grower, quality blooms. *Central Ohio R.S.* (2-2-9′-8) Good large bloom repeats all Summer, slow starter. *Cleveland R.S.* 1(1-2-5′-8) Well-formed blossoms, good repeater. *Lancaster R.C.* 2(2-4-10′-8.1) Blooms continuously, disease-resistant, doesn't like wet weather. *Lima R.S.* 1(1-2-14′-8.7) Fast grower, free-bloomer, long-lasting flowers, very hardy, one of the best Climbers. *Miami Valley R.S.* 1(1-1-10′-8) Excellent color, form and substance, disease-resistant, no outstanding faults. **OKLA.** *Norman R.S.* 2(4-3-8′-8.6). **ORE.** *Medford R.S.* 2(2-2-10′-8)

Very good color, form and healthy plant, does not bloom enough. *Salem R.S.* 1(1-3-7'-7.5) A nice Pillar, large fragrant intermittent bloom. PA. *Breeze Hill T.G.* (1-6-7'-6) Attractive color and form. *Harrisburg R.S.* 1(1-2-6'-7.8) Blooms carried on nice canes have a lasting quality. *Philadelphia R.S.* 2(2-2-12'-8.4) Excellent form and foliage, dull color, doesn't drop clean. TENN. *Nashville R.S.* (8'-9.3) Healthy, vigorous, bloom of excellent form and substance holds well. TEX. *Amarillo R.S.* 1(1-2-7'-8.6) Strong, upright, medium height, large Hybrid Tea-like blooms on long stems, moderate bloomer, good color. *Corpus Christi R.S.* 1(1-3-15'-7.2) Most prolific of the new Climbers, long-lasting full blooms, excellent foliage, long stems. *Dallas R.S.* 1(1-2-8'-7) Vigorous, light red cut flower lasts well, some blackspot. *El Paso R.S.* 2(2-2-10'-9.5) Very vigorous grower, healthy strong foliage and stems, very fragrant, continuous bloomer, nice rich color and form, excellent cut flower, disease-resistant. UTAH *Utah R.S.* 1(1-6-15'-9) One of the best blooming Climbers, deep pink, holds color well. WASH. *Spokane R.S.* 2(2-2-5'-8) Beautiful color, Pillar-type growth. WIS. *Milwaukee R.S.* 1(3-2-14'-9) Beautiful form of bud and flower, lively color, could bloom more. CANADA (British Columbia) *Vancouver R.S.* 3(8-2-10'-8) Good foliage and plant, slow starter, well-shaped bud and bloom, pinkish-red, recurrent but stingy bloomer.

## GOLD CUP F. Golden yellow. (Boerner; int. Jackson & Perkins '58) Pat. 1683; ARA '58; PP 1, 217 Rpts.; Av. ht. 27''; NR 7.4.

ALA. *Twickenham R.S.* 2(3-1-38''-6.1) Not too large, beautiful color and foliage. ARIZ. *Mesa R.S.* 2(4-1-30''-6.3) Nice color holds well, does not bloom enough. *Phoenix R.S.* 4(8-1-24''-7.5) Lots of nicely-formed blooms, good grower. CALIF. *Memorial T.G.* (10-2-20''-6) Free-bloomer, some rust, not vigorous, slight fragrance. *Rose Study Club Oakland* 2(7-1-40''-8) Glossy dark green disease-resistant foliage, many non-fading fragrant blooms, best yellow Grandiflora to date. *Pacific R.S.* 1(1-128''-7.5) Good grower, flowers have good form. *Peninsula R.S.* 3(3-1-24''-8) Beautiful color holds well, slow-starter, some mildew. *Riverside R.S.* (9-6-42''-9) Very good foliage, big blooms hold their color very well. *San Diego R.S.* 1(1-1-29''-8) Continuous show of fine blooms. *San Joaquin Valley R.S.* 1(15-1-36''-7.5) Rich color, shiny foliage, beautiful bud, holds up well in warm weather. COLO. *Colorado Springs R.S.* 1(3-1-24''-6) Not enough bloom, mildews. *Denver R.S.* 5(11-1-24''-7) First bloom abundant, more attractive in bud than in full bloom, blooms short-lasting, subject to blackspot. D.C. *Potomac R.S.* 7(9-1-36''-8.1) Always in bloom, outstanding holly-like foliage, individual flower lacks form but good for mass effect. GA. *Georgia R.S.* 4(9-1-36''-7) Beautiful non-fading blooms on attractive dark green bushy disease-free plant, not enough bloom. ILL. *Greater Peoria R.S.* 1(1-1-18''-7.5) Attractive foliage, bright color, not enough bloom. *Tri-City Men's Rose and Garden Club* 2(15-2-24''-7.5) Slow-growing. IND. *Indianapolis R.S.* 6(7-1-27''-6.8) Tiny, holds color, opens very fast, not profuse bloomer. *St. Joseph Valley R.S.* 2(2-2-36''-7.1) Good foliage, lots of bloom, good color, cool weather rose, not as good as Golden Fleece. *Vincennes R.S.* 2(2-1-8) Good heavy bloom and foliage. IOWA *Des Moines R.S.* 2(3-1-30''-8) Good amount of bloom and color. *Iowa R.S.* 3(8-1-30''-8) Good color, opens too fast, hardy. *Linn County R.S.* 6(9-2-26''-6.5) Nice color, does not hold petals, glossy disease-resistant leaves. KAN. *Wichita R.S.* 2(2-1-24''-7.5) Good bloomer and foliage. KY. *Lexington R.S.* 2(3-2-24''-9) Beautiful buds and bloom, holds color well, glossy disease-resistant foliage. *Louisville Chapter ARS* 5(9-1-25''-6.8) Good color, producer and form, opens too fast, soon fades. LA. *New Orleans R.S.* 1(2-2-36''-7) Good foliage and bloomer, fades in sun. MD. *Maryland R.S.* 3(4-1-24''-7) Good plant, blooms have good color but last only one day. MICH. *Detroit R.S.* 3(7-2-30''-7) Good color, some blackspot, winter-kills. *Greater Lansing R.S.* 4(11-1-30''-7.8) Bright color fades in sun, glossy leaves. *Michigan State University T.G.* (6-2-24''-5.7) Non-fading color, slight "apple blossom" fragrance, only moderate resistance to mildew and blackspot. MINN. *Lyndale Park T.G.* (35-2-18''-8.4) Good foliage and bloomer, disease-resistant, hardy. *Minnesota R.S.* 15(36-1-29''-7.5) Beautiful in bud, non-lasting fragrant flower, glossy leathery emerald-green foliage. MO. *Kansas City R.S.* 1(3-1-18''-5) Vivid color, attractive buds. *Jewel Park T.G.* (5) Slow bloomer, flower opens flat. *Rosarians Midland Empire* 1(3-1-24''-7.5) Good color, nice bud and foliage, clean, could bloom more. *R.S. Greater St. Louis* 5(8-1-18''-7) Needs unfading blooms. *Sedalia R.S.* 2(2-1-24''-8) Disease-resistant foliage, bloom has nice form and color, holds well. MONT. *Sunset Park T.G.* (20-2-20''-8) Sparkling color fades little, charming gold buds, handsome glossy foliage, a great improvement on Goldilocks. NEW ENGLAND *New England R.S.* 3(5-1-28''-8.3) Good color holds, repeats well, clean bushy plant. N.J. *North Jersey R.S.* 13(22-1-21''-7.4) Short plant, beautiful foliage, bright unfading color, production unsatisfactory, usually blooms singly. N.M. *Albuquerque R.S.* 1(2-1-18''-7) Good color holds well in sun, disease-free, plentiful bloom. N.Y. *Cornell University T.G.*

(8-2-20"-8) Excellent color, holds in heat, large flower, nice bud, shiny dark green foliage, very neat, not too vigorous, form of open flower not good. *Greater Buffalo R.S.* 3(4-1-24"-6.5) Loose form, good clear color, blackspots and mildews. *Humboldt Park T.G.* (12-2-24"-8) No blackspot, glossy green foliage, deep golden-yellow buds open into globular medium-size blooms showing stamens of yellow, continuous bloomer, blooms hang on. *Long Island R.S.* 2(4-1-24"-7.8) Good bloomer, beautiful color, flower much better than Goldilocks, blackspots, slow in heat. *Rochester R.S.* 4(6-1-24"-7.5) Good color, glossy foliage. *Schenectady R.S.* 4(8-2-30"-7.6) Color and foliage very good, unable to get large clusters nice shade, slow-growing. *Syracuse R.S.* 2(3-2-30"-7) Leathery green foliage, striking but sparse bloom sprays are irregular in arrangement and do not hold. N.C. *Durham R.S.* 3(8-1-30"-8.5) Profuse bloomer, nice bud and open flower, best yellow Grandiflora, bloom shatters too soon. *Randolph R.S.* 1(2-2-36"-7) Pretty foliage, blooms fade quickly. OHIO *Akron R.S.* 4(29-2-18"-6.8) Holds color, good foliage, some blackspot, opens fast. *Central Ohio R.S.* 2(4-1-28"-7.5) Good color does not fade too badly, flower loses form quickly, fair bloomer, susceptible to blackspot. *Cincinnati R.S.* 2(2-2-24"-8) Very good color. *Cleveland R.S.* 4(19-2-30") Small blooms in clusters, disease-resistant, too-few petals. *Columbus R.C.* 2(2-1-26"-6) Nice bloomer, not floppy. *Euclid R.S.* 1(1-1-36"-8) Good color, abundant fragrant bloom, strong growth, opens fast, slight mildew on necks. *Greater Cincinnati R.S.* 2(2-1-24"-7.8) Good color and form, too-few blooms, blackspots. *Lima R.S.* 2(5-1-30"-8.2) Dark green foliage, holds color, blooms freely, disease-resistant. *Miami Valley R.S.* 3(5-1-24"-7.5) Nice dark color holds. *Ohio State University T.G.* (4-2-15"-4) Disease-resistant good foliage, poor vigor, sparse bloom the entire year. *Park of Roses T.G.* (25-2-24"-7.5) Good foliage somewhat resistant to blackspot, holds color fair, individual bloom not outstanding. *Stark R.S.* 1(1-2-24"-). OKLA. *Norman R.S.* 2(13-2-18"-7.6). *Oklahoma R.S.* 3(7-2-36"-9) Free-bloomer, good plant and foliage. ORE. *Eugene R.S.* 3(3-1-24"-8.7) Makes a striking show with excellent foliage, form of bud and bloom mediocre. *International Rose T.G.* (30-4-36"-7) Very interesting color, foliage contrast good, hangs on, not much flower form. *Medford R.S.* 2(2-1-26"-7.8) Holds color well, disease-resistant foliage. *Salem R.S.* 1(2-1-36"-8) Large bush, excellent color, flowers open fast, a good display. PA. *Breeze Hill T.G.* (3-4-26"-9) Clear color, profuse, nice sprays and foliage. *Harrisburg R.S.* 1(300-1-36"-7.4) Nice sprays, long-lasting buds, retains color, free from blackspot. *Philadelphia R.S.* 2(3-1-18"-7.5) Good color at start but fades, not enough bloom. *Pittsburgh R.S.* 2(14-1-24"-5.3) Not very attractive bush, blackspots. S.C. *Edisto T.G.* (12-2-48"-7) Good color, bud form and foliage, vigorous, not enough flowers. TENN. *Nashville R.S.* 5(12-2-7.9) Healthy, vigorous, unfading color, slow-bloomer, doesn't shed spent bloom. TEX. *Amarillo R.S.* 2(2-1-24"-7) Good foliage, strong stem, good color, some fading. *Corpus Christi R.S.* 1(1-1-36"-9.2) Many large full blooms, strong stems, good foliage, needs fragrance. *Dallas R.S.* 2(3-2-28"-8.5) Good color, very resistant glossy foliage, fades some. *El Paso R.S.* 2(2-1-30"-6.2) Strong healthy foliage and stems, holds well in bud stage, retains color in hot sun, blooms too open and not enough. UTAH *Utah R.S.* 5(30-2-26"-6) Clear color fades, doesn't drop spent blooms. VA. *Eastern Shore R.S.* 1(1-1-30"-8.5) Lovely unfading color, disease-resistant, compact well-shaped bush. *Va. Peninsula R.S.* 1(1-1-24"-5.5) Below-average growth, not many blooms. WASH. *Spokane R.S.* 2(11-2-20"-8) Opens too soon. WIS. *Madison R.S.* 1(2-1-23"-9) Excellent pure color, disease-resistant foliage, well-shaped flower. *Milwaukee R.S.* 1(1-1-36"-7.5) Good color, continuous bloom, very nice foliage, blooms fade slightly. CANADA (British Columbia) *University of B.C. T.G.* (1-2-19"-7) Good color, Grandiflora fades to creamy-yellow, low spreading habit, no mildew, resistance. *Vancouver R.S.* 2(3-2-42"-7) Good foliage, bush and color, sparse-bloomer, loose-petalled. (Nova Scotia) *Buchanan* 3(1-20"-8) Good growth, good deep color, fairly large trusses, not continuous, no faults.

## GOLDEN FLEECE F. Light yellow. (Boerner; int. Jackson & Perkins '55) Pat. 1512; ARA '56; PP 3, 90 Rpts.; Av. ht. 28"; NR 7.1.

ARIZ. *Phoenix R.S.* 3(3-1-20"-6.8) Pale blooms, very little growth. CALIF. *Rose Study Club Oakland* 2(7-3-48"-8.4) Vigorous bushy plants, quite disease-resistant, blooms in graceful clusters, repeats slowly, good for mass planting. *San Diego R.S.* 1(2-3-36"-8) Prolific, large blooms. CONN. *Elizabeth Park T.G.* (9-2-24"-8) Very good plant, slight fragrance. D.C. *Potomac R.S.* 1(1-1-36"-7.9) Size and color of bloom outstanding, not enough bloom. GA. *Georgia R.S.* 2(3-3-36"-6.3) Pretty new color, too few blooms fade quickly, not for our heat. ILL. *Chicago R.S. Reg. 1* (30"-9)

Prolific blooms of good form, attractive shade, disease-resistant, bushy plant. *Greater Peoria R.S.* 1(1-1-24″-5) Well-formed blooms, good color, failed to grow very tall. IND. *Indianapolis R.S.* 1(2-3-18″-7) Good buds, blooms fade and drop soon, not enough blooms for a Floribunda, not much blackspot. *St. Joseph Valley R.S.* 2(2-5-48″-7.9) Good disease-resistant foliage, prolific blooms. IOWA *Des Moines R.S.* 2(3-2-20″-6) Not enough bloom. *Linn County R.S.* 1(3-2-26″-7.5) Good color holds well, no faults. KAN. *Wichita R.S.* 1(1-1-24″-6) Lots of bloom, disease-resistant, small plant, weak necks. MD. *Maryland R.S.* 2(3-30″-7) Weak color, lots of bloom with no form. MICH. *Detroit R.S.* 3(3-2-24″-7) Good color, not for show, weak stem, blackspots. *Greater Lansing R.S.* 2(2-2-30″-7.5) Gardenia-shaped bloom with shading of coral at times, mildew-resistant foliage. *Michigan State University T.G.* (6-4-21″-5) Good petal shape, slight (cold cream) fragrance, color fades, fairly susceptible to blackspot, weak stems. MINN. *Lyndale Park T.G.* (20-5-24″-7) Hardy, good bloomer, disease-free. *Minnesota R.S.* Soft color, not vigorous or winter-hardy. MO. *Rosarians Midland Empire* 1(3-3-30″-8) Good color, petals drop clean, good foliage. NEW ENGLAND *New England R.S.* 3(12-2-26″-7.3) N.H.—Doesn't produce; R.I.—Does well. N.J. *North Jersey R.S.* 9(18-2-27″-7.5) Good color only exceptional feature. N.Y. *Cornell University T.G.* (5-2-25″-8.5) Excellent well-branched habit, good foliage, floriferous all season, nice bud, good flower form, flowers fade in midsummer heat. *Humboldt Park T.G.* (25-4-30″-9.9) Most outstanding yellow Floribunda, always in bloom, bushy plants, dark green leathery foliage is very resistant to disease, need afternoon shade, no faults. *Rochester R.S.* 4(54-3-24″-7) Blooms do not hold well, good color, blackspots quickly. *Schenectady R.S.* 1(1-2-23″-7.5) Free-bloomer, fast blackspotter. *Syracuse R.S.* 3(6-3-28″-7.8) Fine color, good disease-resistant foliage, quite prolific, beautiful bud, fine growth habit. N.C. *Randolph R.S.* 1(1-4-36″-7) Beautiful buds, nice foliage. OHIO *Akron R.S.* 1(2-1-15″-3). *Cincinnati R.S.* 3(6-2-30″-7.5) Very good color if given some shade. *Cleveland R.S.* 1(5-3-24″-7) Nice blooms. *Park of Roses T.G.* (100-3-24″-6) Not vigorous. *Stark R.S.* 1(1-1-30″-8) Not enough bloom. OKLA. *Norman R.S.* 1(5-2-36″-8) Beautiful bloom. ORE. *Eugene R.S.* 3(3-2-36″-7.5) Good grower, open loose bloom, color not clear. *International Rose T.G.* (20-4-36″-7) Clean large blossoms and foliage, off-shade color. *Lewis & Clark T.G.* (11-1-36″-5) Sturdy bush, strong shiny foliage, soft blooms. *Salem R.S.* 1(23-2-30″-9) Free blooming, good color, no disease. PA. *Breeze Hill T.G.* (6-5-28″-8) Profuse nice sprays, very good foliage. *Philadelphia R.S.* 3(6-2-32″-8) Good production, disease-resistant, too few petals. *Pittsburgh R.S.* 1(2-2-12″-6). TENN. *Nashville R.S.* 1(2-3-26″-7) Good plants not vigorous enough. TEX. *Dallas R.S.* 1(1-2-28″-8) Abundant color bloom. UTAH *Utah R.S.* 2(5-3-30″-6) Pale blooms, attractive in bud but not when open. WASH. *Spokane R.S.* 2(2-1-24″-5) Nice very pale flowers, poor form. *Walla Walla R.S.* 2(6-3-30″-8) Light long-lasting bloom. WIS. *Madison R.S.* 2(2-2-52″-6.5) Good color, blackspots easily, not vigorous, not enough bloom. *Milwaukee R..S* 1(1-1-18″-7) Lovely translucent color, lacks vigor. CANADA (British Columbia) *University of B.C. T.G.* (3-2-26″-7) Flowers fade little, light fragrance, only slightly affected by mildew.

## GOLDEN MASTERPIECE HT. Medium yellow. (Boerner; int. Jackson & Perkins '54) Pat. 1284; ARA '54; PP 4, 340 Rpts.; Av. ht. 41″; NR 7.0.

ARIZ. *Mesa R.S.* 4(5-2-36″-7.1) Beautiful buds, not many blooms, sturdy bush, good basal breaks and foliage, opens too fast to large unshapely flower which fades badly. *Phoenix R.S.* 5(5-3-36″-7) Excellent Spring to Fall, large blooms, long stems, not enough good bloom during heat. CALIF. *Memorial T.G.* (12-5-36″-6) 5″ blooms, long stems, petals have good texture, slight fragrance, not a free-bloomer, slow grower. *Rose Study Club Oakland* 2(8-4-60″-6.5) Tall spindly plant, slow-grower, glossy foliage, large pale bloom has poor open form, sparse bloomer. *Pacific R.S.* 2(2-2-36″-7.5) Excellent foliage, straight long stems, holds color well, exhibition variety. *San Diego R.S.* 4(13-3-60″-7.1) Good bush, very fine foliage, poor blooms. *San Joaquin R.S.* 4(5-2-36″-6.5) Sparse bloom, glossy foliage, vigorous plant. *San Mateo County R.S.* 1(1-2-42″-8) Good buds and color, disease-resistant foliage, very sparse bloomer. COLO. *Denver R.S.* 5(25-5-40″-6) Excellent foliage, vigorous, good in late season, lacks substance, leggy, subject to blackspot. D.C. *Potomac R.S.* 5(8-3-42″-7.1) Huge deep yellow blooms on compact plant, waxy, non-resistant foliage, occasional show bloom. GA. *Georgia R.S.* 10(14-3-52″-7.2) Good foliage, gorgeous in shade, huge lovely bloom, nice bud form, better than Mandalay, exhibition variety, good seed parent, not consistent. ILL. *Chicago R.S. Reg. 1* 3(4-2-52″-5.5) Fine bloom, weak neck, foliage subject to blackspot. *Greater Peoria R.S.* 6(5-2-22″-6.5) Good color, too-few petals, blooms too quickly, poor bloomer. *Morgan Park R.S.* 2(4-2-24″-6) Weak bloomer, fades early. *Tri-City Men's Rose and Garden Club* 2(25-4-24″-). IND. *Indianapolis R.S.* 7(11-2-36″-5.6) Good color, large blooms but too few, lacks vigor. *St. Joseph Valley R.S.* 2(7-3-48″-7) Long stems, single bud, good foliage, bloom doesn't last long, good color. *Vincennes R.S.* 2(3-1-48″-6) Profuse, no substance. IOWA *Des Moines R.S.* 8(8-3-30″-7) Good color, few blooms. *Iowa R.S.* 1(2-3-48″-8) Good color, vigorous plant. *Linn County R.S.* 4(4-2-30″-7) Large flower does not hold up, blackspots. KAN. *Wichita R.S.* 2(2-2-42″-7) Good form and color. KY. *Frankfort Chapter ARS* 3(10-4-36″-6) Blackspots easily, not enough bloom, flower opens too fast. *Kentucky R.S.* 4(7-3-42″-7.5) Lovely large bloom, long stem, healthy foliage, not enough blooms. good buds. *Lexington R.S.* 2(2-4-36″-7) Large beautiful blooms and buds, nice foliage, grand color, slow grower. *Louisville Chapter ARS* 12(24-2-33″-6.5) Good form and color, too few large blooms, slow grower, fades fast. LA. *New Orleans R.S.* 2(3-2-60″-8) Large beautiful sparse blooms open fast, bright green foliage. MD. *Maryland R.S.* 2(3-2-52″-7) Very large blooms of good deep color, plenty of blackspot. MICH. *Detroit R.S.* 5(7-2-33″-7.3) Opens too fast, not enough blooms. *Greater Lansing R.S.* 2(2-3-36″-7.5) Beautiful buds and flowers, large foliage, blackspots. *Kalamazoo R.S.* 9(12-2-36″-7) Color holds well, good foliage. *West Michigan Rosarians* 1(2-1-36″-7) Good upright bush, large bloom opens and fades too quickly, weak neck, blackspots easily. MINN. *Lyndale Park T.G.* (35-5-40″-7) Big blooms, not too hardy, blackspots. *Minnesota R.S.* 18(29-2-38″-7.2) Long-tapered bud, good loose bloom, large glossy foliage, weak necks. KAN. *Kansas City R.S.* 3(6-2-40″-8) Beautiful well-formed blooms, some blackspot. MO. *Rosarians Midland Empire* 3(10-3-40″-7) Good color, large bloom opens fast. *R.S. Greater St. Louis* 2(2-2-42″-6) Few large blooms. *Sedalia R.S.* 2(2-2-32″-7) Bloom opens too quickly and fades, fair plant. MONT. *Sunset Park T.G.* (20-3-30″-7) Sunfast lovely buds and very large loose blooms have too many split centers. NEV. *Reno R.S.* 3(12-2-40″-8) Good bright buds open slowly, color fades in sun, no mildew, good grower. NEW ENGLAND *New England R.S.* 6(10-3-38″-6.5) Good bloom when and if. N.J. *North Jersey R.S.* 13(23-3-42″-7.3) Erratic awkward growth, fine color and form. *West Jersey R.S.* 5(10-3-48″-7.8) Vigorous plant, large well-tormed flowers, unfading color holds in hot weather, could bloom more. N.M. *Albuquerque R.S.* 7(10-2-40″-8.2) Large well-formed clear buds, sturdy plant with excellent substance and foliage, always in bloom, unsatisfactory Spring bloom opens floppy. N.Y. *Cornell University T.G.* (10-4-20″-6.5) Clear large flower, good bud and opening, not vigorous, flowers fade badly in Summer heat, not disease-resistant, weak necks. *Humboldt Park T.G.* (55-5-36″-8) Upright growth, glossy waxy light green foliage, no diseases, large bloom, long pointed buds, very long stems, free-blooming, spindly plants, blooms hang on, weak necks, ragged-looking bloom. *Long Island R.S.* 2(2-3-42″-8) Good color and form, vigorous grower. *Niagara Frontier R.S.* 5(11-3-28″-5.9) May be a little gold here, but it is far from a masterpiece. *Rochester R.S.* 9(109-3-48″-7) Color fades in hot sun, wilts quickly, good foliage. *Schenectady R.S.* 7(12-2-36″-7) Beautiful flowers, not enough blooms, weak necks, beautiful foliage, no blackspot or mildew. *Syracuse R.S.* 6(11-3-39″-7.2) Decrease in vigor, good color, opens quickly, does not send up enough new growth, subject to blackspot. N.C. *Durham R.S.* 4(13-2-54″-8.2) Beautiful color, nice green foliage, sparse bloomer. *Randolph R.S.* 2(5-4-60″-7) Beautiful buds and bloom, nice but scant foliage, long stems. OHIO *Akron R.S.* 4(14-3-42″-7.5) Well-formed buds and bloom, good large bloom, blackspots. *Central Ohio R.S.* 5(10-3-36″-6) Nice bud, non-fading flower opens well and loses form, fairly-vigorous bush, shy bloomer, susceptible to blackspot. *Cincinnati R.S.* 2(10-2-48″-7). *Cleveland R.S.* 2(3-3-23″-3). *Columbus R.C.* 2(2-3-24″-5.5) Good color, shy on bloom, fades. *Greater Cincinnati R.S.* 2(5-1-42″-8) Prolific bloomer, lovely buds, open flower, no blackspot. *Lancaster R.C.* 8(11-1-42″-8) Vigorous, upright, good color, poor bloomer, blackspots. *Lima R.S.* 6(9-3-42″-7) Beautiful large well-formed blooms, clear color, good bloom and foliage, blooms too scarce. *Miami Valley R.S.* 4(6-2-36″-7.5) Large bright blooms fade, weak stems. *Ohio State University T.G.* (4-3-33″-7) Excellent abundant foliage, vigorous plant, fragrant, weak flower stems, sparse to medium blooms. *Park of Roses T.G.* (100-3-33″-6.5) High-centered good bloom, poor blackspot resistance. *Stark R.S.* 3(3-2-36″-7.2) Holds its color. OKLA. *Norman R.S.* 3(25-3-50″-8). *Oklahoma R.S.* 4(9-2-48″-8) Beautiful bloom, not plentiful. ORE. *International Rose T.G.* (40-5-72″-7) Clear massive flower, good in warm dry weather. *Lewis & Clark T.G.* (23-3-60″-10) Clean color, many buds on strong plant, repeats. *Medford R.S.* 6(6-2-47″-7.5) Healthy, tall, vigorous bush, glossy foliage, large blooms of good color fade in sun, not enough bloom, some weak stems. *Salem R.S.* 3(29-3-49″-5.6) Strong grower, lacks substance, balls. PA. *Breeze Hill T.G.* (9-6-34″-8) Unfading large flowers, vigorous. *Harrisburg R.S.* 4(1005-2-46″-7.5) Husky grower, sparse bloom, good show rose, strong neck, fades quickly in hot weather, excellent buds, blooms floppy sometimes. *Philadelphia R.S.* 6(7-3-40″-5) Few large blooms of good color on sparse plant, matures poorly. *Pittsburgh R.S.* 2(25-3-36″-7.3)

Blooms not large. *S.C. Edisto T.G.* (12-5-48″-7.5) Good grower, substance, form and color, excellent in Spring and Fall, poor in Summer, some blackspot. TENN. *Nashville R.S.* 3(14-2-30″-7) Sturdy, upright buds of excellent form, not enough bloom. TEX. *Amarillo R.S.* 3(2-2-8) Good substance, color, foliage, bud and flower form, not a continuous bloomer, some blackspot. *Corpus Christi R.S.* 2(4-3-36″-9) Excellent exhibition, color holds, long strong stems, no foliage problems. *Dallas R.S.* 4(10-3-42″-6.5) Good color, huge blooms, waxy foliage, blackspots badly. *El Paso R.S.* 4(5-3-46″-8.5) Vigorous healthy foliage and stems, fades a little in heat, large double blooms, grows better with age, slight fragrance, not enough blooms, grows slowly. UTAH *Utah R.S.* 5(8-3-32″-7.6) Fine blooms hold color, could be bushier and bloom more. VA. *Eastern Shore R.S.* 3(4-2-32″-8) Good healthy plant, will stand dry weather, large well-formed bud, good petal texture, nice in arrangements, strong stems, exhibition-type blooms, holds color well, leggy branches easily broken by wind, subject to blackspot. *Va. Peninsula R.S.* 1(2-1-72″-7) Strong healthy plant, well-formed blooms, holds color well. WASH. *Spokane R.S.* 6(13-3-36″-5) Lovely buds, large flower, likes cool weather. *Walla Walla R.S.* 2(2-3-54″-7) Beautiful buds, long stems, good foliage, not enough bloom. W.VA. *Charleston R.S.* 1(2-2-24″-8) Good upright bush with beautiful blooms. WIS. *Madison R.S.* 3(4-2-36″-7.1) Good color and foliage, vigorous grower, hardy, good form and substance, too-few blooms. *Milwaukee R.S.* 5(6-2-53″-7.3) Tall bush, fine color, blooms one to the stem, good deep green foliage, well-formed buds, poor open flower form. CANADA (British Columbia) *University of B.C. T.G.* (4-2-29″-7) Flowers fade to creamy-yellow sparse-flowering, light fragrance, no mildew resistance. *Vancouver R.S.* 1(2-3-48″-9) Rich unfading color. (Nova Scotia) *Buchanan* (4-4-36″-7) Good color, fragrant, lasts well when cut, not enough bloom.

# GOLDEN SHOWERS C1. Golden-yellow. (Lammerts; int. Germain's '56) Pat. 1557; ARA '57; PP. 2, 260 Rpts.; Av. ht. 7'; NR 7.4.

ALA. *Twickenham R.S.* 2(2-2-4½'-7.5) Beautiful color, free-bloomer, short bloom life. ARIZ. *Mesa R.S.* 1(1-1-4½'-7.2) Rather weak, slender branches, good color in bud, opens too fast. *Phoenix R.S.* 8(8-2-6'-6.8) There are better yellow Climbers and Pillars than this, nice bud, blooms perish quickly, spindly growth. CALIF. *Memorial T.G.* (6-3-10'-9) Free-bloomer, vigorous, slight mildew and fragrance. *Rose Study Club Oakland* 1(1-2-7'-6) Good foliage, bud form and color, opens too fast, burns in heat. *Pacific R.S.* 4(10-2-8'-8.1) Exceptionally clean, well-balanced disease-resistant foliage, heavy Spring bloom of show calibre, some bloom rest of year, long straight stems. *Peninsula R.S.* 2(2-2-7'-6) Good free-blooming Pillar, non-fading, disease–free. *San Diego R.S.* 4(4-2-8'-6.9) Blooms open and fall too quickly. *San Joaquin Valley R.S.* 4(6-2-6'-7.5) Vigorous, shiny, disease-resistant foliage, repeat blooms. *San Mateo County R.S.* 6(7-3-6'-6) Beautiful easily-kept disease-resistant foliage, steady bloomer, flowers fade and last but a day, old petals hold on. COLO. *Denver R.S.* 2(2-1-2½'-6) Fades in sunlight, blooms do not last, sturdy canes, good foliage. D.C. *Potomac R.S.* 3(5-3-7'-7.9) Beautiful Hybrid Tea-type bloom on vigorous Pillar-type Climber, rich color holds well, abundant bloomer. GA. *Georgia R.S.* 6(8-2-7½'-7.4) Glossy disease-resistant foliage, excellent Pillar rose, good deep color holds well in heat, poor form, best for playground or landscape use, blooms open too quickly, sets hits. ILL. *Chicago R.S. Reg. 1* 4(8-1-4½'-7.5) Fine healthy foliage, unfading color. *Greater Peoria R.S.* 3(5-2-7'-7.4) Good color and foliage, blooms consistently, opens fast, fades early. IND. *Indianapolis R.S.* 5(5-2-8'-7.7) Ideal Pillar, good color, excellent foliage, few thorns, disease-resistant, opens very rapidly, fades fast and shatters. *St. Joseph Valley R.S.* 1(1-2-6'-7.1) Beautiful color, freezes back, needs winter protection. *Vincennes R.S.* 1(1-2-4'-5). IOWA *Des Moines R.S.* 7(7-2-4'-7.5) Good color does not last, not enough bloom. *Iowa R.S.* 4(4-2-3½'-6) Poor growth, few blooms. *Linn County R.S.* 2(2-2-7'-7.5) Bushy Pillar, nice color, blooms repeatedly, waxy foliage, hardy. KY. *Kentucky R.S.* 2(2-2-6'-8) Good color, repeat-bloomer, sparse foliage, not much bloom, weak texture. *Lexington R.S.* 2(2-3-10'-8) Continuous bloom, nice color, opens and fades too fast, good foliage. *Louisville Chapter ARS* 4(4-2-6½'-7.5) Good color and foliage, few blooms, opens fast. MD. *Maryland R.S.* 3(4-2-10'-8.5) Lots of decorative blooms all Summer. MICH. *Detroit R.S.* 5(11-2-6'-7.6) Good foliage, sparse bloom, won't climb. *Greater Lansing R.S.* 2(3-2-8'-7.5) Beautiful foliage, lovely color, rather slow to start but excellent after established. *Kalamazoo R.S.* 4(7-2-6½'-8) Fades, not enough bloom. *West Michigan Rosarians* 1(1-1-8.5) Good Pillar, ever-blooming, nice foliage, blooms don't last. MINN. *Lyndale Park T.G.* (5-3-36″-6) Disease-resistant, sparse bloomer. *Minnesota R.S.* 13(17-2-5'-6.9) Beautiful foliage and buds, flower neither pretty nor lasting. MO. *Rosarians Midland Empire* 1(3-2-7'-6.5) Nice foliage, not enough blooms, too lightly-petalled. *R.S. Greater St. Louis* 5(7-2-8'-7.5) Good pale color fades, not enough repeat bloom, blackspots. *Sedalia R.S.* 3(3-2-5'-8) Beautiful foliage, grows well, opens too quickly and fades. NEW ENGLAND *New England R.S.* 3(7-2-6'-8.5) Freezes nearly to the ground but revives well, disease-resistant, constant bloomer. N.J. *North Jersey R.S.* 15(16-2-6½'-7.9) Repeat-bloomer, beautiful foliage, loses form. *West Jersey R.S.* 3(4-2-8'-8.5) Healthy plant, usually in bloom, sharp unfading color. N.M. *Albuquerque R.S.* 4(4-2-6'-7.9) Lovely bud drops petals cleanly, excellent foliage, opens too quickly and fades rapidly, should have full sun. N.Y. *Cornell University T.G.* (2-3-3'-6) Excellent foliage, nice bud, good color, canes winter-kill, intermittent bloom, plants never really get above tall Hybrid Tea stage. *Humboldt Park T.G.* (4-2-7'-9.9) Branching, very vigorous, abundant dark glossy green foliage, no diseases, long strong stems, drops cleanly, uninjured by Winter, growing more as a Pillar than a Climber, no faults. *Long Island R.S.* 1(1-1-6'-7.5) Doing well in a poor spot, very vigorous, resists diseases, blooms intermittently. *Niagara Frontier R.S.* 4(4-2-5'-6.7) Good foliage, color fades badly, sparse bloomer, petals drop quickly. *Rochester R.S.* 3(4-1-6½'-7.5) Free-blooming, good foliage, fades quickly. *Schenectady R.S.* 6(8-2-5'-8.8) Constant bloomer, very healthy and robust plant, flowering not too abundant but lovely in form and color, canes froze back but recovered. *Syracuse R.S.* 6(7-2-7'-7.6) Outstanding color fades after three or four days, strong canes, disease-resistant, lacks substance, good repeater, excellent foliage. N.C. *Durham R.S.* 2(5-2-9'-8.5) Lovely color, blooms well, pretty foliage, blooms fall clean, single flower. OHIO *Akron R.S.* 3(7-2-6'-8.9) Good clean foliage, little stingy on bloom, repeats good color. *Central Ohio R.S.* 3(6-1-6'-9) Vigorous, upright, healthy plant, prolific bloomer, disease-resistant, blooms fade quickly. *Cleveland R.S.* 2(3-2-6½'-7.3) Healthy plant, good repeat-bloomer, fades rapidly. *Forest City R.S.* 5(8-2-5½'-7.5) Strong-growing plant, good foliage, well-formed buds, freebloomer. *Greater Cincinnati R.S.* 3(3-1-7½'-7.8) Good grower, too tall if anything, nice background rose, poor bloomer, not many petals. *Lancaster R.C.* 1(1-3-7'-7.5) Versatile plant, good blooms, glossy foliage, blackspots. *Lima R.S.* 7(11-2-7½'-8) Nice foliage, good bloomer, fades rapidly. *Miami Valley R.S.* 2(3-2-5'-9) Beautiful color, good foliage, blooms all Summer. *Ohio State University T.G.* (1-3-6) Excellent abundant disease-resistant foliage, plant lacks vigor, sparse bloom. *Park of Roses T.G.* (4-2-7½'-7) Prolific bloomer, good foliage, not vigorous enough. *Stark R.S.* 2(2-2-4'-7.5) Glossy foliage. OKLA. *Norman R.S.* 2(9-2-4'-7.6) Doesn't bloom enough. ORE. *International Rose T.G.* (10-4-12'-8) Long buds, clear color, ample foliage, continuous bloom fades somewhat. *Medford R.S.* 4(4-2-7'-7) Healthy glossy foliage, upright growth, blooms open too fast and fade rapidly. *Salem R.S.* 2(2-2-4½'-7.5) Not as good as High Noon. PA. *Breeze Hill T.G.* (1-6-6'-7) Good foliage, large flowers of beautiful color, slight fragrance, fades. *Harrisburg R.S.* 3(404-2-7½'-8.2) Bright color, shiny foliage, blooms all Summer, well-formed flowers blow quickly. *Philadelphia R.S.* 7(7-2-7'-7.5) Disease-resistant, excellent Pillar, doesn't drop petals cleanly. *Pittsburgh R.S.* 5(5-2-6½'-7.4) Foliage best feature, loosely-formed sparse beautiful blooms (mostly one on each stem) fade quickly in Summer heat, needs Winter protection. S.C. *Edisto T.G.* (3-3-7'-7) Good color in bud stage, free Spring-bloomer, flowers lack substance, fade. TENN. *Nashville R.S.* 5(2-7'-6.8) Healthy, vigorous, heavy bloomer, color fades badly, sets fruit. TEX. *Amarillo R.S.* 2(3-2-6'-7) True to color, good substance, foliage, few well-formed blossoms open too quickly. *Corpus Christi R.S.* 1(3-2-6'-5) Scarce bloomer, weak plant, too hot for it. *Dallas R.S.* 2(4-3-6'-7.7) Good foliage and color, husky plant, prolific, resistant. *El Paso R.S.* 1(1-2-6'-8) Strong healthy foliage and profuse bloom, slightly weak necks, color holds well in heat. UTAH *Utah R.S.* 6(15-2-6'-5.2) Good plant, poor bloom fades badly. VA. *Eastern Shore R.S.* 3(3-2-8'-8) Excellent growth, lovely color, no major faults, some slight fading in afternoon sun, blooms the first season, continuous bloom on new growth. *Va. Peninsula R.S.* 1(1-2-6'-5) Good bloomer, color fades, blackspots. WASH. *Seattle R.S.* 3(2-2-7'-7.1) Blooms all season. *Spokane R.S.* 4(4-2-5½'-5) Beautiful foliage, flowers fade and drop too fast. W.VA. *Charleston R.S.* 2(2-2-7'-7.5) Disease-resistant, lovely foliage, recurrent. *Wyo-Mac R.S.* 3(6-2-5'-8) Good foliage, pretty buds, lasting bloom, bushy plant, strong stems, lovely color. WIS. *Madison R.S.* 1(1-1-5'-8.5) Fair growth, hardy, disease-resistant excellent foliage, sparse-bloomer, good form and substance. *Milwaukee R.S.* 2(3-1-6'-7) Fine color, beautiful foliage, open flowers undistinguished. CANADA (British Columbia) *Vancouver R.S.* 4(7-3-9'-8) Good foliage, blooms don't last, disease-resistant, not a free-bloomer.

## GOLDEN WINGS HT. Light yellow. (Shepherd; int. Bosley '53) Pat. 1419; ARA '53; PP 4, 158 Rpts.; Av. ht. 47"; NR 8.3.

ARIZ. *Mesa R.S.* 1(3-1-6) Will not take heat. *Phoenix R.S.* 2(2-1-36"-8) Vigorous growth, abundant bloom, fragrant, good single Shrub. CONN. *Elizabeth Park T.G.*

(2-1-24″-8) Soft papery petals, interesting stamens after petals drop. ILL. *Chicago R.S. Reg. 1* 5(5-5-2-42″-8.5) Excellent single, prolific bloomer, no disease, winters well. *Greater Peoria R.S.* 1(12-1-54″-7) Blooms often, fades fast. *Morgan Park R.S.* 1(1-2-18″-7.4). IND. *Indianapolis R.S.* 3(4-3-50″-9.2) Single Shrub, always plenty of blooms, winterhardy. *St. Joseph Valley R.S.* 2(2-3-42″-8.7) Constantly in bloom, strong healthy bloomer, lovely fragrance. IOWA *Des Moines R.S.* 4(5-2-36″-8) Vigorous plant, hardy, plenty of bloom, fades. *Iowa R.S.* 3(5-2-42″-8.5) Good plant, lots of bloom. *Linn County R.S.* 1(1-2-30″-9) Good single, vigorous, hardy. KY. *Louisville Chapter ARS* 1(1-2-48″-10) Single, hardy, disease-resistant enough to plant as hedge (give plenty of room). MICH. *Detroit R.S.* 7(11-2-48″-8.6) Free-blooming, disease-resistant, vigorous. *Greater Lansing R.S.* 1(1-2-60″-8.8) Good single, no fragrance, vigorous, good foliage, improves with age. *Kalamazoo R.S.* 1(2-1-42″-7) Like all other single roses it does not hold bloom long enough, good color. *West Michigan Rosarians* 3(4-2-60″-8.5) Scant bloom for size of plant, bloom nice when opening but fades badly. MINN. *Minnesota R.S.* 4(8-2-53″-8.9) Vigorous grower, apple-green foliage, almost constant bloomer. KAN. *Kansas City R.S.* 1(3-2-24″-7) Prolific-bloomer, vigorous-grower, good color. MO. *R.S. Greater St. Louis* 2(5-2-48″-8.5) Good single with recurrent bloom, some blackspot. *Sedalia R.S.* 1(1-2-40″-8) Grows well, large bush, good foliage, not quite enough bloom. MONT. *Sunset Park T.G.* (3-1-36″-9) A Dainty Bess yellow flower on a king-sized plant bursting with vigor, blooms steadily, always looks neat and fresh. NEW ENGLAND *New England R.S.* 4(24-3-60″-9.5). N.J. *North Jersey R.S.* 10(17-1-51″-8.6) Superior single Shrub, many sprays, fine bloomer. *West Jersey R.S.* 2(2-3-54″-8) Strong growing Shrub, always in bloom, fades in sun. N.Y. *Humboldt Park T.G.* (5-2-36″-9) Upright, vigorous, abundant light green leathery foliage, no diseases, open flowers show yellow stamens, continuous blooms fall cleanly, moderate spicy fragrance, blooms are not long-lasting enough, lose color. *Niagara Froniter R.S.* 2(4-3-47″-9). *Rochester R.S.* 2(2-2-48″-9) Outstanding single, good color, free-blooming, disease-resistant. *Schenectady R.S.* 1(3-2-48″-9.5) Bountiful five-petalled beauty, fragrant, pest-resistant, Shrub-sized, tremendously hardy, flowers flop in the rain. *Syracuse R.S.* 3(4-1-36″-7) Disease-resistant, fast grower, very good single bloom drops too quickly. N.C. *Durham R.S.* 1(2-4-60″-9.5) Continuous bloom, disease and cold-resistant, lovely single rose, soft color. OHIO *Akron R.S.* 3(4-2-48″-8.5) Vigorous grower, always in bloom, good color, give it plenty of room. *Central Ohio R.S.* 3(6-1-48″-8). Color holds well and is lovely, very free bloomer, bush is spreading and vigorous, healthy, will blackspot some, very hardy bush. *Cincinnati R.S.* 7(3-14-48″-8) Fine Shrub. *Cleveland R.S.* 5(9-3-48″-8.7) Everblooming, lovely, fairly healthy. *Columbus R.C.* 2(2-2-38″-7.3) Very disease-resistant, beautiful bloom, slow grower. *Euclid R.S.* 2(2-2-52″-7.5) Good growing plant, fine single flowers open and fade too fast, Dainty Bess just as good a single. *Forest City R.S.* 6(9-3-60″-8) Hardy Shrub, prolific, best as specimen plant by itself, will blackspot, bloom not long-lasting. *Greater Cincinnati R.S.* 4(6-1-48″-8.2) Lovely stamens, continuous blooms but too sparse, fades to near white after first day, blackspots. *Lancaster R.C.* 2(2-4-78″-8.5) Good Shrub, disease-resistant, blooms fade in sun. *Lima R.S.* 6(11-3-54″-8.5) Strong grower, free-bloomer, good color, disease-resistant. *Medina County R.S.* 4(5-3-54″-9.4) Fool-proof, repeat-blooming, hardy. *Miami Valley R.S.* 3(3-1-36″-9) Hardy, good color, large blooms, beautiful foliage. *Ohio State University T.G.* (4-2-28″-7) Vigorous plant, abundant foliage, good bloom, disease-resistant, dull green foliage, flowers last a very short time. *Stark R.S.* 5(7-2-44″-8). ORE. *International Rose T.G.* (4-3-60″-9) Singular large attractive flowers, stamens good, recurrence good, fades in hot sun, needs its own spot in the garden. *Medford R.S.* 5(6-1-43″-7.7) Lots of bloom, healthy plant, blooms fade, scraggly growth. *Salem R.S.* 3(3-3-45″-8.7) Disease-free foliage, good grower and bloomer, fades some. PA. *Breeze Hill T.G.* (1-1-30″-9) A lovely single rose, blooms continuously but not many at a time. *Harrisburg R.S.* 1(2-1-36″-8) Beautiful flower, blooms all the time but not in a great number, bloom doesn't last very long. *Philadelphia R.S.* 1(1-5-72″-10) A perfect rose. *Pittsburgh R.S.* 6(30-1-34″-8.6) Beautiful blooms, nicely shaped bush, petals on roses do not last too long, color fades but is still beautiful, good foliage, blooms continuously. TENN. *Nashville R.S.* 3(7-1-36″-7.8) Healthy, vigorous, excellent single yellow bush, fades badly in heat, light-colored foliage. TEX. *Dallas R.S.* 1(1-1-38″-8.5) Very prolific, good foliage, color fades. VA. *Eastern Shore of Va. R.S.* 1(1-1-48″-9) No blackspot, very rapid growth, always in bloom, unusual for arrangements, may need to be restrained if rate of growth continues. *Va. Peninsula R.S.* 1(1-2-42″-8) Hardy rapid grower, free-blooming, good color, blooms lack lasting quality, color fades in Summer, will blackspot. WASH. *Spokane R.S.* 4(4-1-42″-5) Mild fragrance. W.VA. *Charleston R.S.* 1(1-2-30″-7). WIS. *Madison R.S.* 3(3-1-67″-8.2) Good growth, color and foliage, disease-resistant, excellent Shrub. *Milwaukee R.S.* 1(1-2-52″-10) Continuous bloom, very hardy, no faults.

**GRAND'MERE JENNY HT.** Yellow blend. (Meilland; int. Conard-Pyle '55) Pat. 1148 ARA '50; PP 4, 185 Rpts.; Av. ht. 36"; NR 7.3.

ALA. *Twickenham R.S.* 1(1-3-28"-6) Lacks vigor. ARIZ. *Mesa R.S.* 1(1-2-41"-8.5) Wonderful bloom, bushy vigorous upright disease-resistant plant. *Phoenix R.S.* 2(2-2-45"-8) Lots of beautiful blooms, sturdy growth, fragrant. CALIF. *Rose Study Club Oakland* 1(3-5-48"-7.3) Good blooms in cool weather don't last long, weak plant for such large flowers, not in class of its parent Peace. *Peninsula R.S.* 1(1-2-48"-8) Vigorous plant, disease-free leathery foliage, excellent color. *San Diego R.S.* 3(6-3-24"-6.5). *San Ioaquin Valley R.S.* (1-1-36"-6.5) Unique color, insufficient size and vigor. *San Mateo County R.S.* 1(4-2-30"-6) Attractive blooms, freely-produced strong stems, nice buds, slow grower, blooms fade quickly. COLO. *Colorado Springs R.S.* 1(6-3-36"-7) Nice small Peace, weak plant. *Denver R.S.* 3(7-3-30"-7) Good in Spring only, heavy bloomer, excellent plant habits, quick breaker. CONN. *Elizabeth Park T.G.* (10-3-30"-8) Excellent plant, no buds or blooms after June. D.C. *Potomac R.S.* 7(13-3-60"-7.9) More colorful and shapely bloom than Peace, disease-resistant foliage, vigorous bush, good Spring exhibition rose, thin in Summer. GA. *Georgia R.S.* 4(4-3-60"-6) Quick with new growth, beautiful color, too few blossoms, not for our heat or the beginner, poor imitation of parent Peace. ILL. *Chicago R.S. Reg. 1* 1(1-1-30"-9) Free-bloomer, healthy plant. *Greater Peoria R.S.* 1(1-1-26"-7.6) Beautiful bloom, a little like a small Peace, good disease-resistant foliage. *Tri-City Men's Rose and Garden Club* 2(4-3-36"-6.5) Shy bloomer, small Peace. IND. *St. Joseph Valley R.S.* 1(1-3-30"-7) Large blooms, but not enough. *Vincennes R.S.* 5(2-19-36"-8) Good exhibition-type bloom better in Spring, needs protection in Winter, mildews and blackspots. IOWA *Des Moines R.S.* 2(2-3-30"-7) Good color, few blooms. *Iowa R.S.* 1(1-3-36"-7) Too-few blooms. *Linn County R.S.* 2(3-2-30"-7.2) Nice coloration, attractive foliage, fairly vigorous. KAN. *Wichita R.S.* 1(1-2-18"-7.5) Not enough blooms. KY. *Frankfort Chapter ARS* 2(6-3-48"-7) Good color, excellent foliage, floppy but delicate bloom. *Louisville Chapter ARS* 1(1-4-36"-8) Good foliage and color, small Peace. LA. *New Orleans R.S.* 4(7-2-42"-7) Good blooms in Spring and Fall, not good in heat, blackspots. MD. *Maryland R.S.* 2(2-3-42"-7) Exceptionally good in Spring. MICH. *Detroit R.S.* 1(1-2-36"-8) Nice foliage, long stems, good color. *Kalamazoo R.S.* 3(3-36"-7) Good bloomer, thrifty bush, some disease. MINN. *Minnesota R.S.* 1(1-3-27"-5). MO. *Rosarians Midland Empire* 3(6-3-36"-7.3) Prefer Peace. *R.S. Greater St. Louis* 2(2-2- ) Weak bush. *Sedalia R.S.* 2(2-3-24"-5). NEV. *Reno R.S.* 2(6-2-30"-5) Lots of bloom on strong stems, nice buds, blooms fade in one day. NEW ENGLAND *New England R.S.* 4(10-3-42"-7.5) Fine bud but poor flower. N.J. *North Jersey R.S.* 10(16-2-24"-6.8) Not vigorous, color not dependable. *West Jersey R.S.* 4(6-2-42"-7.8) Good grower, nice form bloom, could have more of them, some blackspot. N.M. *Albuquerque R.S.* 3(4-2-31"-7.4) Fine color and bud form, strong plant, best bloom in Spring and Fall, color fades in hot sun. N.Y. *Cornell University T.G.* (2-3-25"-7.8) Excellent foliage, beautiful bud, best in cool weather, worst in hot Summers, not too vigorous. *Humboldt Park T.G.* (6-3-24"-7) Blooms freely, double flowers on long strong stems hang on and flop as soon as open, foliage not of best quality. *Long Island R.S.* 1(1-1-42"-8.2) Starts blooming early and continually, exquisite color. *Niagara Frontier R.S.* 1(1-4-34"-8) Subject to blackspot. *Rochester R.S.* 2(2-1-24"-7) Sparse-bloomer, slowgrower, good color. *Schenectady R.S.* 2(4-3-32"-8) Flowers last well both on the bush and for cutting, slight fragrance, good foliage. *Syracuse R.S.* 3(3-3-40"-7.2) Productive growth, good color, lacks substance to hold when open, not enough bloom, good exhibition rose. N.C. *Durham R.S.* 4(8-2-54"-8) More delicate than Peace, good form and foliage, blackspots. OHIO *Akron R.S.* 2(3-4-24"-6.5) Good color, exhibition-type, blackspots, stingy bloomer. *Central Ohio R.S.* 3(5-3-36"-7) Blackspots easily, nice form and foliage, lovely color, not a free-bloomer. *Cleveland R.S.* 1(5-3-48"-8) Robust. *Columbus R.C.* 1(1-2-42"-7) Nice form and foliage, blackspots, not free-flowering. *Forest City R.S.* 4(5-3-30"-7.5) Delicate attractive form and color resembles Peace, rather sparse-bloomer. *Lima R.S.* 2(3-2-30"-8) Good flower and foliage. *Ohio State University T.G.* (3-4-30"-8) Excellent foliage, vigorous, bushy plant, abundant bloom, disease-resistant, little bloom after October. OKLA. *Oklahoma R.S.* 2(6-2-42"-8). ORE. *Eugene R.S.* 3(3-3-30"-7) Scant bloom, color not always good, poor grower, nice buds, form can be good. *International Rose T.G.* (20-5-48"-6) Good color in Spring and Fall, rather loose petals and flowers. *Medford R.S.* 2(5-1-39"-8.5) Beautiful well-formed buds on long stems open into colorful blooms, not affected much by rain, does well in some shade, aphids like it. *Rogue Valley R.S.* 3(4-3-50"-8) Attractive color, good form, disease-resistant, free-bloomer. *Salem R.S.* 4(6-4-32"-8) Free-blooming, showy blooms, good plant and foliage, opens fast. PA. *Breeze Hill T.G.* (3-6-24"-8) Profuse, attractive color, good foliage. *Harrisburg R.S.* 3(503-2-52"-8) Excellent foliage, blooms have good form and substance, good hot weather rose. *Philadelphia R.S.* 8(11-3-38″-7) Good foliage, sparse bloom, flighty, blasts quickly, fades. *Pittsburgh R.S.* 3(18-2-24″-7.6) The shape and color of the shading in the blooms are outstanding, leaves more leathery than Peace. TENN. *Nashville R.S.* 7(14-3-34″-7) Dainty quality bloom, good bud form and color, lacks vigor, blackspots too easily. TEX. *Dallas R.S.* 3(9-4-32″-9.1) Outstanding in every way. *El Paso R.S.* 1(2-1-30″-8.5) Exhibition-type buds, strong healthy foliage, long stems, not too many blooms. UTAH *Utah R.S.* 3(5-2-28″-6.1) Free-bloomer, good cut flower, not as good as Peace. VA. *Eastern Shore R.S.* 1(1-2-36″-8) Outstanding pastel shades blend beautifully. *Va. Peninsula R.S.* 1(1-2-18″-2) Poor grower. WASH. *Seattle R.S.* Blooms open too fast and fade. *Spokane R.S.* 1(1-2-36″-8) Beautiful buds. W.VA. *Charleston R.S.* 1(3-2-36″-5) Exhibition forb, not enough bloom. WIS. *Milwaukee R.S.* 2(3-1-37″-8) Good color blend (more vivid than Peace), scraggly plant, doesn't bloom enough. CANADA (British Columbia) *Vancouver R.S.* 12(15-4-36″-8) A refined Peace, better color, little short on petallage, best in cool weather. (Nova Scotia) *Buchanan* (6-5-40″-9) Splendid bloomer, more free-grower than Peace, clearer color, bushy and branching, doesn't hold form, wonderful sight when in full bloom.

## HANDSOM RED HT. Red blend. (Brownell '54) Pat. 1182; ARA '54; PP 5, 1959, 23 Rpts.; Av. ht. 29″; NR 6.6. Total reports 5 years 86; Av. NR 6.5.

## HENRY FORD HT. Peach-pink. (Howard; int. Howard & Smith '54) Pat. 1218; ARA '54, PP 5, 1959; 73 Rpts.; Av. ht. 38″; NR 6.6. Total reports 5 years 356; Av. NR. 6.2.

## ISOBEL HARKNESS HT. Deep yellow. (Norman; int. Armstrong '57) Pat. 1650; ARA '58; PP 1, 247 Rpts.; Av. ht. 32″; NR 7.3.

ALA. *Twickenham R.S.* 3(4-1-34″-5.3) Beautiful color, poor bloomer, bloom fades. ARIZ. *Mesa R.S.* 3(4-1-42″-8.2) Good bush, blooms, buds and bloomer, holds color. *Phoenix R.S.* 4(5-1-36″-7.5) Good growth and bloom. CALIF. *Memorial T.G.* (12-2-24″-8) Red streak in thick deep yellow petals, moderate fragrance. *Rose Study Club Oakland* Lovely large deep yellow flower on a vigorous free-blooming plant, glossy disease-resistant foliage, holds color well. *Pacific R.S.* 4(7-1-31″-8.7) Lovely buds, color holds well even in heat, heavy bloomer, beautiful glossy foliage, strong sturdy plants. *Peninsula R.S.* 7(7-1-36″-8) Shapely bush with good foliage, non-fading profuse bloom needs more petals. *Riverside R.S.* 6(8-3-36″-7.8) Good strong stock, lovely buds and foliage, not profuse bloomer in heat. *San Diego R.S.* 3(6-2-42″-7.9) Poor keeping quality. *San Joaquin R.S.* 4(9-1-42″-7) Radiant in Spring and Fall, good foliage, exhibition form. *San Mateo County R.S.* 2(4-1-25″-5) Blooms open too fast, plant not too sturdy. COLO. *Denver R.S.* 3(15-2-34″-7.5) Good uniform color, new foliage, flowers last well, form only fair, not enough bloom. D.C. *Potomac R.S.* 4(7-1-42″-7.3) Excellent growing habit, plenty of bloom, deep yellow bud, long stems, some red marking on buds, open flower lacks form. GA. *Georgia R.S.* 6(8-1-36″-7.5) Good color, bud, blooms and foliage, opens too fast and fades in our heat, best in cool weather. ILL. *Chicago R.S. Reg. 1* 3(7-1-33″-7.5) Bloom has good color and form but is rather sparse, healthy plant. *Greater Peoria R.S.* 1(1-1-24″-7.5) Good foliage, excellent blooms, disease-resistant. IND. *Indianapolis R.S.* 1(1-1-15″-6) Very little growth, few blooms, blackspots. IOWA *Des Moines R.S.* 2(2-2-30″-7.5) Good blooms. *Iowa R.S.* 2(3-1-36″-7.1) Not a perfect rose, opens too fast. *Linn County R.S.* 2(2-2-28″-6.5) Nice color and form, opens too fast, sparse bloomer. KAN. *Wichita R.S.* 2(2-1-24″-6.5) Fades, burns badly. KY. *Frankfort Chapter ARS* 7(12-1-28″-5) Blackspots, blooms very soft, no substance. *Louisville Chapter ARS* 4(9-1-31″-7) Good color and form. LA. *New Orleans R.S.* 4(4-1-30″-6) Good true color fades fast, sparse bloom, too-few petals. MD. *Maryland R.S.* 2(3-2-36″-8) Exceptionally-good in Spring, has only decorative blooms in hot weather. MICH. *Detroit R.S.* 5(7-1-30″-6.3) Too loose, opens fast, disease-resistant, fades too soon. *Kalamazoo R.S.* 3(6-2-36″-6.7) Not too vigorous. *Michigan State University T.G.*

(6-2-22″-3.5) Sparse-flowering, somewhat susceptible to blackspot. *West Michigan Rosarians* 1(1-1-48″-9) Beautifully-formed buds, lovely clear color, doesn't fade, prolific bloomer, disease-resistant foliage, too few petals, opens quickly into loose open bloom. MINN. *Lyndale Park T.G.* (25-2-18″-6) Poor bloomer, no vigor. *Minnesota R.S.* 13(16-1-30″-7.5) Good foliage but flower too loose, not enough bloom. MO. *Jewel Park T.G.* (6) Medium bloomer. *Rosarians Midland Empire* 2(4-1-48″-7.5) Nice plant, good bloomer, not enough petals, opens too fast. *R.S. Greater St. Louis* 1(2-2-18″-6) Too-few blooms, not strong plant. *Sedalia R.S.* 2(2-1-20″-6) No plant or foliage, not much bloom. MONT. *Sunset Park T.G.* (12-2-24″-8) A good decorative plant that blooms steadily. NEW ENGLAND *New England R.S.* 5(10-1-30″-7.5) Vt.—very good plant; N.H.—Not vigorous, blackspots easily; Me.—Fragrant, vigorous; R.I.—Good color. N.J. *North Jersey R.S.* 9(17-1-27″-7.2) Fine color, opens fast, blackspots. *West Jersey R.S.* 3(3-2-36″-2) Very nice high centered open bloom, good foliage. N.M. *Albuquerque R.S.* 2(2-1-23″-8.1) Vigorous, healthy, abundant bloom, good color and form, shapely bush, fades. N.Y. *Cornell University T.G.* (7-2-30″-6.5) Good color and form until flower half-open, not too winter-hardy, susceptible to blackspot, flowers fade almost white in Summer and become practically single. *Greater Buffalo R.S.* 3(6-1-36″-7) Long stems, good foliage, not enough for exhibition, some mildew. *Humboldt Park T.G.* (9-2-30″-9.9) Upright, very vigorous plant, abundant large dark leathery green disease-resistant foliage, large globular golden-yellow buds, high-centered double bloom, good lasting quality, drops cleanly, slight spicy fragrance. *Long Island R.S.* 3(3-1-32″-6.9) Excellent bud and bloom, all the usual yellow rose faults. *Niagara Frontier R.S.* 2(2-1-33″-7.5) Needs more petals. *Rochester R.S.* 2(11-2-26″-8) Good color, disease-resistant. *Schenectady R.S.* 1(2-1-24″-8.5) Nice plant, good bloom. *Syracuse R.S.* 3(3-1-24″-7.7) Upright growth, single blooms, good form and color, excellent foliage. N.C. *Durham R.S.* 4(10-3-36″-7.2) Good clear color, sparse bloom, poor substance. *Randolph R.S.* 2(2-2-36″-7) Good bloomer, many blooms, nice foliage. OHIO *Akron R.S.* 4(4-2-32″-6.7) Good non-fading color and foliage, poor grower, not for exhibition. *Central Ohio R.S.* 6(13-1-40″-8) Good color does not fade too fast, good bud, nice flower opens and loses form too fast, vigorous bush, not for exhibition, susceptible to blackspot and mildew. *Cincinnati R.S.* 4(11-1-33″-7.5) Good color, exhibition-type, can't take the heat, blackspots. *Cleveland R.S.* 3(6-2-35″-6.5) Nice large blooms, good color and cut flower, opens fast. *Columbus R.C.* 4(7-1-36″-7.5) Healthy, no form, opens too fast, nice color. *Euclid R.S.* 1(1-1-30″-7.8) Good form and color. *Greater Cincinnati R.S.* 2(4-1-36″-8.5) Opens rapidly to single. *Lancaster R.S.* 1(2-1-30″-7.5) Weak grower, sparse bloomer. *Lima R.S.* 3(4-1-26″-8) Good deep color, free-bloomer, flowers last long after cutting. *Miami Valley R.S.* 3(5-1-30″-8) Nice bright color, good foliage seems disease-resistant, doesn't hold when cut. *Ohio University T.G.* (4-2-18″-5) Disease-resistant, blooms well in July, poor vigor and foliage, affected by early frosts. OKLA. *Norman R.S.* 2(10-2-24″-7.6). *Oklahoma R.S.* 2(6-1-36″-8) Nice foliage. ORE. *Eugene R.S.* 3(14-2-36″-7) Lacks petals, no exhibition form but good garden rose, holds color, good bloomer. *International Rose T.G.* (18-4-42″-7) Good color bud, ample free-flowering bloom, foliage needs protection against blackspot. *Medford R.S.* 5(10-1-30″-8) Disease-resistant, profuse bloom, good color, not fragrant, opens too rapidly. *Rogue Valley R.S.* 2(4-2-30″-8) Good color, free-blooming, disease-resistant. *Salem R.S.* 3(15-2-33″-8) Good dark glossy foliage, decorative showy stamens. PA. *Breeze Hill T.G.* (2-4-30″-7) Nice form and color, blooms well. *Harrisburg R.S.* 1(300-1-48″-8.5) Abundant bloom excellent for cutting, upright, good foliage, resistant to mildew and blackspot. *Philadelphia R.S.* 3(3-1-28″-7) Vigorous, good color and foliage, loose bloom, shallow center, not enough bloom. *Pittsburgh R.S.* 3(13-1-21″-6.7) Fine delicate shade, fair vigor, sparse bloom, both single and in clusters, good sturdy plant. S.C. *Edisto T.G.* (9-2-24″-6) Good form and color of bud, plant lacks vigor, susceptible to blackspot, few flowers. TENN. *Nashville R.S.* 3(11-1-35″-7.3) Healthy, lots of bloom, good color, disbudding is a chore. TEX. *Amarillo R.S.* 1(1-1-30″-8) Good foliage, strong stems, not enough bloom. *Dallas R.S.* 2(4-1-30″-6.7) Good strong color, fragrant, prolific, buds open too fast. *El Paso R.S.* 3(12-1-36″-9) Constant bloomer, glossy healthy foliage, strong long stems, good substance, disease-resistant, lasts when cut, fades in hot sun, good in our heat. UTAH *Utah R.S.* 7(19-2-31″-6.6) Free-blooming, fades, good bush. VA. *Va. Peninsula R.S.* 1(1-1-36″-7) Good plant and blooms, strong canes, very susceptible to blackspot. WASH. *Seattle R.S.* 2(3-1-32″-8.2) Vigorous grower, good remontance. *Spokane R.S.* 4(16-2-24″-8). W.VA. *Charleston R.S.* 1(1-1-48″-8.5) Good performance, clear yellow blooms do not fade, attractive when full blown. WIS. *Madison R.S.* 2(2-1-31″-8.5) Disease-resistant foliage, long-lasting flower, not vigorous enough, could bloom more. *Milwaukee R.S.* 1(1-1-24″-7.5) Good color and form, sparse bloom, small plant. CANADA (British Columbia) *University of B.C. T.G.* (10-2-44″-8) Clear flowers fade to creamy yellow, bloom 6″ or more in diameter, medium fragrance, vigorous, comparatively disease-resistant. *Vancouver R.S.* 4(7-3-48″-7) Good foliage, bush and color, flowers don't last, not much form. (Nova Scotia) *Buchanan* (3-1-22″-6) Lovely bloom, long shapely buds, excellent color, does not hold form too long, no faults.

## JIMINY CRICKET F. Orange blend. (Boerner; int. Jackson & Perkins '54) Pat. 1346; ARA '55; PP 4, 352 Rpts.; Av. ht. 36"; NR 7.5.

ALA. *Twickenham R.S.* 4(16-2-42"-7.8) Bright cheerful color. ARIZ. *Mesa R.S.* 2(2-2-42"-7.5) Good bush, lovely color, few petals, doesn't last. *Phoenix R.S.* 5(11-3-36"-8.3) Beautiful color, constant bloomer, could have more petallage. CALIF. *Memorial T.G.* (12-5-20"-7) Outstanding orange-pink color, 20 petals, 2" blooms, free-blooming, early mildew and rust, slight fragrance. *Rose Study Club Oakland* 6(12-3-33"-7.3) Attractive tangerine buds and flowers come generously on bushy compact plant, disease-resistant bronzy-green foliage. *Pacific R.S.* 1(1-2-24"-5) Good color, poor bloomer. *Peninsula R.S.* 1(1-3-36"-8) Bright clean flower always in bloom, vigorous, fades. *Riverside R.S.* 7(11-3-30"-7.8) Good strong plant, flowers hold color very well in our hot dry climate, no aphids or mildew. *San Joaquin Valley R.S.* 3(17-3-24"-7) Vigorous, upright plant, excellent color, all-season bloom, one of the best Floribundas. *San Mateo County R.S.* 2(2-1-27"-5) Blooms open too fast and color fades too quickly, mildews badly. COLO. *Denver R.S.* 3(27-4-30"-8.8) Always in bloom, well-shaped bush, excellent foliage, vigorous, does not burn, wonderful color, resistant to mildew. CONN. *Elizabeth Park T.G.* (28-5-24"-8) Good plant. D.C. *Potomac R.S.* 4(3-3-48"-7.2) Bright orange bloom, excellent plant and foliage, not enough bloom, flower opens too fast. GA. *Georgia R.S.* 6(13-4-48"-6.3) Nice compact bush, holds foliage well, blooms open too quickly in heat and color fades too fast, not as good as Spartan in same color class. ILL. *Chicago R.S. Reg. 1* 3(8-3-30"-7.5) Worthwhile plant and blooms. *Greater Peoria R.S.* 5(5-2-32"-7) Good grower, nice form, good color, could bloom more, fades rapidly. *Morgan Park R.S.* 1(1-3-24"-7) Slow developing, poor flowers. IND. *Indianapolis R.S.* 6(16-2-36"-7.5) Bright color, fragrant, buds and blooms have good form, too-few blooms, lack substance. *St. Joseph Valley R.S.* 4(9-2-36"-7.7) Vigorous grower, good foliage. *Vincennes R.S.* 1(2-2-48"-6) Plenty of foliage, no disease, scanty bloom. IOWA *Des Moines R.S.* 7(22-3-30"-8) Prolific bloomer, fades. *Iowa R.S.* 3(4-2-24"-6.4) Small flowers, profuse bloomer. *Linn County R.S.* 4(6-3-28"-8) Vigorous plant, hardy, blooms frequently, dark disease-resistant foliage. KAN. *Wichita R.S.* 4(5-3-42"-8) Blooms well, disease-resistant, prolific grower. KY. *Kentucky R.S.* 4(8-2-7) Blooms all the time, loses leaves immediately after bloom. *Lexington R.S.* 2(3-2-36"-7.2) Nice color, healthy plant, resistant to disease, fades fast. *Louisville Chapter ARS* 12(17-2-40"-7.8) Good color, foliage, constant bloomer, hardy plant, opens fast, fades, little substance. LA. *New Orleans R.S.* 2(4-3-36"-9) Disease-resistant, good bloomer, holds color. MD. *Maryland R.S.* 2(3-4-54"-8) Very prolific, husky bush, good buds, opens too quickly. MICH. *Detroit R.S.* 5(9-2-24"-6.8) Fine foliage, fades fast, not enough breaks. *Kalamazoo R.S.* 5(13-3-40"-7.5) Good bloomer, nice color. *Michigan State University T.G.* (6-5-32"-5.7) Holds color well, slight fragrance, vigorous, not resistant to blackspot. *West Michigan Rosarians* 2(3-2-36"-7) Nice plant, blooms do not last long. MINN. *Lyndale Park T.G.* (35-4-24"-6.8) Very hardy, flowers fade, blackspots. *Minnesota R.S.* 10(31-3-30"-7.7) Rugged plant, strong stems, disease-resistant, petals drop soon. MO. *Jewel Park T.G.* (10) Very good bloomer, no faults. *Rosarians Midland Empire* 1(3-3-8.5). *R.S. Greater St. Louis* 6(10-3-48"-7) Opens too fast, not enough bloom, no disease. *Sedalia R.S.* 9(7-4-33"-7.5) Excellent foliage and plant, intermittent rather than continuous bloomer. MONT. *Sunset Park T.G.* (12-2-20"-8) Hardy, healthy, good constant bloom. NEV. *Reno R.S.* 16(26-4-30"-6) Blooms open very fast, color fades some in the sun, good grower, some mildew. NEW ENGLAND *New England R.S.* 6(16-3-36"-7.5). N.J. *North Jersey R.S.* 15(21-3-40"-8.3) Permanent favorite for color, form, plant. *West Jersey R.S.* 4(6-3-39"-8.1) Strong plant, usually in bloom, holds color well. N.M. *Albuquerque R.S.* 6(12-2-36"-7.9) Brilliant orange flowers continually in bloom, fragrant. N.Y. *Cornell University T.G.* (8-4-28"-7) Good distinctive color, good but sparse foliage, loose open habit, susceptible to blackspot, flower form not too good. *Humboldt Park T.G.* (39-5-36"-8) Abundant medium-sized foliage, coral-pink buds in clusters, medium to small open semi-double blooms drop cleanly, good-lasting quality, blackspots. *Long Island R.S.* 2(3-2-42"-7.5) Large showy bush with plenty of bloom and lovely disease-free foliage, not much better than Fashion. *Niagara Frontier R.S.* 3(3-3-38"-7.6) Good color, constantly in bloom, too fragile. *Rochester R.S.* 4(5-2-36"-7) Excellent foliage, outstanding color, blackspots early, flowers fade, mildews easily. *Schenectady R.S.* 7(9-2-26"-7) Very good color, continuous but not to abundant flowers. *Syracuse R.S.* 7(9-2-32"-7.9) Very hardy, disease-resistant, frequent bloomer, pretty color, best in Fall. N.C. *Durham R.S.* 2(10-3-6) Too vigorous, no substance or form, pretty color, sparse bloomer. *Randolph R.S.* 3(10-3-60"-8) Excellent bloomer, very disease-resistant, good color, blooms last only a short time. OHIO *Akron R.S.* 6(26-42"-8.2) Beautiful foliage, good growth and color, slight mildew. *Central Ohio R.S.* 1(2-2-30"-7) Lots of good-colored bloom, glossy disease-resistant foliage, some blackspot. *Cincinnati R.S.*

12(17-3-36″-7) Nice bloomer. *Cleveland R.S.* 3(10-4-40″-7.4) Always in bloom, good buds, poor lasting quality. *Columbus R.C.* 1(1-2-48″-7) Beautiful bloom, petals fall quickly, does not hold its form. *Euclid R.S.* 1(1-3-42″-7) Not enough bloom. *Forest City R.S.* 5(10-3-42″-7) Better than average bloom, good color, ordinary foliage. *Greater Cincinnati R.S.* 3(3-2-30″-7) Medium bloomer, beautiful buds, blackspots. *Lancaster R.C.* 4(9-3-36″-8) Spreading bushy, continuous bloomer, blackspots. *Lima R.S.* 5(11-2-36″-7.9) Nice bloom, good color, not very vigorous. *Miami Valley R.S.* 5(10-3-42″-8) Good bloom, disease-resistant foliage, *Ohio State University T.G.* (4-5-27″-7) Vigorous, bushy plant, excellent foliage, very abundant bloom in June and July, disease-resistant, fair to poor quality later bloom. *Park of Roses T.G.* (150-4-39″-7.5) Good upright growth habit, prolific bloom, blackspot-susceptible. *Stark R.S.* 3(3-3-35″-7.9). OKLA. *Norman R.S.* 1(2-3-52″-9) Fine plant. ORE. *International Rose T.G.* (40-4-48″-8) Good color, masses of bloom, fragrant. *Lewis & Clark T.G.* (21-3-24″-10) Fast growth, heavy bloom, bright foliage. *Medford R.S.* Unusual bright color, bushy plant, glossy foliage addicted to some mildew, blooms fade. *Rogue Valley R.S.* 3(6-3-30″-8) Outstanding color, symmetrical bush, prolific bloomer, very attractive in garden. *Salem R.S.* 2(3-5-38″-6.5) Beautiful buds, poor open flower. PA. *Breeze Hill T.G.* (6-6-42″-10) Vigorous, profuse, interesting color. *Harrisburg R.S.* 2(503-3-42″-8.2) Wonderful color does not fade, continuous bloomer, good border rose, sometimes clashes with other colors. *Philadelphia R.S.* 4(7-3-45″-8.7) Prolific bloomer, strong plant, spreads, opens fast in heat. *Pittsburgh R.S.* 3(12-3-24″-7.8) Good color, free-blooming, excellent foliage, could have more vigor. S.C. *Edisto T.G.* (30-5-36″-8) Good color, bushy disease-resistant plant, continuous bloom, little shy on bloom quantity. TENN. *Nashville R.S.* 4(9-3-39″-8.1) Healthy, vigorous, good quality and quantity of bloom. TEX. *Amarillo R.S.* 5(3-2-30″-8) Prolific bloomer, hardy, disease-resistant, color clashes. *Corpus Christi R.S.* 3(3-2-24″-6) Mildews. *Dallas R.S.* 4(11-3-36″-6.5) Good foliage, blooms in showy clusters, vigorous, some blackspot. *El Paso R.S.* 4(4-3-38″-8) Strong glossy foliage and stems, beautiful bud, rich color coral, blooms open quickly and are ugly, sparse bloomer during Summer, likes partial shade. UTAH *Utah R.S.* 8(39-3-35″-7.7) Always in bloom, attractive buds, healthy bush, lovely bronze foliage. VA. *Eastern Shore R.S.* 1(1-3-54″-7.5) Lovely unusual color, nice fragrance, sparse bloomer, blackspots. *Va. Peninsula R.S.* 3(3-2-48″-7.2) Good grower, free-blooming, holds color, disease-resistant. WASH. *Spokane R.S.* 5(21-3-30″-8) Brilliant coloring, vigorous, lots of bloom from June until frost. *Walla Walla R.S.* 1(1-4-36″-8) Good color in bud, disease-resistant foliage. W.VA. *Charleston R.S.* 2(1-2-36″-7) Good bloomer, but many better. *Wyo-Mac R.S.* brilliant color, bloomed only twice last year. *Milwaukee R.S.* 2(3-3-42″-7.2) Large bush, 3(5-2-42″-10) Blooms freely, beautiful and colorful blooms, very bushy, nice foliage, bright new color, individual flowers not attractive, flowers fade, poor relative of Spartan. CANADA (British Columbia) *University B.C. T.G.* (4-2-30″-7) Salmon-red flowers with yellow center fade to salmon-pink, prolific bloomer, no mildew-resistance. *Vancouver R.S.* 5(8-4-42″-7.5) Very good color and foliage, not a continuous bloomer.

## JUNE BRIDE Gr. White tinged cream. (Shepherd; int. Bosley '57) ARA '57; PP 2, 159 Rpts.; Av. ht. 49″; NR 7.5.

ARIZ. *Phoenix R.S.* 3(3-2-45″-8) Lovely-shaped bud, vigorous growth, nice for cutting, could use more petals. CALIF. *Pacific R.S.* 1(1-2-48″-7) Foliage and bush form very good, bloom habit average, good fragrance, some blooms exceptional, but not as advertised. *Peninsula R.S.* 1(1-2-72″-8) Profuse bloom, vigorous, bloom too small. *San Diego R.S.* 1(3-1-96″-5) Mildews badly, blooms almost single. *San Joaquin Valley R.S.* 1(1-2-24″-6) Does not bloom enough, not vigorous. COLO. *Denver R.S.* 1(2-1-24″-6) Few blooms have a tendency to ball and not open. D.C. *Potomac R.S.* (48″-7.9) Nice blooms last well. *Georgia R.S.* (6-32-78″-8.2) Tremendous growth, good foliage, cluster-type bloom, flower lasts when cut, small tapered buds, vigorous bush, almost a Climber, shy bloomer. GA. 4(4-2-48″-8.5) Good form, fragrant, slow-opening, long-lasting bloom, large clusters, balls, plant too big for small flower, needs too much disbudding to obtain satisfactory flower. ILL. *Chicago R.S. Reg. 1* 4(7-1-60″-9.5) Beautiful bud and flower, fragrant, steady bloomer, vigorous healthy plant, some blackspot and mildew. *Greater Peoria R.S.* 2(2-1-50″-6.6) Good form, disease-resistant, sparse bloom, not good in rainy season. IND. *Indianapolis R.S.* 3(6-2-45″-7) Good substance in dry weather, cannot stand wet weather, fine bloomer, attractive bud, vigorous growth. *Vincennes R.S.* 2(2-1-36″-7) Very profuse, discolors, frail plant, few blooms. *St. Joseph Valley R.S.* 2(3-1-48″-8.3) Continuous bloomer. IOWA *Des Moines R.S.* 2(3-2-36″-6) Few blooms. *Iowa R.S.* 1(1-3-24″-5) Sparse bloom. *Linn County R.S.* 3(5-2-46″-8) Nice white, vigorous plant, disease-resistant. KAN. *Wichita R.S.* 3(3-2-36″-7.5) Good white, fine form. KY. *Lexington R.S.* 1(1-2-42″-4) Blooms burn in heat, subject to thrips and mildew. *Louisville Chapter ARS* 1(1-1-48″-7.5). MICH. *Detroit R.S.* 8(12-1-60″-7.5) Good growth, disease-resistant, vigorous, good bloom. *Greater Lansing R.S.* 1(1-2-36″-8) Not too double, pointed bud, vigorous disease-resistant foliage. *Kalamazoo R.S.* 5(7-2-54″-7.8) Nice bloom, good bloomer, hardy bush. *West Michigan Rosarians* 3(3-2-66″-8). MINN. *Minnesota R.S.* 8(15-

2-46″-7) Creamy-white, disease-resistant, average bloomer. MO. *Kansas City R.S.*
2(3-60″-8.5) Good bloomer, vigorous grower, glossy foliage. *Sedalia R.S.* 1(1-2-
50″-7.7) Good form, lasts very well, grows too tall to stand alone ( needs support or
pruning). N.C. *Charlotte R.S.* 3(3-1-48″-6) Good strong bush. NEW ENGLAND *New
England R.S.* 3(9-2-50″-8) Tall, fast-growing, few constant flowers. N.J. *North Jersey R.S.*
5(10-2-35″-6.6). N.M. *Albuquerque R.S.* 3(4-1-42″-7.9) Vigorous growth, constantly in bloom, lovely color, good bud form, susceptible to thrip, slow to start. N.Y.
*Greater Buffalo R.S.* 2(2-2-40″-7.5) Balls in wet weather, single-stemmed blooms, average
bush and bloom. *Long Island R.S.* 2(2-1-48″-8) Lovely long-lasting blooms, good foliage,
dislikes hot weather, lacks continuity of bloom. *Niagara Frontier R.S.* 2(3-1-44″-8)
Vigorous growth, excellent foliage, prolific bloom in June, wonderful fragrance, not
many blooms after the first, cream color instead of pure white. *Rochester R.S.* 3(4-2-36″-7.5)
Fine pointed bud, strong grower, disease-resistant. *Syracuse R.S.* 4(6-2-40″-7.8) Form
good, blooms well, disease-resistant, mildews at times, Hybrid Tea-type. N.C. *Durham R.S.*
1(2-2-48″-7) Disappointing hue, pretty open flower, good growth, not as good as other
whites, flower too small. OHIO *Akron R.S.* 2(4-2-50″-6.8) Good form and foliage, sparse
bloomer. *Central Ohio R.S.* 6(8-2-60″-7.5) Lovely bloom holds well on bush or as cut flower,
outstanding shape and fragrance, slow grower, some blackspot, blooms ball easily, not
enough bloom. *Cincinnati R.S.* 5(11-2-42″-8) Good strong plants, lots of bloom, very
good white. *Cleveland R.S.* 5(9-2-60″-7) Fragrant, heavy bloomer, good in arrangements.
*Columbus R.C.* 2(2-2-48″-7) Good form and color, holds well, slow grower, not enough
bloom. *Euclid R.S.* 1(2-2-60″-7.5) Nice plant, good color, too-few blooms and canes.
*Forest City R.S.* 5(7-2-54″-7) Tall grower, free-bloomer, good fragrance, tendency to
bloom in clusters, makes good specimen plant. *Greater Cincinnati R.S.* 5(9-1-48″-8.2)
Perfect clusters creamy-white bloom almost constantly in bloom. *Lancaster R.C.* 1(1-3-84″-
8.5) Vigorous, upright, prolific bloomer, disease-resistant, prefers dry weather. *Lima R.S.*
4(4-2-48″-8.5) Good form, fragrant, show-opening, long-lasting bloom, large clusters,
disease-resistant. *Medina County R.S.* 2(3-2-66″-9) Fine color, resistant to blackspot.
*Miami Valley R.S.* 5(8-2-45″-8) Excellent creamy-white, good grower, bloom and foliage,
some blooms ball. *Ohio State University T.G.* (4-2-33″-8) Vigorous, bushy plant, flowers
well until October, excellent disease-resistant foliage. *Stark R.S.* 3(3-2-56″-7.9) Tall
bush, constant bloom. OKLA. *Norman R.S.* 2(3-2-36″-6). ORE. *Eugene R.S.* 2(2-2-54″-7.2)
Lots of bloom, does not always open well in our climate, good grower. *Salem R.S.*
1(1-2-60″-2) Mildews, balls, poor blooms. PA. *Breeze Hill T.G.* (3-4-36″-8) Attractive bud
form, profuse. *Harrisburg R.S.* 1(20-1-60″-8.4) Good high-centered show rose, leathery
foliage, upright. *Philadelphia R.S.* 1(1-2-5) Won't grow or bloom much. *Pittsburgh R.S.*
1(3-2-24″-9) Very nice clear color, good bud, blooms well in clusters, some fragrance.
TENN. *Nashville R.S.* 6(19-2- ) Healthy, vigorous plant, very free-blooming, fine color,
thrips like it too. TEX. *Amarillo R.S.* 1(1-1-36″-8) Good foliage, strong stems, blooms
profusely. *Corpus Christi R.S.* 1(1-2-24″-6.5) Very sweet blooms, foliage mildews
and turns yellow, very few blooms. *El Paso R.S.* 1(1-2-38″-6) Good buds in
clusters, tall lanky growth, weak necks, very few blooms, green foliage, small stems.
VA. *Va. Peninsula R.S.* 2(2-2-57″-7.5) Good grower, well-formed buds, beautiful creamy-
white color, disease-resistant, not enough blooms. W.VA. *Charleston R.S.* (60″-7) Good
to grow and show, best in Fall. *Wyo-Mac R.S.* 2(4-2-60″-9) Profuse bloomer, good foliage,
an outstanding white for this region. WIS. *Madison R.S.* 3(4-1-56″-7) Good grower,
foliage nothing outstanding, too-few blooms, mildews. *Milwaukee R.S.* 2(2-2-27″-7.7)
Beautifully-shaped bud and bloom, good foliage, not vigorous.

## KONRAD ADENAUER HT. Dark red. (Tantau; int. Jackson & Perkins '55) Pat. 1452; ARA '56; PP 3, 78 Rpts.; Av. ht. 37″; NR 7.5

ALA. *Twickenham R.S.* 1(1-2-30″-6) Blooms sparsely. ARIZ. *Phoenix R.S.* 4(4-1-36″-7.5)
Lots of medium-sized fragrant blooms, short stems. COLO. *Denver R.S.* 1(1-2-18″-7)
Very double high-centered bloom opens slowly, lovely color, sprawly plant, blackspots
badly. CALIF. *Peninsula R.S.* 1(1-3-48″-6)Good color and form, weak stems, sparse
bloom, blind wood. *San Diego R.S.* 1(1-2-37″-6.5) Blooms ball except in very hot
weather. D.C. *Potomac R.S.* 2(3-2-48″-7.4) Good bush and foliage, dark red flower,
fragrant, bud and flower form not outstanding. GA. *Georgia R.S.* 4(6-3-66″-7.9) Excellent color, exhibition-type, disease-resistant, likes heat, balls in wet weather. IOWA
*Des Moines R.S.* 1(1-3-36″-9) Fragrant, good color and foliage. *Iowa R.S.* 1(1-3-60″-9)
Strong grower, not exhibition quality. KAN. *Wichita R.S.* 1(1-2-36″-6.5) Disease-
resistant, double blooms, color fades. KY. *Louisville Chapter ARS* 1(1-3-40″-8)
Exhibition form and substance, vigorous, profuse bloomer, spreading, some double centers,
mildews. MD. *Maryland R.S.* 3(4-2-54″-8) Very large and full, best from late Spring
through Fall. MICH. *Detroit R.S.* 2(3-2-36″-7.8) Disease-resistant, does not fade.
*Kalamazoo R.S.* 2(2-2-30″-6) Balls in cool weather, nice color, many petals, high center,
good form. *Michigan State University T.G.* (5-3-28″-5) Holds color well, long-lasting

bloom, moderate "old-rose" fragrance. MINN. *Lyndale Park T.G.* (35-2-36″-7.8) Good
color, fragrant, blackspots. *Minnesota R.S.* 8(11-2-28″-8) Sturdy bush, medium red
blooms, fragrant. MO. *Sedalia R.S.* 1(1-2-49″-8) Good plant, blooms well, does not stand
our heat or sun (burns and fades). N.J. *North Jersey R.S.* 4(5-3-40″-7.9) Good color,
resistant to blackspot, blues, confused center, fragrant, poor growth. N.Y. *Cornell University T.G.* (5-3-30″-7.5) Excellent foliage, open, not too floriferous.
*Humboldt Park T.G.* (10-3-36″-8.7) Upright, branching, very large full high-
centered blooms with very good lasting quality, long stems, very vigorous plant,
abundant large resistant foliage, very large globular deep dark red bud, double petallage, drop cleanly, delectable fragrance, continuous and abundant flowering, some
balling when weather is warm. *Long Island R.S.* 2(2-3-57″-8.6) Very strong plant,
abundant very fragrant flowers last well in water. *Rochester R.S.* 2(3-1-24″-7.5) Rich
color, very fragrant, balls occasionally. *Schenectady R.S.* 2(2-2-20″-7.7) Very large
fragrant blooms, (sometimes almost too heavy for size of bush), slow growth. N.C.
*Randolph R.S.* 1(1-3-48″-7) Nice disease-resistant foliage. OHIO *Central Ohio R.S.*
2(3-2-28″-7) Good color, does not blue, very fragrant, shy bloomer, blackspots some.
*Lancaster R.C.* 1(1-1-16″-5.6) Spindly plant. *Lima R.S.* 5(10-3-36″-8.3) Good bloomer,
holds its color, vigorous, disease-resistant. *Ohio State University T.G.* (4-4-30″-7) Disease-
resistant, vigorous plant, large leaves, flowers abundantly in June and July, foliage
rather sparse, flowers in Fall on short spur-like growth. *Stark County R.S.* 2(2-2-42″-7.7).
ORE. *International Rose T.G.* (20-4-48″-8) Large pointed buds, many petals, fragrant,
exhibition posibilities, mildews in Fall. *Salem R.S.* 2(5-3-36″-7) Doesn't like the heat,
good early in season, good foliage. PA. *Breeze Hill T.G.* (3-4-28″-7) Very large fragrant
flowers of good color and form, weak stems. TENN. *Nashville R.S.* 2(4-2-44″-7.9)
Healthy, vigorous, fragrant, could bloom more, better in hot weather. TEX. *Amarillo R.S.*
1(1-1-8) Very good plant and bloomer. *El Paso R.S.* 4(4-2-36″-8) Strong healthy
growth, slightly fragrant, full buds, rich color does not fade easily, weak stems,
grows slowly at first, mildews easily. UTAH *Utah R.S.* 1(1-5-20″-5) Wonderful
flowers, but too few. WASH. *Seattle R.S.* 3(8-2-38″-6.8) Large well-shaped blooms, a
warm weather rose, doesn't hold color. W.VA. *Charleston R.S.* 1(3-3-36″-4) Healthy plant,
blooms ball in cool weather. *Wyo-Mac R.S.* 1(1-2-24″-6) Beautiful blooms, short stems,
strong. CANADA (Nova Scotia) *Buchanan* (3-1-35″-8) Good fragrance, red bloom, free-
bloomer, good grower, lovely foliage (sometimes sparse), bushy plant.

## LADY ELGIN HT. Reddish-apricot. (Meilland; int. Conard-Pyle '57) Pat. 1469; ARA '57; PP 2, 231 Rpts.; Av. ht. 41″; NR 7.5.

ALA. *Twickenham R.S.* 1(3-2-36″-8.5) Good show form, distinctive color. ARIZ.
*Mesa R.S.* 2(4-1-54″-7.3) Nice buds and bloom, stingy bloomer. *Phoenix R.S.* 3(4-2-36″-7.8)
Beautiful orange-blend, fragrant, good form and growth, fades some during heat. CALIF.
*Rose Study Club Oakland* 2(4-1-42″-6.9) Beautiful orange-blend coloring, good grower,
blooms well, mildews slightly, needs good root development to do its best. *Pacific R.S.*
2(3-2-42″-8.7) Exhibition form, blooms of unusual color, upright bush, Peace-like foliage,
sparse bloomer, opens fast. *Peninsula R.S.* 9(10-1-60″-8) Vigorous, upright plant, long strong
stem, good color and form, tender foliage mildews. *San Diego R.S.* 2(4-1-45″-7.9)
Wonderful orange color. *San Joaquin Valley R.S.* (48″-7.5) Excellent color, vigorous
plant, exhibition form, steady bloom. *San Mateo County R.S.* 3(5-2-36″-8) Excellent
color and bloom form, vigorous grower, shy bloomer, needs a year to get started, mildews
badly. COLO. *Denver R.S.* 1(10-1-24″-8) Good light pink, high center, has substance,
lasts well when cut, delightful fragrance. D.C. *Potomac R.S.* 5(10-2-60″-8) Beautiful
orange-yellow, exhibition blooms on long cutting canes, vigorous, upright bush, reddish-
green foliage, some blackspot and mildew. GA. *Georgia R.S.* 9(16-1-54″-7.4) Good vigorous
plant, unusual new color, best in cool weather, long stems, sparse Summer bloomer,
tender sensitive foliage blackspots. ILL. *Greater Peoria R.S.* 2(2-1-30″-8) Large blooms,
good foliage and growth, shy on blooms, tends to blackspot. *Tri-City Men's Rose & Garden
Club* 2(3-2-30″-6.8). IND. *Indianapolis R.S.* 2(2-1-40″-7.4) Large bud, nice gold-
orange blooms, vigorous, shy bloomer. *St. Joseph Valley R.S.* 3(7-2-48″-8.6) Sturdy upright plant, excellent color and form, good bud and bloom substance, holds up well when
cut, slightly fragrant. *Vincennes R.S.* 1(3-1-36″-7) Lovely bud, shapely, not enough bloom.
IOWA *Des Moines R.S.* 3(4-2-30″-8) Good color and form, short of bloom. *Iowa R.S.*
1(2-2-36″-8) Good color, few blooms. *Linn County R.S.* 3(4-2-32″-7.6) Vigorous, nice
orange blend. KAN. *Wichita R.S.* 1(1-1-24″-5.9) Fades, poor growth and foliage. KY.
*Kentucky R.S.* 1(3-1-36″-8) Beautiful color, not enough bloom. *Louisville Chapter ARS*
2(2-1-36″-8) Good form, vigorous. LA. *New Orleans R.S.* 1(1-2-24″-4) Long-lasting
bloom, relatively disease-free, poor grower. MD. *Maryland R.S.* 3(7-2-48″-8) Beautiful
blooms on long stems, many canes. MICH. *Detroit R.S.* 6(9-1-36″-7.4) Mildews, good
form and substance, lasting bloom, small foliage. *Kalamazoo R.S.* 5(6-1-36″-7.5) Strong
canes. *West Michigan Rosarians* 2(7-2-36″-6.5) Beautiful blooms, mildews badly. MINN.
*Minnesota R.S.* 6(7-2-39″-7.4) Beautiful color and quality bloom, susceptible to mildew
and blackspot. MO. *Rosarians Midland Empire* 2(3-2-48″-8) Good color, large blooms, nice

upright growth, no faults. *R.S. Greater St. Louis* 2(2-2-30″-7.5) Good exhibition bloom, but too few. *Sedalia R.S.* 3(3-2-36″-7) Beautiful blooms, excellent form, foliage requires extra care, should produce more bloom. NEV. *Reno R.S.* 2(2-2-30″-7) Excellent color, attractive blooms, slow grower, too-few blooms, mildews badly. NEW ENGLAND *New England R.S.* 7(12-1-40″-7.5) Vt.—scarce bloomer, fades quickly. N.H.— does well in some areas. Me.—vigorous, continuous bloom. Mass.—outstanding color, few blooms. N.J. *North Jersey R.S.* 18(38-1-40″-7.3) Color and exhibition form admired, generally shy bloom, blackspotter. *West Jersey R.S.* 5(6-1-52″-8.6) Good foliage, large blooms hold color well, few flowers, not much fragrance. N.Y. *Greater Buffalo R.S.* 2(5-2-30″-8.5) Clear color, long single bloom stems, excellent foliage, good form. *Humboldt Park T.G.* (5-2-30″-8) Coppery-yellow urn-shaped buds supported on long strong stems, large double blooms, continuous bloom fades quickly, no blackspot. *Long Island R.S.* 3(4-1-44″-6.8) Bloom unbeatable in color class, holds very well when cut, foliage catches everything but measles. *Rochester R.S.* 5(5-1-42″-7.5) Good color, limited bloom, good upright grower, blooms drop too quickly, mildews early, does not stand heat. *Schenectady R.S.* 5(5-1-37″-7.3) Beautiful color, bud and flower, no blackspot or mildew, not too many blooms. *Syracuse R.S.* 4(6-1-37″-8.4) Exhibition quality, good foliage and new growth, attractive color, some blackspot, could stand more bloom. N.C. *Charlotte R.S.* 2(2-1-30″-8) Blackspots. *Durham R.S.* 2(3-1-36″-9) Free grower and bloomer, long stems, strong neck. OHIO *Akron R.S.* 4(5-1-40″-8.3) Good exhibition type, fine foliage. *Randolph R.S.* 2(3-2-60″-8.5) Good growth, form and foliage, mildews. *Central Ohio R.S.* 2(3-1-34″-7) Flower good color, fades quickly, very slow grower, shy bloomer, some blackspot. *Cleveland R.S.* 3(12-1-40″-7.7) Fine color, strong growth, exhibition type. *Columbus R.C.* 2(5-2-60″-8) Foliage gets light. *Euclid R.S.* 3(4-1-36″-8) Very good form, fine plant, nice foliage, good exhibition flower. *Forest City R.S.* 5(6-1-30″-8) Good bloom, form and color, good exhibition rose, sparse bloomer, tendency to grow upright. *Lancaster R.C.* 3(6-3-52″-6.5) Vigorous upright grower, unusual color blooms, blackspots badly. *Lima R.S.* 4(6-2-42″-7) Large high-centered bloom, lovely color, vigorous. *Medina County R.S.* 1(1-1-36″-8.5) Nice buds and foliage. *Miami Valley R.S.* 3(6-1-40″-8.5) Outstanding color, vigorous growth and foliage, long stems, holds color. ORE. *Eugene R.S.* 1(1-1-36″-7) Rare coloring, good growth habit, mildews. *International Rose T.G.* (104-60″-7) Good color, long stems, vigorous, mildews. *Medford R.S.* 3(5-1-56″-8.1) Beautiful color, nice form, slow-opening large bloom on long straight stems, very vigorous, some mildew. *Salem R.S.* 2(3-3-45″-8.1) Upright plant, good color and flowers. PA. *Breeze Hill T.G.* (2-2-30″-7) Attractive color and form, good foliage, fairly profuse. *Harrisburg R.S.* 3(1004--2-47″-9) Good show rose, large blooms of good color and form, good foliage, fairly profuse. *Harrisburg R.S.* 3(1004-2-47″-9) Good show rose, large blooms of good color and form, strong necks, nice foliage, burns in hot sun, mildews. *Philadelphia R.S.* 5(10-2-28″-7.6) Fair bloomer and plant, fades fast. *Pittsburgh R.S.* 1(3-2-24″-7.5) Not vigorous enough. TENN. *Nashville R.S.* 1(3-2-34″-6.5). TEX. *Amarillo R.S.* 2(2-2-36″-7) Rapid grower, average bloomer, color and substance not desirable. *Dallas R.S.* 2(4-1-30″-7) Strong upright growth, outstanding color, blooms last well, some blackspot. *El Paso R.S.* 3(3-1-38″-8) Strong straight stems, upright bush, healthy green foliage, long well-formed buds, beautiful color, good bloomer, in Spring and Fall, very little bloom during the Summer. VA. *Eastern Shore R.S.* 5(5-1-48″-7) Good bloomer, no mildew, likes shade, excellent color, strong stems, good textured petals, mildews and blackspots, not too many blooms. *Va. Peninsula R.S.* 1(1-1-36″-5) Good color, not enough blooms. WASH. *Seattle R.S.* 6(12-2-42″-7.1) Good color, vigorous, tends to mildew. *Spokane R.S.* 3(3-1-24″-2) Disappointing color (sickly orange). W.VA. *Charleston R.S.* 1(3-3-36″-6) Poor bloomer, upright plant, good foliage. *Wyo-Mac R.S.* 1(2-1-30″-8) Beautiful color, excellent substance, lovely foliage. WIS. *Madison R.S.* 4(6-1-45″-7.8) Good color, substance and form, vigorous, disease-resistant, not enough bloom. CANADA (British Columbia) *Vancouver R.S.* 5(15-3-42″-7) Very good color, exhibition form, fragrant, mildews badly if neglected. HAWAII *Kona* (1-1-71″-9) Exceptionally-vigorous, always in bud or flower, few thorns, medium-sized bloom, luscious apricot, each bloom gets larger, some blackspot and mildew.

## LADY LUCK HT. Rhodamine-pink. (Miller; int. Elmer '56) Pat. 1579; ARA '57; PP 2, 27 Rpts.; Av. ht. 33″; NR 7.3.

CALIF. *Rose Study Club Oakland* 1(5-1-48″-7.8) Beautiful medium-size flower and bud, long stems, good disease-free foliage. *Pacific R.S.* 3(3-1-42″-8.5) Moderate bloom, exquisite color, well-shaped bush. *San Diego R.S.* 3(4-1-36″-7.6) Very fine exhibition blooms in Spring. CONN. *Elizabeth Park T.G.* (2-1-20″-5) Too small, few blooms. IOWA *Linn County R.S.* 1(1-1-24″-7) Fair plant. KAN. *Wichita R.S.* 1(1-1-24″-7) Good blooms, color and form. MINN. *Minnesota R.S.* 3(4-2-26″-7.6) Bloom has beautiful form and unfading color, doesn't bloom enough.

NEW ENGLAND *New England R.S.* 1(3-2-36″-6) Blackspots easily. N.M. *Albuquerque R.S.* 2(9-2-30″-8) Grand performer, elegant buds, faint lavender tinge, open rose has good form, fragrant, not a vigorous grower, mildews. N.Y. *Humboldt Park T.G.* 5(2-24″-8.8) Leathery medium size dark green foliage, large deep flesh-pink large full high-centered long-pointed blooms with good-lasting quality and strong fruity fragrance, no disease, good specimen show rose, plants not vigorous enough, leggy growth. OHIO *Akron R.S.* 1(17-2-24″-8) Beautiful buds, large First Love with more form. *Lima R.S.* 1(4-2-42″-7.8) Long bud, high-centered light and dark pink bloom, grows better in full sun, some blackspot. *Miami Valley R.S.* 3(4-2-48″-7.8) Good color and grower, excellent buds, not enough blooms. *Ohio State University T.G.* (4-3-18″-5) Blooms well in June, disease-resistant large foliage, not vigorous, sparse bloom except in June. ORE. *International Rose T.G.* (10-2-36″-8) Fine form in bud, opalescent-pink color, stems bend over at times. *Lewis & Clark T.G.* (6-1-30″-5) Too tall, poor color. UTAH *Utah R.S.* 2(8-1-28″-6.1) Good fragrance, keeps when cut.

## LA JOLLA HT. Pink blend. (Swim; int. Armstrong '54) Pat. 1103; ARA '54; PP 4, 231 Rpts.; Av. ht. 44″; NR 7.6.

ALA. *Twickenham R.S.* 4(4-2-36″-6.2) Improves with age, long pointed buds. ARIZ. *Mesa R.S.* 4(2-3-48″-8.9) Unfading, good bush, lovely buds and flowers. *Phoenix R.S.* 3(6-3-42″-7.5) Dainty beautiful coloring, fragrant, excellent in Spring and Fall, opens too fast in heat. CALIF. *Rose Study Club Oakland* 3(8-3-60″-7.4) Dainty orange-pink bloom, vigorous, tall, rather leggy, bloom fades in sun, mildews. *Pacific R.S.* 3(3-2-37″-8.1) Good color blend, long-lasting when cut, plant has good form, some weak necks, drops foliage after blooming period. *Peninsula R.S.* 6(7-2-48″-8) Exquisite form and color, disease-free foliage on shapely bush, weak stems on repeat bloom. *Riverside R.S.* 9(14-5-36″-7.8) Good strong stems and foliage, holds color well, hardy in our Summer heat. *San Diego R.S.* 4(10-2-50″-7.8) Exhibition blooms, best in filtered light. *San Joaquin Valley R.S.* 2(3-4-48″-8) Excellent for warm weather, vigorous plant with good foliage, exhibition blooms on long stems. *San Mateo County R.S.* 4(7-4-48″-8) Beautiful exhibition form in Spring, fine color, disease-resistant, shy bloomer, weak neck, too little foliage, poor Summer bloom. COLO. *Denver R.S.* 4(24-4-40″-7) Vigorous, good foliage and bloom when it comes, flower color not outstanding. CONN. *Elizabeth Park T.G.* (10-5-24″-5) Attractive plant, weak stems for heavy bloom. D.C. *Potomac R.S.* (48″-7.3) Beautiful well-formed open delicate pink and orange blend fragrant flowers, good foliage, not a free-bloomer. GA. *Georgia R.S.* 10(19-3-72″-7.6) Well-blended pastel, long-lasting cut blooms, needs disbudding. ILL. *Chicago R.S. Reg. 1* 3(7-2-48″-8) Fine vigorous plant produces continuous bloom, exquisite blend flower. *Greater Peoria R.S.* 2(2-2-36″-7.2) Fairly prolific, long stems, vigorous well-clothed plant, best in cool weather (fades in heat), balls, good bloomer, nice buds, good color, doesn't hold form, some mildew and blackspot. IND. *Indianapolis R.S.* 2(2-3-36″-6.3) Vigorous, very pretty blooms when you get them, but form not always good. *St. Joseph Valley R.S.* 2(5-5-42″-7.7) Beautiful form, 15-20 buds at a time, cool weather rose, balls. *Vincennes R.S.* 2(2-2-51″-8) Fine, prolific, no disease. IOWA *Iowa R.S.* 2(2-3-42″-7.5). KAN. *Wichita R.S.* 2(4-2-36″-7.5) Good foliage, vigorous grower, good bloom. KY. *Frankfort Chapter ARS* 7(12-3-45″-7.5) Nice exhibition bloom, good foliage, fades in hot weather. *Kentucky R.S.* 2(3-236″-7) Good exhibition rose, scarce bloomer. *Lexington R.S.* 1(1-4-48″-7.7) Good for cutting, sparse bloomer, nice foliage, vigorous grower. *Louisville Chapter ARS* 4(4-2-42″-7.2) Good color shape and substance, few blooms, fades. LA. *New Orleans R.S.* 1(2-4-54″-7) Vigorous grower, disease-free, bloom quality good only in cool weather. MD. *Maryland R.S.* 3(3-3-54″-8) Very good in Spring. MICH. *Detroit R.S.* 5(6-2-42″-7.6) Good form, fair bloom, strong stems. *Kalamazoo R.S.* 9(17-3-36″-8.5) Nice plant, good form, weak necks, could bloom more, nice in Spring. *Michigan State University T.G.* (6-6-22″-6) Disease-resistant, weak necks, no fragrance. MINN. *Minnesota R.S.* 5(16-2-38″-7.4) Good form and color, petals don't like rain. MO. *Rosarians Midland Empire* 2(5-2-54″-7.9) Good grower, nice bloom (but a little shy). *R.S. Greater St. Louis* 2(3-4-42″-7) Beautiful bloom, not strong plant, not good in hot weather. NEW ENGLAND *New England R.S.* 5(9-3-40″-7.5) Fairly vigorous, good color, some fragrance, not very disease-resistant. N.J. *North Jersey R.S.* 10(17-3-36″-7.5) Exquisite coloring and form. N.Y. *Greater Buffalo R.S.* 2(3-3-30″-8.2) Fragrant, good color in hot weather, poor in wet weather, disease-resistant, excellent form. *Humboldt Park T.G.* (6-4-30″-8) High-centered, peach-pink large double blooms, very resistant, slight fruity fragrance, not abundant enough foliage, sparse blooms, weak flower necks. *Long Island R.S.* 1(1-2-36″-7.8) Perfect blooms. *Niagara Frontier R.S.* 3(8-3-31″-7.5) Vigorous plants, good foliage, good quantity of exhibition-type blooms. *Rochester R.S.* 5(25-3-48″-8) Good color, sturdy upright growth, good foliage. *Schenectady R.S.* 1(1-2-36″-6) Pretty bud and bloom, disease-resistant. *Syracuse R.S.* 2(2-1-33″-7.5) Fine color, excellent foliage, sparse bloom, disease-resistant. N.C. *Durham R.S.* 1(1-2-80″-9.5) Beautiful color blend, nice foliage, good bloomer and substance, very fragrant. OHIO *Akron R.S.* 1(12-4-48″-8). *Central Ohio R.S.* 4(16-3-48″-8) Beautiful bloom, vigorous healthy plant, color best in Fall and Spring (Summer flowers fade and lack texture and substance), not enough bloom. *Cincinnati R.S.* 1(1-2-48″-8) Very vigorous, attractive blooms. *Cleveland R.S.* 2(3-3-27″-7) Enduring bloom, nice compact bush. *Columbus R.C.* 3(3-2-42″-

7.8) Healthy plant, good bloom, mildews, weak stems. *Euclid R.S.* 1(1-4-30″-7.5) Nice bloom and foliage, skimpy on flowers, slow grower. *Greater Cincinnati R.S.* 4(4-1-42″-7.5) Pretty blend, nice shape, medium bloomer. *Lima R.S.* 5(8-2-36″-7.9) Good bloomer, well-formed foliage, good texture, good in Spring and Fall. *Miami Valley R.S.* 4(10-2-40″-8) Outstanding color (especially in Spring and Fall), long stems. OKLA. *Norman R.S.* 2(12-4-36″-7.6). *Oklahoma R.S.* 1(2-2-36″-8) Good plant, beautiful blooms. ORE. *International Rose T.G.* (12-4-54″-8) Profusion of good roses fade out in too much heat. *Lewis & Clark T.G.* (18-4-36″-5) Good bush and foliage, fades in hot weather. *Medford R.S.* 4(5-2-41″-8.2) Pretty in bud and full-bloom, better in Spring and Fall. *Rogue Valley R.S.* 3(3-3-54″-7) Good color and form, but not enough bloom. *Roseburg R.S.* 3(3-3-66″-8) Heavy blooms, disease-resistant strong growth. *Salem R.S.* 3(4-4-36″-7) Good color and form, fine plant, sparse bloomer. PA. *Harrisburg R.S.* 3(305-3-54″-7.4) Good color in early bloom, long stems, good form, blooms freely, vigorous, Summer blooms thin. *Philadelphia R.S.* 3(4-3-45″-7.5) Good foliage, strong canes, weak stems, blooms spot with age. *Pittsburgh R.S.* 1(1-3-24″-6) Moderate bloomer, color varies, weak stems, best in Fall, open spreading habit. S.C. *Edisto T.G.* (9-5-36″-7) Good form, color and substance, fairly-vigorous plant, can't take the Summer sun. TENN. *Nashville R.S.* 3(9-2-41″-7.8) Good vigor, form and lasting quality, light bloomer, does well with afternoon shade. TEX. *Amarillo R.S.* 7(9-54″-7) Distinctive varigated bloom (but not enough) which fades badly, good disease-resistant foliage. *Dallas R.S.* 1(3-4-48″-7.8) Lovely color, very good form, glossy resistant foliage. *El Paso R.S.* 1(1-3-25″-6.2) Good healthy foliage, fine bud color, does not bloom enough, slow growing, weak plant. UTAH *Utah R.S.* 3(13-4-36″-5.3) Fair-formed blooms, color not smooth, weak neck, plant not husky. VA. *Va. Peninsula R.S.* 1(1-2-66″-7) Vigorous growth, strong stems, good blooms, does not bloom freely. WASH. *Seattle R.S.* 4(4-3-40″-7.1) Buds better than blooms, fades. *Spokane R.S.* 4(6-2-36″-10) Good buds and open bloom, best in hot weather. *Walla Walla R.S.* 2(4-4-54″-8) Good blooms of exhibition form and delicate color. W.VA. *Charleston R.S.* 1(3-2-48″-7) Exhibition-quality, good clear color. WIS. *Milwaukee R.S.* 2(3-2-43″-7.2) Nice color blend, interesting unusually-good form. CANADA (British Columbia) *Vancouver R.S.* 4(16-4-48″-7) Color good at times (variable and fades), sturdy bush, good form, center petals short.

## LAS VEGAS HT. Salmon-pink. (Whisler; int. Germain's '56) Pat. 1486; ARA '56; PP 3, 59 Rpts.; Av. ht. 36″; NR 7.4.

ARIZ. *Mesa R.S.* 1(1-1-36″-8) Nice buds and bloom. *Phoenix R.S.* 2(2-2-40″-7.3) Large showy blooms, lovely color and foliage, heat fades blooms slightly. CALIF. *Pacific R.S.* 1(1-2-18″-0) Poor grower, fades, rusts. *Peninsula R.S.* 1(1-2-24″-7) Vigorous bush, beautiful bloom, mildews, rusts badly. *San Joaquin Valley R.S.* 1(1-1-36″-7.5) Good form and color. D.C. *Potomac R.S.* 2(3-2-48″-7.9) Really worthwhile new rose of exhibition quality, vigorous-growing Charlotte Armstrong-colored rose, flower form similar to Texas Centennial, open flower fades. GA. *Georgia R.S.* 3(3-1-60″-7.5) Vigorous, well-shaped bush, disease-free, too few blooms, a lot like Mission Bells. IND. *St. Joseph Valley R.S.* 1(2-1-42″-8) 6″ flowers, tall bush, good color. IOWA *Linn County R.S.* 1(1-1-24″-7) Nice bloom (but not enough), not vigorous. KAN. *Wichita R.S.* 1(2-1-30″-8). LA. *New Orleans R.S.* 1(1-1-24″-7). MD. *Maryland R.S.* 2(2-1-30″-7.5) Spring blooms are a knockout, many basal breaks. MINN. *Minnesota R.S.* 4(7-2-30″-7.7) Large beautiful pink and apricot blend, sparse bloomer. MO. *Rosarians Midland Empire* 1(1-2-18″-6.8) Nice blooms, shy bloomer, no growth. NEW ENGLAND *New England R.S.* 1(1-1-40″-8). N.J. *North Jersey R.S.* 6(11-1-25″-7.5) Stingy bloomer, husky plant, nice color and form. N.M. *Albuquerque R.S.* 2(6-2-45″-8) Wonderful plant, beautiful bud and flower form with good substance, plenty of floppy blooms, very fleeting. N.Y. *Long Island R.S.* 1(1-1-48″-8) Seems to have everything—vigor, fine foliage, disease-resistance and a constant crop of gorgeous pink blooms. *Syracuse R.S.* 1(1-1-30″-6.5) Attractive color, good disease-resistant foliage, sparse blooms. N.C. *Durham R.S.* 2(3-1-36″-9) Best of the new roses tested for color, form, stem, substance, profuse bloomer, no faults. OHIO *Akron R.S.* 3(4-1-36″-7.9) Beautiful good growth, blackspots. *Central Ohio R.S.* 1(1-1-24″-7) Healthy plant, lovely bud shape, beautiful color. *Cleveland R.S.* 1(1-1-42″-6.5) Promising exhibition rose, healthy. *Euclid R.S.* 3(5-1-48″-8) Good pink, fine form, vigorous plant, good for exhibition. *Lancaster Rose Club* 2(2-1-48″-7.5) Vigorous, upright, disease-resistant, fair bloomer, exhibition-type at times. *Lima R.S.* 1(2-1-36″-7.5) Good form and color. *Miami Valley R.S.* 2(5-1-30″-7.5) Color and form very good in bud, won't hold when cut, high center. OKLA. *Norman R.S.* 1(1-1-36″-7.6). *Oklahoma R.S.* 2(6-2-30″-6) Beautiful but scarce bloom, poor plant. PA. *Breeze Hill T.G.* (3-5-36″-7) Attractive flowers on long stems. *Harrisburg R.S.* 2(801-2-48″-8.6) Above-average, high-centered bud, long stems, dark disease-resistant foliage. TEX. *Dallas R.S.* 1(1-2-32″-6.5) Excellent flower of unusual color, blackspots, soft foliage. *El Paso R.S.* 2(1-1-38″-7) Strong healthy foliage and long stems, large bud, lovely colors, slow grower, sparse bloomer. WIS. *Madison R.S.* 1(1-1-48″-7.5) Fair growth, good hardiness, foliage, form and substance, sparse bloomer.

## LEMON CHIFFON HT. Medium yellow. (Swim; int. Arp '54) Pat. 1241; ARA '55; PP 4, 36 Rpts.; Av. ht. 23"; NR 6.1.

**ALA.** *Twickenham R.S.* 2(4-2-21"-5.8) Pretty color, opens too quickly, blackspots easily. **ARIZ.** *Mesa R.S.* 1(1-1-36"-7.2) Fairly good color, nice plant, good bloomer. **CONN.** *Elizabeth Park T.G.* (3-4-15"-7) Fair foliage, size and flower. **GA.** *Georgia R.S.* 2(2-2-36"-6.5) Good high-centered bud, cool color, weak bush with little vigor. **IND.** *St. Joseph Valley R.S.* 1(2-3-24"-6.9) Good color, poor weak bush. **IOWA** *Linn County R.S.* 1(1-1-20"-6.7) Good color, not vigorous. **MICH.** *Detroit R.S.* 1(2-2-12"-6) Low growth. *Michigan State University T.G.* (5-2-21"-7.5) Holds color very well, very fragrant, not free-flowering. **MINN.** *Minnesota R.S.* 3(5-2-18"-5). **MO.** *R.S. Greater St. Louis* 1(1-2-18"-6) Too few blooms, not too robust a plant. **N.J.** *North Jersey R.S.* 1(1-2-12"-3) Poor plant and form, good color. **N.Y.** *Humboldt Park T.G.* (2-2-1). *Rochester R.S.* 1(10-1-26"-6.5) Clear color, blackspots, limited bloomer, weak plant. *Syracuse R.S.* 1(2-3-12"-6) Good color, plants sprawl, no stems. **N.C.** *Durham R.S.* 1(2-2-12"-3) Poor growth sparse bloomer. **OHIO** *Euclid R.S.* 1(1-2-6) Nice deep color, good bloom, spreading plant (hard to control), fades fast. *Lancaster R.C.* 1(1-2-36"-7.5). *Miami Valley R.S.* 3(6-2-24"-6) Fair bloomer in Spring, not too strong, sprawling plant, weak necks. **ORE.** *International Rose T.G.* (20-4-36"-6) Citrus fragrance, deep color, dark green foliage, not enough good bloom. *Lewis & Clark T.G.* (12-1-36"-8) Long-pointed buds with bright foliage, good form. **PA.** *Breeze Hill T.G.* (3-7-26"-8) Bright color, profuse. **TENN.** *Nashville R.S.* 3(9-3-18"-6) Excellent color, fragrant, weakness for cold weather, light bloomer. **TEX.** *Corpus Christi R.S.* 1(1-3-42"-8) Excellent foliage, lots of bloom, nice fragrance, buds open too quickly, few petals. *Dallas R.S.* 1(6-4-24"-4.5) Good clear color, weak plant, subject to disease. **UTAH** *Utah R.S.* 1(1-3-24"-6.5) Beautiful blooms. **WASH.** *Spokane R.S.* 1(1-3-30"-10) Beautiful color, good bloomer. **W.VA.** *Charleston R.S.* 1(3-3-36"-5) Sprawling low bush, light bloomer. **WIS.** *Madison R.S.* 1(1-2-24"-7.7) Fair growth, disease-resistant, fair hardiness, good foliage, intermittent bloom.

## LINDA PORTER HT. Clear pink. (Dot; int. Bobbink & Atkins '57) Pat. 1507; ARA '57; PP 2, 43 Rpts.; Av. ht. 31"; NR 7.1.

**ARIZ.** *Mesa R.S.* 1(1-1-36"-6.9) Poor bush, few blooms, doesn't like heat. *Phoenix R.S.* 2(2-2-24"-6.8) Beautiful blooms, fragrant, not enough vigor or bloom. **CALIF.** *San Joaquin Valley R.S.* 1(1-1-24"-7) Good color and form, holds well in warm weather. **D.C.** *Potomac R.S.* 2(3-2-36"-7.8) Huge pink bloom with many petals, good strong canes and foliage, fragrant, not enough bloom or growth. **GA.** *Georgia R.S.* 1(1-2-36"-7) Good color on a good bush. **ILL.** *Chicago R.S. Reg. 1* 1(1-3-22"-7) Beautiful sparse camellia-like bloom, poor growth. **IOWA** *Des Moines R.S.* 1(1-1-30"-7) *Linn County R.S.* 1(1-2-24"-7) Nice form and color, sparse bloomer. **MINN.** *Minnesota R.S.* 7(10-2-33"-6.6) Beautiful bloom, very poor growth habit, sparse bloomer. **MO.** *Rosarians Midland Empire* 1(1-1-36"-8). **NEW ENGLAND** *New England R.S.* 1(1-1-40"-6.9) Not enough blooms. **N.J.** *North Jersey R.S.* 4(7-1-27"-6.7) Good bloom, but inclined to be shy. **N.Y.** *Humboldt Park T.G.* (5-2-24"-8) Large leathery green foliage, disease-resistant, large very double clear pink flower with apricot shading, only moderate vigor, not branching enough, leggy growth. **N.Y.** *Niagara Frontier R.S.* 1(1-2-24"-6) Only two good blooms in two years, blackspots. *Schenectady R.S.* 1(1-1-15"-8.4) Blooms very good but small, small plant. *Syracuse R.S.* 1(1-1-12"- ). **N.C.** *Durham R.S.* 2(4-2-48"-9) Beautiful color, good substance, plenty of petals, good foliage. **OHIO** *Akron R.S.* 1(2-2-24"-7) Large stingy blooms, low grower. *Cleveland R.S.* 1(1-1-24"-6) Nice color, lots of petals. *Euclid R.S.* 1(1-1-24"-7) Beautiful stingy blooms, nice shade, good form, slow grower. *Lancaster R.C.* 1(3-2-48"-7.2) Vigorous, upright, disease-resistant, fine pink exhibition bloom, sparse bloomer. *Lima R.S.* 1(1-1-28"- ) Plant not large enough to hold large full double blooms. **ORE.** *Medford R.S.* 1(2-1-36"-8.2) Good form, color and substance, opens slowly, good for exhibition and as cut flower, buds faulty at times. **PA.** *Breeze Hill T.G.* 6(4-28"-7) Huge flowers of good form and color, scant bloom. *Philadelphia R.S.* 2(4-2-33"-7) Exhibition possibilities, weak plant, shy bloomer, lacks strong branching. **TENN.** *Nashville R.S.* 1(1-1-36"-6) Doesn't bloom enough. **TEX.** *Amarillo R.S.* 2(2-1-8.2) Beautiful buds and color, perfect bloom, disease-resistant, weak stems. **WASH.** *Seattle R.S.* 2(2-1-27"-6.4). **W.VA.** *Charleston R.S.* 1(3-3-36"-5) Bloom has good form and color, upright plant, good foliage, not enough bloom. **WIS.** *Madison R.S.* 1(1-1-36"-8.5) Beautiful exhibition flower, disease-resistant, could bloom more.

## LITTLE DARLING F. Yellow with pink. (Duehrsen; int. Elmer '56) Pat. 1581; ARA '57; PP 2, 100 Rpts.; Av. ht. 40"; NR 8.5.

**CALIF.** *Rose Study Club Oakland* 4(11-2-58"-8.8) Lovely color, free-blooming, vigorous growth, some main shoots 8-10' high, beautiful disease-free foliage. *Pacific R.S.* 2(5-1-27"-9.5) Beautiful buds on long strong stems, profuse bloomer, even old open blooms have class, strong leathery foliage, no mildew. *Peninsula R.S.* 9(16-2-54″-8) Glorious color and form, vigorous, lasts well as cut flower, disease-resistant. *San Diego R.S.* 2(2-1-35″-8) Very pleasing blooms. *San Joaquin Valley R.S.* (36″-8) Flower form and color lives up to the name. *San Mateo County R.S.* 1(1-1-36″-10) Beautifully-shaped buds, good foliage, disease-resistant. COLO. *Denver R.S.* 1(20-1-24″-7) Attractive multicolor, especially the buds and partly-opened flower, vigorous, uneven growth, not enough blooms. D.C. *Potomac R.S.* 2(2-1-36″-8) Breath-taking color, blooms in good spray heads, good substance to individual flower. GA. *Georgia R.S.* 6(9-1-48″-8.2) Strong grower, perfect buds, outstanding color, disease-free foliage, too leggy, too much foliage for amount of bloom. ILL. *Chicago R.S. Reg. 1* 2(2-1-48″-8.5) Vigorous disease-free plant with attractive prolific bloom. *Indianapolis R.S.* 1(1-1-36″-9) Good color and form, might bloom more, disease-resistant. *St. Joseph Valley R.S.* 1(1-1-60″-9) Very vigorous, beautiful shiny foliage, blooms last long on plant. IOWA *Linn County R.S.* 1(2-1-20″-8) Good in all respects. KAN. *Wichita R.S.* 1(1-1-30″-8.5) Beautiful foliage and bloom. KY. *Louisville Chapter ARS* 1(1-1-24″-8) Good bud form and color, no outstanding faults. MD. *Maryland R.S.* 3(3-1-36″-8) Exquisitely-shaped and colored blooms. MICH. *Detroit R.S.* 3(3-1-24″-8.1) Mildews, good color and form. MINN. *Minnesota R.S.* 9(50-1-33″-8.4) Vigorous, excellent bud, flower and foliage, speckles in wet weather, fading flowers not too attractive, almost always in bloom. MO. *Rosarians Midland Empire* 1(1-1-40″-8) Good bi-color, small bloom. NEV. *Reno R.S.* 9(23-3-36″-9) Holds its beautiful color, beautifully-shaped buds, good disease-resistant foliage, fine strong canes. N.J. *North Jersey R.S.* 1(2-1-30″-9.5) Vigorous, perfect form, consistent bloom. N.M. *Albuquerque R.S.* 7(17-2-35″-8.9) Peace in miniature, leggy plant. N.Y. *Humboldt Park T.G.* (5-2-42″-8) Medium to small coppery-pink buds, medium deep to light pink intermittent blooms of good lasting quality, no insect or disease injury. *Long Island R.S.* 1(3-1-48″-8.2) Delightful blooms on a very healthy bush, long and limber canes. *Rochester R.S.* 1(20-2-35″-8) Good blend, free-flowering, clean foliage. OHIO *Akron R.S.* 1(7-1-18″-8) A good corsage rose. *Cleveland R.S.* 1(1-1-42″-9) Wonderful color and form, too long between blooming splurges. *Miami Valley R.S.* 2(4-2-54″-9) Excellent form and color, good disease-resistant foliage, excellent for corsages and arrangements. *Ohio State University T.G.* (4-1-21″-6) Vigorous husky plant, abundant large to medium disease-resistant foliage, bloom not too abundant, weak flower stem. ORE. *Eugene R.S.* 3(3-1-42″-8.5) Good color and form of both bud and bloom, perfect foliage, main stems spread. *International Rose T.G.* (20-4-48″-9) Petite bud form, attractive color, ample bloom, corsage and arrangement rose, tall at times, canes cascade pendulate. *Lewis & Clark T.G.* (9-1-60″-10) Good all-round plant. *Medford R.S.* 1(1-1-36″-8.3) Beautiful form and color blend, scarce bloom. *Salem R.S.* 1(2-1-30″-9.5) Excellent bush, perfect buds, luscious color, extremely healthy. PA. *Harrisburg R.S.* 1(500-1-60″-9.6) Vigorous, profuse, disease-resistant, outstanding quality flowers, wonderful show rose. TEX. *Dallas R.S.* 1(3-1-36″-8) Very vigorous, free-flowering, excellent form and color, resistant. *El Paso R.S.* 2(1-1-36″-9) Beautiful small buds, vigorous, fast grower, healthy glossy foliage, holds well as a cut flower, prettiest Floribunda to date. UTAH *Utah R.S.* 2(11-1-33″-7.2) Beautiful dainty fragrant blooms, plant could improve. WASH. *Seattle R.S.* 6(13-2-40″-9) Blooms have good form and color. *Spokane R.S.* 1(1-1-44″-10) Much like a Shrub. CANADA (British Columbia) *Vancouver R.S.* 4(5-1-42″-9) Free-bloomer, no serious faults.

## LIVING HT. Vermilion to scarlet. (Lammerts; int. Consolidated '56) Pat. 1463; ARA '58; PP 2, 158 pts.; Av. ht. 42″; NR 7.3.

ARIZ. *Phoenix R.S.* 2(2-1-45″-7.5) Vigorous growth, exquisite color, bud and form, excellent for cutting, opens fast. CALIF. *Rose Study Club Oakland* 1(2-2-38″-7.8) Spectacular color fades in hot weather, bush well covered with disease-resistant foliage, opens rather quickly. *Pacific R.S.* 1(3-1-40″-9) Outstanding vivid color, tall upright growth shows Grande Duchesse Charlotte parentage, blooms open fast. *Peninsula R.S.* 7(9-2-48″-7) Vivid, unfading color, flower opens quickly, vigorous, disease-free, fragrant, *San Diego R.S.* 2(3-1-60″-7.5) Spectacular buds. *San Mateo County R.S.* 4(8-2-48″-8) Beautiful color, good form in bud, long-lasting, strong grower, too-few petals, opens too fast. D.C. *Potomac R.S.* 2(3-1-42″-7.9) Beautifully-formed bud, brilliant Red Emperor color, good foliage. GA. *Georgia R.S.* 4(4-1-48″-6.1) Beautiful form and color bloom on unattractive bush, too few petals for our heat, too short-lasting, not winter-hardy. ILL. *Chicago R.S. Reg. 1* 2(2-1-42″-7) Beautiful orange-red blend. *Greater Peoria R.S.* 2(2-1-31″-7.5) Long tapered buds, light green foliage, opens fast in full sunlight, sparse bloomer, weak stem. IND. *Indianapolis R.S.* 1(1-1-20″- ). *St. Joseph Valley R.S.* 1(1-2-48″-8) Tall bush, opens too fast, not enough petals. *Vincennes R.S.* 2(1-2-48″-8) Not prolific enough. IOWA *Linn County R.S.* 3(4-2-30″-6) Good only in Spring and Fall, single in warm weather. KY. *Kentucky R.S.* 1(1-1-24″-6) Beautiful buds, healthy foliage and plant. *Louisville Chapter ARS* 3(15-1-44″-7.2) Good color, needs more foliage. LA. *New Orleans R.S.* 2(3-2-48″-8.5) Beautiful color, good form, fragrant, too-few petals, weak necks. MD. *Maryland R.S.* 2(4-2-36″-8) Color and form excellent, could grow and bloom more. MICH. *Detroit R.S.* 7(13-2-42″-6.7) Winter-kills, weak stems, opens too quickly. *Greater Lansing R.S.* 2(2-2-30″-7.8) Tall, slender flower, most unusual buds, pretty orange-red, good disease-resistant foliage, good blooms all season. *Kalamazoo R.S.* 5(7-1-42″-7.8) Good foliage and color, not enough bloom, opens too fast, best in Spring and Fall. *Michigan State University T.G.* (10-1-35″-5) Excellent color, bud form very attractive, disease-resistant, fully-open blooms have a loose appearance, weak necks, no fragrance. MINN. *Minnesota R.S.* 9(21-1-41″-7.5) Buds attractive but flower opens too fast, spindly growth. MO. *Rosarians Midland Empire* 2(4-2-45″-8.2) Blooms well, disease-free, needs more petals. *R.S. Greater St. Louis* 1(1-2-42″-7) Not enough of the fine blooms. NEV. *Reno R.S.* 4(6-2-40″-8) Well-shaped buds, attractive color, vigorous grower, too-few petals, some mildew. NEW ENGLAND *New England R.S.* 3(6-2-40″-7.6) N.H.—not vigorous, loose blooms; Me.—vigorous, abundant floppy blooms; Mass.—hardy, clean, few blooms. N.J. *North Jersey R.S.* 3(4-1-26″-7) Good color and plant, few petals. N.M. *Albuquerque R.S.* 1(3-2-44″-8.1) Profuse bloomer, vivid coloring, healthy plant, long tapering buds, opens too quickly in heat. N.Y. *Niagara Frontier R.S.* 2(3-2-42″-8) Lovely vibrant color, prolific bloomer, fine plant. *Schenectady R.S.* 1(1-1-54″-8.5) Long buds, fragrant, no blackspot or mildew, not bushy, outstanding color when open, floppy flowers. *Syracuse R.S.* 1(1-1-36″-7) Striking color, weak stems, lacks substance in open stage. N.C. *Charlotte R.S.* 3(7-1-24″-7). OHIO *Akron R.S.* 6(13-2-42″-7.2) Good foliage, grower and color, leggy plant, bloom opens fast. *Central Ohio R.S.* 1(2-2-42″-7.3) Blooms very attractive, good form, bush rather spreading, blooms lack petalage, bush lacks vigor. *Cincinnati R.S.* 2(3-2-36″-7) Not enough blooms. *Cleveland R.S.* 5(21-2-54″-9.4) Most beautiful of all buds, great bloom color, single blooms on long stems, exhibition rose, healthy. *Columbus R.C.* (36″-7.3) Attractive bloom, good form, lacks petalage. *Euclid R.S.* 3(4-2-48″-7.1) Good color, not too many blooms, flowers open too fast, not a good exhibition flower. *Forest City R.S.* 6(12-2-42″-7) Good bloom color, long stems, exhibition-quality, good disease-resistant foliage. *Lancaster R.C.* 5(6-2-48″-7.3) Decorative in the garden, upright, bushy, good bloomer, too-few petals. *Lima R.S.* 6(8-2-36″-7) Beautiful color, long tapering bud, lasts well when cut. *Ohio State University T.G.* (3-3-36″-6) Vigorous plants, disease-resistant, fair amount of bloom, good foliage, fragrant flower, lacks leaves at base. *Park of Roses T.G.* (50-2-60″-9) Prolific nice quality bloom, hardy, no faults. *Stark R.S.* 4(11-2-37″-7.7) Lovely color. OKLA. *Norman R.S.* 2(7-2-40″-7.6). ORE. *Eugene R.S.* 2(2-2-42″-8.1) Good foliage, unusual vivid color, long-lasting large bloom, excellent buds, very sparse bloomer. *International Rose T.G.* (40-8-72″-8) Outstanding color, foliage, bloom recurrence, best in cool weather, sun fades color. *Medford R.S.* 6(7-2-47″-8) Long tapering buds, vibrant color, opens too fast, disease-resistant foliage, could bloom more. *Rogue Valley R.S.* 1(1-1-48″-8.9) Excellent color and form, disease-resistant, long cutting stems. *Salem R.S.* 1(2-2-30″-7.5) Stingy orange flowers on single stems, good plant. PA. *Harrisburg R.S.* 1(1-1-40″-3) Bloomed twice. S.C. *Edisto T.G.* (24-3-42″-7) Form and color of bud attractive (like Grande Duchesse Charlotte) but better flower, shy on vigor and flowers, best in Spring and Fall. TENN. *Nashville R.S.* 2(3-2-38″- ) Vivid color, excellent bud form, plant seems to lack vigor, light bloomer. TEX. *Amarillo R.S.* 2(1-1-36″-7) Good bloomer, beautiful healthy plant, blossoms open too fast, coloring not always the same. *Corpus Christi R.S.* 1(1-2-60″-9.5) Long pointed buds open slowly, long-lasting striking color, long stems, grows fast. *Dallas R.S.* 4(6-1-36″-6.4) Beautiful color, good foliage and bud, flower lacks substance. UTAH *Utah R.S.* 1(5-1-48″-5) Too-few petals, fades fast. VA. *Va. Peninsula R.S.* 1(1-2-78″-7) Vigorous growth, good foliage and color, disease-resistant, blooms open too fast. WASH. *Seattle R.S.* 2(3-2-42″-6.5) Brilliant color bud, open blooms fade. *Spokane R.S.* 1(1-1-36″-5) Not exhibition type. W.VA. *Charleston R.S.* 2(3-1-48″-8) Beautiful red blend, good grower, bloom opens quickly. WIS. *Madison R.S.* 1(1-2-48″-8.4) Good hardiness, good disease-resistant foliage, intermittent bloomer, unusual color, fair form.

## LOVE SONG HT. Pink blend. (Fisher; int. Conard-Pyle '55) Pat. 1360; ARA '56; PP 3, 296 Rpts.; Av. ht. 29″; NR 6.5.

ALA. *Twickenham R.S.* 1(1-2-24″-5) Sparse bloom, little vigor. ARIZ. *Mesa R.S.* 1(1-3-24″-7) Poor bloomer, large blooms of good color, small bush, no mildew. *Phoenix R.S.* 2(2-2-40″-6.5) Good foliage, attractive scarce bloom sunburns. CALIF. *Rose Study Club Oakland* 2(8-2-33″-6.1) Poor growth with die-back, scant bloom opens poorly, split-center flowers. *Pacific R.S.* 2(2-2-12″-3.5) Grows exceptionally slow, very few beautiful bi-color blooms, subject to die-back. *Peninsula R.S.* 7(9-2-36″-5) Poor grower, good color, confused centers, sparse bloom. *Riverside R.S.* 5(5-6-24″-6.7) Foliage seems to burn in our heat, blooms freely, grows very slowly. *San Joaquin Valley R.S.*

1(1-3-30″-6) Poor growing habit, few beautiful blooms. *San Mateo County R.S.* 7(11-3-30″-2) Attractive color, poor grower, shy bloomer, split center blooms, fades quickly, mildews and rusts. COLO. *Colorado Springs R.S.* 1(4-2-36″-9) Strongest blend available, few if any faults. *Denver R.S.* 4(4-2-18″-5) Beautiful rose, good foliage, fragrant, dies-back. CONN. *Elizabeth Park T.G.* (9-3-20″-5) Vigorous stems and foliage, but not enough of them, slow grower. D.C. *Potomac R.S.* 6(15-3-36″-7.5) Beautiful pink and yellow bi-color blooms of good size, open flower form good, waxy foliage, poor grower, crooked necks on bloom, plant deteriorates. GA. *Georgia R.S.* 10(17-2-38″-6.6) Exhibition bloom of many petals, beautiful leathery foliage, sunburns, split-centers, sparse bloomer. ILL. *Greater Peoria R.S.* 5(5-2-26″-7.2) Large blooms, beautiful color, good foliage, some split centers, too-few blooms, slow grower. *Tri-City Men's Rose & Garden Club* 3(8-3-36″-7.8) Few good blooms. IND. *Indianapolis R.S.* 5(8-2-24″-6.4) Good color, does not grow well, winter-tender. *St. Joseph Valley R.S.* 2(2-2-30″-6.5) Colorful large flower, good foliage, not enough basal shoots, poor bloomer. *Vincennes R.S.* 2(2-2-18″-6) Fine blooms, but no growth. IOWA *Des Moines R.S.* 3(3-2-30″-7.5) Vigorous plant, large bloom. *Iowa R.S.* 2(3-2-24″-6) Large bloom, slow growth. *Linn County R.S.* 3(6-2-24″-6.4) Large flowers, nice color, sparse bloomer. KAN. *Wichita R.S.* 3(3-1-24″-7) Great rose, beautiful bloom, good foliage. KY. *Frankfort Chapter ARS* 3(8-2-28″-6.5) Very good color in Spring, split centers, not too hardy, shy bloomer. *Kentucky R.S.* 6(11-2-30″-6) Few nice large blooms, lacks vigor, nice foliage. *Louisville Chapter ARS* 3(3-2-22″-5.3) Nice color and shape, weak, few blooms. LA. *New Orleans R.S.* 4(6-2-24″-6) Nice bloom, will not grow, blackspots, infrequent bloomer. MD. *Maryland R.S.* 3(6-2-30″-7) Bloom very large and attractive, healthy but not vigorous plant. MICH. *Detroit R.S.* 5(72-24″-6.8) Good color, poor grower, blooms ball, crooked necks. *Kalamazoo R.S.* 8(16-2-30″-7) Nice rose and color, not enough bloom, some disease, good foliage, slow grower. *West Michigan Rosarians* 1(1-1-24″-8) Very large pink flower with yellow reverse, good green foliage, slow grower. MINN. *Minnesota R.S.* 11(18-2-28″-6.9) Full-petalled bloom, centers tend to split, glossy foliage. KAN. *Kansas City R.S.* (2-2-24″-9.5) Good foliage and color, few blossoms. MO. *Rosarians Midland Empire* 2(4-2-26″-8) Beautiful blooms, not a prolific bloomer. *R.S. Greater St. Louis* 4(7-2-18″-6) Beautiful flowers on poor plant, but too few. *Sedalia R.S.* 1(1-2-28″-7) Large blooms, color does not hold, plant lacks vigor, not enough bloom. NEV. *Reno R.S.* 2(6-3-30″-5) Large beautiful flowers, poor grower and bloomer, fades quickly, mildews and rusts. NEW ENGLAND *New England R.S.* 7(16-3-30″-7.7) Few blooms, good color. N.J. *North Jersey R.S.* 13(19-2-20″-5.7) Feeble plant, gorgeous colors when you get them, quartered. *West Jersey R.S.* 4(8-1-30″-7.5) Very good foliage, large fade-proof blooms, free-blooming. N.Y. *Cornell University T.G.* (9-3-30″-7.8) Excellent foliage, vigorous, very large flower with many petals (best on opening in cooler weather) fades badly. *Greater Buffalo R.S.* 2(4-2-12″-7) Single stem blooms with intense coloring and beautiful form, does not send up canes long enough for the huge bloom. *Long Island R.S.* 5(6-1-28″-7) Large beautiful blooms, weak foliage, mildews, winter-kills. *Niagara Frontier R.S.* 5(8-3-28″-6.6) Beautiful bi-color buds, very large many-petalled blooms most of which are ragged and with split centers, plants refuse to grow large enough to support the big blooms. *Rochester R.S.* 5(5-1-18″-7) Good blooms of good form, excellent pink bi-color, bush small for size of blooms, does not like heat. *Schenectady R.S.* 3(3-2-18″-7.1) Big blooms, dwarf bush, beautiful in Spring, not too good a bloomer. *Syracuse R.S.* 2(2-2-24″-6.5) Attractive color, disease-resistant foliage, sparse bloomer, poor repeat performer. N.C. *Charlotte R.S.* 3(4-2-30″-8) Not a heavy bloomer. *Durham R.S.* 1(1-2-48″-7.5) Beautiful bi-color large blossoms with good susbtance, not very hardy, not a free-bloomer. *Randolph R.S.* 2(3-2-36″-6) Large flower, fine color, scant bloom. split center. OHIO *Akron R.S.* 6(9-2-30″-7.6) Good color, form and foliage, upright, exhibition-type, stingy bloom, some blackspot and mildew. *Central Ohio R.S.* 2(4-2-30″-6) Good large bloom, nice open flower, winter-kills, slow grower, not enough blooms, short stems. *Cincinnati R.S.* 8(18-3-36″-7) Too much die-back. *Cleveland R.S.* 5(6-2-26″-6.4) Nice occasional bloom, good color and good foliage, poor grower. *Columbus R.C.* 3(3-1-24″-4) Good bud, no substance, wilts quickly. *Euclid R.S.* 1(2-2-24″-6.5) Nice flower and foliage, split center, stingy on flowers, very slow grower. *Lancaster R.C.* 2(2-3-33″-7.3) Sparse bloomer. *Lima R.S.* 3(6-2-30″-8) Much the same coloring as Flirtation, but better bush, good bloom and foliage, slow to repeat bloom. *Miami Valley R.S.* 2(4-3-24″-7) Good color, sparse bloomer, many split centers. *Ohio State University T.G.* (4-3-33″-5) Dark glossy green foliage, abundant bloom in June, July and August, disease-resistant, weak flower stem. plant lacks vigor and bushiness. *Stark R.S.* 3(3-2-30″-7.1) Lovely bi-color. ORE. *Eugene R.S.* 4(7-3-24″-6.8) Occasional striking bloom but many are poor, glossy foliage, rather poor plant. *International Rose T.G.* (20-5-36″-7) Huge bi-color flowers best in Spring and Fall, short stems in Summer. *Medford R.S.* 4(7-2-29″-7.4) Well-shaped bud, full beautiful blossom, glossy foliage, doesn't bloom enough. *Roseburg R.S.* 3(4-4-48″-6) Beautiful scarce bloom in Spring, slow grower, disease-resistant. *Salem R.S.* 3(3-2-33″) Long-lasting exhibition blooms with good color, glossy foliage, stingy. PA.

*Breeze Hill T.G.* (1-3-24″-4) Color only nice as it opens, scant bloom. *Harrisburg R.S.* 3(904-3-32″-6.7) Good bi-color, blooms well in June, poor grower, sparse bloomer, large blooms, foliage like Peace, upright, blights easily. *Philadelphia R.S.* 7(13-2-21″-6.5) Good color, poor grower, sparse bloomer, lacks vitality. *Pittsburgh R.S.* 4(21-3-30″-6.6) Lovely bloom color does not last, not vigorous, blackspots badly, poor bloomer. TENN. *Nashville R.S.* 2(5-2-28″-6.6) Beautiful bloom, plants seem weak, light bloomer. TEX. *Amarillo R.S.* 2(3-1-72″-6.5) Not strong bush, not enough bloom. *Corpus Christi R.S.* 1(1-3-36″-8.2) Exquisite bloom, subtle peach and pink tones, more petals than Tiffany, blooms scarce, slow grower. *Dallas R.S.* 3(8-2-32″-7.3) Good color, fine glossy foliage, huge blooms, short stems, many split centers. *El Paso R.S.* 4(4-1-30″-7) Large full bloom, good color, holds well as cut flower, strong disease-resistant foliage, slow-growing, sparse blooms, split centers, dies-back. UTAH *Utah R.S.* 2(3-3-20″-3.5) Good color, fine glossy foliage, bushy plant, too-few blooms, fades too soon. VA. *Eastern Shore R.S.* 3(3-2-36″-6) Good bloom, healthy plant, blooms last well, vigorous bush, stems not straight, crooked neck, no growth. *Va. Peninsula R.S.* 3(3-2-22″-4.3) Beautiful color, good quality bloom, very poor grower, weak plant, sparse blooms. WASH. *Seattle R.S.* 7(15-2-30″-6.4) Occasional good bloom, split centers, S necks, not for our climate. *Spokane R.S.* 8(8-2-30″-8) Attractive foliage, few large flowers, slow-growing. W.VA. *Charleston R.S.* 3(4-2-18″-5). *Wyo-Mac R.S.* 1(1-3-36″-5) Beautiful but not many blooms. WIS. *Madison R.S.* 5(10-2-39″-8.4) Large blooms good for exhibition, good foliage, fair growth, hardy, not enough blooms, split centers. *Milwaukee R.S.* 2(2-2-30″-8) Beautiful form and color, good foliage, small plant, lovely spectacular bloom when there is any. CANADA (British Columbia) *Vancouver R.S.* 2(7-3-36″-7.5) Good foliage, blooms and bush, not enough flowers, best in Fall.

## MARDI GRAS HT. Medium red. (Jordan; int. Jackson & Perkins '54) Pat. 1139; ARA '52; PP 5, 1959, 68 Rpts.; Av. ht. 39″; NR 7.5. Total reports 5 years 218; Av. NR 7.3.

## MERRY WIDOW Gr. Chrysanthemum-crimson to rose-red. (Lammerts; int. Germain's '58) Pat. 1711; ARA '58; PP 1, 57 Rpts.; Av. ht. 42″; NR 7.8.

ALA. *Twickenham R.S.* 2(1-1-33″-7.3) Vigorous growth, good bloom, above-average form. ARIZ. *Mesa R.S.* 1(1-1-60″-8) Blooms freely, nice bud. *Phoenix R.S.* 3(3-1-24″-7.5) Good growth and bloom, moderate fragrance. CALIF. *Memorial T.G.* (10-2-40″-9) 4″ bloom, lighter-colored bud, very free-blooming, petals do not fall. *Rose Study Club Oakland* 1(3-4-60″-7.5) Lovely bud and flower, generous blooms on a vigorous tall bush, poor form when fully open, mildews and rusts easily. *Pacific R.S.* 1(1-1-48″-8.5) Disease-resistant foliage, well-formed plant, produces mostly-single blooms on long strong stems, good bud form, lacks substance. *Peninsula R.S.* 3(5-1-42″-8) Flowers last well, some mildew and blind wood, fragrant. *San Diego R.S.* 3(7-1-48″-8.5) Good color, no side buds. *San Joaquin Valley R.S.* 1(1-1-36″-8) Tapered, well-formed buds, good color and foliage, vigorous plant. GA. *Georgia R.S.* 1(1-1-54″-7.8) Beautiful velvety bud and bloom perfect for lapel, leggy, weak stemmed-plant, some mildew. IND. *Indianapolis R.S.* 2(4-1-45″-7.7) Excellent long stems, high-centered blooms of good substance, outer petals droop, blooms constantly. *St. Joseph Valley R.S.* 1(1-1-42″-8.2) Tall bush, fragrant 5″ flowers. IOWA *Iowa R.S.* 1(3-1-36″- ) Good buds and bloom. KAN. *Wichita R.S.* 2(2-1-36″-5.6) Good grower and foliage, bloom burns. KY. *Louisville Chapter ARS* 1(1-1-54″-7) Beautiful bud, nice foliage, too-few blooms, unattractive open blossom. MICH. *Detroit R.S.* 4(5-1-36″-7.2) Good color holds, profuse single blooms. *Michigan State University T.G.* (26-3-42″-10) Holds color very well, blooms open slowly, excellent form from bud to full blown, moderate but continuous flowering, blooms borne singly, very fragrant (tea), only slightly susceptible to mildew. MO. *Rosarians Midland Empire* 1(1-1-48″-7.7) Good grower, nice red blooms, no faults. *Sedalia R.S.* 1(1-1-38″-8.5) Excellent plant, lots of bloom. N.J. *North Jersey R.S.* 6(7-1-27″-7) Well-shaped buds, nice color, good foliage, not generous. N.M. *Albuquerque R.S.* 1(2-2-42″-8) Exquisite form, high-centered buds, open flower rather fleeting, fool-proof foliage. N.C. *Durham R.S.* 1(2-1-48″-8) Long tapering blood-red bloom on excellent stem, good foliage, uniform growth habit, sparse bloomer. OHIO *Akron R.S.* 2(2-1-38″-8) Good form and color, exhibition-type, vigorous, single stems. *Central Ohio R.S.* 1(3-1-48″-8) Prolific bloomer with good color, healthy vigorous plant, very disease-resistant. *Lancaster R.C.* 1(2-4-72″-8) Vigorous, upright, velvety blooms, too-few clusters. ORE. *International Rose T.G.* (18-3-72″-6) Long clear bud form and color, one flower on each long stem. *Medford R.S.* 1(1-1-68″-8.5) Very vigorous, blooms similar in color and form to Chrysler Imperial only smaller, blooms almost all the time, some mildew. *Rogue Valley R.S.* 1(1-1-54″-8.5) Beautiful color, good form, floriferous, symmetrical, disease-resistant, vigorous. PA. *Breeze Hill T.G.* (3-4-32″-9) Most attractive color and form, heavy foliage, stiff stems, keeps color well. *Harrisburg R.S.* 1(1-1-54″-8) Well-formed blooms, repeats well, good grower, no trace of disease. TENN. *Nashville R.S.* 3(6-1-60″-8.1) Healthy, vigorous, large quantity of blooms blue some, fast-opening. TEX. *Amarillo R.S.* 2(2-1-48″-8.2) Good growth, color, foliage and stem, bloom size not regular. *Corpus Christi R.S.* 1(1-1-36″-8.5) Lovely buds open slowly, long stems, resembles Mirandy, scarce bloomer. *El Paso R.S.* 1(1-1-40″-9) Fast grower, good foliage, prolific bloomer, lovely color does not fade like most of the reds, strong healthy growth. WIS. *Madison R.S.* 2(2-1-40″-7.2) Good color, form and foliage, lasts long, not vigorous, stingy blooms. *Milwaukee R.S.* (32″-9) Beautiful bud and flower, could bloom more.

**MIAMI HT.** Yellow and red. (Meilland; int. Conard-Pyle '54) Pat. 977; ARA '54; PP 5, 1959, 71 Rpts.; Av. ht. 29″; **NR 6.2.** Total reports 5 years 320; **Av. NR 6.1.**

**MIDNIGHT HT.** Very deep red. (Swim; int. Armstrong '56) Pat. 1542; ARA '57; PP 2, 178 Rpts.; Av. ht. 37″; **NR 6.7.**

ALA. *Twickenham R.S.* 1(6-2-48″-8.2) Beautiful color, long stems, very fragrant. ARIZ. *Mesa R.S.* 3(3-1-36″-6.8) Beautiful unfading fragrant bloom, poor bud, color and bloom form. *Phoenix R.S.* 5(5-2-40″-7.5) Velvet blooms burn during heat, strong fragrance, not enough petals. CALIF. *Rose Study Club Oakland* 2(8-1-55″-6.7) Beautiful form and color when it first opens, requires heat and subdued light to do well, strong damask, fragrance, burns quickly in hot sun. *Pacific R.S.* 4(4-2-47″-7.4) Unusually dark urn-shaped buds, vigorous disease-resistant plant, profuse bloomer, full-blown rose is washed out and doesn't hold. *Peninsula R.S.* 4(4-2-48″-6) Good blooms, best in bud, mildews. *Riverside R.S.* 4(5-8-30″-5.6) Mildews, sun cooks the flowers. *San Diego R.S.* 4(6-1-62″-7.7). *San Joaquin Valley R.S.* Vigorous, upright growth, resistant to mildew, beautiful velvety bloom loses size and petalage in warm weather. COLO. *Colorado Springs R.S.* 1(8-2-36″-6) Nice color, sparse blooms. *Denver R.S.* 2(2-2-26″-5) Beautiful but sparse bloomer, foliage O.K., burns in sun. GA. *Georgia R.S.* 4(6-2-42″-6) Best in cool weather, good bush, small flower, poor form, blackens in sun, not for this area, poor lasting quality. ILL. *Chicago Reg R.S.* 1 4(4-2-6.5) Slow sparse bloomer, weak plant, bloom attractive but of poor form. *Greater Peoria R.S.* 1(1-2-24″-6.5) Good blooms in Summer and Fall, open flowers darken around the edges, mildews badly. IND. *Indianapolis R.S.* 2(4-2-27″-5.6) Poor growth, few blooms with no form, not enough petals, blackspots. *St. Joseph Valley R.S.* 2(4-3-30″-7.2) Dark bud, healthy glossy foliage, opens fast, too-few petals. IOWA *Des Moines R.S.* 3(3-2-24″-5) Good color, too-few blooms. *Iowa R.S.* 2(2-2-30″-5) Burns easily, small flowers. *Linn County R.S.* 1(1-2-30″-6). KY. *Lexington R.S.* 1(1-1-40″-6.9) Vigorous grower, good bloom in Spring, fine bud form, petals burn on edges. *Louisville Chapter ARS* 2(3-2-33″-7.3) Lovely dark bud and flower, good glossy foliage, sunburns and mildews. LA. *New Orleans R.S.* 3(3-1-36″-5) Not enough bloom, does not grow well. MICH. *Detroit R.S.* 4(4-2-30″-6.1) Not enough bloom, small flowers. *Greater Lansing R.S.* 1(1-2-36″-7) Deep red, urn-shaped bud, little or no fragrance, average foliage and height, quite resistant to disease. *Kalamazoo R.S.* 3(4-2-40″-7.5) Vigorous, not a show rose, blackspots. MINN. *Minnesota R.S.* 8(12-1-37″-7.6) Small fragrant bloom, susceptible to mildew. MO. *Rosarians Midland Empire* 2(5-2-30″-5) Deep color, poor plants, not prolific, too-few petals. *R.S. Greater St. Louis* 2(3-3-36″-6) Not enough growth or bloom, poor form. *Sedalia R.S.* 2(2-2-30″-7.5) Good foliage, nice plant, opens quickly and sunburns. NEW ENGLAND *New England R.S.* 4(6-2-30″-7) Poor performer. N.J. *North Jersey R.S.* 10(19-1-33″-6.6) Dark red bud opens fast, good plant, disappointing bloom size. *West Jersey R.S.* 3(3-2-24″-6.8) Good color, does not blue, too-few blooms, medium-size canes with sparse foliage. N.M. *Albuquerque R.S.* 4(4-2-37″-7.1) Good color and bud form, fragrant, bloom does not fade in heat, opens too fast, not enough petals, small blooms. N.Y. *Greater Buffalo R.S.* 1(1-1-30″-7.5) Satiny flowers, stiff slender stems, not very vigorous plant. *Humboldt Park T.G.* (5-2-36″-9.8) Upright, very vigorous plant, very resistant foliage, large abundant urn-shaped buds, drops cleanly, moderate fruity fragrance, abundant continuous bloom. *Long Island R.S.* 1(1-2-48″-6.9) Healthy, form and number of petals varies widely with weather. *Niagara Frontier R.S.* 3(5-2-42″-6.7) Small blooms, not enough petals, mildews freely, fragrant. *Rochester R.S.* 3(3-1-15″-7.5) Flowers almost black, bloomed three times, some mildew. *Schenectady R.S.* 1(1-1-36″-7). *Syracuse R.S.* 2(2-2-33″-7.4) Good form, small bloom, foliage susceptible to blackspot and mildew. N.C. *Durham R.S.* 2(4-2-54″-7) Profuse bloomer, good vigor, fragrant, more shapely plant than Charles Mallerin. OHIO *Akron R.S.* 2(3-2-8) Good color, not exhibition-type, opens fast. *Central Ohio R.S.* 2(3-2-42″-6) Lovely bloom, weak plant, few blooms, plant mildews easily. *Cincinnati R.S.* 5(11-2-28″-6.5) Good fragrance. *Cleveland R.S.* 2(10-3-38″-7.2) Wonderful color, good garden variety, healthy, short bud, few petals, loose blooms. *Columbus R.C.* 4(4-2-48″-6) Good color, opens too fast, small blooms. *Lancasster R.C.* 5(6-2-33″-5.7) Skimpy foliage, poor bloomer. *Lima R.S.* 3(3-3-36″-6.9) Some blooms small, not disease-resistant. *Miami Valley R.S.* 2(3-2-30″-7.5) Good color, stand heat, too-thin petalage, blooms too small. *Ohio State University T.G.* (4-3-36″-7) Blooms well in June, August and September, excellent foliage, very vigorous and bushy, holds leaves to base of plant, fragrant, affected by early frost. *Stark R.S.* 1(1-1-30″-7) Profuse, good bloom. OKLA. *Norman R.S.* 1(1-2-36″-6.5). ORE. *International Rose T.G.* (20-2-48″-6) Medium dusky-red buds and flowers, fair resistance. *Medford R.S.* 4(8-2-38″-5.6) Small attractive blackish-red bud, small and unattractive open bloom burns, mildews, blooms hang on. *Rogue Valley R.S.* 4(5-2-52″- ) Outstanding form and color, fragrant, could have more blooms, lots of mildew. *Salem R.S.* 2(3-2-37″-8) Long buds, black-red, very fragrant, stingy. PA. *Breeze Hill T.G.* (3-5-34″-8) Early, profuse, nice color and form, good stems. *Harrisburg R.S.* 1(1-2-30″-6) Good color, few blooms, poor foliage. *Philadelphia R.S.* 2(3-2-40″-6.7) Good color, fair plant, small loose blooms. TENN. *Nashville R.S.* 5(7-2-33″-6.6) Vigorous hardy plant, fragrant, almost black, opens fast, not good in warm weather. TEX. *Amarillo R.S.* 3(3-3-36″-8) Very good black-red, profuse bloomer, good sturdy foliage. *Corpus Christi R.S.* 1(1-3-36″-9) Most beautiful foliage of any rose, fragrant lovely bloom fades quickly, not very double. UTAH *Utah R.S.* 3(4-2-31″-3.8) Good color, too-few blooms, bush too small. VA. *Va. Peninsula R.S.* 2(2-2-48″-7) Small tight buds open quickly, blooms do not last very long. WASH. *Seattle R.S.* 2(4-3-52″-8.1) Lacks petalage. *Spokane R.S.* 3(3-2-36″-8) Velvety petals, fragrant, semi-single. W.VA. *Charleston R.S.* 1(3-2-36″-5) Upright medium-sized plant, heavy bloomer. WIS. *Madison R.S.* 2(2-2-40″-6.9) Good color, poor form, good hardy foliage, small flowers, poor substance. *Milwaukee R.S.* 2(2-1-28″-7) Beautiful color and buds, small flowers, color fades rapidly. CANADA (British Columbia) *Vancouver R.S.* 1(6-3-36″-7) Good color, small bloom. HAWAII *Kona* (1-1-46″-7) Improves with age, floriferous, easily damaged by wind.

## MONTEZUMA Gr. Light red. (Swim; int. Armstrong '55) Pat. 1383; ARA '56; PP 3, 568 Rpts.; Av. ht. 48″; NR 8.5.

ALA. *Twickenham R.S.* 2(3-2-45″-9) Beautiful color, continuous bloom, vigorous. ARIZ. *Mesa R.S.* 5(6-2-48″-8.9) Excellent bush, long-lasting non-fading bloom, outstanding color, form and foliage. *Phoenix R.S.* 6(9-2-48″-8.8) Outstanding color and form, stands heat. CALIF. *Memorial T.G.* (6-4-60″-10) Good cutter, free-blooming, 4″ flower, lovely orange-red color, long-lasting, cut 25 half-opened blooms from one bush same day, slight fragrance. *Rose Study Club Oakland* 4(12-2-55″-8.3) Vivid color, beautiful bud, flower has crisp substance, lasts long on bush or cut, bush improves greatly with age, blooms fade on outer edge in heat. *Pacific R.S.* 6(11-2-47″-9.2) Exceptional foliage, free blooming habit, excellent cut flower, attractive color. *Peninsula R.S.* 7(11-2-48″-8) Outstanding plant with disease-free foliage, good color and form, lasts well as cut flower, fades. *Riverside R.S.* 8(12-5-66″-9.5) A favorite for our climate, good form, long-lasting flowers, no mildew. *San Diego R.S.* 5(11-2-60″-8.6). *San Joaquin Valley R.S.* 9(28-2-54″-9). *San Mateo County R.S.* 8(15-3-60″-9) Good color, growth and bloomer, new growth must be protected from mildew in cool weather. COLO. *Colorado Springs R.S.* 3(14-2-30″-7) Beautiful buds, fades in sun, nice plant, good for cutting, poor producer. *Denver R.S.* 7(34-4-48″-9) Moderate bloomer, nice foliage, attractive color and form, never drops petals, holds color, sometimes balls a little. CONN. *Elizabeth Park T.G.* (15-4-24″-8) Good grower, attractive color. D.C. *Potomac R.S.* 6(12-3-60″-9.2) Big high-centered bloom on long stems, holly-like foliage on vigorous plant, second only to Queen Elizabeth, cut roses keep longest of all. GA. *Georgia R.S.* 13(35-2-52″-8.6) Perfectly-shaped bush, beautiful disease-resistant foliage, perfect form in bud and bloom, high center, long-lasting when cut, outstanding orange-red color, no faults. ILL. *Chicago R.S. Reg. I* 7(16-2-48″-9.2) Striking color, excellent form, prolific bloomer, vigorous healthy plant. *Greater Peoria R.S.* 7(7-1-47″-8.4) Good color and form, does not fade, vigorous grower, keeps well when cut, some blackspot, blooming periods far apart. *Morgan Park R.S.* 3(3-2-24″-8.3) Good bloomer. *Tri-City Men's Rose and Garden Club* 1(24-3-30″-8.5) Makes a good showing. IND. *Indianapolis R.S.* 5(7-2-49″-8.3) Beautiful burnt-orange buds and blooms, long-lasting, do not open after cutting, strong plant, disease-resistant. *St. Joseph Valley R.S.* 4(11-2-42″-8.8) Flowers last well when cut, strong, healthy, vigorous, lots of bloom, balls in cool weather. *Vincennes R.S.* 2(4-2-48″-8) Wonderful long-lasting blooms except in

hot sun, hardy, good cut rose, few specimen blooms. IOWA *Des Moines R.S.* 5(6-2-48″-8.5)
Good color and form, plenty of bloom. *Iowa R.S.* 4(12-1-30″-7.5) Blooms last well.
*Linn County R.S.* 6(10-3-40″-8.6) Orange-rose color, nice bud form, vigorous grower,
long-lasting bloom, disease-resistant. KAN. *Wichita R.S.* 11(23-3-48″-8.5) Good bloomer,
flowers last. KY. *Frankfort Chapter ARS* 10(30-2-60″-8) Outstanding color and form,
profuse bloomer, good foliage. *Kentucky R.S.* 9(20-2-53″-8.8) Good form, cutting quality,
long-lasting blooms, lovely color, good bloomer. *Lexington R.S.* 1(1-2-48″-7) Vigorous grower,
good foliage, attracts thrips, fades, some mildew. *Louisville Chapter ARS* 13(18-2-44″-8.3)
Long-lasting beautiful bud and flower, vigorous growing, too-few blooms. LA. *New Orleans
R.S.* 6(16-2-60″-9) Beautiful color, good grower, nice disease-resistant foliage. MD.
*Maryland R.S.* 4(6-2-54″-8.5) Well-formed blooms, never see the center, first-rate petals
hang on. MICH. *Detroit R.S.* 9(12-2-36″-8.2) Free-bloomer, strong plant, good stems,
disease-resistant. *Greater Lansing R.S.* 4(4-2-42″-8.5) Artistic very double flower, lovely
orange color, no fragrance, large plant, vigorous, hardiest rose grown. *Kalamazoo R.S.*
13(49-3-54″-8) Fades, good form, nice disease-resistant foliage. *Michigan State University
T.G.* (6-3-33″-5.6) Large bud, disease-resistant, petals burn in heat, balling tendency, no
fragrance. *West Michigan Rosarians* 4(4-4-48″-9). MINN. *Lyndale Park T.G.* (35-4-48″-7.5)
Good bloomer, outstanding color, blackspots, blooms fade. *Minnesota R.S.* 19(46-2-35″-8.2)
Outstanding vigorous growth, sturdy stems, long-lasting blooms. MO. *Kansas City R.S.*
3(7-2-60″-9) Good color, continuous bloomer, some blackspot. *Rosarians Midland Empire*
3(8-2-45″-8) Vivid color, prolific bloomer, good foliage, upright growth. *R.S. Greater
St. Louis* 6(10-2-42″-8) Long-lasting blooms of fine color, wish there were more of them,
good plant and foliage. *Sedalia R.S.* 4(4-3-48″-8.5) Excellent form and color, holds well,
balls occasionally, not quite enough vigor. MONT. *Sunset Park T.G.* (10-3-30″-9) Sturdy
upright plant produces steady flow of well-shaped long-lasting showy flowers, does especially
well in mid-Summer and Fall. NEV. *Reno R.S.* 18(38-4-72″-9) Excellent strong grower,
blooms profusely, does not fade, mildews in Fall like Spartan. NEW ENGLAND *New
England R.S.* 8(26-2-30″-8.2) N.H.—not tall in colder areas, persistent blooms. N.J.
*North Jersey R.S.* 18(34-3-47″-8.6) Excellent exhibition form and cut flowers, vigorous.
*West Jersey R.S.* 5(9-2-48″-8.3) Rugged disease-resistant plant, blooms last when cut.
N.M. *Albuquerque R.S.* 3(6-3-41″-9.1) Vigorous, long-lasting rose, good non-fading color,
form and foliage. N.Y. *Cornell University T.G.* (6-4-36″-8) Unusual color, best in cool
weather, good form and foliage, tends to ball in wet weather, best blooms early in
season. *Greater Buffalo R.S.* 6(18-2-48″-9) Vigorous, heavy canes, long-lasting flower,
very disease-resistant. *Humboldt Park T.G.* (5-4-30″-8.5) Upright, vigorous plant, abundant
large very resistant foliage, some blooms in clusters, others single, deep coral-pink buds
brighten when opening, continuous blooms, petals fade and hang on.. *Long Island R.S.*
5(5-2-40″-8) Good color, bud, bloom and foliage, vigorous, long-lasting blooms, good cut
flowers, no fragrance. *Niagara Frontier R.S.* 6(10-2-42″-8.3) Healthy, slow-growing plant,
fine blooms, but not enough of them. *Rochester R.S.* 9(31-2-39″-8.5) Interesting orange-
red color, extra-good disease-resistant foliage, blooms hold well. *Schenectady R.S.*
2(2-2-30″-7) Nice flower and foliage, not as upright as other Grandifloras, flower fades,
poor bush, lovely color, good bloomer. *Syracuse R.S.* 5(5-2-48″-8.1) Very vigorous bush,
good bloomer, disease-resistant, good exhibition rose, very unusual color, nice foliage.
N.C. *Charlotte R.S.* 2(3-3-36″-7). *Durham R.S.* 13(39-2-54″-8.5) Beautiful coral color,
wonderful for arrangements, long-lasting, tends to ball. *Randolph R.S.* 2(4-2-60″-7) Beautiful long-lasting buds and bloom, abundant strong foliage. OHIO *Akron R.S.* 6(12-3-42″-8.3)
Outstanding color, exhibition-type sparse blooms hold form and color, slight blackspot,
water-marks. *Central Ohio R.S.* 6(10-2-48″-8.8) Lovely bloom, good color, excellent
form and substance, free-bloomer, healthy, strong vigorous-growing bush, discolors in mid-Summer, bush a little too spreading. *Cincinnati R.S.* 11(31-2-54″-9)
*Cleveland R.S.* 7(19-2-50″-8.5) Excellent bloom, stems, foliage, growth, color, Hybrid Tea-
size blooms in clusters. *Columbus R.C.* 5(10-2-48″-8.2) Excellent form, good foliage, large
blooms, too-few flowers. *Euclid R.S.* 4(4-1-54″-8.5) Excellent form, good color and
foliage, could have more blooms. *Forest City R.S.* 4(6-2-42″-9) Good strong upright
plant, good bloomer, exceptional color. *Greater Cincinnati R.S.* 7(9-1-42″-8.5) Good
growing plant, beautiful form of both bud and flower, attractive color, generous bloom.
*Lancaster R.C.* 9(15-2-54″-8.4) Vigorous, upright, large foliage, abundant non-fading
blooms. *Lima R.S.* 9(22-3-48″-9) Free-bloomer, long-lasting flowers, good color and texture,
disease-resistant. *Miami Valley R.S.* 5(10-2-48″-9) Excellent holding quality, outstanding
color, good form. *Ohio State University T.G.* (4-1-27″-7) Vigorous, bushy, abundant
large glossy disease-resistant leaves, blooms well only in July. *Park of Roses T.G.*
(75-3-46″-8) Good color and quality of bloom, not too susceptible to blackspot, not too
vigorous. *Stark R.S.* (42″-7.7) Fine grower, single blooms, good exhibition rose. OKLA.
*Norman R.S.* A favorite here. *Oklahoma R.S.* 3(12-2-48″-9) Free-bloomer, strong plant.
ORE. *Eugene R.S.* 4(5-3-60″-8.7) Soft pleasing flame color, true exhibition form, strong
plant, good producer. *International Rose T.G.* (40-6-60″-9) Fine bud form, disbud for
exhibition, good color, foliage and plant, fades somewhat. *Lewis & Clark T.G.* (10-2-60″-8)

PINK PEACE HT
Francis Meilland; introduced Conard-Pyle Co., West Grove, Pa. Plant Patent
1759. Described page 253.

FASHIONETTE F
E. S. Boerner; introduced Jackson & Perkins, Newark, N.Y. Plant patent 1563.
Described page 245.

OF THE PUDDING**                                                 **213**

Beautiful bud and bloom, fine foliage, too high. *Medford R.S.* 6(10-2-50″-8.9) Excellent form, color and size, prolific bloom, healthy foliage, some fading. *Rogue Valley R.S.* 3(5-2-60″-9) Good color, form and foliage, long stems, disease-resistant. *Roseburg R.S.* 2(3-3-72″-8) Good color, excellent quality when disbudded, good foliage, fades. *Salem R.S.* 4(6-3-47″-9.2) Glowing color, continuous bloomer, exhibition quality, healthy plant. PA. *Breeze Hill T.G.* (3-6-40″-7) Very profuse, good foliage, interesting color. *Harrisburg R.S.* 2(1003-2-57″-9.2) Bloom opens slowly, withstands heat and sunlight, excellent foliage, good grower, excellent show rose, hardy. *Philadelphia R.S.* 8(13-2-42″-8) Vigorous grower, good bloom form and color, withstands heat. *Pittsburgh R.S.* 4(10-2-42″-7.4) Excellent bush, rich color, many blooms, good foliage, slight fading. S.C. *Edisto T.G.* (10-4-42″-8.5) Good color, free-flowering, vigorous, some blackspot. TENN. *Nashville R.S.* 8(24-3-50″-7.6) Magnificent form and color, blooms keep well, adequate production, cold weather-tender. TEX. *Amarillo R.S.* 5(3-42″-8.9) Good bloomer, healthy, vigorous foliage, good form and color, blooms last for days. *Corpus Christi R.S.* 1(1-3-24″-8.7) Exceptional color, lovely full buds, slow to open, very long-lasting, foliage mildews very easily. *Dallas R.S.* 3(9-3-45″-7.3) Glorious color, form and foliage, prolific short stems, fades badly. *El Paso R.S.* 6(7-2-60″-9) Rich healthy foliage, good substance in stem and blooms, true to color, prolific bloomer during the entire season, disease-resistant, long straight stems. UTAH *Utah R.S.* 10(38-3-50″-8.4) Wonderful bush and plant, fine color, fades slightly, slight mildew. VA. *Eastern Shore R.S.* 3(4-2-48″-9) Vigorous bush, good foliage, especially long-lasting cut flowers, disease-resistant. *Va. Peninsula R.S.* 3(4-2-58″-8) Vigorous growth, good foliage, good color, free-bloomer, color fades. WASH. *Seattle R.S.* 5(10-3-45″-8.9) Good blooms on a good plant. *Spokane R.S.* 10(21-2-36″-5) Perfect for arrangements, many exhibition-type blooms. *Walla Walla R.S.* 3(12-4-54″-9) Grows well, good color and form. W.VA. *Charleston R.S.* 2(6-2-48″-8) Long-lasting blooms on healthy plants, unusual color, no faults. *Wyo-Mac R.S.* 5(20-2-48″-9.2) Outstanding performer, unfading color, good as cut flower, luxurious growth. WIS. *Madison R.S.* 6(15-2-42″-8.3) Good form, beautiful color, good foliage, long-lasting blooms, vigorous growth, disease-resistant, not enough blooms. *Milwaukee R.S.* 5(11-2-54″-8.8) Unusual fine color, good form, large plant, good dark foliage, nice bushy canes, vigorous, fades in hot weather. CANADA (British Columbia) *Vancouver R.S.* 10(21-4-54″-8.5) Very good form and color, leathery disease-resistant foliage, floriferous, vivid color changes, long-lasting.

**MOONSPRITE F.** Yellow and cream. (Swim; int. Armstrong '56) Pat. 1450; ARA '57; PP 2, 44 Rpts.; Av. ht. 28″; NR 7.8.

ARIZ. *Mesa R.S.* 1(3-1-30″-7.6) Nice bloomer, nice flower, does not fade badly. *Phoenix R.S.* 2(2-2-24″-7.5) Compact growth, dainty buds, good form, fragrant. CALIF. *Pacific R.S.* 1(1-2-36″-9) Attractive producer, keeps well. *Peninsula R.S.* 1(2-1-24″-7) Shapely plant, performs best in Spring, shy bloomer. *San Joaquin Valley R.S.* (2-3-36″-8) Good plant with fine foliage, good for landscaping, blooms in large clusters. CONN. *Elizabeth Park T.G.* (4-3-20″-5) Pleasing appearance, buds on short stems. D.C. *Potomac R.S.* 2(3-3-36″-7.4) Neat grower, glossy foliage, small flower, many petals, yellow-gold center fades to white, good for edging, not a mass bloomer. GA. *Georgia R.S.* 1(10-2-36″-8.8) Well-shaped plant, free-bloomer, pleasing color, no disease, sets hips. IND. *Vincennes R.S.* 1(1-1- ). IOWA *Linn County R.S.* 1(1-1-20″-6). KY. *Louisville Chapter ARS* 3(5-2-37″-8) Profuse bloom, good color, form and substance, healthy foliage, sprawling habit. MICH. *Detroit R.S.* 1(1-2-30″-7.5) Abundant bloom, holds color well. *Greater Lansing R.S.* 1(1-2-18″-7.5) Beautiful light rosette, fragrant, very bushy, excellent foliage, perfect for lasting bouquets. *Kalamazoo R.S.* 1(1-3-42″-7.5) Good different bloom. MINN. *Minnesota R.S.* 6(12-1-27″-8.7) Good for foreground, excellent form, bushy, vigorous plant, abundant bloom. N.J. *North Jersey R.S.* 5(11-2-28″-7.5) Dependable. N.Y. *Humboldt Park T.G.* (5-2-18″-9) Branching vigorous plant, abundant large to medium bloom, very leathery foliage very resistant to disease, ovoid-shaped ivory-yellow buds, medium full globular double yellow to ivory blooms in clusters fade when finishing, winter-kills to 4″. OHIO *Cleveland R.S.* 1(1-1-13″-6) Attractive blooms, poor growth. *Euclid R.S.* 1(1-2-24″-7.5) Nice blooms, beautiful clusters on spray, center flowers in cluster fade too quickly. *Ohio State University T.G.* (4-3-27″-6) Vigorous, bushy plant, excellent foliage, blooms abundantly in June and July, disease-resistant, fragrant, very little bloom from September on, weak flower stems. ORE. *International Rose T.G.* (2-4-24″-8) Nice bud form, clean fresh flowers, always in bloom. *Salem R.S.* 1(2-3-30″-7) Plenty of bloom on good plant, unattractive color. PA. *Breeze Hill T.G.* (3-5-28″-8) Very profuse, nice color as it opens, good plant and foliage. *Philadelphia R.S.* 1(1-2-18″-7) Good flower, slow grower, weak plant, not enough bloom. TENN. *Nashville R.S.* 2(9-2-33″-8.8) Healthy, vigorous, constant bloomer, fades rapidly to white. TEX. *Amarillo R.S.* 1(1-1-9) Prolific bloomer, beautiful buds, long-lasting. UTAH *Utah R.S.*

1(2-4-28″-9) Lots of bloom. WASH. *Walla Walla R.S.* 1(1-2-36″-7) Very cute, tiny. WIS. *Madison R.S.* 2(2-1-27″-8.2) Good bloom, form and foliage, disease-resistant, fair substance, attractive bud, good in cool weather.

**PAGEANT HT.** Red and yellow. (Boerner; int. Jackson & Perkins '54) Pat. 1252; ARA '54; PP 5, 1959, 59 Rpts.; Av. ht. 30″; **NR 6.5.** Total reports 5 years 233; **Av. NR 5.8.**

**PEACEFUL HT.** Pink blend. (Boerner; int. Jackson & Perkins '56) Pat. 1599; ARA '56; PP 3, 76 Rpts.; Av. ht. 32″; **NR 6.6.**

ARIZ. *Phoenix R.S.* 3(3-1-24″-6.5) Few beautiful blooms, weak bush. CALIF. *Rose Study Club Oakland* 2(8-2-45″-6.4) Rather weak, slow-growing plant, beautiful large fragrant blooms of exhibition quality but sparse quantity, weak stems. *San Mateo County R.S.* 1(2-3-36″-2) Only one good bloom in a year, plant lacks vigor. D.C. *Potomac R.S.* 2(3-2-6.5) Poor plant, one or two large blooms on a weak stem twice a year. GA. *Georgia R.S.* 4(6-2-52″-6.2) Above-average bloom size and color, weak necks, requires constant disbudding, too-few blooms. ILL. *Greater Peoria R.S.* 3(3-1-36″-6.9 Good color, large blooms, not enough blooms. IND. *St. Joseph Valley R.S.* 1(1-2-36″-7.2) Tall bush, large 5″ bloom, blackspots easily. IOWA *Linn County R.S.* 1(1-2-28″-7.5) Vigorous. KY. *Louisville Chapter ARS* 2(2-1-33″-6) Good color and form, poor producer, weak necks, does not grow well. MICH. *Detroit R.S.* 1(1-1-30″-7.6) Nice bloom, does not grow well. *Kalamazoo R.S.* 1(2-2-36″-7.8) Nice blooms, good form. *Michigan State University T.G.* (5-3-31″-9.3) Holds color well, open flower of pleasing form, disease-resistant, moderate fragrance (cold cream), 3½″ blooms, light color. MINN. *Minnesota R.S.* 3(4-1-22″-6.7) Waxy foliage, strong stems hold striking pink 50-petalled blossoms. MO. *R.S. Greater St. Louis* 1(1-1-12″-5) Too peaceful. NEV. *Reno R.S.* 2(6-3-30″-4) Blooms only in June, weak leggy plant, weak stems, mildews in cool weather. NEW ENGLAND *New England R.S.* 4(6-1-30″-7.5) Vt. and N.H.—sparse bloom, weak necks; Me. and Mass.—few large fragrant flowers. N.J. *North Jersey R.S.* Blackspots, weak plant, bloom not worth the trouble. *West Jersey R.S.* 6(8-2-24″-5) Plants never look very healthy, leaves spot and fall off (not blackspot), good pink flowers of enormous size, too big for the stem. N.Y. *Greater Buffalo R.S.* 3(6-1-18″-8) Large leathery leaves, huge heavy flower, some blackspot and mildew. *Richester R.S.* 2(3-3-38″-8) Large blooms of excellent color, good foliage. *Echenectady R.S.* 1(2-3-16″-7) Color outstanding quality, not tall, heavy heads, weak necks. *Syracuse R.S.* 2(2-2-26″-7) Very large, double, good pink, fragrant, poor foliage, blackspots, thin stems. N.C. *Charlotte R.S.* 4(5-2-60″-8) Blooms have substance, too large for supporting stem. OHIO *Akron R.S.* 3(4-2-20″-6.2) Good blooms, weak neck, blackspots, stingy. *Cleveland R.S.* 2(4-2-33″-7.9) Large pleasing blooms of exhibition size and form, bushy plant, heavy canes. *Lancaster R.C.* 2(2-3-30″-5.8) Weak necks, poor bloom. OKLA. *Oklahoma R.S.* 1(3-2-36″-8) Large blooms. ORE. *International Rose T.G.* (18-4-36″-6) Huge exhibition buds, good flower form, needs disbudding, has foliage problems. *Lewis & Clark T.G.* (5-1-48″-5) Sparse bloom in hot weather. PA. *Philadelphia R.S.* 1(2-2-36″-9) Wonderful bloom and color, good producer, plant too spindly for so large a bloom. TENN. *Nashville R.S.* 2(4-2-32″-7.8) Beautiful immense blooms, rosy-pink blend. TEX. *Corpus Christi R.S.* 1(1-1-24″-7) Nice blooms, good full color, mildews easily, too-few blooms, slow grower. *Dallas R.S.* 1(3-1-30″-7.5) Good full blooms, good color, soft foliage. *El Paso R.S.* 1(1-1-36″-7.8) Beautiful full blooms, good color does not fade, low-growing bushy plant, weak stems, not too vigorous. UTAH *Utah R.S.* 1(1-5-24″-5) Lovely blooms, small bush. WASH. *Spokane R.S.* 1(1-2-24″-5) Beautiful exhibition rose, wish it bloomed more freely. W.VA. *Charleston R.S.* 1(2-2-24″-3). *Wyo-Mac R.S.* 1(1-1-48″-10) Beautiful bloom and color, long stems, blooms freely, no faults. WIS. *Madison R.S.* 1(1-1-30″-7.4) Good color and disease-resistant foliage, too-few blooms.

**PENNSYLVANIAN HT.** Salmon-buff to seashell-pink. (Ohlhus; int. Conard-Pyle '54) Pat. 936; ARA '54; PP 5, 1959, 43 Rpts.; Av. ht. 40″; **NR 7.3.** Total reports 5 years 214; **Av. NR 7.2.**

**PIGMY RED F.** Red. (Boerner; int. Jackson & Perkins '54) Pat. 1319; ARA '54; PP 5, 1959, 15 Rpts.; Av. ht. 15″; **NR 6.6.** Total reports 5 years 97; **Av. 5.7.**

**PINK CAMEO Cl. Min.** Rose-pink. (Moore; int. Sequoia '54) Pat. 1451; ARA 1451; PP 5, 1959, 23 Rpts.; Av. ht. 3′; **NR 7.9.** Total reports 5 years 63; **Av. NR 8.0.**

**PINK CHIFFON F.** Pink, darker at center. (Boerner; int. Jackson & Perkins '58) Pat. 1564; ARA '58; PP 1, 23 Rpts.; Av. ht. 28″; **NR 8.1.**

CALIF. *Rose Study Club Oakland* 2(8-1-36″-8.2) Lovely delicate pink and white blooms, good producer, upright spreading foliage, fragrant flower fades in sun. *San Joaquin Valley R.S.* 2(3-1-24″-6.7). KY. *Louisville Chapter ARS* 1(4-2-36″-7.8) Disease-resistant, good form, pale in hot weather. MICH. *Michigan State University T.G.* (6-1-30″-10) Continuous flowering, excellent color, disease-resistant, semi-weak necks, no fragrance, quilled effect in fully-open blooms. N.J. *North Jersey R.S.* 2(2-1-34″-8.5) Fine plant. N.Y. *Humboldt Park T.G.* (6-1-21″-9.9) Branching vigorous plant, abundant medium very resistant foliage, large to medium urn-shaped blush-pink buds, medium full high-centered pale pink blooms supported on medium length strong stems, petals drop cleanly, intermittent bloom. *Rochester R.S.* 1(20-1-28″-7) Good foliage, rich pink flower lasts well, good fragrance, slow starter. OHIO *Cincinnati R.S.* 1(1-1-24″-8) No serious faults. *Cleveland R.S.* 1(7-3-36″-7.9) Sturdy plant, blooms all Summer, weak color in heat. *Lancaster R.C.* 1(2-1-36″-7) Vigorous, upright, good foliage, light pink full blooms in clusters. *Ohio State University T.G.* (4-2-27″-7.8) Very abundant flowering until September, vigorous bushy plant, small to medium-size dark green glossy disease-resistant leaves, weak flower stems, malformed flowers (looks like thrip damage). OKLA. *Oklahoma R.S.* 1(4-2-36″-9) Fine plant, profuse bloomer. ORE. *Lewis & Clark T.G.* (10-1-24″-8) Good foliage, bloom and color. *Rogue Valley R.S.* 1(2-1-30″-8.5) Dainty color, beautiful plant, disease-resistant. PA. *Breeze Hill T.G.* (3-4-22″-8) Delicate color, graceful, nice form, blooms well, fades much. S.C. *Edisto T.G.* (6-1-24″-7.5) Good bushy plant, fine form, substance and blush-pink color, shy on flowers. UTAH *Utah R.S.* 2(4-2-24″-8.4) Lovely color, continuous bloomer. WASH. *Spokane R.S.* 1(10-1-16″-8) Nice scent, full of bloom at all times. WIS. *Madison R.S.* 1(2-1-30″-8.8) Beautiful bud, fine bush, excellent long-lasting color.

**PINK FAVORITE HT.** Medium pink. (Peterson & Dering '56) Pat. 1523; ARA '56; PP 3, 244 Rpts.; Av. ht. 34″; **NR 8.2.**

ALA. *Twickenham R.S.* 1(2-1-36″-9) Blooms freely, waxy disease-resistant foliage. CALIF. *Rose Study Club Oakland* 2(2-1-42″-7) "Hard" color fades quickly, good show form, disease-resistant foliage. *Pacific R.S.* 1(1-1-30″-8.5) Beautiful disease-resistant foliage, different color, good amount of bloom. *Peninsula R.S.* 4(4-1-48″-8) Glossy foliage, vivid color, good form, fairly vigorous, fades. *San Diego R.S.* 6(31-2-42″-7.8) Wonderful foliage, blooms best in Spring. *San Joaquin Valley R.S.* 3(5-1-30″-6.8) Lovely color. *San Mateo County R.S.* 2(3-2-30″-10) Lovely color, good substance, disease-resistant, beautiful foliage, well-shaped plant, too-few petals, poor hot weather bloom. COLO. *Colorado Springs R.S.* 1(6-1-36″-8) Nice plant, good foliage, nice blooms, does not last too long after cutting. *Denver R.S.* 3(14-2-30″-8) Nice color, with substance, excellent shiny disease-resistant foliage, vigorous, 3-4 blooms on same stem, must be disbudded. D.C. *Potomac R.S.* 4(8-2-42″-8.5) Low compact plant, prolific bloomer, holly-like foliage, no disease, good long-stemmed flowers, fine flower form, color not clear. GA. *Georgia R.S.* 5(8-1-45″-7) Exhibition rose in cool weather, dark glossy foliage, not good in heat; burns and too single in Summer. ILL. *Chicago R.S. Reg. 1* 5(10-2-36″-8) Glossy leaves, vigorous disease-free bush, profuse bloom (too often in clusters). *Greater Peoria R.S.* 4(5-4-28″-8.8) Excellent form and color, glossy waxy disease-resistant foliage, exhibition blooms, prefers cool weather. *Tri-City Men's Rose and Garden Club* 4(12-2-36″-8.4) Too-few petals, good June bloom, fades in hot weather. IND. *Indianapolis R.S.* 2(6-1-26″-8.6) Long buds, good form, disease-resistant, could have more vigor. *St. Joseph Valley R.S.* 1(1-1-39″-8.4) Beautiful foliage, slightly fragrant, good blooms. *Vincennes R.S.* 2(2-1-24″-8) Wonderful foliage, good substance. IOWA *Des Moines R.S.* 1(1-1-30″-7.5). *Iowa R.S.* 3(7-1-30″-8.2) Beautiful foliage, sparse bloom. *Linn County R.S.* 2(4-1-30″-7.4) Good bloom and form, dark waxy green foliage. KAN. *Wichita R.S.* 1(1-1-24″-8.5) Good foliage, long-lasting blooms, best Hybrid Tea. KY. *Kentucky R.S.* 4(6-2-36″-8.5) Lovely foliage and bloom formation, disease-free, blooms well in hot weather. *Lexington R.S.* 1(1-1-36″-8.8) Shiny holly-like foliage, excellent grower, slight fragrance, buds open too fast. *Louisville Chapter ARS* 2(2-1-30″-8.1) Good foliage and color, opens too soon, needs more bloom. LA. *New Orleans R.S.* 1(2-1-30″-7) Bush not hardy, sparse bloom, flower has good substance. MD. *Maryland R.S.* 2(4-2-42″-9) Very large bloom, good form, foliage near perfection. MICH. *Detroit R.S.* 6(11-2-36″-8.5) Good foliage, exhibition bloom, good form and growth. *Kalamazoo R.S.* 6(10-1-36″-8) Nice bloom and glossy foliage, exhibition-type rose. *West Michigan R.S.* 1(2-1-24″-7.9) Nice foliage, thrifty plant, blooms look promising as show stock. MINN. *Lyndale Park T.G.* (25-3-26″-8.5) Beautiful foliage, very good bloomer, disease-free. *Minnesota R.S.* 8(15-1-34″-7.6) Glossy foliage, fruity fragrance, bloom has beautiful color and form, scanty bloom. MO. *Kansas City R.S.* 2(5-2-30″-9) Large bloom, glossy disease-resistant foliage. *Rosarians Midland Empire* 2(5-2-30″-8) Beautiful foliage, nice color, wish it would grow taller. *R.S. Greater St. Louis* 2(2-1-24″-7) Nice bloom, not too good growth. MONT. *Sunset Park T.G.* (20-1-20″-8) Wonderful foliage on a good plant, pleasing well-modelled bud and bloom. NEV. *Reno R.S.* 2(2-3-24″-8) Beautiful color, good substance, glossy foliage, blooms poor in hot Summer, disease-resistant. NEW ENGLAND *New England R.S.* 2(2-1-26″-8). N.J. *North Jersey R.S.* 18(37-1-29″-8.2) Outstanding disease-resistant foliage, reliable producer, fine bloom, good color. N.M. *Albuquerque R.S.* 1(2-2-30″-8.1) Blooms of good form, disease-resistant, good color, too low-growing. N.Y. *Greater Buffalo R.S.* 1(4-1-24″-9) Exhibition form, vigorous grower, clear color, very disease-resistant. *Long Island R.S.* 1(1-1-24″-9) Extraordinary form, color and texture of bloom. *Niagara Frontier R.S.* 4(5-1-34″-7.5) Nice fragrant blooms open too soon. *Schenectady R.S.* 1(1-1-24″-7.5) Foliage shines, buxom bloom is not distinctive enough. *Syracuse R.S.* 1(1-2-36″-8 8) Outstanding dark green shiny foliage, very good bloom and color. *Rochester R.S.* 2(2-1-36″-8.4) Flower of excellent substance and form, not good hot weather rose. N.C. *Durham R.S.* 1(1-1-60″-8) Vigorous, well-shaped bud, color not clear, petallage sparse at first. OHIO *Akron R.S.* 4(30-1-24″-7.2) Glossy foliage, exhibition-type, low growth, no blackspot or mildew. *Central Ohio R.S.* 8(20-2-36″-8.5) Beautiful glossy disease-resistant foliage, vigorous upright bush, bloom has good form, color and substance, not enough bloom. *Cincinnati R.S.* 1(1-1-30″-7.8) Excellent form and color, fine glossy foliage. *Cleveland R.S.* 2(6-1-26″-7.7) Husky grower, beautiful foliage, nice bud form, many blooms, healthy. *Columbus R.C.* 4(10-2-32″-7.5) Good bloomer, disease-resistant, hardy. *Euclid R.S.* 1(3-1-36″-9) Shows great promise as a show rose, glossy attractive disease-resistant foliage, little mildew. *Forest City R.S.* 3(6-1-30″-8) Good strong plant and form, large bloom, fine leathery foliage. *Greater Cincinnati R.S.* 3(4-1-30″-8.5) Beautiful buds, full flowers, large bushy plant, not too many blooms, no blackspot. *Lancaster R.C.* 9(18-2-33″-8.1) Vigorous, upright, excellent glossy foliage, too-few good blooms. *Lima R.S.* 5(8-1-36″-8.9) Excellent foliage, good form, bud and beautiful color, inclined to bloom in clusters. *Medina County R.S.* 1(1-1-36″-8.8) Very attractive free-bloomer, fades too rapidly. *Miami Valley R.S.* 9(14-2-36″-8.5) Excellent color, good form and substance, glossy foliage, exhibition form, disease-resistant, needs constant disbudding. ORE. *Eugene R.S.* 2(5-1-36″-8.7) Strong-growing plant, lots of bloom in fine form. *International Rose T.G.* (40-6-60″-9) Exhibition form, apple-like foliage, resistant to foliar troubles, too much sun fades blooms. *Medford R.S.* 14(25-1-35″-8.7) Excellent exhibition rose, glossy disease-resistant foliage, bushy growth, not affected by hot weather. *Rogue Valley R.S.* 5(12-2-50″-9) Beautiful color, disease-resistant, many blooms, excellent foliage and form. *Roseburg R.S.* 5(19-1-36″-8) Good early bloom, abundant good stems and foliage, very fragrant beautiful flowers, disease-resistant, rapid growth. *Salem R.S.* 5(26-1-33″- ) Good flowers, glossy foliage, fades in hot sun. PA. *Philadelphia R.S.* 3(4-3-30″-7.7) Good show rose, disbud early, best foliage yet developed, not enough bloom. TENN. *Nashville R.S.* 2(4-2-32″-7.9) One of the better pinks, large well-formed blooms and buds, some blackspot. TEX. *Amarillo R.S.* 1(1-1-8) True color, prolific bloomer, colorful foliage, blooms not consistent in design. *Dallas R.S.* 3(3-2-36″-8.2) Good waxy foliage and form, resistant, slow grower. UTAH *Utah R.S.* 1(1-1-30″-8) Husky plant, blooms too large for stem, fades in sun. WASH. *Seattle R.S.* 12(45-2-42″-8.8) Good exhibition bloom, beautiful foliage, vigorous grower, best in June. *Spokane R.S.* 7(19-2-30″-8) Lovely long-lasting blooms, usually produced singly without disbudding. *Walla Walla R.S.* 1(1-2-48″-9) Outstanding bloomer, excellent foliage. W.VA. *Charleston R.S.* 1(3-1-48″-9) Perfect form, glossy foliage. WIS. *Madison R.S.* 1(1-1-35″-8) Waxy disease-resistant foliage, flower not exceptional. *Milwaukee R.S.* 1(1-1-24″-8) Beautiful color and form, good looking foliage, slow to start. CANADA (British Columbia) *Vancouver R.S.* 4(10-2-42″-8) Grand foliage, color sometimes harsh, well-shaped exhibition blooms do not last on the show bench, color fades.

**PINK FROST HT.** Pink blend. (Swim; int. Arp '54) Pat. 1269; ARA '55; PP 4, 58 Rpts.; Av. ht. 34″; **NR 7.1.**

ARIZ. *Phoenix R.S.* 2(2-2-24″-6) Very attractive color, fragrance and form, weak plant. COLO. *Denver R.S.* 1(6-2-30″-7) Excellent color and form when flowers open, last well when cut, many petals, ball early in season, susceptible to mildew and red spider. CONN. *Elizabeth Park T.G.* (5-2-36″-5) Good plant but too open and leggy, lower and younger stems weak for bloom. D.C. *Potomac R.S.* 2(2-3-48″-7.4) A real good bloomer, excellent for cutting and landscape effect, very fragrant, urn-shaped bud, large open flower of little form. GA. *Georgia R.S.* 2(3-2-54″-7.3). IND. *Indianapolis R.S.* 1(3-1-36″-9) Good color, very fragrant, good form, vigorous, slight blackspot. IOWA *Linn County R.S.* 1(1-3-36″-7) Good color, sparse bloom. MICH. *Kalamazoo R.S.* 1(1-3-48″-7.5) Good color, nice buds. *Michigan State University T.G.* (5-2-28″-6.5) Color holds well, moderate fragrance (Damask rose), somewhat weak stems, not resistant to mildew, shy Fall bloomer. MINN. *Lyndale Park T.G.* (35-2-30″-6) Balls, not winter-hardy. *Minnesota R.S.* 8(19-2-34″-7.2) Globular blooms, strong Damask fragrance, unattractive buds, sprawls. MO. *R.S. Greater St. Louis* 1(2-2-24″-7) Lovely flowers but too few on not too good a plant. N.J. *North Jersey R.S.* 1(1-5-24″-7) Fair plant, nice bloom. N.Y. *Cornell University T.G.* (2-2-22″-6.5) Nice pink, large flower, not vigorous, susceptible to blackspot, "tubby" bud. *Humboldt Park T.G.* (4-2-30″-9.9) Upright, branching, very vigorous, normal large leathery dark foliage resistant to disease, large to medium globular buds, large full high-centered globular light pink blooms, strong fruity fragrance, free-flowering, long strong stems, intermittent blooms. *Rochester R.S.* 1(5-2-30″-7.5) Good color, sparse globe-shaped blooms. *Syracuse R.S.* 1(1-2-48″-8) Fine blooms on fine plant, would like more bloom. OHIO *Akron R.S.* 2(7-2-24″-7.9) Good plant, large exhibition-type blooms. *Cleveland R.S.* 1(2-2-28″-8) Fragrant blooms, large as Peace, clean foliage. *Lancaster R.C.* 4(9-2-42″-7.6) Vigorous, spreading grower, free-blooming, large flower. *Forest City R.S.* 3(4-2-24″-6) Spreads rather than growing upright, good form and color of bloom, disease-resistant. *Miami Valley R.S.* 1(2-2-42″-7.5) Plenty of bloom, large pink flowers, good form. *Ohio State University T.G.* (4-2-24″-5) Fair amount of bloom in June and July, disease-resistant, fragrant, glossy green sparse foliage, plant lacks vigor, sparse flowering after July. OKLA. *Oklahoma R.S.* 1(3-3-30″-7) Fragrant, blackspots. ORE. *International Rose T.G.* (20-3-48″-7) Plenty of large well-formed buds and flowers, irregular growth habit. *Medford R.S.* 2(3-2-46″-7.8) Best in the Spring, lovely blooms with loads of fragrance, vigorous, "twiggy" growth. PA. *Breeze Hill T.G.* (4-4-28″-8) Fragrant, beautiful color and form, fairly profuse. S.C. *Edisto T.G.* (4-3-48″-8.5) Very dependable, vigorous, good continuity of bloom, color and substance, bud form could be better. TENN. *Nashville R.S.* 3(5-3-33″-6.9) Healthy, lots of fragrant double blooms don't open too well in cool weather. TEX. *Corpus Christi R.S.* 1(1-3-24″-8) Few wonderful cool weather exhibition-quality blooms with wonderful fragrance, slow grower, foliage mildews. *Dallas R.S.* 3(10-3-33″-7) Good blooms, foliage and color, not vigorous. UTAH *Utah R.S.* 2(11-2-24″-4.7). WASH. *Seattle R.S.* 2(2-1-30″-7.5) Fragrant, susceptible to mildew. W.VA. *Charleston R.S.* 1(3-2-36″-6) Upright plant with good blooms on long stems. WIS. *Madison R.S.* 1(1-2-60″-8.7) Excellent growth, hardy, good disease-resistant foliage, excellent form, substance, good bloomer.

## PINK LUSTRE HT. Pink. (Verschuren; int. Jackson & Perkins '57) Pat. 1641; ARA '58; PP 2, 90 Rpts.; Av. ht. 36″; NR 7.6.

ARIZ. *Phoenix R.S.* 3(4-1-36″-7) Fragrant, good form and color. CALIF. *Rose Study Club Oakland* 1(2-1-42″-7.2) Well-formed bud and bloom, fine color holds well, exhibition-form, plant has moderate vigor, sparse bloomer, needs time to develop into a well-rooted plant. COLO. *Denver R.S.* 2(2-2-54″-9) Excellent form, color, texture, substance, lasting quality, good growth habit, moderately vigorous, shy bloomer. D.C. *Potomac R.S.* (48″-8.4) Outstanding flower form, color and substance, good foliage, not many blooms but each one perfect. GA. *Georgia R.S.* 2(5-2-54″-8) Good bloom form, tight centers, clear color, strong stems, vigorous growth, not enough cane breaks, bloom large for neck. ILL. *Chicago R.S. Reg. 1* 1(1-2-24″-7) Sparse but attractive bloom, subject to disease, not a good plant. IND. *Indianapolis R.S.* 1(2-2-30″-8.5) Good form, color, some split centers. *St. Joseph Valley R.S.* 1(2-1-36″-7.5) 35-40 petals, beautiful. IOWA *Des Moines R.S.* 2(2-1-30″-7) Good form and color. *Iowa R.S.* 1(1-2-24″-7) Nice form and color. *Linn County R.S.* 2(2-1-30″-7.5) Nice bud, good form. KAN. *Wichita R.S.* 1(3-3-30″-7.5) Beautiful flowers, good color. KY. *Kentucky R.S.* 1(2-1-28″-9). Loads of gorgeous blooms, delicately-formed buds. *Lexington R.S.* 1(1-2-7.9) Beautiful large bloom, nice color, doesn't bloom enough. *Louisville Chapter ARS* 1(1-1-36″-8) Good color, form, foliage. MICH. *Detroit R.S.* 5(6-1-30″-7.7). *Kalamazoo R.S.* 7(13-1-36″-8) Tall bush, disease-resistant, nice bloom, vigorous. MINN. *Minnesota R.S.* 1(1-2-26″-7.5) Exhibition-form, delicate color stands out, sparse bloomer. MO. *Rosarians Midland Empire* 1(1-1-36″-7). *R.S. Greater St. Louis* 2(1-1-24″-6). *Sedalia R.S.* 1(1-2-30″-7.2) Plant does not grow as well as it should, buds and blooms nice clear color, not enough bloom. NEW ENGLAND *New England R.S.* 2(3-1-42″-8). Mass.—Blackspots readily. N.J. *North Jersey R.S.* 5(5-2-26″-7.1) Very beautiful but infrequent unsteady bloom. *West Jersey R.S.*

3(4-1-42″-7.5) Good color holds well, healthy vigorous plant, not enough bloom. N.M. *Albuquerque R.S.* 2(2-1-45″-8.4) Sturdy plant, vigorous growth, lovely clean color reminiscent of some of the old-fashioned types, good form in all stages of bloom, grows fast. N.Y. *Cornell University T.G.* (2-2-28″-6.5) Good bud, delicate color has too much gray, good flower form, weak necks, poor substance. *Greater Buffalo R.S.* 1(3-1-18″-8) Unusual color, very good bloom form, disease-resistant. *Rochester R.S.* 1(2-2-42″-7.5) Good bloom and foliage. *Schenectady R.S.* 1(1-3-42″-10) Excellent all-season bloomer, good foliage. *Syracuse R.S.* 3(3-2-32″-8.2) Nice large good keeper, good foliage. OHIO *Akron R.S.* 4(4-2-30″-7.2) Good color, form and foliage, sparse bloomer. *Central Ohio R.S.* 4(6-1-42″-8) Large bloom with good exhibition form, color and substance, vigorous grower, disease-resistant, not enough bloom, bush not attractive, sprawls. *Columbus R.C.* 3(5-1-42″-8.1) Good form and bloom, good substance, sprawling bush. *Greater Cincinnati R.S.* 1(1-2-24″-9) Really charming color with a luminous undertone, fragrant, not as many flowers as some. *Lancaster R.C.* 2(2-2-60″-8.1) Vigorous, disease-resistant, pure exhibition flower. *Lima R.S.* 2(4-2-30″-7) Large high-centered flower, could bloom more freely, disease-resistant. *Ohio State University T.G.* (4-2-15″-5) Blooms well in June and July, large fragrant flowers, disease-resistant small foliage, plant lacks vigor, sparse bloom after July. OKLA. *Oklahoma R.S.* 1(3-1-36″-9). ORE. *Medford R.S.* 1(1-1-45″-7.5) Vigorous, spreading growth, large double exhibition blooms, but not enough of them, some mildew. PA. *Breeze Hill T.G.* (2-2-28″-7) Good color and form, fairly profuse. *Harrisburg R.S.* 1(400-1-48″-9) Vigorous, upright, radiant color, good show rose. TENN. *Nashville R.S.* 1(3-3-8) Healthy, vigorous, outstanding exhibition-type, not too many blooms. TEX. *Corpus Christi R.S.* 1(1-2-36″-7) Lovely full bloom, perfect color shade, has foliage problems. *Dallas R.S.* 2(4-2-7.7) Good bloom color, fragrant, shy bloomer. *El Paso R.S.* 1(1-2-60″-7.5) Strong, healthy, upright bush, well-shaped buds, lovely color shade, large full blooms, too few blooms. VA. *Eastern Shore R.S.* 2(2-1-38″-8) Lovely blooms, vigorous growth, nice disease-resistant foliage. *Va. Peninsula R.S.* 1(1-1-36″-7.6) Strong healthy plant, good foliage, good bloom holds color very well, susceptible to blackspot. WASH. *Spokane R.S.* 4(4-1-36″-5) Other pinks have better bloom, good form.

## PRESIDENT EISENHOWER HT. Bright rose-red. (Hill; int. Conard-Pyle '53) Pat. 1217, ARA '53; PP 5, 1959, 158 Rpts.; Av. ht. 32″; NR 7.0. Total reports 5 years 702; Av. NR 6.7.

## QUEEN ELIZABETH Gr. Medium pink. (Lammerts; int. Germain's '54) Pat. 1259; ARA '55; PP 4, 686 Rpts.; Av. ht. 63″; NR 8.9.

ALA. *Twickenham R.S.* 4(6-2-6.5) Blooms freely, vigorous grower, weak plant. ARIZ. *Mesa R.S.* 6(8-2-60″-9) Good upright plant, holds color well, excellent bloomer, wonderful bush and foliage, glorious color. *Phoenix R.S.* 7(12-2-72″-8.7) Has fragrance, form, color and vigor, could have more petals. CALIF. *Memorial T.G.* (10-5-60″-10) Free 4″ longlasting lovely bloom, very vigorous. *Rose Study Club Oakland* 5(16-3-85″-9) Good form, lovely soft pink color, fine disease-free foliage, extremely-vigorous plant, free-bloomer, fragrant. *Pacific R.S.* 8(16-3-72″-9.3) Vigorous, upright plant, good bloomer, different color shade, beautiful bloom in all stages, good as a cut rose. *Peninsula R.S.* 8(28-3-84″-9) Glowing color, very vigorous, disease-free, blooms well singly and in clusters, susceptible to wind burn. *Roverside R.S.* 9(34-3-72″-9.5) Blooms almost year-round, no mildew, good foliage. *San Diego R.S.* 6(17-3-84″-8.5). *San Joaquin Valley R.S.* 10(28-4-72″-9). *San Mateo R.S.* 12(22-3-72″-8) Very vigorous, beautiful long-lasting color, excellent foliage, free-bloomer, no foliage troubles, poor flower form, almost too vigorous for a small garden. COLO. *Colorado Springs R.S.* 4(13-2-54″-9) Disease-resistant, good canes and foliage, abundant non-fading blooms, good color, hardy plant. *Denver R.S.* 8(69-3-48″-9.5) Perfect color, profuse bloomer, good substance, vigorous, resists mildew. CONN. *Elizabeth Park T.G.* (6-4-36″-5) Tall, uniform height would make it more desirable, stems too slender. D.C. *Potomac R.S.* 6(15-3-94″-10) Tall, covered with beautiful flowers all season, no blackspot or mildew. GA. *Georgia R.S.* 20(86-3-80″-8.8) Exquisite true color doesn't fade, vigorous, husky plant, abundant bloomer, healthy foliage, good substance. ILL. *Chicago R.S. Reg. 1* 7(19-3-60″-9) Attractive prolific bloom, vigorous disease-free bush. *Greater Peoria R.S.* 8(10-2-61″-8.7) Beautiful clear color, dark green foliage, prolific bloomer, disease-resistant, good grower, would be more satisfactory for cut flowers if there were more leaves close to the bloom. *Morgan Park R.S.* 3(3-2-48″-9.3) Excellent bloomer, disease-resistant. *Tri-City Men's Rose and Garden Club* 5(4-31″-8.9). IND

*Indianapolis R.S.* 8(15-3-64″-9.2) Excellent grower and bloomer, disease-resistant. *St. Joseph Valley R.S.* 6(14-3-60″-9) Strong, healthy plant, good bloomer, attractive lasting blooms. *Vincennes R.S.* 4(14-3-60″-8) Profuse bloomer, hardy, no disease. IOWA *Des Moines R.S.* 10(24-3-60″-9) Vigorous plant, lots of bloom, disease-resistant. *Iowa R.S.* 8(28-3-60″-9.1) Good foliage, nice buds and bloom, strong grower. *Linn County R.S.* 7(19-2-54″-9) Vigorous, nice bud and form, holds color when open, blooms repeatedly. KAN. *Wichita R.S.* 9(21-2-60″-8.5) Good form, color and grower, disease-resistant. KY. *Frankfort Chapter ARS* 12(20-3-60″-8.5). *Kentucky R.S.* 7(20-2-72″-9.1) Beautiful color, opens too flat, blooms all the time, too tall, bad foliage down low. *Lexington R.S.* 2(4-4-66″-9.5) Vigorous, beautiful buds and flower, heavy textured foliage. *Louisville Chapter ARS* 16(22-2-72″-9.1) Good blooms and bush, vigorous abundant bloom, tends to blackspot. LA. *New Orleans R.S.* 6(8-3-72″-9) Good bloomer and grower, fine foliage. MD. *Maryland R.S.* 4(5-2-60″-9) Terrific tall bush with many basal canes, free-bloomer. MICH. *Detroit R.S.* 9(19-2-72″-9). *Greater Lansing R.S.* 2(2-2-48″-8) Lovely shape, deep color, perfect globular buds, fragrant, disease-resistant. *Kalamazoo R.S.* 12(31-3-66″-8.7) Good bush and form, nice foliage, holds color. *Michigan State University T.G.* (21-3-43″-10) Excellent color holds well, beautiful form, long-lasting blooms, slight fragrance (cold cream), slightly susceptible to blackspot. *West Michigan Rosarians* 3(6-2-60″-8.5) Vigorous plant, lovely bloom. *Lyndale Park T.G.* (20-4-50″-8.2) Vigorous grower, good bloomer and color, disease-free, hardy. MINN. *Minnesota R.S.* 18(40-2-49″-8.7) Vigorous bush, clear bloom, too long between blooming. MO. *Kansas City R.S.* 4(20-3-60″-9.5) Vigorous grower, good color, disease-resistant. *Rosarians Midland Empire* 4(18-3-66″-9). *R.S. Greater St. Louis* 7(15-3-84″-8.5) Fine long-lasting flowers, grows too tall, most flowers at end of long canes. *Sedalia R.S.* 10(8-4-60″-9) Blooms profusely, hardy disease-resistant plant. MONT. *Sunset Park T.G.* (12-3-48″-9) Terrific plant, heavy resistant foliage, long-lasting flowers, blooms better each year. NEW ENGLAND *New England R.S.* 9(40-3-54″-9). N.J. *North Jersey R.S.* 23(52-2-60″-8.7) Superior plant, unusual cutting rose for exhibition, superb color. *West Jersey R.S.* 6(10-3-66″-8.5) Tall vigorous plant, always in bloom, fades quickly. N.M. *Albuquerque R.S.* 7(16-3-66″-9.3) Vigorous grower, constant bloom cycles, marvelous color and substance, stands sun, straight thick stems, leathery foliage, too tall, erratic form sometimes. N.J. *Cornell University T.G.* (18-7-48″-9) Excellent vigor, foliage, bud, coloring, growth habit, disease-resistance. *Greater Buffalo R.S.* 4(8-3-48″-9) Beautiful sprays of clear flowers, very disease-resistant, continuous bloom, vigorous plant. *Humboldt Park T.G.* (13-4-72″-9.9) Tall everblooming rose, healthy foliage, no faults. *Long Island R.S.* 9(14-2-54″-9.5). *Niagara Frontier R.S.* 4(11-3-68″-8.5) Beautiful clear long-lasting blooms, well-shaped plant, *Rochester R.S.* 12(21-2-60″-9) Good color, strong grower, disease-resistant. *Schenectady R.S.* 10(23-2-51″-9) Vigorous, upright plant, disease-resistant, starts rather slowly, fine bloomer, canes freeze back but recover by late Summer. *Syracuse N.Y.* 8(13-3-54″-8.8) Wonderful foliage, good form, strong grower, nice bloom, disease-resistant. N.C. *Charlotte R.S.* 6(10-3-72″-9) Good bloomer, healthy, rather tall and spindly. *Durham R.S.* 13(27-2-66″-8.7) Lovely unfading color, profuse bloomer, dark green foliage, too small blooms. *Randolph R.S.* 3(3-3-66″-9) Strong upright growth, free-bloomer, beautiful bud and flower, good foliage. OHIO *Akron R.S.* 9(28-3-60″-9.1) Needs room, slight mildew. *Central Ohio R.S.* 6(14-3-60″-9.3) Strong, vigorous grower, disease-resistant, prolific bloomer, very attractive blooms of good form, color and substance. *Cincinnati R.S.* 6(28-3-61″-9) Clear blooms, long stems, free-bloomer, good foliage, grows too tall. *Cleveland R.S.* 6(12-2-52″-8) Fine color and all-around performance. *Columbus R.C.* 5(9-3-60″-8.5) Good bloom, plant and foliage. *Euclid R.S.* 3(6-2-54″-8.6) Good plant, nice disease-resistant foliage, many fine blooms. *Forest City R.S.* 10(18-3-54″-9) Good upright-growing plant, good bloomer, well-formed buds, pure color, exhibition quality, disease-resistant. *Greater Cincinnati R.S.* 7(12-2-60″-9) Good color, form and bloomer, almost constant bloom, grows very tall. *Lancaster R.C.* 8(17-3-72″-8.8) Vigorous, upright, free-bloomer, Hybrid Tea-form flowers. *Lima R.S.* 10(23-3-60″-9) Very vigorous, good form and color, disease-resistant. *Medina County R.S.* 3(3-2-48″-8.7) Highest quality bloom. *Miami Valley R.S.* 11(18-3-60″-9) Outstanding color, excellent foliage, non-fading in Spring and Fall, some fading in sun and Summer. *Ohio State University T.G.* (4-3-54″-8.5) Very vigorous plant, more upright than bushy growth habit, dark glossy green foliage, large bud, abundant disease-resistant lower leaves drop in late Summer. *Park of Roses T.G.* (150-4-66″-9) Good quality bloom, strong vigorous growth, good foliage, little blackspot. *Stark R.S.* 6(13-2-60″-8.8). OKLA. *Norman R.S.* 4(14-3-48″-8.6). *Oklahoma R.S.* 3(9-2-54″-9) Fine plant and bloom. ORE. *Eugene R.S.* 6(15-2-72″-9) High bloom production, pleasing color, excellent plant, blooms only on upper part. *International Rose T.G.* (40-6-96″-9) Fine color, good bush form, clean flowers and foliage, terrific plant. *Lewis & Clark T.G.* (10-3-72″-8) Vigorous grower, fine foliage, many long-lasting blooms. *Medford R.S.* 11(16-2-52″-9) Vigorous, upright, very healthy foliage, entrancing color. *Rogue Valley R.S.* 4(5-3-64″-9.5) Beautiful color, form and long stems, good foliage, many long-lasting blooms. *Roseburg R.S.* 4(9-4-84″-9) Abundant bloom, beautiful color, good disease-resistant foliage, but too dense.

*Salem R.S.* 4(35-3-53″-8.8) Vigorous grower, profuse bloomer, holds color well, clean foliage. PA. *Breeze Hill T.G.* (3-7-36″-10) Tall, profuse, well-formed buds, lovely color. *Harrisburg R.S.* 3(1003-2-72″-9.4) Strong grower, beautiful buds, long stems, does not fade, blooms freely all Summer, a good show rose, bloom a little small in comparison to bud. *Philadelphia R.S.* 11(19-3-72″-9.5) Excellent form, color and foliage, strong lasting flower, blooms only at top. *Pittsburgh R.S.* 6(17-3-65″-8.9) Good grower, many blooms, vigorous, strong canes, disease-resistant, good form and color. S.C. *Edisto T.G.* (10-5-48″-8.5) Vigorous upright grower, excellent color, good form and substance. TENN. *Nashville R.S.* 10(40-4-65″-9.3) Healthy, extremely vigorous, good producer, excellent cut flower. TEX. *Amarillo R.S.* 9(25-60″-9) Strong disease-resistant plant, rare color, good foliage, excellent substance. *Corpus Christi R.S.* 2(4-3-48″-9.2) Wonderful foliage, lots of blooms on single stems. *Dallas R.S.* 6(12-3-63″-8.6). *El Paso R.S.* 7(12-2-72″-9.5) Strong, upright, healthy bush, disease-resistant, straight long stems, excellent cut flower, lovely color holds well. UTAH *Utah R.S.* 8(26-3-60″-8.9) Excels in color, substance and foliage, plants could have better form. VA. *Eastern Shore R.S.* 4(6-2-60″-9) Excellent foliage, lovely color, long stems, lots of new basal canes, hardy plant, disease-resistant. *Va. Peninsula R.S.* 6(8-3-69″-9.7) Very vigorous, fine foliage, excellent clear color, free-bloomer, long stems, lasts well when cut, no faults. WASH. *Seattle R.S.* 7(19-2-60″-8.8) Vigorous grower, good color, no faults. *Spokane R.S.* 10(65-3-48″-10). *Walla Walla R.S.* 3(10-4-80″-9) Very strong-growing plant, disease-resistant foliage. W.VA. *Charleston R.S.* 9(13-3-60″-9.5). *Wyo-Mac R.S.* 6(20-2-54″-8.2) Beautiful blooms, good foliage, large strong stems, everbloomer, slow grower. WIS. *Madison R.S.* 7(21-2-67″-9.3) Good disease-resistant foliage, good color, hardy bush, long-lasting flower. *Milwaukee R.S.* (68″-9.1) Lovely color, unique ruffled bloom form, large plant, good bushy canes, nice foliage, magnificent grower, constant profuse bloom, no faults. CANADA (British Columbia) *Vancouver R.S.* 13(25-3-72″-9.5) Cut flowers have lasting quality, clean color, excellent plant symmetry and all-round excellence. (Nova Scotia) *Buchanan* (2-1-12″-5) Lovely flower, no fragrance, not good grower, flowers in July, no sign of repeat crop.

**REDCAP F.** Red. (Swim; int. Armstrong '54) Pat. 1292; ARA '54, PP 5, 1959, 65 Rpts.; Av. ht. 38″; **NR 7.2.** Total reports 5 years 287; Av. NR 7.6.

**RED EMPRESS LCl.** Irisdescent spirea-red. (Mallerin; int. Conard-Pyle '57) Pat. 1573; ARA '57; PP 2, 39 Rpts.; Av. ht. 7′; **NR 7.7.**

ALA. *Twickenham R.S.* 1(1-2-10′-7) Blooms recurrently, does well under adverse weather conditions. ARIZ. *Mesa R.S.* 1(1-2-10′-8). CALIF. *Rose Study Club Oakland* 1(2-1-7′-7.8) Fine large deep-colored flower of good form opens slowly but lasts, vigorous plant. *San Mateo County R.S.* 1(1-2-6′-8) Good fragrant long-lasting blooms, strong grower, fine strong canes, not as good as Cl. Chrysler Imperial. D.C. *Potomac R.S.* 2(2-2-8′-7.5) Vigorous grower, repeat-bloomer, Hybrid Tea-type bloom, deep color. IND. *Indianapolis R.S.* 1(1-2-4′-7.5) Good non-burning large blooms, no disease. *St. Joseph Valley R.S.* 1(1-1-8′-8) Very good Climber, continuous bloom, no fragrance, good color, holds shape and color. IOWA *Des Moines R.S.* 1(1-2-3′-7) Fine bud, few long-lasting blooms. *Iowa R.S.* 1(1-2-6′-7) Beautiful bud, few blooms. *Linn County R.S.* 1(2-2-9′-7.5) Vigorous, shy bloom. KY. *Louisville Chapter ARS* 1(1-2-8′-7.9) Good fragrant bloom, upright grower. MD. *Maryland R.S.* 3(3-2-10′-8) Disease-resistant plant, blooms have good form and color. MICH. *Detroit R.S.* 2(3-1-6½′-7.7) Good form and color, not enough bloom. MO. *Rosarians Midland Empire* 1(5-1-10′-8) Good foliage and bloom, not too recurrent bloom. *R.S. Greater St. Louis* 1(1-2-12′-7) Good ever-blooming Climber, NEV. *Reno R.S.* 2(2-3-6′-8) Beautiful long-lasting fragrant blooms, large fast-growing canes, poor bloomer. NEW ENGLAND *New England R.S.* 4(7-2-6′-8) Large fragrant flowers on fairly vigorous plant. N.J. *North Jersey R.S.* 1(1-1-6′-5) Doesn't repeat well, good color. N.Y. *Humboldt Park T.G.* (5-2-6½′-9) Outstanding color with stamens showing when fully open, high-centered blooms with good lasting quality, abundant flowers drop cleanly, no blackspot, flowers intermittently, only tips freeze. OHIO *Cincinnati R.S.* 3(4-2-3½′-7.5). *Lima R.S.* 2(4-1-10′-8.5) Vigorous bush, good foliage, lovely bloom, no faults. ORE. *International Rose T.G.* (2-2-8′-7) Long stems, singular bloom, good long tapered buds and color, repeat bloom not as heavy as in Spring. *Medford R.S.* 1(1-1-12′-8.5) Nice bloom and color, blooms continuously, burns in hot weather. PA. *Philadelphia R.S.* 1(1-2-7′-7.5) Good form and Spring bloom, poor repeat. *Pittsburgh R.S.* 1(1-2-6′-8). TENN. *Nashville R.S.* 2(2-2-9′-8) Medium Climber, some blackspot. TEX. *Corpus Christi R.S.* 1(1-2-6′-6.5) Nice bright scarce blooms, climbs slowly.

**RED FAVORITE F.** Bright red. (Tantau; int. Conard-Pyle '53)
Pat. 1189; ARA '52; PP 5, 1959, 45 Rpts.; Av. ht. 33″ **NR 7.8.**
Total reports 5 years 231; **Av. NR 7.5.**

**RED WONDER F.** Dark red. (de Ruiter; int. Conard-Pyle '54)
Pat. 1341; ARA '55; PP 4, 24 Rpts.; Av. ht. 39″; **NR 7.6.**

COLO. *Denver R.S.* 1(10-4-28″-6) Nice rich color, showy at peak, best late, thin growth, not enough bloom. D.C. *Potomac R.S.* 2(4-2-60″-7.6) Large flowers (one to a stem), good substance, not enough bloom. MICH. *Kalamazoo R.S.* 1(1-3-42″-6.5) Blackspots, not enough bloom. MO. *Rosarians Midland Empire* 1(3-3-24″-7) Good color, shy bloom. *R.S. Greater St. Louis* 1(1-2-36″-7) Odd-shaped long-lasting flowers do not fade. NEW ENGLAND *New England R.S.* 3(6-4-30″-7). N.J. *North Jersey R.S.* 2(3-3-53″-8.5). *West Jersey R.S.* 4(24-4-48″-9) Fragrant bright bloom, disease-free, no faults. N.Y. *Humboldt Park T.G.* (6-3-24″-8) Upright, very vigorous growth, full blooms, single petals drop cleanly, leggy plants, intermittent bloom. OHIO *Akron R.S.* 1(1-2-36″-8) Outstanding bush, could recur more. *Ohio State University T.G.* (4-4-36″-8) Abundant bloom all season, excellent disease-resistant foliage to base of plant, strong flower stem. PA. *Breeze Hill T.G.* (3-6-28″-7) Fairly profuse, good foliage and bud form, brilliant color. *Philadelphia R.S.* 3(5-3-38″-8) Odd color, good plant. WASH. *Spokane R.S.* 1(1-2-42″-10) Nice large foliage. CANADA (Nova Scotia) *Buchanan* (2-3-12″-2).

**RONDO HT.** Red blend. (Tantau; int. Jackson & Perkins '55)
Pat. 1454; ARA '55; PP 4, 24 Rpts.; Av. ht. 34″; **NR 6.3.**

ARIZ. *Phoenix R.S.* 2(2-1-36″-6.5) Attractive lasting scarce blooms, unusual color. CALIF. *Rose Study Club Oakland* 3(9-2-50″-6.5) Beautiful vivid orange color, always in bloom, good flower form, strong upright grower, spreading, disease-resistant foliage. GA. *Georgia R.S.* 2(2-2-30″-7) Excellent color, good bloomer, poor bud form, small bloom. ILL. *Greater Peoria R.S.* 1(1-3-36″-7.3) Good clear orange eye-catching color, not good in cool weather. KY. *Louisville Chapter ARS* 1(1-2-24″-6.5) Slow growth, few blooms. N.J. *North Jersey R.S.* 2(2-2-18″-2). N.Y. *Cornell University T.G.* (5-2-26″-7.5) Superb color on opening, brilliant flowers fade badly, blackspots, not vigorous. *Humboldt Park T.G.* (19-3-20″-9) Deep pink ovoid buds borne on long stems, moderate fruity fragrance, glowing coral-pink blooms drop cleanly, continuous bloomer, tips freeze. *Rochester R.S.* 3(14-2-30″-7.5) Beautiful orange color, sparse bloomer, good foliage. OHIO *Akron R.S.* 2(2-3-36″-7.8) Good color, blackspots. *Stark R.S.* 1(1-2-15″-4) Lacks vigor, not much bloom. ORE. *International Rose T.G.* (20-3-36″-7) Good orange-brick color, magentas at finish, ample bloom. PA. *Breeze Hill T.G.* (3-5-26″-6) Lovely bud form, brilliant color, fairly profuse. *Philadelphia R.S.* 1(1-3-5) Unique color, won't bloom or grow much. *Pittsburgh R.S.* 1(1-3-72″- ) Good color, poorly-formed flower. TENN. *Nashville R.S.* 1(1-4-30″-7) Novel orange, fairly fragrant, not much bloom. W.VA. *Charleston R.S.* 1(1-4-36″-3).

**ROSE MARIE REID HT.** Medium pink. (Whisler; int. Germain's
'56) Pat. 1487; ARA '56; PP 3, 36 Rpts.; Av. ht. 42″; **NR 7.6.**

CALIF. *Pacific R.S.* 2(2-2-48″-8) Strong sturdy bush, clean foliage, good bloomer, Charlote Armstrong-type bloom. *Peninsula R.S.* 7(7-2-48″-6) Vigorous plant, rusts, poor substance, needs heat for best bloom. IND. *St. Joseph Valley R.S.* 1(1-3-48″-8.5) Very tall bush, large flower, prolific bloom. IOWA *Linn County R.S.* 1(2-2-40″-8) Exhibition bloom, good foliage, vigorous, nice bud and open flower. KY. *Louisville Chapter ARS* 1(1-2-42″-7.5) Many petals, excellent color, few blooms. MICH. *Detroit R.S.* 1(1-3-36″-8) Large plant, long strong stems, flowers hold. *Kalamazoo R.S.* 2(3-2-36″-8.5) Exhibition-type bloom. MINN. *Minnesota R.S.* 6(10-2-37″-8) Large full fragrant bloom, stingy bloomer. N.J. *North Jersey R.S.* 1(1-3-40″-7.8) Repeats well, promising bud, disappointing open bloom. N.M. *Albuquerque R.S.* 1(1-2-42″-8.2) Fragrant well-formed blooms on sturdy healthy plant, could bloom more. *Central Ohio R.S.* 1(1-1-46″-7.5) Good color, nice long stems, holds color well, possible show rose, too-few blooms. *Greater Cincinnati R.S.* 1(1-3-48″-9) Huge flowers with good color, nice buds, no blackspot until late in season. OKLA. *Oklahoma R.S.* 2(6-1-24″-7) Strong plant, good bloomer, mildews. ORE. *Medford R.S.* 1(1-3-56″-7) Upright growth, strong canes, does not bloom as profusely as Queen Elizabeth. PA. *Breeze Hill T.G.* (3-5-40″-8) Large clear flowers of nice form on good stems, vigorous. TEX. *Amarillo R.S.* 3(7-2-48″-9.2) Large unfading blossom of good substance, good foliage. *Dallas R.S.* 1(2-3-30″-6.5) Large full blooms, good color, stingy, foliage discolors. Wis. *Madison R.S.* 3(3-2-40″-7.3) Good disease-resistant foliage, vigorous, good form and substance, hardy, sparse bloomer.

## ROUNDELAY Gr. Dark red. (Swim; int. Armstrong '54) Pat. 1280; ARA '54; PP 4, 285 Rpts.; Av. ht. 47″; NR 8.0.

ALA. *Twickenham R.S.* 2(5-2-39″-8) Camellia-like long-lasting bloom, profuse bloomer, not as cold-hardy as others. ARIZ. *Mesa R.S.* 3(3-3-48″-8.7) Good foliage, long stems, disease-resistant, beautiful flowers (often exhibition quality). *Phoenix R.S.* 5(8-2-48″-8.1) Stands heat, constant bloomer, holds color, healthy foliage. CALIF. *Memorial T.G.* (12-5-72″-10) Long-lasting, very vigorous, long stems, continuous bloom, no faults. *Rose Study Club Oakland* 3(11-3-60″-7.9) Free-blooming, vigorous growth, good show rose, nice color holds well, good cutting rose, burns in hot sun, fragrant, disease-resistant foliage. *Pacific R.S.* 2(3-2-45″-8.7) Vigorous plant, disease-resistant foliage, good bud form in Spring, open bloom holds well, attractive old-fashioned form, excellent fragrance, light mudding of color in full-blown rose. *Peninsula R.S.* 3(3-3-84″-8.5) Large disease-free foliage, color good only in heat, good cut flower. *San Diego R.S.* 2(5-2-63″-8.5) Beautiful color and form. *San Joaquin Valley R.S.* 4(3-3-60″-7.5). *San Mateo County R.S.* 6(18-4-48″-8) Excellent plant, beautiful disease-resistant foliage, fast repeat-bloomer, good color in protected gardens (browns badly elsewhere). COLO. *Colorado Springs R.S.* 2(7-3-36″-7.5) Good color, hardy, good bloom for cutting. *Denver R.S.* 5(58-3-40″-8) Showy rich color, good foliage, vigorous, burns in sun, resistant to mildew, good bloomer. CONN. *Elizabeth Park T.G.* (30-5-30″-5) Good plant, dark blotch or crease on outer petals when opens. D.C. *Potomac R.S.* 2(3-3-60″-7.9) Lovely bloom, disease-resistant plant, fragrant, needs protection from afternoon sun or will burn. GA. *Georgia R.S.* 9(20-3-60″-8) Dark vivid color, vigorous, long-lasting cut blooms, disease-free foliage, burns in 90° weather, too-few bottom breaks, requires either constant pruning or support. ILL. *Chicago R.S. Reg. I* 3(5-2-48″-8) Fine husky plant, dull blooms turn brown with age. *Greater Peoria R.S.* 3(3-1-48″-7.8) Outstanding deep color holds well, sparse bloomer. *Morgan Park R.S.* 1(1-2-18″-7.5). IND. *Indianapolis R.S.* 4(5-2-39″-7.4) Resistant, too small and flat, blooms burn in sun. *St. Joseph Valley R.S.* 3(5-7-42″-8.2) Slight fragrance, flowers tend to fade. *Vincennes R.S.* 3(4-2-48″-7) Only two canes, good in all respects. IOWA *Des Moines R.S.* 4(5-2-36″-8) Good color and bloom. *Iowa R.S.* 3(6-3-36″-7.9) Fine color, not enough bloom. *Linn County R.S.* 3(4-2-40″-7.5) Perfect bud form, double flower blues in hot weather, disease-resistant. KAN. *Wichita R.S.* 4(8-1-36″-8) Good growth and foliage, flower burns badly. KY. *Kentucky R.S.* 6(28-3-48″-9.5) Beautiful deep velvet bloom, disease-resistant, prolific bloomer, spicy fragrance. *Lexington R.S.* 1(1-1-36″-6.8) Good disease-free foliage, good buds, zinnia-type bloom, weak stems. *Louisville Chapter ARS* 9(13-2-63″-8.5) Disease-resistant, good color, vigorous, productive, slow starter. MD. *Maryland R.S.* 2(3-2-7) Very good bush, dull color, beetles don't touch it. MICH. *Detroit R.S.* 5(6-2-54″-8.3) Disease-resistant, fine color and form, good repeat bloom. *Kalamazoo R.S.* 3(3-8-42″-8) Good color, nice foliage, could bloom more. *Michigan State University T.G.* (6-4-45″-3) Good disease-resistant foliage, moderate fragrance, fades to an objectionable color with blackening and burning of petals. MINN. *Lyndale Park T.G.* (30-5-48″-8) Very hardy, disease-free, good bloomer, blooms blacken when old. *Minnesota R.S.* 7(8-2-36″-7.2) Shapely bush, black-red buds, not floriferous. MO. *Rosarians Midland Empire* 2(6-3-45″-7.7) Nice blooms, not enough flowers, could have better foliage. *R.S. Greater St. Louis* 2(3-4-78″-7) Fine color, fragrant, a blue ribbon winner. *Sedalia R.S.* 3(3-3-36″-7.7) Beautiful bloom, good color and form, not quite enough plant. NEV. *Reno R.S.* 10(18-4-48″-8) Beautiful blooms, fast repeat bloomer, beautiful disease-resistant foliage, fast growing canes, blooms brown in the heat of Summer. NEW ENGLAND *New England R.S.* 3(6-4-60″-8.5) Vigorous with good continuity, burns black in heat. N.J. *North Jersey R.S.* 17(24-2-47″-7.5) Healthy dependable plant, blooms burn and water spot. *West Jersey R.S.* 2(3-2-54″-8) Vigorous healthy plant, usually in bloom, small flower holds well. N.M. *Albuquerque R.S.* 2(3-2-18″-7.7) Beautiful flowers, many petals, opens like a camellia, slow starter. N.Y. *Cornell University T.G.* (8-5-35″-8.5) Colorful large flowers, good bud, floriferous all season, good substance, flowers burn and turn purplish in Summer heat. *Humboldt Park T.G.* (10-2-42″-8) Upright, very vigorous growth, abundant dark green leathery foliage, very deep color, double full globular bloom, continuously in flower, long strong stems, urn-shaped buds, blooms remain on plant, and have burnt look when done. *Long Island R.S.* 1(4-1-48″-9) Prolific, exquisite color, form and substance, disease-resistant foliage. *Niagara Frontier R.S.* 4(5-2-39″-7.5). *Rochester R.S.* 1(20-3-40″-8) Upright vigorous grower, good fragrance, small flower. *Syracuse R.S.* 1(4-3-48″-8) Nice foliage, nice color when first open, flowers brown and fade, disease-resistant. N.C. *Charlotte R.S.* 8(10-2-48″-8). *Durham R.S.* 4(12-2-66″-9.4) Real rose fragrance, plenty of petals, good form in all stages, profuse bloomer, good hot weather rose. *Randolph R.S.* 1(1-4-72″-8) Upright strong growth habit, long-lasting bloom, slight tendency to weak necks. OHIO *Akron R.S.* 2(32-2-40″-7.8) Deep color, good grower and foliage, heat fades blooms. *Central Ohio R.S.* 4(13-3-54″-8) Vigorous upright bush, disease-resistant, good color blooms have poor form and sunburn readily, not enough bloom. *Cincinnati R.S.* 5(10-3-40″-8) Long-lasting, free-blooming, Japanese beetles shy away. *Cleveland R.S.* 4(14-2-40″-7.9) Blooms in clusters, deep color, beautiful form, healthy growth. *Columbus R.C.* 2(4-3-51″-8) Vigorous, good plant, good color, no form, sunburns. *Forest City R.S.* 6(8-2-30″-7.5) Good form, deep color, long-lasting bloom, good disease-resistant foliage. *Greater Cincinnati R.S.* 4(8-3-45″-8.5) Good color, erect stem, splendid foliage, blooms all Summer, sparse canes. *Lancaster R.C.* 1(1-4-54″-8) Vigorous, upright, good color, blackspots. *Lima R.S.* 6(8-2-48″-7.9) Nice form, rich color, good bloomer. *Miami Valley R.S.* 3(8-3-45″-8) Good bloom, color and foliage, fragrant, nice in all stages of bloom. *Ohio State University T.G.* (4-5-30″-7) Excellent foliage, good bloom until October, disease-resistant, deep rich color, strong fragrance, loses foliage from base of plant. *Stark R.S.* 4(5-2-48″-7.5). OKLA. *Norman R.S.* 2(8-3-48″-9). ORE. *Eugene R.S.* 4(6-3-60″-8.5) Vigorous grower, prolific bloomer, disease-resistant, browns in sun. *International Rose T.G.* (40-5-72″-7) Lots of bloom, fine for cutting, good resistance, many repeat blooms, blues and burns in poor weather. *Medford R.S.* 2(4-2-33″-8.5) Nice form, good color, vigorous, not as tall as other Grandifloras, likes a little shade, some sun-fading, petals hang on. *Salem R.S.* 3(4-5-45″-8) Good plant, foliage and blooms, blues with age. PA. *Breeze Hill T.G.* (3-7-40″-8) Nice color, form and foliage, blooms well, vigorous. *Harrisburg R.S.* 1(700-3-60″-9.5) Good show rose, beautiful dark color, free-blooming, exceptional foliage. *Philadelphia R.S.* 2(2-3-30″-6.5) Pleasing color, not enough growth or bloom. S.C. *Edisto T.G.* (12-5-48″-8) Good color, form and substance, vigorous, upright growth, shy bloom quantity. TENN. *Nashville R.S.* 10(31-3-48″-8.9) Healthy, very vigorous, excellent producer of long-lasting deep rich blooms, excellent form. TEX. *Amarillo R.S.* 5(14-48″-9) Fine dark color, big upright plant, keeps turning blooms out. *Corpus Christi R.S.* 1(1-3-48″-9.3) Gorgeous long-lasting blooms, long stems, prolific grower and bloomer, blooms blue as they fade. *Dallas R.S.* 3(8-3-55″-9) Always in bloom, good in every way. *El Paso R.S.* 3(3-2-48″-8.5) Fairly good bloomer, healthy leathery foliage, large full buds, holds well as cut flower, slightly weak necks, slow starter, improves with age. UTAH *Utah R.S.* 4(6-3-40″-6.4) Beautiful dark color, vigorous bush, stingy bloomer. VA. *Va. Peninsula R.S.* 4(4-3-69″-7.8) Good foliage, strong grower, deep velvety color, disappointing form and color of full-blown bloom. WASH. *Spokane R.S.* 7(20-3-48″-8) Good dark color, not as showy as Carrousel, fragrant. *Walla Walla R.S.* 1(1-4-60″-7) Very prolific bloomer, excellent quality. W.VA. *Charleston R.S.* 1(3-2-48″-8) Deep color, pretty from bud till petals fall. WIS. *Madison R.S.* 2(2-2-57″-8.1) Good dark color, no disease, good form, hardy, good foliage, flower blackens with age, not enough blooms. *Milwaukee R.S.* 2(3-3-48″-8.8) Gorgeous dark color and form, spray-spots, not very hardy. CANADA (British Columbia) *Vancouver R.S.* 2(3-3-48″-8) Disease-resistant, vigorous, lots of bloom, fragrant.

**SIREN F.** Orange-red. (Kordes; int. Jackson & Perkins '53) Pat. 1197; PP 5, 1959, 81 Rpts.; Av. ht. 33″; **NR 7.6.** Total reports 5 years 342; **Av. NR 7.6.**

**SPARTAN F.** Medium red. (Boerner; int. Jackson & Perkins '55) Pat. 1357; ARA '56; PP 3, 454 Rpts.; Av. ht. 37″; **NR 8.5.**

ALA. *Twickenham R.S.* 1(1-1-48″-8) Beautiful color. ARIZ. *Mesa R.S.* 4(11-2-48″-8.5) Beautiful consistent bloomer. *Phoenix R.S.* 5(8-2-36″-9) Outstanding color stands heat, profuse bloomer, healthy bush. CALIF. *Memorial T.G.* (12-4-38″-9) 3-4″ vigorous double bloom, good cutter, moderate fragrance, continuous blooms, no faults. *Rose Study Club Oakland* 3(14-4-52″-8.9) Many fine blooms on vigorous, well-foliaged plant, beautiful color blooms fade little, disease-resistant, prolific bloomer, good lasting cut flower. *Pacific R.S.* 3(3-2-30″-8.3) Vigorous growth, prolific bloomer, companion color to Montezuma, disease-resistant, many long stems. *Peninsula R.S.* 4(5-2-36″-7) Lacks general vigor, good color and form, rusts badly, fades. *San Diego R.S.* 1(1-1-38″-8.1). *San

*Joaquin Valley R.S.* 5(10-3-42″-8.9) Excellent bloom, **good** all-weather rose. *San Mateo County R.S.* 3(4-2-40″-9) Holds its beautiful orange-red color, very showy profuse bloomer, resents our cool nights, some mildew. COLO. *Colorado Springs R.S.* 1(6-1-24″-8) Beautiful color, profuse bloom. *Denver R.S.* 4(53-4-23″-8) Profuse showy double orange-scarlet long-lasting blooms do not fade, nice foliage. CONN. *Elizabeth Park T.G.* (29-4-28″-8) Good in all aspects. D.C. *Potomac R.S.* 4(7-3-96″-9) Best orange-red Floribunda to date, constant bloomer, cut flower lasts well, robust grower, excellent foliage, no disease, beautiful plant even without blooms. GA. *Georgia R.S.* 9(28-2-48″-9) Vigorous bush, eye-catching orange-red color, excellent form, long-lasting, disease-resistant, could bloom more. ILL. *Chicago R.S. Reg. 1* 3(3-2-30″-8) Healthy foliage, flowers borne singly, similar to Montezuma in color. *Greater Peoria R.S.* 5(11-2-30″-7.9) Good color and form, lots of flowers, blackspots. *Tri-City Men's Rose and Garden Club* 3(10-3-36″-8.6) Good bloom, hardy, lasts. *Indianapolis R.S.* 6(14-3-36″-8.7) Vivid color, good form in bud and flower, sturdy plants, fragrant. *St. Joseph Valley R.S.* 3(10-5-30″-8.8) Large compact bush, many blooms, good foliage, attractive color, blackspots. *Vincennes R.S.* 1(1-1-24″-8) Perfect blooms. IOWA *Des Moines R.S.* 5(16-3-24″-9) Good color, plenty of bloom. *Iowa R.S.* 7(25-2-30″-8.7). Linn *County R.S.* 6(27-8.3) Well-formed bud and open bloom, nice disease-resistant foliage. KAN. *Wichita R.S.* 7(9-2-30″-8.5) No faults. KY. *Frankfort Chapter ARS* 15(40-4-36″-8) Outstanding color and form. *Kentucky R.S.* 5(58-2-42″-9) Prolific bloomer, free of ordinary diseases, easy to care for. *Lexington R.S.* 2(4-2-24″-9) Outstanding color and form, good foliage, beautiful buds and bloom. *Louisville Chapter ARS* 15(54-1-32″-9.1) Hardy, vigorous plant, productive, good color, bloom could be better. LA. *New Orleans R.S.* 2(7-3-48″-8.5) Good color, tall bush. MD. *Maryland R.S.* 3(5-2-42″-8) Free-bloomer, good form and color, blooms small during hot weather. MICH. *Detroit R.S.* 6(8-2-36″-8.5) Excellent bush and bloom, disease-resistant. *Greater Lansing R.S.* 3(10-3-30″-8) Fine bud and bloom, average disease-resistant foliage, fragrant. *Kalamazoo R.S.* (36″-8.8) Good bloom, disease-free, flower holds. *Michigan State University T.G.* (98-4-28″-8.6) Outstanding color, best in cool weather, color holds well, vigorous, disease-resistant, heavy Damask rose fragrance. *West Michigan Rosarians* 1(2-2-30″-8.5) Beautiful plant, nice blooms, repeats well. MINN. *Lyndale Park T.G.* (35-3-30″-8.2) Very good bloomer, outstanding color, disease-free. *Minnestota R.S.* 14(36-2-27″-7.9) Makes good border rose, beautiful tangerine buds, full-petalled bloom. MO. *Kansas City R.S.* 1(3-1-20″-8) Good color and bloomer, disease-resistant. *Rosarians Midland Empire* 3(16-3-32″-8.8) Beautiful flowers, clean, good grower. *R.S. Greater St. Louis* 6(13-3-54″-8.5) Large many-petalled flower. *Sedalia R.S.* 3(3-3-30″-8.5) Excellent form and color, opens slowly and lasts well, good plant and foliage. NEV. *Reno R.S.* 9(24-4-48″-8) Beautiful orange-red color does not fade in the hottest Summer, very showy, steady bloomer, no mildew. NEW ENGLAND *New England R.S.* 6(26-3-40″-8) Better-than-average disease resistance, free bloom, usually fragrant. N.J. *North Jersey R.S.* 20(85-3-38″-8.3) Excellent color and plant. *West Jersey R.S.* 5(12-3-42″-8.3) Excellent color and plant. *West Jersey R.S.* 5(12-3-42″-8.8) Strong healthy plants, disease-free, profuse bloomer, long-lasting beautiful flowers. N.M. *Albuquerque R.S.* 4(6-2-28″-7.7) Distinctive non-fading color, excellent disease-free prolific plant, well-shaped bud, not' hardy in severe weather, slow-starter, dislikes reflected heat. N.Y. *Cornell University T.G.* (20-3-30″-8.8) Large flower of excellent color, floriferous, disease-resistant, poor spray, fades badly. *Humboldt Park T.G.* (21-3-24″-9) Very vigorous, upright, branching plant, abundant disease-resistant foliage, deep coral-pink buds, small to medium clustered blooms hang on and fade when done. *Long Island R.S.* 6(6-2-39″-8) Color, form, vigor and foliage tops, few blooms. *Niagara Frontier R.S.* 2(5-3-37″-8.2) Nice color, grows well, full flower good, husky plants almost constantly in bloom. *Rochester R.S.* 8(56-2-36″-8) Vigorous disease-resistant foliage, distinctive color, fragrant. *Schenectady R.S.* 9(22-2-28″-8.5) Very healthy plant, beautiful color, buds open slowly, prolific. *Syracuse R.S.* 9(19-3-37″-8.2) Distinctive color, blooms constantly, good disease-resistant foliage. N.C. *Charlotte R.S.* 5(6-1-24″-7) Healthy, good color. *Durham R.S.* 11(37-2-54″-9.6) Outstanding long-lasting cut flower, profuse bloomer, vigorous, nice single bloom. *Randolph R.S.* 3(62-48″-9) Good grower, abundant long-lasting bloom, fine disease-resistant foliage. OHIO *Akron R.S.* 7(46-2-30″-7.5) Good in mass planting, good disease-resistant foliage. *Central Ohio R.S.* 4(10-2-48″-8) Blooms have attractive form and color, very free-flowering, vigorous, disease-resistant plant. *Cincinnati R.S.* 7(21-2-36″-8) Best salmon shade. *Cleveland R.S.* 6(31-3-38″-9) Striking color, prolific, rich insect-free disease-resistant foliage. *Columbus R.C.* 4(8-2-54″-8.2) Good color, some blackspot. *Euclid R.S.* 1(1-1-36″-9) Abundant bloom, good color and foliage, blooms hold, strong growth. *Forest City R.S.* 9(27-3-38″-9) Outstanding color, long-lasting bloom, disease-resistant, good exhibition-type cutting rose. *Greater Cincinnati R.S.* 2(5-1-30″-8) Nice color doesn't fade, very little blackspot, fair bloomer, weak stems. *Lancaster R.C.* 8(24-3-33″-8.4) Vigorous, upright, profuse bloomer, needs more blooms in clusters. *Lima R.S.* 8(13-2-36″-8.7) Vigorous, excellent color does not fade, keeps well, disease-resistant. *Miami Valley R.S.* 7(24-2-48″-9) Very vigorous, beautiful color, disease-resistant, not for exhibition. *Park of Roses T.G.*

(150-4-45″-9.5) Excellent bloom, good disease-resistant foliage, good growth habit, no faults. *Stark R.S.* 5(6-2-27″-7.8) Excellent color, disease-free foliage. OKLA. *Norman R.S.* 3(28-4-36″-8.6) Very floriferous. ORE. *Eugene R.S.* 4(6-2-24″-8.5) Real fragrance, pleasing full vivid red-orange blooms. *International Rose T.G.* (40-5-52″-9) Good color, single and spray Hybrid Tea-form bloom recurrence, color could hold longer. *Medford R.S.* 11(20-2-32″-8.6) Striking color, vigorous, bushy, disease-resistant, many blooms come one to a stem. *Rogue Valley R.S.* 4(6-3-32″-8.9) Rich striking color, prolific bloomer, disease-resistant. *Roseburg R.S.* 2(2-1-30″-9) Profuse bloom, beautiful color, very good disease-resistant foliage. *Salem R.S.* 5(8-3-34″-8.2) Healthy plant, excellent buds and blooms, color fades a bit. PA. *Breeze Hill T.G.* (9-4-30″-10). *Harrisburg R.S.* 2(3-1-48″-9) Vigorous, free-bloomer, beautiful color, excellent buds and flowers, fine foliage. *Philadelphia R.S.* 5(11-3-40″-8.6) Good bloom holds well in heat, needs room. *Pittsburgh R.S.* 3(77-2-33″-8.1) Vigorous plant, good color, many blooms hold, some blackspot. S.C. *Edisto T.G.* (24-4-48″-9) Vigorous grower, floriferous, attractive color, good flower form. TENN. *Nashville R.S.* 6(21-3-34″-8.8) Profuse bloomer, orange-red color holds well, some blackspot. TEX. *Amarillo R.S.* 5(6-1-24″-8.5) Prolific bloomer, enticing color, stems not too strong. *Corpus Christi R.S.* 1(1-3-36″-9.3) Lovely foliage, gorgeous long-lasting blooms, most unusual striking color, stems not always sturdy. *Dallas R.S.* 6(13-3-40″-8.5) Good color, blooms well, vigorous, some blackspot. *El Paso R.S.* 2(2-2-34″-9) Vigorous grower, beautiful rich color, fully-double bloom, healthy green foliage, blooms profusely during the Summer, fades slightly. UTAH *Utah R.S.* 9(52-3-32″-8.3) Vigorous growth, lots of fine blooms, good foliage, constantly improving. VA. *Eastern Shore R.S.* 3(4-3-48″-9) Vigorous growth, unusual color, good bloomer, very vigorous bush with wide spread, disease-resistant, blackspots. *Va. Peninsula R.S.* 1(1-2-46″-8) Average grower, good color, average disease-resistant foliage. WASH. *Seattle R.S.* 3(6-2-36″-8.2). *Spokane R.S.* 8(43-3-36″-10) Unusual color, blooms continuously, buds prettier than open flower. *Walla Walla R.S.* 2(8-3-36″-9) Fine foliage and bloom. W.VA. *Charleston R.S.* 1(1-3-36″-6) Good bloom color, healthy. WIS. *Madison R.S.* 6(13-2-33″-8.2) Beautiful color, disease-resistant, good form and foliage, not enough blooms. *Milwaukee R.S.* 5(22-3-8.9) Un-usual color, lovely form, healthy bush, profuse repeat bloom, occasional scraggly plant, long-lasting bloom, mildews. CANADA (British Columbia) *University B.C. T.G.* (3-2-31″-7) Salmon-pink flowers fade to pink, light fragrance, mildews. *Vancouver R.S.* 5(12-4-36″-8) Excellent color, good symmetrical bush, fragrant, flowers last well. (Nova Scotia) *Buchanan* (3-3-24″-7) Good color doesn't fade, not continuous.

## SPECTACULAR Cl. Orange-red. (Mallerin; int. Jackson & Perkins '57) Pat. 1416; ARA '57; PP 2, 45 Rpts.; Av. ht. 6½′; NR 7.5.

ARIZ. *Phoenix R.S.* 2(2-1-6′-7) Good growth, few recurrent blooms during Summer. CALIF. *Memorial T.G.* (1-3-4′-4) Not vigorous. *San Joaquin Valley R.S.* 3(3-3-7½′-7.9) Vigorous, striking color, does not bloom enough. IND. *St. Joseph Valley R.S.* 1(1-2-8′-7.9) Get this Climber if you like Independence, an eye-catcher, large blooms. IOWA *Des Moines R.S.* 2(4-2-6′-8) Strong cane, withstands cold, holds color well. *Iowa R.S.* 1(1-2-4′- ) Few spectacular blooms. KY. *Louisville Chapter ARS* 1(1-3-12′-8) Hardy, vigorous, nice Spring flower form and substance, some mildew and blackspot, slow to spread. MINN. *Minnesota R.S.* 1(1-1-5′-6.5) Weak stem, not many blooms. MO. *Rosarians Midland Empire* 1(2-2-10′-7.6) Grows like Paul's Scarlet Climber, a lot cleaner, does not repeat in the Fall. *R.S. Greater St. Louis* 1(1-2-10′-6) Lovely Independence color, but not much recurrent bloom. NEW ENGLAND *New England R.S.* 2(6-2-5′-7.5) Too-few blooms, slow starter. N.J. *North Jersey R.S.* 2(2-1-4½′-7.9) Not a repeater, marvelous color, good plant. *West Jersey R.S.* 1(1-2-9′-7) Good remontant Climber, pretty flowers, good bloomer. N.Y. *Cornell University T.G.* (1-4-5¼′-6.5) Good color on opening, very slow grower, not overly vigorous, not continuously in flower, blooms burn badly during hot weather. *Humboldt Park T.G.* (2-2-7′-9) Branching plants, vigorous abundant dark green leathery disease-resistant foliage. ovoid bright buds, abundant intermittent open globular semi-double blooms drop cleanly. *Schenectady R.S.* 1(2-2-3′-7.5). *Syracuse R.S.* 4(4-2-8′-8.2) Large cluster of gorgeous blooms, very vigorous growth, good foliage, would like more repeat bloom. N.C. *Durham R.S.* 1(6-2-8′-8) Generous Spring bloomer, no Summer bloom, each branch festooned with roses in all stages. OHIO *Akron R.S.* 3(3-2-4′-7.2) Grows well, vigorous, good foliage, does not recur. *Cleveland R.S.* 1(2-2-7′-7) Superb color form and size. *Lima R.S.* 1(2-2-6′-8) Beautiful blooms, color and foliage. ORE. *Medford R.S.* 1(1-2-9′-7.5) More vigor this year but did not bloom as much as last, glossy disease-resistant foliage, blooms similar to Paul's Scarlet Climber but with Independence color. *Salem R.S.* 1(1-1-4′-7) Fades quickly and badly in hot sun, good bud form and color. PA. *Breeze Hill T.G.* (1-4-3'-6) Brilliant color, long stems, diesback in Winter. *Philadelphia R.S.* 1(1-1-4'-8) Bud holds well. *Pittsburgh R.S.* 1(1-2-6'-8) Nice color, good bloom, very good new growth, little mildew. TEX. *Amarillo R.S.* 3(1-2-8'-8) Good color, foliage and stems, true to size, not enough bloom. UTAH *Utah R.S.* 1(1-4-14'-9). VA. *Eastern Shore R.S.* 1(1-1-4'-6) Nice color, disease-resistant foliage, sparse bloomer, very poor grower. WASH. *Spokane R.S.* 1(1-2-6'-8) Beautiful blooms. WIS. *Milwaukee R.S.* 1(1-1-6'-7) Beautiful color, not enough bloom. CANADA (British Columbia) *Vancouver R.S.* 1(1-2-8'-9) Color like Independence, long-lasting recurrent bloom, good abundant foliage. (Nova Scotia) *Buchanan* (3-1-8'-8) Wonderful color, not everblooming as yet, needs to be pruned to first 5-leaflet leaf (not just dead flower cut off), hardy, pliable canes, like a sheet of flame when in bloom.

## STERLING SILVER HT. Lavender with silver sheen. (Fisher; int. Jackson & Perkins '55) Pat. 1433; ARA '56; PP 1, 111 Rpts.; Av. ht. 29"; NR 7.2.

ALA. *Twickenham R.S.* 2(1-1-32"-7.3) Good color, vigorous, no blackspot. ARIZ. *Mesa R.S.* 3(5-1-24"-6) Small plant and blooms, flowers fade, not enough of them, nice buds and open flower, needs partial shade. *Phoenix R.S.* 3(4-1-24"-7.5) Stately blooms, color holds. CALIF. *Memorial T.G.* (5-2-18"-7) Attractive color, very fragrant, not a freebloomer. *Rose Study Club Oakland* 3(6-1-41"-8.3) Nearly every bloom perfect, interesting new color, disease-resistant foliage, good grower and bloomer, fine cutting rose. *Pacific R.S.* 1(1-1-24"-10) Well-branched and shaped bush, disease-resistant, beautiful color, bloom has both form and fragrance, profuse bloomer. *Peninsula R.S.* 4(5-1-36"-8) Good form and color, holds well as cut bloom, spindly plant. *San Diego R.S.* 2(2-1-30"-5.4) Highly susceptible to mildew. CONN. *Elizabeth Park T.G.* (14-2-15"-5) Good plant in bloom. D.C. *Potomac R.S.* 2(3-1-36"-7.6) Beautiful light clear color, good plant, fragrant, not a tall grower. GA. *Georgia R.S.* 3(4-1-48"-7.5) Exhibition-quality, vigorous plant, disease-resistant foliage, good bud, bloom, form, size and color on tall strong stems, slowopening, not enough bloom. ILL. *Chicago R.S. Reg. 1* (24"-7) Lovely color, not enough blooms. *Greater Peoria R.S.* 2(4-1-36"-7.6) Blooms well except in hot weather, diseaseresistant, opens too fast. IND. *Indianapolis R.S.* 1(1-1-48"-6) Fair bloomer, leggy. *St. Joseph Valley R.S.* 2(2-1-42"-8.1) Very fragrant, good substance, beautiful color in Fall. *Vincennes R.S.* 1(1-1-36"-9) No faults, each bloom graceful and shapely. IOWA *Iowa R.S.* 1(1-1-16"- ) Poor growth, many petals, lasts well. KY. *Kentucky R.S.* 2(2-1-42"-7) Large pointed buds, too-few blooms, mildews. *Louisville Chapter ARS* (25"-6.6) Unusual color, good form, blackspots, slow grower, weak. LA. *New Orleans R.S.* 1(2-2-42"-9) Good substance, good for exhibition. MD. *Maryland R.S.* 2(2-1-18"-5) Good form and color, bush will not grow. MICH. *Detroit R.S.* 3(4-1-18"-7.1) Good color, fragrance, hard to winter, no fading. *Kalamazoo R.S.* 1(1-1-24"-7) Good bloom. *Michigan State University T.G.* (6-1-24"-4) Pleasing color, good form, long-lasting, very fragrant (tea) shy bloomer, susceptible to disease. MINN. *Lyndale Park T.G.* (15-2-18"-6) Good fragrance and bud, blackspots, not hardy. *Minnesota R.S.* 4(4-1-28"-8) Good color, fine bud and flower form, small blooms in hot weather. MO. *R.S. Greater St. Louis* 1(2-1-30"-7) Lovely bud color fades in open bloom, disappointing growth, not enough bloom. NEW ENGLAND *New England R.S.* 1(1-1-30"-9) Exceptional color and flower form. N.J. *North Jersey R.S.* 5(11-1-25"-6.5) Not vigorous, poor open bloom, needs afternoon shade. *West Jersey R.S.* 4(8-1-36"-7.5) Well-formed medium-size bloom, keeps well when cut, fades in sun, good growing plant, free-bloomer. N.M. *Albuquerque R.S.* 4(4-1-16"-7.5) Good form and substance, clear lasting color, deep green disease-resistant foliage, small plant. N.Y. *Cornell University T.G.* (3-1-20"-6.5) Unusual color finishes poorly, good flower form, sparse bloom in late Summer, weak necks. *Greater Buffalo R.S.* 3(9-1-24"-8.7) Clear color, good form, excellent for arrangements, small bloom, blackspots. *Humboldt Park T.G.* (5-2-10"-2) Pretty blooms, ovoid large to medium buds, strong rich fragrance, petals drop cleanly, very poor vigor. *Rochester R.S.* 1(15-2-26"-6) Full-petalled bloom, too much yellow in color. *Schenectady R.S.* 1(5-1-38"-8) Few rival its fragrance or substance, perfect in half-opened stage, finishes somewhat flat, occasional mildew. N.C. *Durham R.S.* 1(1-2-18"-2). *Randolph R.S.* 1(1-1-36"-7) Beautiful lasting bloom, good foliage. OHIO *Akron R.S.* 3(5-1-30"-8.1) Fair growth. *Central Ohio R.S.* 2(4-1-36"-6.5) Nice bud, good opening color fades quickly, very susceptible to blackspot. *Cleveland R.S.* 1(1-2-24"-7) Lovely color, delicate fragrance. *Forest City R.S.* 4(4-1-24"-8) Good form, clean near-blue color. *Lancaster R.C.* 2(5-2-30"-7.1) Unusual color, high-centered fragrant bloom, poor grower. *Lima R.S.* 1(1-1-24"-7.5) Nice form, unusual long-lasting color. *Medina County R.S.* 1(1-1-26"-7) Interesting color. *Ohio State University T.G.* (4-1-14"-4) Fragrant flower, good color during entire length of bloom, disease-resistant, plants not vigorous, low flower production, plants not bushy. *Park of Roses T.G.* (25-2-33″-6.5) Weak spindly plant, blackspots badly. OKLA. *Norman R.S.* 1(1-1-28″-8) Nice foliage, holds color well. *Oklahoma R.S.* 2(4-2-30″-8). ORE. *Eugene R.S.* 2(2-1-24″-7.5) Light nice clean color, good form, long-lasting bloom, plant not too strong. *International Rose T.G.* (10-2-30″-6) Good bud, attractive open flower, slow vigor, mildews. *Lewis & Clark T.G.* (6-2-18″-8) Excellent form, good color and foliage. *Medford R.S.* 2(2-1-30″-6.9) True color, small exhibition blooms on a not-too-vigorous plant, does best in Spring and Fall, very few blooms in middle of Summer, red spider mites love it. PA. *Breeze Hill T.G.* (2-2-24″-7) Excellent form, good color as it opens, fairly profuse. *Harrisburg R.S.* 1(1500-1-42″-8.5) Outstanding different color, good foliage, compact growth, well-formed bud, good show rose. *Philadelphia R.S.* 2(3-2-24″-6.5). TENN. *Nashville R.S.* 3(4-1-30″-7.3) Healthy, fair bloomer. TEX. *Corpus Christi R.S.* 1(1-1-30″-8) Scarce lovely fragrant bloom, sturdy plant. UTAH *Utah R.S.* 2(3-2-24″-8) Vigorous, prolific bloomer, fragrant. VA. *Va. Peninsula R.S.* 1(1-1-24″-5.6) Very slow grower, not many blooms, susceptible to blackspot. WIS. *Madison R.S.* 1(1-1-36″-8.1) Good foliage, hardy, good growth, intermittent bloom, well-formed rose, unusual color. *Milwaukee R.S.* Lovely perfect buds and bloom, dreamy color, healthy bush, very few blooms, small plant, very susceptible to blackspot.

## SUMATRA F. Vivid signal-red. (Mallerin; int. Conard-Pyle '57) Pat. 1572; ARA '57; PP 2, 84 Rpts.; Av. ht. 30″; NR 7.5.

ALA. *Twickenham R.S.* 1(1-2-33″-6). ARIZ. *Mesa R.S.* 1(1-2-60″-8.5) Good plant, fair bloomer, beautiful flowers. *Phoenix R.S.* 2(3-2-33″-7.8) Vivid outstanding color, good foliage and form. CALIF. *Rose Study Club Oakland* 2(8-2-42″-7.5) Striking new orange-red shade, semi-double flat flowers in large sprays, best in Spring, mildews, repeats rather slowly. *Pacific R.S.* 1(2-1-24″-7.5) Average foliage, heavy spring bloom, not much bloom after that, sheds clean. *San Joaquin Valley R.S.* 1(1-1-24″-8) Color and vigor makes this rose outstanding, clusters of coral-red blooms. *San Mateo County R.S.* 1(2-2-30″-5) Beautiful color, needs more bloom, poor plant, weak grower. D.C. *Potomac R.S.* 4(7-2-36″-7.5) Outstanding orange-red large flower clusters of semi-double blooms, good foliage, flower lacks form. GA. *Georgia R.S.* 1(1-1-12″-5). IND. *Indianapolis R.S.* 1(1-2-30″-7) Good color, fair vigor, not good repeat-bloomer, slight blackspot. IOWA *Des Moines R.S.* 1(1-1-24″-7). *Iowa R.S.* 1(3-2-30″-7) Loose sparse blooms. KAN. *Wichita R.S.* 1(1-1-42″-7) Outstanding different color, blackspots. KY. *Kentucky R.S.* 1(2-2-43″-7) A show in the Spring, mildews. *Lexington R.S.* 1(1-1-36″-8.5) Nice foliage, good grower, gorgeous color, prolific. *Louisville Chapter ARS* 1(1-2-30″-8) Good bud and flower, striking color. MD. *Maryland R.S.* 3(5-1-30″-8) Blooms as freely as an azalea in the Spring, very bushy. MICH. *Detroit R.S.* 5(7-1-18″-7) Good color fades. *Kalamazoo R.S.* 1(1-1-24″-8) Good bloomer, much like Spartan. MINN. *Minnesota R.S.* 5(7-2-27″-7.7) Unusual color, good bush form, could bloom more. MO. *Sedalia R.S.* 1(1-2-30″-7.5) Bright single blooms last several days, plant not vigorous enough, intermittent bloom. NEV. *Reno R.S.* 1(2-2-24″-4) Beautiful flower color fades quickly, weak stems, winter-kills easily, very weak grower. NEW ENGLAND *New England R.S.* 2(5-2-36″-8) Handsome flower fades, good production and foliage. N.J. *North Jersey R.S.* 6(9-2-25″-6.7) Good color, stingy bloomer, not disease-resistant. *West Jersey R.S.* 5(20-2-36″-8.5) Very good unusual color, always in bloom, disease-free. N.Y. *Cornell University T.G.* (13-2-23″-8) Excellent foliage, opening color outstanding, many flowers all season, nice form, old flowers do not drop, color finishes very badly. *Greater Buffalo R.S.* 1(1-1-24″-8.5) Vigorous plant, continuous bloom, disease-resistant. *Humboldt Park T.G.* (5-2-20″-8) Bushy, vigorous, dark green leathery foliage, very good lasting quality blooms drop cleanly, disease-free foliage has purple to brown cast late in season. *Syracuse R.S.* 2(2-2-36″-8.5) Fine plant, lots of good bloom. N.C. *Charlotte R.S.* 2(3-1-24″-6) Good color, not a strong grower or bloomer. *Durham R.S.* 2(4-2-42″-8.6) Profuse bloomer, striking color, pretty open flower, fragrant, extra-good plant. OHIO *Akron R.S.* 2(3-2-24″-7.3) Good color, foliage, blooms constantly, slight blackspot. *Cincinnati R.S.* 3(7-2-33″-8) Similar to Spartan, picks up more disease. *Lima R.S.* 1(1-2-30″-7.2). *Ohio State University T.G.* (4-27″-7) Very bushy, vigorous plant, excellent dark green disease-resistant foliage, fair flower production, slightly fragrant, spray burns in August. OKLA. *Norman R.S.* 3(3-3-30″-7.6). ORE. *International Rose T.G.* (2-4-36″-6) Good color and plant habit, fades quickly, needs half-day shade. *Lewis & Clark T.G.* (12-1-30″-5) Poor plant and growth, mildews. PA. *Breeze Hill T.G.* (3-4-30″-8) Profuse large flowers of exquisite color, nice foliage, fades. *Harrisburg R.S.* 1(600-1-36″-9) Compact growth, abundant bloom, dark foliage, nice appearance all Summer, brilliant orange seed hips. *Philadelphia R.S.* 4(7-2-30″-8) Excellent plant, good bloom, blues. *Pittsburgh R.S.* 2(3-2-30″-7.8) Beautiful color, few blooms, heavy foliage. TEX. *Dallas R.S.* 1(1-2-36″-8.5) Very colorful, good foliage, some blackspot. *El Paso R.S.* 1(3-1-30″-9) Dark green healthy foliage and stems, holds color well in full sun, excellent bloomer. UTAH *Utah R.S.* 2(3-3-26″-7.7) Nice bright blooms, likes partial shade. WIS. *Madison R.S.* 1(1-2-36″-8.5) Good growth, foliage, form and substance, unusual color, disease-resistant, lots of blooms.

## SUMMERTIME HT. Pink. (Boerner; int. Jackson & Perkins '57) Pat. 1541; ARA '57; PP 2, 61 Rpts.; Av. ht. 31″; NR 7.7.

ARIZ. *Phoenix R.S.* 3(4-1-20″-6.7). CALIF. *Rose Study Club Oakland* 2(6-2-50″-7.9) Lovely bud and abundant fragrant bloom, upright spreading bush, moderate vigor. COLO. *Denver R.S.* 1(1-2-18″-7.5) Resistant to mildew, blooms stay out for more than a week, good repeater. CONN. *Elizabeth Park T.G.* (9-3-30″-8) Strong grower, slightly scented. GA. *Georgia R.S.* 1(1-1-7). ILL. *Chicago R.S. Reg. 1* 4(5-1-36″-8.5) Very fragrant, well-shaped blooms, disease-free bush. IOWA *Des Moines R.S.* 2(2-1-24″-7) Clear large bloom. *Iowa R.S.* 1(2-2-24″-7) Nice clear color. *Linn County R.S.* 1(1-1-24″-7) Double petals, long-lasting infrequent bloom, beautiful when open. KAN. *Wichita R.S.* 3(3-1-24″-6.8) Disease-resistant, profuse bloomer, fades. KY. *Kentucky R.S.* 1(2-1-24″-10) Beautiful show rose, no faults. *Louisville Chapter ARS* 2(3-2-27″-7) Good color, disease-resistant foliage, bush stunted and weak. MICH. *Detroit R.S.* 1(1-1-24″-7) Perfect blooms, but not enough. *Kalamazoo R.S.* 2(6-1-36″-8) Good form and flowers. MINN. *Minnesota R.S.* 1(1-2-27″-9.5) Perfectly-formed lovely pink blooms, weather-resistant. MO. *Rosarians Midland Empire* 1(2-2-30″-7) Prolific Spring bloomer, bush not sturdy, sparse foliage, little bloom in hot weather, fades in sun. NEW ENGLAND *New England R.S.* 2(3-2-32″-8) Good repeat-bloomer, not an attractive plant. N.J. *North Jersey R.S.* 3(3-2-26″-8) Fine bloom, excellent production, dependable plant. *West Jersey R.S.* 5(14-2-48″-8.8) Very fragrant well-formed bloom, healthy plant, always in bloom. N.Y. *Long Island R.S.* 1(1-1-18″-7). *Rochester R.S.* 1(1-1-24″-8) Beautiful bloom, good fragrance, poor bud. *Schenectady R.S.* 2(6-2-34″-8.3) Good color and bloom. *Syracuse R.S.* 2(2-2-22″-6) Poor buds, beautiful but sparse bloom, poor grower. OHIO *Akron R.S.* 2(3-1-30″-8). *Greater Cincinnati R.S.* 1(1-2-24″-8) Charming camellia-type flowers almost constantly in bloom, small flowers unless disbudded. *Ohio State University T.G.* (3-3-27″-7) Vigorous, bushy plant, disease-resistant, blooms well in June, July and August, fragrant, poor foliage. OKLA. *Oklahoma R.S.* 1(2-1-30″-7). ORE. *International Rose T.G.* (18-4-48″-7) Exhibition form, tea fragrance, profuse bloom, needs disbudding, acts like a Floribunda after Spring bloom. *Lewis & Clark T.G.* (9-1-48″-10) Tall plant, excellent foliage, long pointed buds open to fine bloom. *Medford R.S.* 2(2-1-30″-8) Small well-formed silvery-pink prolific buds and blooms, vigorous, bushy plant, some mildew. *Rogue Valley R.S.* 3(5-2-30″-8) Excellent color and form, good bloomer, long-lasting, disease-resistant. PA. *Breeze Hill T.G.* (3-5-30″-6) Pretty form and color, fairly profuse. TENN. *Nashville R.S.* 2(6-3-30″-7.8) Excellent light color. TEX. *Dallas R.S.* 2(4-2-35″-8) Good healthy plant, flowers well, willowly stems. VA. *Eastern Shore R.S.* 1(2-3-24″-6) Well-shaped buds, nice fragrance, slow grower, too-few blooms.

## SUN KING HT. Light yellow. (Meilland; int. Conard-Pyle '54) Pat. 1342; ARA '55; PP 4, 59 Rpts.; Av. ht. 34″; NR 6.2.

CALIF. *San Mateo County R.S.* 3(4-3-36″-2) Beautiful exhibition-type bloom, color fades, weak leggy plant, sparse bloomer. D.C. *Potomac R.S.* 4(7-3-48″-7.4) Beautifully-formed blooms of many petals, good cutting canes, color fades, little new growth, not many blooms. GA. *Georgia R.S.* 2(3-2-48″-8.5) Beautiful form, good clear color, best in cool weather, ranks next to Eclipse, could bloom more. ILL. *Greater Peoria R.S.* 1(1-3-36″-6) Beautiful color, poor foliage. *St. Joseph Valley R.S.* 1(3-3-42″-6.8) Tall like Peace, slightly fragrant, good flowers don't hold up. IOWA *Linn County R.S.* 1(1-2-36″-7.5) Good color. KY. *Kentucky R.S.* 1(2-3-42″-7) Beautifully-shaped big bud, color bleaches to white, lovely foliage, tall, leggy, few blooms. MD. *Maryland R.S.* 2(2-2-42″-7) Nice color, good form, upright bush. MINN. *Minnesota R.S.* 1(1-3-30″-6.5) Exhibition flower, but not enough bloom. MO. *Rosarians Midland Empire* 2(3-3-39″-6.5) Exhibition bloom, but sparse. *R.S. Greater St. Louis* 1(1-2-30″-7) Lovely pale blooms turn nearly white. NEV. *Reno R.S.* 1(2-2-30″-3) Large beautiful bloom, color fades, spindly weak plant, poor bloomer. NEW ENGLAND *New England R.S.* 4(6-3-36″-7) Weak plant, few blooms. N.J. *North Jersey R.S.* 8(11-2-23″-4.9) Poor plant, lacks bloom. N.Y. *Humboldt Park T.G.* (6-3-30″-2) Upright, good height, large globular blooms, long strong stems, blooms hang on, sparse foliage looks terrible as season advances, intermittent blooms. *Niagara Frontier R.S.* 5(7-3-26″-6) Weak grower, few blooms. *Rochester R.S.* 1(1-2-54″-

6.5) Sparse bloomer, fades. *Syracuse R.S.* 2(4-2-26″-6.5) Blooms of nice form
and color, sparse bloomer, not vigorous, blackspots. OHIO *Akron R.S.* 3(4-2-20″-7.3)
Exhibition-type, not hardy. *Cincinnati R.S.* 1(1-2-36″-7.5) Fine sparse pale exhibition
blooms. *Lancaster R.C.* 2(3-3-40″-6) High-centered bloom, poor bloomer, plants lack
vigor. OKLA. *Norman R.S.* 1(1-3-32″-6.2). PA. *Breeze Hill T.G.* (1-4-20″-7) Lovely
color and form, nice foliage, fairly profuse. *Philadelphia R.S.* 4(5-2-30″-6.8) Needs
sun and moisture for repeat bloom, leggy, good flower. TENN. *Nashville R.S.* 2(2-4-36″-7.3)
Outstanding form and substance, few blooms. TEX. *Dallas R.S.* 1(3-5-38″-6) Superb
form, fair foliage, much die-back, stingy. VA. *Eastern Shore R.S.* 2(2-2-48″-7) Good
bloomer, exhibition-type, upright plant, no mildew, grows better in partial shade, slow
grower. CANADA (British Columbia) *Vancouver R.S.* 1(1-3-36″-8) Large pointed clear
buds and blooms, good form does not last long, some die-back.

## SUNLIGHT HT. Aureolin-yellow. (Meilland; int. Conard-Pyle '58) Pat. 1576; ARA '59; PP 1, 47 Rpts.; Av. ht. 38″; NR 7.4.

ARIZ. *Mesa R.S.* 1(1-1-48″-7.5) Good plant and blooms, fair bloomer. CALIF. *Rose
Study Club Oakland* 1(2-1-42″-8.2) Vigorous, upright, bushy plant, good bloomer,
disease-resistant, good color. *Peninsula R.S.* 3(4-1-48″-7) Non-fading, compact plant,
tender foliage, some rust. *San Mateo County R.S.* 1(2-2-36″-8) Free-bloomer, holds color
well, good plant, disease-resistant, blooms could be larger. ILL. *Greater Peoria R.S.*
1(1-1-42″-8.3) Vigorous grower, doesn't fade, holds form well, could bloom more often,
blackspots. IND. *Indianapolis R.S.* 2(2-2-30″-7) Good blooms, but too few. KY. *Kentucky
R.S.* 1(3-1-30″-7) Pretty color, very little bloom. MD. *Maryland R.S.* 2(4-2-42″-8)
Good deep color, upright bush, vigorous. MINN. *Minnesota R.S.* 5(7-1-38″-7.5) Upright,
vigorous growth, long pointed deep buds, abundant continuous blooms. MO. *Rosarians
Midland Empire* 1(3-1-36″-7.9) Nice clean blooms open fast. *R.S. Greater St. Louis*
1(1-1-36″-7) Wonderful bloom on upright-growing plant. NEW ENGLAND *New England
R.S.* 2(2-2-34″-7.5) Good form, fragrant, moderately vigorous. N.J. *North Jersey R.S.*
5(5-1-30″-6.8). *West Jersey R.S.* 3(5-1-30″-7) Nice light color fades in sun, healthy,
good growing plant, could bloom more. N.Y. *Long Island R.S.* 1(1-1-18″--7) Holds
color (Peace blood evident in bloom), foliage like all other yellow roses, blackspots badly.
*Richester R.S.* 1(1-1-30″-7.6) Bright deep color, good form, sparse bloomer. *Schenectady
R.S.* 1(1-1-48″-9) Beautiful color does not fade, fragrant, plenty of bloom, no blackspot
or mildew, no faults. OHIO *Akron R.S.* 1(1-1-60″-8.5) Slight mildew. *Cleveland R.S.*
2(11-1-50″-8.9) Strong color, long bud, good form and growth, shows Eclipse parentage.
*Lancaster R.C.* 2(4-1-48″-7.3) Fair bloomer, mildews. *Ohio State University T.G.*
(4-1-24″-5) Flowers fairly abundantly in July and August, good disease-resistant foliage,
vigorous bushy plant. ORE. *International Rose T.G.* (20-1-36″-7) Long tapered buds, good
color, fragrant, mildews. PA. *Breeze Hill T.G.* (2-3-32″-8) Good color fades very little, nice
form and foliage. *Philadelphia R.S.* 4(4-2-28″-7.2) Good substance, fair bloomer. VA.
*Eastern Shore R.S.* 1(1-2-60″-8) Beautiful bud opens to full 40-45 petal bloom, tall
vigorous plant, flowers borne on long stems, good foliage. WIS. *Madison R.S.* 1(1-1-50″-9)
Beautiful large exhibition-type flower, disease-resistant foliage, could bloom more. HAWAII
*Kona* (1-1-44″-6) Lovely clear soft color, looks like a miniature Peace, improves with
age, too many thorns too close together, few flowers fade very rapidly.

## TEXAN F. Rose-red. (Lindquist; int. Howard '56) Pat. 1471; ARA '56; PP 2, 134 Rpts.; Av. ht. 39″; NR 8.0.

ARIZ. *Mesa R.S.* 3(3-1-48″-8.8) No faults, Hybrid Tea-quality flowers from bud to
bloom. *Phoenix R.S.* 4(4-2-30″-8.8) Profuse bloomer, beautiful fragrant buds and
blooms, strong growth, excellent foliage. CALIF. *Memorial T.G.* (10-3-22″-4) Very fragrant,
rusts. *Rose Study Club Oakland* 2(9-3-49″-7.3) Vigorous grower, disease-resistant foliage,
scant Hybrid Tea-type fragrant bloom, color holds well. *Peninsula R.S.* 2(2-2-36″-6) Good
form and color, rusts and mildews, some blind wood. *Riverside R.S.* 6(8-2-48″-9.5) Brilliant
color, good thick leaves and buds. *San Diego R.S.* 2(8-3-48″-8.1) Loves hot weather.
*San Joaquin Valley R.S.* 2(3-2-48″-6.5) Does not hold in hot weather, not too vigorous.
*San Mateo County R.S.* 4(8-2-48″-8) Excellent strong-growing plant, disease-resistant
foliage, good bloomer, too tall. COLO. *Colorado Springs R.S.* 2(5-3-30″-7.5) Very good
plant, not enough blooms. *Denver R.S.* 3(53-3-36″-7) Good early, holds color and bloom
well, flower edges turn white in hot weather. CONN. *Elizabeth Park T.G.* (2-9-2-30″-8)
Excellent plant, weak stem for bloom, main bloom on lower part of plant. D.C. *Potomac R.S.*
2(3-2-54″-8.4) Good form, grower, foliage, large bloom, makes a good show rose. GA.
*Georgia R.S.* 5(8-2-48″-8) Good color and form, large Hybrid Tea-type bloom, dark

green disease-free foliage. ILL. *Chicago R.S. Reg. 1* 1(1-2-48″-9) Beautiful bright color, always in bloom. IND. *Indianapolis R.S.* 3(3-2-37″-8.1) Good form and color, blooms monthly like a Hybrid Tea, sulks at times. *St. Joseph Valley R.S.* 1(1-1-40″-8.2) Large prolific beautiful 3¼″ flowers of 25-28 petals. IOWA *Des Moines R.S.* 1(1-2-24″-6.5) Few blooms. *Linn County R.S.* 5(7-2-30″-8) Vigorous growth, nice pointed bud, full bush, disease-resistant. KAN. *Wichita R.S.* 3(3-2-36″-7.5) Good form, healthy, slow repeater, good grower. KY. *Kentucky R.S.* 1(1-2-24″-10) Pretty, no faults. *Louisville Chapter ARS* 3(4-1-38″-8.2) Excellent bud and bloom, good color, hardy plant. MICH. *Kalamazoo R.S.* 3(4-2-48″-8) Blooms freely, nice color and foliage. *Michigan State University T.G.* (5-4-38″-10) Good form, holds color well, slight "tea" fragrance, slight susceptibility to blackspot, blackens slightly in heat. MINN. *Lyndale Park T.G.* (20-3-36″-7.8) Good color, lots of bloom, hardy, disease-free. *Minnesota R.S.* 7(9-2-38″-7.7) Good performer, upright growth, does not blue. MO. *Rosarians Midland Empire* 1(1-1-36″-8) Very good odor. *R.S. Greater St. Louis* 2(3-2-30″-7.5) Lots of bloom on healthy plant. NEV. *Reno R.S.* 3(3-3-48″-8) Very healthy plant, grows tall, good bloomer, holds color well, disease-resistant. NEW ENGLAND *New England R.S.* 2(11-1-30″-9) Rusts. N.J. *North Jersey R.S.* 1(2-1-30″-7.5) Plenty of flowers. N.M. *Albuquerque R.S.* 1(1-1-18″-7) Wonderful color, many petals, blooms in profusion. N.Y. *Cornell University T.G.* (12-2-34″-7.8) Vigorous, excellent foliage, large flower, fine bud and color, floriferous, blooms in spurts, early effect is best. *Humboldt Park T.G.* (9-2-36″-9) Very vigorous, upright branching plant, abundant large dark green leathery foliage, dark velvet ovoid buds in clusters, flower petals drop cleanly, blues when finishing, some plants had a touch of blackspot. *Long Island R.S.* 2(3-1-32″-8.5) Most attractive flower, blooms frequently, vigorous grower, disease-resistant. *Rochester R.S.* 1(25-2-36″-7.5) Good dark velvety flower, disease-resistant. OHIO *Akron R.S.* 3(7-1-30″-9) Sparse bloom. *Central Ohio R.S.* 3(5-2-42″-8.5) Strong healthy vigorous free-blooming bush, blooms have good color and form, too many stems have only one bloom. *Cleveland R.S.* 1(1-1-24″-7) Nice color, good bloomer. *Columbus R.C.* 2(3-2-39″-7.5) Healthy, strong, good color and form. *Euclid R.S.* 1(1-2-40″-8.5) Very good plant, grows well, good foliage and bloom. *Greater Cincinnati R.S.* 1(1-1-36″-7.9) Blooms all Summer, doesn't fade, no blackspot, nice color, not many blooms in Fall. *Lima R.S.* 5(12-2-33″-7.5) Perfect form, always in bloom, doesn't fade, lasts after cutting, no faults. *Medina County R.S.* 1(1-2-48″-8.7) Very showy free-bloomer. *Ohio State University T.G.* (15-3-27″-7) Good bushy plant, vigorous flowers, good until September, disease-resistant, shows slight spray burn in August. *Stark R.S.* 1(1-3-22″-7) Lots of bloom, but not particularly beautiful. ORE. *International Rose T.G.* (20-4-48″-6) Profusion of bloom on huge trussses, color best in cool weather, subject to foliar diseases. *Lewis & Clark R.S.* (15-1-36″-8) Good color, form and bright foliage. *Medford R.S.* 4(7-2-46″-8.2) Well-formed blooms have unusual shade, vigorous, tall grower, disease-free. *Salem R.S.* 3(23-3-42″-7) Good bush and foliage, abundant bloom balls some early. PA. *Breeze Hill T.G.* (3-5-36″-8) Vigorous, profuse, good clear color, pretty form. S.C. *Edisto T.G.* (12-3-36″-7) Vigorous grower, good color and form, a little shy on Summer bloom. TENN. *Nashville R.S.* 4(14-2-44″-8.2) Dazzling velvety flower, almost constantly in bloom. TEX. *Amarillo R.S.* 2(4-2-48″-8) Good bloomer and foliage, size varies, stems not strong enough. *Corpus Christi R.S.* 1(3-3-24″-9.2) Excellent foliage, gorgeous bright long-lasting fragrant blooms. *Dallas R.S.* 2(6-2-38″-8) Blooms well, vigorous, good color, dull foliage. *El Paso R.S.* 5(16-2-46″-9) Healthy green foliage, strong stems in spray or single bloom, good color for the heat, blooms well all year, does not fade or shatter. UTAH *Utah R.S.* 3(5-2-44″-7.2) Good blooms, clear color, extra good bushes, but very stingy. WASH. *Spokane R.S.* 1(1-2-36″-8). WIS. *Madison R.S.* 1(1-2-48″-8.8) Good growth, hardy, excellent foliage, good bloomer, excellent form, substance and color. *Milwaukee R.S.* 1(3-4-7) No faults.

## THE DUKE HT. Solferino-purple. (Peterson & Dering '56) Pat. 1522; ARA '56; PP 3, 56 Rpts.; Av. ht. 27″; NR 7.1.

ARIZ. *Mesa R.S.* 1(1-1-7.2) Nice buds, not enough bloom. *Phoenix R.S.* 2(2-3-24″-7.5) large bloom, decorative bi-color, medium growth, good foliage. CALIF. *Peninsula R.S.* 2(2-1-18″-6) Generally lacks vigor, large bloom has poor form. COLO. *Denver R.S.* 1(10-2-26″-6) Continuous bloomer, good color, full blooms, mediocre form. GA. *Georgia R.S.* 1(1-2-19″-6) Outstanding bloom on sprawling plant not in proportion to heavy flower. IOWA *Des Moines R.S.* 1(1-1-24″-7) Good color, few blooms. *Linn County R.S.* 1(2-1-42″-7.5) Split centers, heavy bloomer. KY. *Kentucky R.S.* 1(1-3-30″-5). *Louisville Chapter ARS* 2(2-1-45″7) Wonderful color, good bloomer, cool weather rose. MICH. *Detroit R.S.* 2(22-36″-8.7) Good form, strong stems, hard to winter. *Kalamazoo R.S.* 2(5-1-30″-8) Vigorous, double blooms, good foliage. MINN. *Lyndale Park T.G.* (20-3-36″-8)

Very large double flower, good color, disease-free. *Minnesota R.S.* 11(18-1-27″-7.7) Large, full, exhibition bloom, dull foliage, short stems. MO. *R.S. Greater St. Louis* 1(1-1-12″-5) Poor growth and bloom. MONT. *Sunset Park T.G.* (20-1-26″-8) Huge showy blooms on a healthy spreading plant. N.J. *North Jersey R.S.* 8(10-1-24″-7) Large but infrequent bloomer, low grower. OHIO *Akron R.S.* 1(24-1-18″-6.9) Nice form. *Central Ohio R.S.* 3(4-1-28″-7) Large bloom with excellent color, lovely full bloom, vigorous bush resistant to disease, slow-grower, sparse bloom. *Lima R. S.* 2(2-2-36″-7.4) Large very double slow-opening blooms, good foliage, fragrant. *Ohio State University T.G.* (4-1-15″-5) Good bloom only in July, sparse disease-resistant large leaves, plants lack vigor. ORE. *International Rose T.G.* (20-4-42″-6) Good opening color, huge flowers, short stems in Summer, some mildew. *Lewis & Clark T.G.* (7-1-24″-5) Faded soft bloom, poor foliage. *Medford R.S.* 1(1-1-24″-6) Nice color, bloom has no form, weak bush, blooms too heavy for stem. *Salem R.S.* 1(24-1-30″-4) Mildews badly. PA. *Breeze Hill T.G.* (3-5-24″-6) Fairly profuse large flowers of bright color and good form. TEX. *Dallas R.S.* 1(2-1-24″-8.5) Good foliage and plant, blooms well, good cut flower. WASH. *Seattle R.S.* 2(2-2-24″-5.5) No good qualities. *Spokane R.S.* 2(2-2-24″-10) Long stems, strong fragrance. WIS. *Madison R.S.* 1(1-1-28″-9) Exquisite bloom, good form.

# TIFFANY HT. Pink blend. (Lindquist; int. Howard '54) Pat. 1304; ARA '55; PP 4, 686 Rpts.; Av. ht. 48″; NR 8.8.

ALA. *Twickenham R.S.* 3(5-2-45″-8.7) Fine quality and quantity bloom. ARIZ. *Mesa R.S.* 4(7-2-48″-8) Nice bloomer, outside petals fade, fragrant beautiful blooms. *Phoenix R.S.* 6(8-2-42″-8.7) Good exhibition rose, fragrant, lovely delicate color. CALIF. *Memorial T.G.* (12-5-40″-8) Very fragrant 4″ bloom, long stems, good cutter, lovely color. *Rose Study Club Oakland* 6(15-3-48″-7.9) Beautiful bloom of exhibition form, fragrant, vigorous plant, disease-resistant foliage, fine warm weather rose, good cutter, improves with age. *Pacific R.S.* 5(8-3-48″-8.7) Beautiful blend and form combined with fragrance, long straight stems, moderately strong plant, exhibition-type bloom, could be more prolific. *Peninsula R.S.* 7(14-3-60″-8) Vigorous upright grower, good disease-free foliage, fragrant bloom has good color and form, performs best in warm weather. *San Diego R.S.* 7(46-3-60″-8.7) Magnificent in Summer and Fall. *San Joaquin Valley R.S.* 4(9-4-60″-9) Exhibitor's rose, does well in warm weather, disease-resistant. *San Mateo County R.S.* 8(20-3-48″-9) Good flower form, substance and color, fragrant, good plant, many basal shoots, some blind shoots, some balling in wet weather. COLO. *Colorado Springs R.S.* 3(13-4-36″-7.5) Beautiful well-shaped blooms, strong stems, not a prolific bloomer. *Denver R.S.* 9(99-5-40″-8.9) Good bloomer, excellent form and color, has substance, long stems for cutting, vigorous, pleasing fragrance, poor plant habits. CONN. *Elizabeth Park T.G.* (32-6-20″-8) Excellent plant. D.C. *Potomac R.S.* 8(25-3-60″-10) Beautiful form with lots of substance, tops for shows, long cutting canes, upright bush, fragrant, no faults. GA. *Georgia R.S.* 18(80-3-66″-8.7) Exhibition bloom, good substance and color, tall upright bush, likes heat. ILL. *Chicago R.S. Reg. 1* 4(7-3-52″-8.5) Very lovely fragrant bloom of fine form, erect disease-free bush. *Greater Peoria R.S.* 9(15-2-54″-8.6) Good form, color and foliage, some blackspot. *Morgan Park R.S.* 3(3-1-24″-8) Good reliable bloomer. *Tri-City Men's Rose and Garden Club* 4(16-3-36″-8.8) Good canes, pointed bud. IND. *Indianapolis R.S.* 8(15-3-41″-8.6) Good grower and bloomer, beautiful bud, lovely fragrant flower. *St. Joseph Valley R.S.* 4(10-2-60″-8.9) Vigorous upright plant, fine exhibition fragrant blooms. *Vincennes R.S.* 6(20-2-48″-9.5) Lovely blooms, vigorous, hardy, no disease, plenty of substance, no faults. IOWA *Des Moines R.S.* 7(11-3-48″-8.5) Good bloom, long stems. *Iowa R.S.* 8(36″-8.7) Good form and color, steady bloomer, fine foliage. *Linn County R.S.* 3(11-3-54″-8.5) Long bud, nice when open, some fragrance, long stems, disease-resistant. KAN. *Wichita R.S.* 7(12-2-48″-8.5) Nice shape, good blooms and color, very fragrant, vigorous. KY. *Frankfort Chapter ARS* 8(30-4-48″-8) Long stems, free-bloomer. *Kentucky R.S.* 19(54-3-48″-10) Lovely color, vigorous, lasts when cut, slightly leggy. *Lexington R.S.* 3(6-7-42″-9) Very fragrant exhibition rose, exquisite buds, good grower. *Louisville Chapter ARS* 17(43-2-54″-9.4) Outstanding in every way. LA. *New Orleans R.S.* 3(6-2-60″-8.5) Good color, long stems, exhibition bloom best in cool weather, fades in our Summer heat. MD. *Maryland R.S.* 4(7-2-54″-8.5) Good most of the time, exhibition form, sturdy bush. MICH. *Detroit R.S.* 8(16-248″-8.6) Disease-resistant, excellent exhibition bloom. *Kalamazoo R.S.* 9(19-3-48″-8.5) Good substance, exhibition-type blooms. *Michigan State University T.G.* (6-5-38″-6) Excellent color, large blooms, very fragrant (like clove-spiced hot tea), shy bloomer, weak neck, not fully disease-resistant. *West Michigan Rosarians* 2(6-2-42″-8.5) Good in all ways. MINN. *Lyndale Park T.G.* (35-5-40″-8.5) Long stems for cutting, good color, bud and flower, disease-free. *Greater Lansing R.S.* 2(6-3-48″-8.5) Free-blooming urn-shaped bud, pink tinged with gold, fragrant, vigorous plant, well-shaped, almost perfect form. MINN. *Minnesota R.S.* 17(42-3-38″-8.6) Blooms consistently of show quality, hardy, could bloom more. MO. *Kansas City R.S.* 4(16-3-60″-9.2) Good grower, free-bloomer, beautiful color. *Rosarians Midland Empire* 4(28-3-60″-9) Good color and bloomer, upright grower. *R.S. Greater St. Louis* 7(12-4-72″-9) Outstanding exhibition rose on tall-growing plant. *Sedalia R.S.* 5(6-3-58″-8.5) Lovely form and color especially in full bloom, good plant, not enough bloom. MONT. *Sunset Park T.G.* (12-3-28″-9). NEV. *Reno R.S.* 17(30-3-60″-9) Excellent flower form, substance and non-fading color, very fragrant, fast grower, repeat-bloomer, some mildew. NEW ENGLAND *New England R.S.* 12(40-3-40″-8.8) Not hardy in colder areas. N.J. *North Jersey R.S.* 24(60-3-54″-9.1) Superlative aristocrat for exhibition and garden. *West Jersey R.S.* 5(12-3-54″-8.5) Beautiful well-formed flower holds well, healthy plant, plenty of bloom. N.M. *Albuquerque R.S.* 8(14-2-35″-9.1) Sturdy bush, bloom has excellent form and color, holds up in extreme heat, fragrant, good leathery foliage on fine thick stems, bloom cycles not frequent enough. N.Y. *Cornell University T.G.* (4-4-40″-8.5) Excellent bud, good flower form, fine color, blooms throughout season, good foliage, medium vigor. *Greater Buffalo R.S.* 12(38-3-48″-9) Long single-stem bloom, upright thrifty plant, good form. *Humboldt Park T.G.* (25-4-42″-9) Upright, very vigorous plant, very resistant, abundant large light green leathery foliage, glowing pink with shades of salmon at base of large double flowers with tea fragrance, long strong-stemmed plant, some yellowing of basal leaves but no disease. *Long Island R.S.* 9(10-2-43″-8.4) Good in all aspects. *Niagara Frontier R.S.* (39″-8.3) Vigorous plant, good form, fragrant, does not open well in cool wet weather. *Rochester R.S.* 12(55-2-48″-8.5) Exhibition-type bloom, lasting quality, erect grower, good foliage. *Schenectady R.S.* 9(15-2-35″-8.1) Good high show buds, not good-lasting bloom, vigorous and healthy. *Syracuse R.S.* 9(17-3-41″-8.6) Excellent in all ways, vigorous, disease-resistant, wonderful exhibition rose, some blackspot. N.C. *Charlotte R.S.* 4(7-1-48″-8) Well-formed blooms of lasting quality. *Durham R.S.* 17(38-2-66″-9.4) Superb fragrance, heavy-bloomer, high-centered bud, good all-year exhibition type in July and August, unfading. *Randolph R.S.* 3(9-3-72″-9) Strong upright growth, excellent form bud, long-lasting bloom color, generous bloomer, thick disease-resistant foliage. OHIO *Akron R.S.* 9(40-3-33″-8.5) Outstanding exhibition bloom, fades. *Central Ohio R.S.* 8(26-3-48″-9) Healthy, vigorous, disease-resistant plant, excellent attractive foliage, upright grower, beautiful bloom of good color, substance, exhibition form and quality, prolific bloomer. *Cincinnati R.S.* 21(64-3-51″-9) Has everything. *Cleveland R.S.* 6(17-3-43″-8) Fine show rose, pointed long-lasting buds, strong grower, upright, blooms through Summer heat, poor color and weak necks in Fall. *Columbus R.C.* 7(30-3-60″-8.7) Upright, good form and color, slight mildew. *Euclid R.S.* 3(8-3-48″-9.1) Good plant, long stems, one of the finest show roses. *Forest City R.S.* 10(24-3-36″-9) Exhibition-quality bloom, disease-resistant, upright grower, fragrant. *Greater Cincinnati R.S.* 6(14-2-48″-8.9) Exquisite buds, good open flower blooms frequently, fine sturdy plant, fragrant, not too many blooms. *Lancaster R.C.* 10(38-3-48″-9) Large, slow-opening, good substance, exhibition rose, disease-resistant. *Lima R.S.* 9(22-3-48″-8.9) One bloom to a stem, good form and color, upright, disease-resistant, does not refrigerate well. *Medina County R.S.* 2(2-3-48″-8.8) Excellent color and bloom form. *Miami Valley R.S.* 19(20-3-40″-9) Excellent exhibition rose, beautiful color, upright plant, disease-resistant. *Ohio State University T.G.* (4-5-9) Very vigorous plant, disease-resistant, abundant large foliage and bloom, very large flower. *Stark R.S.* 6(8-6-40″-8.5) Good for exhibition and arranging. OKLA. *Norman R.S.* 4(15-3-40″-9) Splendid in hot weather, could bloom more. *Oklahoma R.S.* 4(11-2-48″-9)ˎ. ORE. *International Rose T.G.* (40-5-60″-9) Very good bud form, single stems, fine color, ample bloom, rains damage this rose, best in warm weather. *Medford R.S.* 17(29-2-41″-8.4) Long stems, exhibition blooms need no disbudding, excellent healthy foliage, does best in warm weather, could bloom more. *Rogue Valley R.S.* 4(6-3-54″-9) Good color, disease-resistant foliage, long stems, excellent form. *Roseburg R.S.* 3(4-3-60″-8) Beautiful blooms, good disease-resistant foliage. *Salem R.S.* 5(35-3-43″-7.9) Exhibition form, good color and foliage, balls in early season. PA. *Breeze Hill T.G.* (15-6-36″-10) Excellent color, form and vigor, profuse, fragrant. *Harrisburg R.S.* 2(5-3-45″-8.9) Vigorous, long stems, good color and substance, blooms freely. *Philadelphia R.S.* 10(18-3-42″-8.5) Excellent form, color and foliage, cut flowers last, could bloom more often. *Pittsburgh R.S.* 6(15-3-36″-8.3) Show-type perfectly formed blooms on long stems, unaffected by Summer heat, fair vigor, good foliage, lovely coloring. S.C. *Edisto T.G.* (30-5-42″-9) Strong grower, good exhibition type, color fades somewhat in Summer. TENN. *Nashville R.S.* 37(9-3-9.1) Healthy, vigorous, exhibition blooms. TEX. *Amarillo R.S.* 8(19-3-48″-9) Good grower, heavy dark green disease-resistant foliage, large beautiful fragrant blooms keep well. *Corpus Christi R.S.* 1(1-3-36″-9.2) Nice compact plant, lovely blooms, excellent fragrance, long-lasting, too-few blooms. *Dallas R.S.* 4(8-3-45″-8.4) Good in every way. *El Paso R.S.* 5(12-3-52″-9) Strong healthy upright grower, leathery foliage, good substance, excellent exhibition rose, very fragrant, beautiful large true-colored buds, cold weather bloomer. UTAH *Utah R.S.* 8(29-3-39″-8.4) True exhibition blooms, fine color and fragrance, long stems, only lacks good branching. VA. *Eastern Shore R.S.* 3(5-2-50″-9) Good upright bush, nice strong stem, large bud, exquisite bloom, excellent petal texture, disease-resistant. *Va. Peninsula R.S.* 4(6-3-59″-8.5) Vigorous growth, good foliage, beautiful color, fragrant, exhibition-type. WASH. *Seattle R.S.* 5(8-3-42″-8.3) Good bloom, vigorous plant. *Spokane R.S.* 9(28-3-36″-8) All it needs is more bloom, good form. *Walla Walla R.S.* 4(5-2-60″-8) Outstanding in every way. W.VA. *Charleston R.S.* 6(15-3-48″-9.5) Healthy, productive, charming, graceful, blue ribbon-type. *Wyo-Mac R.S.* 3(4-2-54″-10) Beautiful blooms, long strong stems, fine foliage. WIS. *Madison R.S.* 5(8-2-38″-8.8) Good form, beautiful color, good disease-resistant foliage, could bloom more in Summer. *Milwaukee R.S.* 3(6-3-48″-9.2) Color, form, fragrance, good looks to the end, strong plant, good canes and foliage. CANADA (British Columbia) *Vancouver R.S.* 12(21-3-48″-9) Long buds, well-formed blooms, fragrant, clear color, best in warm weather, variable color in early Spring.

**TIMMIE ARKLES F.** Apple blossom-pink. (Boerner; int. Jackson & Perkins '54) Pat. 1320; ARA '54; PP 5, 1959, 12 Rpts.; Av. ht. 32″; **NR 6.5.** Total reports 5 years 40; **Av. NR 6.5.**

**TINKER BELL Min.** Bright pink. (de Vink; int. Conard-Pyle '54) Pat. 1293; ARA '54; PP 5, 1959, 38 Rpts.; Av. ht. 10″; **NR 8.3.** Total reports 5 years 131; **Av. NR 8.1.**

**TUDOR HT.** Strawberry-red, finishing scarlet. (Verschuren; int. Jackson & Perkins '54) Pat. 1223; ARA '54; PP 5, 1959, 23 Rpts.; Av. ht. 38″; **NR 6.9.** Total reports 5 years 109; **Av. NR 6.7.**

**TWILIGHT HT.** Lavender-lilac. (Boerner; int. Jackson & Perkins '55) Pat. 1434; ARA '55; PP 4, 107 Rpts.; Av. ht. 29″; **NR 6.1.**

ALA. *Twickenham R.S.* 2(1-1-33″-4.8) Very different foliage. ARIZ. *Phoenix R.S.* 3(4-2-36″-6.5) Too-few perfect blooms, burns. CALIF. *Rose Study Club Oakland* 1(3-4-16″-6.3) Occasional beautiful bloom, best in warm climate, weak plant, sparse blooms ball in damp weather, burn in sun. *Pacific R.S.* 1(1-2-36″-7) Good form in Spring, good coloring, average foliage, many blooms quarter or split, cannot take damp misty weather. *Peninsula R.S.* 3(3-3-36″-5) Lacks vigor, blooms have good form, ball in cool weather, muddy color, shy bloomer. *San Diego R.S.* 2(2-1-48″-6.5) Good form and color. *San Mateo County R.S.* 1(12-24″-2) Buds ball and mildew, not one good bloom. D.C. *Potomac R.S.* 2(2-2-42″-7) Shapely bloom, color can be outstanding, good for flower arrangement, grows well, balls badly, should bloom more. ILL. *Greater Peoria R.S.* 2(2-1-29″-7) Perfect blooms, unusual color, blooms well, not a rampant grower, fades. IND. *Indianapolis R.S.* 1(1-1-12″-7) Blooms pretty but frail with weak necks. *St. Joseph Valley R.S.* 1(2-2-30″-6.9) Good prolific bloom in Fall, fades in hot weather, balls badly. *Vincennes R.S.* 1(1-1-24″-6) Each bloom has a confused and split center. IOWA *Des Moines R.S.* 3(3-3-36″-6) Good color, balls, blackspots. *Iowa R.S.* 2(4-1-30″-7) Dirty color, balls. *Linn County R.S.* 2(3-1-24″-7.5) Beautiful bi-color, bud opens hard, black-spots easily. KAN. *Wichita R.S.* 2(2-3-24″-6.5) Slow grower. KY. *Louisville Chapter ARS* 3(6-1-26″-5.5) Disease-resistant, too-few good blooms. MD. *Maryland R.S.* 3(3-2-36″-6) Very good color and form, most blooms ball, healthy. MICH. *Detroit R.S.* 2(2-2-36″-7) Fragrant, healthy, vigorous plant, color fades. *Kalamazoo R.S.* 1(1-1-24″-5). MINN *Minnesota R.S.* Flowers ball, not good performer. MO. *Rosarians Midland Empire* 1(1-2-22″) Balls and fades badly. *R.S. Greater St. Louis* 3(5-3-30″-7.5) Only occasional good flowers, balls and browns too often. N.J. *North Jersey R.S.* 5(6-2-24″-5.8) Unusually poor plant and production. *West Jersey R.S.* 3(4-2-24″-6) Fair foliage, slow-starter, poor color blooms, not attractive. N.M. *Albuquerque R.S.* 2(2-1-18″-7) Good bud, profuse bloomer, slow to start, fades very fast, balls. N.Y. *Cornell University T.G.* (1-3-19″-5) Fair flower size, unusual opening color, weak plants, color finishes poorly, only good early in season, might be better in semi-shade. *Long Island R.S.* 3(4-3-32″-5.3) Nice blooms in Fall, overall characteristics poor. *Niagara Frontier R.S.* 2(3-2-36″-6.7) Strong healthy plant, profuse bloomer, unusual color, flowers seldom open well, malformed or browned on the edges, a few are very pretty. *Rochester R.S.* 2(3-1-29″-6) Bushy plant, unusual color, balls in wet weather. *Syracuse R.S.* 4(5-2-36″-7.6) Good color and form, fragrant, plenty of bloom, good foliage, fades too quickly. N.C. *Durham R.S.* 1(1-1-36″-5) Too small a bud, shatters too easily. OHIO *Akron R.S.* 4(4-3-30″-7.7) Novel color, stingy bloom, balls in hot weather. *Cleveland R.S.* 2(6-2-27″-7) Unusual coloring, clean foliage. *Euclid R.S.* 1(1-2-40″-7) Very good buds in Fall or late Summer, good foliage, fades and discolors, balls a little when wet. *Forest City R.S.* 3(3-3-30″-7) Another novelty, better bloom in cool weather. *Greater Cincinnati R.S.* 1(1-1-18″-7.5) Nice color with pale reverse, weak stems, blackspots. *Lima R.S.* 2(2-2-27″-6) Flowers don't last, many never open, grows better in shade. *Stark R.S.* 1(1-1-24″-1) White rose with lavender spots. ORE. *Eugene R.S.* 2(4-2-24″-7) Can be beautiful but often disappointing, color fades, weak plant. *Lewis & Clark T.G.* (9-1-30″-5) Good color. *Medford R.S.* 3(4-2-26″-4.7) Unusual color in ideal weather; burns in hot weather and balls in damp weather, defoliates easily. *Salem R.S.* 1(1-3-24″-1). PA. *Breeze Hill T.G.* (3-5-28″-8) Blooms well all season, attractive color. *Harrisburg R.S.* 1(3-3-24″-6) Blooms well, flower not too large, low bush, slow grower. *Philadelphia R.S.* 2(3-2-24″-6) Good color, balls. TEX. *Dallas R.S.* \1(1-2-20″-4)! Good foliage, intriguing color, blooms ball. *El Paso R.S.* 1(1-2-36″-7.5) Strong healthy foliage and stems, good color, abundant very fragrant blooms, some balling in the Summer months. UTAH *Utah R.S.* 1(1-1-24″-5). VA *Va. Peninsula R.S.* 1(1-1-24″-5.6) Very slow grower, weak canes, poor foliage, too-few blooms. WASH. *Seattle R.S.* 2(2-2-26″-7.2) Unusual color. *Spokane R.S.* 2(2-1-18″-5) Good color. W.VA. *Charleston R.S.* 1(2-3-36″-4) Unusual color, poor bloomer. *Wyo-Mac R.S.* 1(1-2-24″-7) Beautiful buds and color, blackspots easily. WIS. *Milwaukee R.S.* 1(1-1-24″-7) Unusual pretty bloom, few blooms. CANADA (British Columbia) *Vancouver R.S.* 3(8-3-36″-6) Color seldom good. HAWAII *Kona* (1-2-31″-5) Occasional beautiful buds, many flowers most of the year, prey to every insect and disease, ugly twiggy bush.

## TWINKLES Min. White. (Spek; int. Jackson & Perkins '54) Pat. 1407; ARA '55; PP 5, 1959, 16 Rpts; Av. ht. 7″; NR 8.3. Total reports 5 years 42; Av. NR 8.2.

## TZIGANE HT. Yellow blend. (Meilland; int. Hennessey '56) Pat. 1188; ARA '55; PP 3, 50 Rpts.; Av. ht. 32″; NR 7.6.

CALIF. *Peninsula R.S.* 1(1-1-36″-8) Beautiful bi-color, good form, vigorous. *San Joaquin Valley R.S.* 1(1-1-24″-7) Good substance, exciting color variation, not a vigorous-grower. D.C. *Potomac R.S.* 3(4-3-42″-8) Unbelievable color, outstanding odor, quilted open flower, waxy foliage, needs more vigor and blooms. ILL. *Greater Peoria R.S.* 1(1-1-36″-7.4) Good coloring, nice buds, good foliage, fine grower, color fades, blackspots. IND. *Vincennes R.S.* 1(2-2-24″-8) No faults in shade, scant bloom in sun, no disease, hardy. IOWA *Linn County R.S.* 1(2-1-36″-7.5) Heavy bloomer, good foliage, split centers. KAN. *Wichita R.S.* 1(2-1-42″-8.5) Vigorous grower, leathery foliage. LA. *New Orleans R.S.* 2(3-1-30″-8) Grand foliage, blackspots. MD. *Maryland R.S.* 3(4-2-7.5) Gorgeous color and form, sulks in hot weather. MICH. *Detroit R.S.* 2(5-1-42″-6.7) Good bi-color, quick repeat, poor in hot weather. *Kalamazoo R.S.* 1(3-2-33″-8) Good color, nice foliage, some blackspot. MO. *Rosarians Midland Empire* 1(1-1-30″-8). NEW ENGLAND *New England R.S.* 2(7-3-36″-8.2) Good color, blackspots badly. N.J. *North Jersey R.S.* 5(11-1-24″-6.9). N.C. *Durham R.S.* 1(1-1-42″-8.5) Good grower, retains color very well, needs afternoon shade. OHIO *Central Ohio R.S.* 2(4-1-28″-8) Disease-resistant leathery foliage, bloom has excellent form and color, exhibition-form flower, plant likes shade and cool weather. *Columbus R.C.* 1(2-1-36″-8) Disease-resistant, excellent form, not too free-blooming. *Lancaster R.C.* 1(1-2-48″-7.5) Brilliant bi-color, split centers, fades in sun. *Miami Valley R.S.* 2(4-3-24″-8) Gorgeous color, perfect form, few blooms, slow grower. OKLA. *Norman R.S.* 1(1-1-36″-8) Leathery foliage, brilliant bi-color in Fall. ORE. *Salem R.S.* 1(1-4-30″-8) Beautiful foliage, wonderful buds, flowers fade! gracefully. PA. *Philadelphia R.S.* 3(4-3-30″-6.7) Lovely dazzling color bloom, needs pampering. TEX. *Dallas R.S.* 4(10-2-33″-7.5) Beautiful form, color and foliage, can't stand heat, mildews. WASH. *Seattle R.S.* 5(9-2-32″-7.7) Best in cool weather. WIS. *Milwaukee R.S.* 1(1-2-7) Beautiful color, beautiful foliage, fat bud. CANADA (British Columbia) *Vancouver R.S.* 2(7-5-36″-7.5) Good foliage, bush and color, flowers do not last. (Nova Scotia) *Buchanan* (3-5-40″-8) Good red and yellow flower opens too quickly and loses form.

# WHITE BOUQUET F. White. (Boerner; int. Jackson & Perkins '57) Pat. 1415; PP 2, 275 Rpts.; Av. ht. 25"; NR 7.5.

ALA. *Twickenham R.S.* 2(2-2-35"-5.5) Doesn't bloom enough, very weak grower. ARIZ. *Mesa R.S.* 2(2-1-36"-8) Good bush, pure flowers, good blooming Spring and Fall. *Phoenix R.S.* 3(5-2-30"-8) Fragrant, lovely buds and blooms, lasting, compact bush, good foliage. CALIF. *Memorial T.G.* (6-2-30"-8) Very fragrant, free-blooming (50 blooms at one time on one bush). *Rose Study Club Oakland* 2(8-2-20"-7.9) Prolific bloomer, well-shaped bud and flower won't take warm weather, good spreading foliage. *Pacific R.S.* 2(2-1-30"-7.5) Good form, holds well as a cut flower, bush not too strong. *Riverside R.S.* 6(8-1-30"-9.5) Does well in the heat, blooms all season, good foliage, blooms keep well. *San Diego R.S.* 3(5-2-27"-8.1). *San Joaquin Valley R.S.* 2(3-2-36"-6.6) not enough bloom, good foliage. *San Mateo County R.S.* 2(3-2-30"-9) Profuse bloomer, lasts well, good dark green disease-resistant foliage, more cream than white. COLO. *Colorado Springs R.S.* 1(6-2-24"-9) Beautiful blooms, small Tea rose form, sturdy, always in bloom. *Denver R.S.* 5(18-2-20"-7) Pleasing fragrance, long-lasting bloom, no mildew or blackspot, lacks vigor and substance. CONN. *Elizabeth Park T.G.* (18-2-14"-5) Good bud and bloom, poor vigor. D.C. *Potomac R.S.* 4(8-2-24"-9.6) Neat compact plant, excellent foliage, pure camellia-type flower, lots of substance and fragrance. GA. *Georgia R.S.* 2(5-2-36"-7.5) Good bush, bloom too slow repeating. ILL. *Chicago R.S. Reg. 1* 3(4-1-24"-7) Pretty gardenia-like flower, susceptible to mildew and blackspot. *Greater Peoria R.S.* 3(5-1-27"-7.6) Pure bloom, reblooms fast. *Tri-City Men's Garden and Rose Club* 2(9-3-36"-7.6). IND. *Indianapolis R.S.* 4(8-2-19"-6.3) Too-few blooms. *St. Joseph Valley R.S.* 2(4-4-24"-7.4) Strong healthy grower. IOWA *Des Moines R.S.* 4(5-2-24"-7) Good bloom, weak plant. *Iowa R.S.* 3(7-2-24"-6) Poor growth. *Linn County R.S.* (24"-7.5) Lots of bloom, blackspots easily. KAN. *Wichita R.S.* 4(7-1-18"-6.5) Good bloomer, slow growth, blackspots. KY. *Kentucky R.S.* 2(3-2-22"-8) Blooms well, nice flower formation. *Lexington R.S.* 1(2-1-18"-9.5) Beautiful flower, lovely foliage, good bloomer, doesn't yellow. *Louisville Chapter ARS* 8(24-1-22"-7.8) Very good color blooms, good grower, few low blooms, blackspots. LA. *New Orleans R.S.* 1(2-2-42"-9) Alabaster-white, good bush, long-lasting flower. MD. *Maryland R.S.* 3(3-1-24"-8) Good repeater, fine in cool weather, blackspots very much. MICH. *Detroit R.S.* 2(6-2-18"-7.5) Always in bloom, sprawls, blackspots. *Greater Lansing R.S.* 4(8-2-24"-8) Pure flower, almost perfectly-formed, disease-resistant. *Kalamazoo R.S.* 2(2-2-30"-8) Lots of bloom in Spring, nice color, some blackspot. *Michigan State University T.G.* (2-4-21"-3) Buds not clear, weak necks, not resistant to blackspot. MINN. *Lyndale Park T.G.* (30-3-24"-6.5) Blackspots. *Minnesota R.S.* 11(22-2-24"-7.4) Dark glossy foliage, perfect gardenia-blooms, fragrant. *Kansas City R.S.* 2(4-2-22"-8) Prolific bloomer, good foliage, disease-resistant. *Rosarians Midland Empire* 2(9-2-24"-8) Good blooms in Spring, everything nice about it, disease-resistant, could bloom more. *R.S. Greater St. Louis* 4(6-2-18"-6) Not enough bloom, poor growth, some blackspot. *Sedalia R.S.* 5(5-2-16"-7) Nice bloom lasts well, small plant grows slowly, foliage just fair. MONT. *Sunset Park T.G.* (10-2-24"-9) Large semi-double bloom with attractive contrasting stamens, fairly productive plant. NEV. *Reno R.S.* 4(15-3-48"-8) Cream-white buds, long stems, blooms steadily, fine strong canes with beautiful dark foliage, does not fade in Summer heat, disease-resistant. NEW ENGLAND *New England R.S.* 5(14-2-24"-7.5) Good Spring bloom, lacks vigor. N.J. *North Jersey R.S.* 11(28-2-23"-7.4). *West Jersey R.S.* 5(10-2-30"-8.5) Very fine flowers much like a camellia, plenty of bloom all Summer, healthy foliage, good growing plant. N.M. *Albuquerque R.S.* 2(3-2-24"-7.7) Profuse blooms, good form, clear color, small flowers, slow to repeat. N.Y. *Humboldt Park T.G.* (9-3-18"-6) Branching plants, lemon-white ovoid buds borne in clusters, medium to open clusters, of semi-double blooms on short stems, poor foliage during Summer, dirty white appearance when finishing. *Long Island R.S.* 3(8-2-17"-7.6) Good color, plenty of well-rounded blooms hold well, subject to disease, slow getting started. *Rochester R.S.* 4(18-2-24"-7.5) Large flowers of good form, singly or in clusters. *Schenectady R.S.* 3(13-2-27"-7.1). *Syracuse R.S.* 6(9-2-26"-7.3) Beautiful bud and bloom, good disease-resistant foliage, sparse bloomer, doesn't winter-over. N.C. *Charlotte R.S.* 3(4-1-18"-5). *Randolph R.S.* 2(2-2-36"-8) Good grower and bloomer, gardenia-like fragrant blooms. OHIO *Akron R.S.* 4(16-2-24"-7.2) Bushy. *Central Ohio R.S.* 3(6-2-30"-7.8) Good pure color, lovely large flower when open, lasts well after cutting, healthy vigorous bush, not enough bloom. *Cincinnati R.S.* 9(29-2-21"-7.5) Ought to hang on, good low compact plant with beautiful bloom. *Cleveland R.S.* 2(11-2-20"-8) Fine color, good size, quality bloom. *Columbus R.C.* 1(1-2-30"-7) Good healthy plant, not enough bloom follow-up. *Euclid R.S.* 1(1-3-36"-8.8) Lots of long-lasting bloom, good foliage. *Greater Cincinnati R.S.* 5($-2-18"-7.6) Flower lovely in shape and substance, very sparse blooms, too low-growing, poor plants, not healthy enough, blackspots. *Lancaster R.C.* 2(2-3-24"-7.5) Poor grower, large blooms, blackspots. *Lima R.S.* 3(5-2-24"-7.5) Lovely small gardenia-type, low bush, slow grower.

*Miami Valley R.S.* 4(8-2-24″-8) Disease-resistant, not too tall. *Ohio State University T.G.* (4-3-21″-7) Vigorous flowering habit throughout entire Summer, disease-resistant medium-sized dark green glossy leaves, strong stems, plant not too vigorous. *Stark R.S.* 1(1-1-30″-9) Good foliage, prolific bloom, pure flower. OKLA. *Norman R.S.* 3(5-2-24″-8) Long-lasting camellia-like blooms. *Oklahoma R.S.* 2(6-1-30″-8). ORE. *Eugene R.S.* 4(5-1-24″-8) Very clean color, resists rain, heavy bloomer, long-lasting flower, low bushy growth. *International Rose T.G.* (40-4-24″-7) Good long bud, pinwheel-like clean flowers, good contrast of foliage, blooms rest then come back again. *Lewis & Clark T.G.* (10-1-24″-5) Too many soft open blooms. *Medford R.S.* 8(11-2-30″-7.2) Very good foliage. PA. *Breeze Hill T.G.* Profuse lovely flowers and buds. *Harrisburg R.S.* 2(501-1-27″-8.6) Vigorous, good foliage, profuse bloom. *Philadelphia R.S.* 5-11-2-20″-8) Large clear compact bloom, good repeat, good in partial shade. *Pittsburgh R.S.* Constant bloomer, no blackspot. S.C. *Edisto T.G.* (6-3-18″-5) No vigor, won't grow. TENN. *Nashville R.S.* 6(16-2-20″-7.5) Healthy, vigorous, plenty of bloom, low-growing plant. TEX. *Amarillo R.S.* 2(2-2-24″-8) Large blooms. *Dallas R.S.* 4(10-2-24″-8) Good bushy plant, prolific, low-grower, some blackspot. *El Paso R.S.* 5(52-24″-8) Good healthy foliage, many blooms all year, weak stems, opens quickly to full bloom, not a good cutting rose, slow to start, some mildew. UTAH *Utah R.S.* 9(21-2-23″-7.6) Small plants, beautiful foliage and blooms, spicy fragrance. VA. *Eastern Shore R.S.* 1(1-2-24″-7) Flowers lovely in both bud and open, stingy bloomer, small bush, no vigor. WASH. *Seattle R.S.* 3(7-2-24″-6.8). *Spokane R.S.* 2(2-2-24″-5) Flowers too large for bush. *Walla Walla R.S.* 2(3-2-30″-8) Nice blooms, fine foliage. W.VA. *Charleston R.S.* 4(8-2-24″-8) Low-growing. WIS. *Madison R.S.* 4(4-1-27″-8) Good flower, rather bushy, good foliage, good bloom in June but very little the rest of the year, disease-resistant. WIS. *Milwaukee R.S.* 2(6-2-22″-8) Beautiful bud, large clear flower, blackspots. CANADA (British Columbia) *Vancouver R.S.* 3(8-3-30″-7) Good foliage, pure blooms stand wet weather, continuous bloomer, mildews and blackspots.

# WILDFIRE F. Medium red. (Swim; int. Armstrong '55) Pat. 1381; ARA '56; PP 3, 73 Rpts.; Av. ht. 34″; NR 8.2.

CALIF. *Memorial T.G.* (12-4-30″-9) Free-blooming, vigorous. *Rose Study Club Oakland* 1(5-1-36″-7.8) Vigorous bush, disease-resistant foliage, free-bloomer, non-fading single flower. *Pacific R.S.* 1(1-2-24″-6) Good blooms of good color, not a strong grower. *San Diego R.S.* 2(4-3-60″-8.7) Cut blooms have very good keeping qualities. *San Joaquin Valley R.S.* 1(6-3-42″-6) Good foliage and color. *San Mateo County R.S.* 1(4-4-30″-9) A sheet of almost too much fiery color, good plant, some rust, very little fragrance. COLO. *Colorado Springs R.S.* 1(20-4-28″-8) Showy fiery color, good bloomer, vigorous. CONN. *Elizabeth Park T.G.* (10-3-15″-5) Pleasant bloom when opening up, but not too attractive after. GA. *Georgia R.S.* 1(3-3-8.8). IND. *St. Joseph Valley R.S.* 2(2-4-36″-8.1) Prolific blooms, good foliage, large clusters of 7-9 petals hold color. IOWA *Linn County R.S.* 1(2-3-36″-7.8) Long-lasting single bloom, fairly vigorous. MICH. *Kalamazoo R.S.* 2(1-3-48″-8.5) No faults. *Michigan State University T.G.* (6-5-28″-9.3) Very floriferous, holds color very well, disease-resistant, slight fragrance at half-open stage. MINN. *Lyndale Park T.G.* (35-4-36″-8.3) Very good bloomer, holds color good in hot weather, hardy, vigorous grower. *Minnesota R.S.* 6(12-3-31″-8.7) Brilliant single bloom, profuse long-lasting bloomer. MO. *Rosarians Midland Empire* 1(3-3-48″-9) Good color, tall grower. *R.S. Greater St. Louis* 2(3-3-30″-5) Good bush, few flowers. MONT. *Sunset Park T.G.* (12-3-28″-8) Free-blooming, hardy, healthy plant. NEV. *Reno R.S.* 2(20-2-30″-8) Small buds open slowly, blooms fade quickly, blooms steadily, very little fragrance, grows better in semi-shade. N.J. *North Jersey R.S.* 5(12-2-36″-7.9) Lively color, good plant, single type. N.M. *Albuquerque R.S.* 1(12-2-9) Mass of repeat bloom, vigorous plants, wonderful color holds well in sun. N.Y. *Cornell University T.G.* (2-4-25″-8) Brilliant single flowers, vigorous, disease-resistant, upright, continuous bloom, flowers not at best in mid-Summer heat. *Humboldt Park T.G.* (10-3-36″-8) Upright, vigorous plants, abundant leathery dark green resistant foliage, semi-double blooms, cherry-red petals drop cleanly, slight tea fragrance, freezes to 6″ above ground. OHIO *Akron R.S.* 1(12-3-24″-7.5) Few petals, good bush. *Cincinnati R.S.* 1(1-1-24″-7.5) Very colorful plant, blooms drop clear. *Lancaster R.C.* 2(2-2-33″-7) Large clusters of brilliant blooms, not winter-hardy. *Ohio State University T.G.* (4-4-39″-8) Excellent foliage, abundant flowering throughout the entire season, bushy vigorous plant, disease-resistant. OKLA. *Norman R.S.* 1(4-3-36″-8). ORE. *Eugene R.S.* 8(12-2-36″-9) Fiery mass of color, good foliage, heavy stems support big heads of bright bloom, nice repeater. *International Rose T.G.* (20-4-48″-8) Continual bloom, huge sprays of attractive color. *Medford R.S.* 1(1-1-36″-8.5) Excellent blooms, good foliage, quite resistant to aphids and fungus. *Rogue Valley R.S.* 3(6-4-30″-8.6) Excellent color and lasting quality, prolific bloomer. *Harrisburg R.S.* 1(2-2-48″-8.6) Beautiful color, vigorous grower, free-bloomer, flowers "blow" quickly. *Philadelphia R.S.* 2(3-2-33″-

8.3) Excellent bloom and plant, performs well in heat, good repeat. S.C. *Edisto T.G.* (10-4-36″-7) Good in Spring, lacks bloom continuity. TENN. *Nashville R.S.* 1(1-3-30″-7.7) Lots of bright single blooms. TEX. *Dallas R.S.* 2(7-2-36″--9.7) Continuous bloomer, good color, very vigorous. UTAH *Utah R.S.* 3(14-3-30″-8.3) Brilliant color, lots of blooms, good bush. WASH. *Seattle R.S.* 2(3-2-30″-9) Always in bloom, good bedder. *Spokane R.S.* 2(4-1-36″-8) Outstanding brilliance, not many petals. *Walla Walla R.S.* 1(2-3-36″-9) Outstanding clusters of single roses always in bloom. WIS. *Milwaukee R.S.* 1(2-2-5) Very ordinary. CANADA (British Columbia) *Vancouver R.S.* 1(1-3-36″-9) Semi-single brilliant blooms, good bush, free-bloomer.

# CONTRIBUTORS

Akron Rose Society, Akron, Ohio; L. W. Nigh.
Albuquerque Rose Society, Albuquerque, N.M.; Mrs. George L. Doolittle.
Amarillo Rose Society, Amarillo, Tex.; Mrs. Joe J. Miller.
Breeze Hill Garden, Harrisburg, Pa.; Margaret R. Snyder.
Buchanan, William C., Sydney, Nova Scotia, Canada.
Central Ohio Rose Society, Columbus, Ohio; Howard J. Ward.
Charleston Rose Society, Charleston, W.Va.; Mrs. L. M. Ross.
Charlotte Rose Society, Charlotte, N.C.; W. B. Kluttz.
Chicago Rose Society, Region 1, Chicago, Ill.; Roscoe C. Nash.
Cincinnati Rose Society, Cincinnati, Ohio; W. M. Burgess.
Cleveland Rose Society, Cleveland, Ohio; E. J. Husselman.
Colorado Springs Rose Society, Colorado Springs, Colo.; Earl H. Zimmer.
Columbus Rose Club, Columbus, Ohio; J. T. Edwards.
Cornell University Test Garden, Ithaca, N.Y.; Robert E. Lee.
Corpus Christi Rose Society, Corpus Christi, Tex.; Mrs. A. W. Crow.
Dallas Rose Society, Dallas, Tex.; Oscar J. Chase.
Denver Rose Society, Denver, Colo.; Mrs. Clarence Jones.
Des Moines Rose Society, Des Moines, Iowa; Earl Thomas.
Detroit Rose Society, Detroit, Mich.; F. S. Howell.
Durham Rose Society, Durham, N.C.; Mrs. Robert H. Pate.
Eastern Shore Rose Society, Exmore, Va.; Mrs. Garrett Sanderson.
Edisto Gardens, Orangeburg, S.C.; A. C. Dibble.
Elizabeth Park Test Garden, Hartford, Conn.; Charles Meli.
El Paso Rose Society, El Paso, Tex.; Mrs. W. E. Powell.
Euclid Rose Society, Euclid, Ohio; John Kern.
Eugene Rose Society, Eugene, Ore.; Mrs. Charles M. Andreason.
Forest City Rose Society, Cleveland, Ohio; C. C. Roach.
Frankfort Rose Chapter, Frankfort, Ky.; John L. Allen.
Georgia Rose Society, Atlanta, Ga.; T. J. Donaldson, Jr.
Greater Buffalo Rose Society, Buffalo, N.Y.; Mrs. Arvin Putzbach.
Greater Cincinnati Rose Society, Cincinnati, Ohio; Mrs. H. Auburn.
Greater Lansing Rose Society, East Lansing, Mich.; M. Detloff.
Greater Peoria Rose Society, East Peoria, Ill.; Ted C. Alberssen.
Greenwell, Miss Amy, Captain Cook (Kona), Hawaii.
Harrisburg Rose Society, Harrisburg, Pa.; Margaret R. Snyder.
Humboldt Park Test Garden, Buffalo, N.Y.; Richard Lensen.
Indianapolis Rose Society, Indianapolis, Ind.; Ralph B. Kling.
Iowa Rose Society, Des Moines, Iowa; Ralph Oldham.
International Rose Test Garden, Portland, Ore.; R. C. Kalmbach.
Jewel Park Test Garden, St. Louis, Mo.; Henry Ochs.
Kalamazoo Rose Society, Kalamazoo, Mich.; Robert M. Heistand.
Kansas City Rose Society, Kansas City, Mo.; Mrs. William Bugg.
Kentucky Rose Society, Louisville, Ky.; Wm. T. Bayne.
Lancaster Rose Club, Lancaster, Ohio; Ralph A. Felton.
Lewis and Clark College Test Garden, Portland, Ore.; T. H. Thorburn.
Lexington Rose Society, Lexington, Ky.; Mrs. James M. Burgin.
Lima Rose Society, Lima, Ohio; Mrs. Charles J. Smith.

Linn County Rose Society, Cedar Rapids, Iowa; B. O. Bruce.
Long Island Rose Society, Long Island, N.Y.; Arthur Liers.
Louisville Chapter ARS, Louisville, Ky.; Leroy D. Isaacs.
Lyndale Park Test Garden, Minneapolis, Minn.; Gregory J. Lucking.
Madison Rose Society, Madison, Wis.; Gilbert Raether.
Maryland Rose Society, Baltimore, Md.; Ernest W. Schwartz.
Medford Rose Society, Medford, Ore.; Eldred W. Peyton.
Medina County Rose Society, Medina, Ohio; Roy E. Shepherd.
Memorial Rose Test Garden, Santa Barbara, Calif.; Col. Oscar C. Warner.
Mesa Rose Society, Mesa, Ariz.; R. E. Love.
Miami Valley Rose Society, Dayton, Ohio; E. Lee Cox.
Michigan State University Test Garden, East Lansing, Mich.; Richard F. Stinson.
Milwaukee Rose Society, Milwaukee, Wis.; Mrs. Henry A. Weil.
Minnesota Rose Society, St. Paul, Minn.; Mrs. William S. Sweeney.
Morgan Park Rose Society, Chicago, Ill.; H. H. Morrison.
Nashville Rose Society, Nashville, Tenn.; I. W. Grizzard.
New England Rose Society, Boston, Mass.; Karl P. Jones.
New Orleans Rose Society, New Orleans, La.; E. Kleinschmidt.
Niagara Frontier Rose Society, Buffalo, N.Y.; Frank G. Oliver.
Norman Rose Society, Norman, Okla.; Mrs. E. L. Lucas.
North Jersey Rose Society, Montclair, N.J.; John F. Walton.
Ohio State University Test Garden, Columbus, Ohio; Dr. L. C. Chadwick.
Oklahoma Rose Society, Oklahoma City, Okla.; C. T. Baker.
Pacific Rose Society, Pasadena, Calif.; Mr. and Mrs. George W. Horn.
Park of Roses, Columbus, Ohio; Foster Franks.
Peninsula Rose Society, Redwood City, Calif.; Herbert E. Vasconcelles.
Philadelphia Rose Society, Philadelphia, Pa.; J. Homer Smith.
Phoenix Rose Society, Phoenix, Ariz.; Mrs. James O. Long.
Pittsburgh Rose Society, Pittsburgh, Pa.; Hugh L. Cobb.
Potomac Rose Society, Washington, D.C.; J. Benjamin Williams.
Randolph Rose Society, Asheboro, N.C.; Mrs. Edgar B. Cole.
Reno Rose Society, Reno, Nev.; Al Russell.
Riverside Rose Society, Riverside, Calif.; Jean Symons.
Rochester Rose Society, Rochester, N.Y.; Mrs. Herbert H. Morse.
Rogue Valley Rose Society, Grants Pass, Ore.; Ernest E. Vehrs.
Rosarians of the Midland Empire, St. Joseph, Mo.; Edward J. Hausman.
Roseburg Rose Society, Roseburg, Ore.; Mrs. Mable Hafer.
Rose Society of Greater St. Louis, St. Louis, Mo.; Frank R. McMath.
Rose Study Club of Oakland, Oakland, Calif.; John Paul Edwards.
St. Joseph Valley Rose Society, South Bend, Ind.; Nicholas L. Stuart.
Salem Rose Society, Salem, Ore.; Ollie Schendel.
San Diego Rose Society, San Diego, Calif.; Clive N. Pillsbury.
San Joaquin Valley Rose Society, Fresno, Calif.; Mrs. Clement A. Tavares.
San Mateo County Rose Society, San Mateo, Calif.; Iva Newman.
Schenectady Rose Society, Schenectady, N.Y.; John A. Bliss.
Seattle Rose Society, Seattle, Wash.; W. R. Nelson.
Sedalia Rose Society, Sedalia, Mo.; E. E. Brummet.
Spokane Rose Society, Spokane, Wash.; Mrs. E. K. Pearson.
Stark Rose Society, Canton, Ohio; Mrs. A. J. Shahan.
Sunset Park Test Garden, Missoula, Mont.; S. M. Trenouth.
Syracuse Rose Society, Syracuse, N.Y.; Harold G. Munroe.
Tri-City Men's Rose and Garden Club, Moline, Ill.; George L. Baker.
Twickenham Rose Society, Huntsville, Ala.; W. T. Bledsoe.
University of British Columbia Test Garden, Vancouver, Canada; Freek Vrugtman.
Utah Rose Society, Salt Lake City, Utah; Mrs. W. R. Middlemiss.
Vancouver Rose Society, Vancouver, British Columbia, Canada; Archie Selwood.
Vincennes Rose Society, Vincennes, Ind.; Victor K. Langford.
Virginia Peninsula Rose Society, Hampton, Va.; Floyd Bradd.
Walla Walla Rose Society, Walla Walla, Wash.; M. L. Harmon.
West Jersey Rose Society, Haddonfield, N.J.; Mrs. Maurice R. Sinclair.
West Michigan Rosarians, Grand Rapids, Mich.; Robert J. Philip.
Wichita Rose Society, Wichita, Kan.; Floyd Raynes.
Wyo-Mac Rose Socety, Welch, W.Va.; Mrs. J. B. Crozier.

## GARDEN CHAPEL

These bushes dazzle like candle-blossoming altars.
The paths are chancels where the ministering snails slow pace.
The trees are choirs where bird-winged angels chorus.
The sun his matin, nones, and vesper prayers descants.
And all the roses' faces shine delight.
Kissed by the night, the dew, the wind, the day.
They sway upon their spires like angels poised
And breathe their incense from bright cherub lips
And whisper secrets to the bees, and dance
Their incandescent lights among the leaves.
From what stars blew the fires that course these veins?
Man cannot know, man cannot pierce the veil
Of beauty woven in rose petal's tremulous shell.
Man cannot touch the mystery, can only wonder,
Look distantly, with half-averted eyes
Lest the pure dazzle of it blind him, and
In slow awe bow his soul in love and prayer
Before the rosebush altars . . .

                                        Robert Palfrey Utter
                                        San Francisco, Calif.

# New Roses of the World

**ALICE MANLEY HT.** (Joseph H. Hill Co. '58) Unnamed seedling x *Golden Rapture*. Lemon-yellow, large, long pointed bud opening to large, high-centered, very double mimosa-yellow bloom with slight fragrance. Petals hang on, good lasting quality. Abundant, leathery, holly-green, resistant leaves. Vigorous, upright growth. Continuous, abundant flowering. Greenhouse only.

**ALLOTRIA F.** (M. Tantau '58) *Fanal* x *Tantau's Triumph* seedling. Ovoid, medium bud. Large, orange-red, full, double flowers with slight fragrance, borne in clusters. Very good lasting quality. Resistant, large, leathery, dark green foliage on vigorous, upright plant. Few thorns. Profuse bloom.

**ANGEL WINGS HT.** (R. V. Lindquist; int. Howard Rose Co. '58) *Golden Rapture* x *Girona*. Large ovoid bud. Large, high centered, semi-double flower with good lasting qualities. Base bright yellow, shading to white, edged Spinel-pink. Long strong stems. Moderate fragrance. Leathery, semi-resistant foliage. Vigorous, upright plant with continuous bloom.

**APPEAL HT.** (N. Fletcher; int. R. Tucker & Sons '57) *Ena Harkness* x *Treasure*. High-centered, double, blossom-pink flower, overlaid with orange at base. Very strong old-rose fragrance. Very free-blooming. Vigorous, very hardy plant with glossy, bronze leaves.

**BABY JAYNE Cl. Min.** (R. S. Moore; int. Germain's '57) *Violette* x *(Carolyn Dean x Tom Thumb)*. Small, short, pointed buds open to clustered, fuchsine-pink, full, very double small flowers of good lasting quality. Old flowers drop off. Abundant, leathery, glossy, resistant foliage. Few thorns. Vigorous, compact, bushy growth. Arching branches 3-4' high. Free, intermittent blooming.

**BACCHUS HT.** (A. Dickson & Sons' '51) Parentage not given. Moderately-large, semi-double, bright rose-red flower with a sweet scent. Free-blooming. Strong, hardy growth. Medium green foliage.

**BALLET HT.** (Wilhelm Kordes; int. S. McGredy & Son '58) Parentage not given. Large, deep pink bloom. Very free-flowering. Hardy growth. Tough, medium green leaves.

**BELLINA F.** (G. von Abrams; int. Peterson & Dering '58) *Pinocchio* x *(Fashion x Orange Triumph)*. Pointed, medium, clustered pink buds flushed cardinal-red. Full, very double, medium flowers. Good lasting quality. Moderate fragrance. Leathery foliage on bushy plant of compact, moderate growth. Abundant bloom.

**BLACK BOY M.** (Wilhelm Kordes '58) *World's Fair* x *Nuits d'Young*. Large, velvety-red, ovoid bud. Very double, full, intense blackish-crimson flower with strong fragrance and very good lasting

240

qualities. Medium, abundant, leathery, wrinkled, light green, resistant leaves. Vigorous, bushy, upright growth. Many thorns. Abundant bloom.

**BLUE BOY M.** (Wilhelm Kordes '58) *Louis Gimard* x *Independence*. Large, ovoid buds. Double, very large, full, high-centered, reddish-violet flower of very good lasting quality and strong fragrance. Resistant, glossy, abundant, light green leaves. Few thorns. Vigorous, upright, bushy growth. Profuse bloom in May and June. Very hardy.

**BLUSHING JEWEL Min.** (Dennison Morey; int. Jackson & Perkins '59) Sport of *Dick Koster* x *Tom Thumb*. Small globular buds, opens into small, open, double, bluish-white flower finishing blush-pink. Good lasting quality and moderate fragrance. Small, glossy, resistant leaves. Few thorns on moderate, dwarf plant (6-8″). Continuous bloom.

**BRIGHTNESS HT.** (Fryers Nurseries '58) Sport of *Doreen*. Large, full, bright scarlet-and-gold flower with good fragrance. Very free-blooming. Vigorous growth. Glossy foliage.

**BRILLIANCE F.** (E. S. Boerner; int. Jackson & Perkins '59) Unnamed seedling x *Independence*. Medium, ovoid buds. Clustered, medium, double, cupped, reddish *Fashion*-colored flower with good lasting quality and moderate fragrance. Abundant, glossy, resistant leaves on vigorous, bushy plant. Abundant, continuous bloom. Greenhouse only.

**CALYPSO F.** (E. S. Boerner; int. C. W. Stuart '57) *Geranium Red* x *Fashion*. Medium, globular, very dark chrysanthemum-crimson bud. Geranium-lake-colored, large, open, cupped, double flower. Good lasting quality. Strong fragrance resembles *Crimson Glory*. Abundant, leathery, glossy, dark green, resistant leaves. Many thorns. Very vigorous, upright, bushy plant with abundant, continuous bloom.

**CANDY CANE Cl. Min.** (Moore: int. Sequoia '58) Unnamed seedling x *Zee*. Small, ovoid, pointed pink bud opens to small, semidouble, open pink to light rose-red flower with white stripes. Outside of petal solid color. Blooms are borne several together and have good lasting quality and slight fragrance. Small, normal green foliage on a vigorous, climbing, upright plant. Free-blooming.

**CAPRIOLE F.** (Mathias Tantau '56) *Red Favorite* x *Fanal*. Large, long-pointed buds open to semi-double, large, open flowers borne in clusters. Very good lasting quality, slight fragrance. Abundant, leathery, resistant leaves. Few thorns. Vigorous, upright bushy growth. Profuse bloom for about five weeks.

**CHANTRÉ HT.** (Wilhelm Kordes '58) *(Luis Brinas x Spek's Yellow)* x *Anthéor*. Very large, long-pointed, orange-gold bud. Orange and golden-yellow, very large, open, double flower with strong fragrance. Resistant, abundant, leathery, wrinkled, large foliage. Many thorns. Very vigorous, upright bushy plant with abundant bloom.

**CHARLOTTE WHEATCROFT F.** (Wheatcroft Bros.' Ltd. '58) Parentage not given. Brilliant scarlet, single flowers borne in clusters. Very free-blooming. Dark, glossy green foliage on very hardy plant.

**CHERRY GLOW Gr.** (H. C. Swim; int. C. R. Burr & Co., Inc. '59) *Floradora* x *First Love*. Medium buds open to double, cupped, dark red flowers of good lasting quality, moderate fragrance, borne singly and several together. Leathery, glossy foliage mildews. Vigorous, upright, bushy growth. Abundant, continuous bloom.

**CHRISTIAN DIOR HT.** (Francis Meilland; int. Universal Rose Selection '58) *(Independence x Happiness)* x *(Peace x Happiness)*. Large, ovoid bud. Slight fragrance. Very long-lasting, full, high-centered, very large, double, brilliant crimson-red flower. Glossy, leathery, resistant leaves. Few thorns. Very vigorous, upright plant with abundant, continuous bloom.

**CHRISTINE GANDY F.** (G. de Ruiter; int. Gandy's Roses Ltd. '58) Parentage not given. Semi-double, claret-red flowers with fairly strong fragrance borne in clusters. Free-blooming. Bushy plant with dark green leaves.

**CL. BETTINA ClHT.** (Francis Meilland; int. Universal Rose Selection '58) Sport of *Betinna*.

**CL. ELLI KNAB ClHT.** (M. Tantau; int. Kordes '53) Sport of *Elli Knab*.

**CL. GRAND'MERE JENNY ClHT.** (Francis Meilland; int. Universal Rose Selection '58) Sport of *Grand'mere Jenny*.

**CL. MARJORIE le GRICE ClHT.** (Mathias Tantau; int. Kordes '56) Sport of *Marjorie le Grice*.

**CL. QUEEN ELIZABETH ClGr.** (Milton Whisler; int. Germain's Inc.) Sport of *Queen Elizabeth*.

**COGNAC F.** (Mathias Tantau '56) *Alpine Glow* x *Mrs. Pierre S. duPont*. Large, ovoid buds borne in clusters. Large, open, semi-double, cognac-yellow blooms of good lasting quality. Abundant, resistant, glossy leaves. Few thorns on upright, bushy plant of moderate vigor. Abundant bloom. Tips freeze.

**COLIBRI MIN.** (Francis Meilland; int. Universal Rose Selection '58) *Goldilocks* x *Perla de Montserrat*. Small, ovoid buds. Full, open, small, double, very vivid orange-yellow flowers suffused with coral on the edges borne several together. Long-lasting. Slight fragrance.

Small, abundant, glossy, resistant leaves on dwarf plant of moderate growth. Abundant, continuous bloom.

**COOLNESS F.** (E. S. Boerner; int. Jackson & Perkins '59) Unnamed *Glacier* seedling x unnamed *Starlite* seedling. Medium, ovoid, cream buds borne several together and in clusters. Opens to double, full, medium, clear-white flower of good lasting quality and moderate fragrance. Resistant, leathery, glossy leaves on vigorous, bushy, compact plant with few thorns. Profuse, continuous bloom. Greenhouse only.

**CORAL GEM F.** (E. S. Boerner; int. Jackson & Perkins '59) Unnamed *Pinocchio* seedling x *Fashion*. Medium, ovoid bud. Medium, open, cupped, double, light coral-pink flower of very good lasting quality and moderate fragrance. Resistant, leathery leaves on vigorous, bushy plant with many thorns. Abundant, continuous bloom. Greenhouse only.

**CRI-CRI MIN.** (Francis Meilland; int. Universal Rose Selection '58) *(Alain* x *Independence)* x *Perla de Alcanada*. Small, globular buds opening into small full, open, very double rose-carmine blooms which turn rose-Neyron borne several together. Very long-lasting. Slight fragrance. Petals hang on. Moderate, compact, bushy, dwarf growth. Leathery, abundant, resistant leaves. Few thorns. Abundant, continuous bloom.

**DAME de COEUR HT.** (Louis Lens '58) *Peace* x *Independence*. Cherry-red, open, full flower with slight fragrance. Continuous bloom. Very vigorous plant with abundant foliage.

**DAWNLIGHT F.** (T. E. Motose; int. George B. Hart, Inc. '58) *Cl. Summer Snow* x *Summer Snow*. Small, pink, ovoid buds borne in clusters. Small, double, cupped Bengal-rose flowers fade to pinkish cream as they age. Very good lasting quality. Slight fragrance. Light green, leathery leaves mildew. Vigorous, bushy, compact, well-branched plant. No thorns. Profuse, continuous bloom.

**DELIGHTFUL PINK F.** (E. S. Boerner; int. Jackson & Perkins '59) *Chic* x *Demure*. Medium, ovoid buds borne in clusters. Deep pink to rose-pink, medium, cupped, double flower with good lasting quality and moderate fragrance. Dark green, smooth, resistant foliage. Vigorous, upright bush grows to 2-2½'. Profuse, abundant bloom. Greenhouse only.

**DIAMOND JEWEL Min.** (Dennison Morey; int. Jackson & Perkins '59) Sport of *Dick Koster* x *Tom Thumb*. Small, globular buds borne several together and in clusters. Small, cupped, globular, double flower begins white and finishes blush-pink. Good lasting quality. Moderate fragrance. Small, resistant, glossy, light green, foliage on moderate, dwarf plant (6-8"). Abundant, continuous bloom.

**DICKSON'S FLAME F.** (Alex Dickson & Sons, Ltd. '58) *Independence* seedling x *Nymph*. Semi-double, pure, unfading scarlet flame flower with slight fragrance borne in clusters. Very perpetual and free-blooming. Very disease-resistant foliage. Vigorous, hardy plant.

**DIRIGENT HMsk.** (Mathias Tantau '56) *Fanal* x *Karl Weinhausen*. Large, long pointed buds borne in clusters. Blood-red, open, semi-double flower with good lasting qualities and slight fragrance. Large, leathery leaves. No thorns. Vigorous, upright bush. Abundant bloom for four weeks.

**DISCOVERY Gr.** (G. de Ruiter; int. Blaby Rose Gardens '58) *(Peace* x *Christopher Stone)* x unnamed Floribunda seedling. Large, full-pointed flower borne singly and in clusters. Rose bud opens dawn-pink, tinted apricot. Strong scent. Very free-blooming. Healthy, strong foliage on hardy, very strong bush.

**DONY ROBIN F.** (Francis Meilland; int. Universal Rose Selections '58) *Goldilocks* x *Fashion*. Medium, pointed buds darker than cupped, medium, semi-double salmon flowers retouched with Madder-red borne several together and in clusters. Slight fragrance. Small, sparse, leathery, resistant foliage. Compact, vigorous, bushy plant. Few thorns. Abundant, continuous, long-lasting bloom.

**DORIS NORMAN F.** (Albert Norman; int. R. Harkness & Co. '58) *Paul's Scarlet Climber* x *Mary*. Double, Hybrid Tea-form, wide, brilliant light orange-scarlet flowers borne several together. Very free-blooming. Leaves purple when young, dull-green when old. Very bushy, hardy plant.

**DUBONNET Pol.** (R. G. Jelly; int. E. G. Hill Co. '58) Sport of *Stoplite*. Small buds open to cardinal-red, double, full, high-centered flowers of good lasting quality borne singly and several together. Slight fragrance. Petals hang on. Vigorous, upright plant with abundant, leathery, resistant leaves. Free, continuous bloom. Greenhouse only.

**DUKAT Cl.** (Mathias Tantau '55) *Mrs. Pierre S. duPont* x *Golden Glow*. Large, long-pointed buds open to large, open, double, gold-yellow, clustered flowers with good lasting quality and slight fragrance. Leathery, glossy foliage. Very vigorous climber. Profuse bloom. Tips freeze.

**EVE HT.** (Jean Gaujard; int. Gandy's Roses, Ltd. '59) Cross of two unnamed seedlings. Large, long, pointed buds open to salmon-coppery, open, double flower with very good lasting quality and moderate fragrance. Glossy, dark green, resistant, abundant foliage. Upright, bushy plant with profuse, continuous bloom.

HEAT WAVE F
H. C. Swim; introduced Armstrong Nurseries, Ontario, Calif. Plant patent
applied for. Described page 247.

ANGEL WINGS HT
R. V. Lindquist; introduced Howard Rose Co., Hemet, Calif.
Described page 240.

**FAIR LADY HT.** (E. S. Boerner; int. Jackson & Perkins '59) *Golden Masterpiece* x *Tawny Gold*. Medium, ovoid to pointed, apricot bud. Large, high-centered, double, pink flowers with apricot center borne singly and several together with very good lasting quality and moderate fragrance. Resistant, glossy leaves on vigorous, upright plant. Abundant, continuous flowering. Greenhouse only.

**FANTAN HT.** (Francis Meilland; int. Conard-Pyle '58) *(Pigalle x Prelude)* seedling x *(Prelude x Pigalle)* seedling. Medium, pointed, ovoid bud. Burnt-orange, cupped, high-centered, double flower with very good lasting quality and slight to moderate fragrance. Leathery, resistant leaves. Much-branched, upright, vigorous plant. Free, continuous bloom.

**FASHIONETTE F.** (E. S. Boerner; int. Jackson & Perkins '58) Unnamed seedling x *Fashion*. Medium, cupped to flat, double, coral-pink to *Fashion*-colored flower with very good lasting quality and moderate fragrance. Resistant, leathery, glossy leaves. Continuous bloom on vigorous, upright bush.

**FEU ROUGE F.** (Mathias Tantau '56) *Red Favorite* x *Fanal*. Medium, ovoid bud. Clustered, semi-double, open, red flowers with good lasting quality and slight fragrance. Glossy, resistant foliage on vigorous, upright plant. Profuse bloom for a few weeks.

**FIRE KING F.** (Francis Meilland; int. Universal Rose Selection '58) *Moulin Rouge* x *Fashion*. Medium, pointed buds. Full, high-centered semi-double geranium-red flowers suffused with vermilion-red. Very long lasting quality. Borne several together and in custers. Vigorous, upright plant with abundant, leathery leaves and abundant, continuous bloom.

**FIRE OPAL F.** (E. S. Boerner; int. Jackson and Perkins '54) *Goldilocks* x unnamed orange Polyantha. Distinct bud with white mid-rib on outside. Medium, cupped, semi-double, orange-scarlet bloom with a red-toned base. No bluing. Vigorous, open, upright, bushy plant (2½-3'). Profuse, continuous bloom with very good lasting quality. Strong fragrance. Leathery, resistant foliage. Greenhouse only.

**FIRST CHOICE F.** (H. Morse & Son's '58) *Masquerade* x *Sultane*. Single, fiery orange-scarlet flower with yellow center and sweet fragrance borne in clusters. Very free-flowering. Hardy plant.

**FLORIMEL F.** (Fryers Nurseries Ltd. '58) *Pinocchio* x unnamed seedling. Dainty Hybrid Tea-type, bright silvery-pink flower opens to deep rose-pink. Borne in clusters. Exceptionally free-blooming. Foliage glossy on vigorous, very free-growing plant.

**FUGUE Cl.** (Francis Meilland; int. Universal Rose Selection '58) *Alain* x *Guinee.* Medium, globular buds borne several together. Medium, open, double, garnet-red and velvet scarlet flower. Very long lasting. Slight fragrance. Leathery, resistant leaves on vigorous climbing plant with few thorns. Less vigor than *Guinee,* but more flowers. Abundant, intermittent bloom.

**GAY JEWEL Min.** (Dennison Morey; int. Jackson & Perkins '59) Sport of *Dick Koster* x *Tom Thumb.* Small, globular buds borne several together and in clusters. Small, light rose-pink, cupped, double bloom of good lasting quality with moderate fragrance. Dark green, wrinkled, resistant foliage. Moderate, dwarf plant (6-8″). Abundant, continuous flowering.

**GILLIAN HT.** (Verschuren; int. Gandy's Roses Ltd. '58) Parentage not given. Long, pointed soft coral-pink flower borne singly. Free-bloomer. Bronze-green foliage on hardy bush.

**GLEAMING F.** (E. B. Le Grice '58) *Goldilocks* x *Spek's Yellow.* Semi-single, deep lemon-yellow, very free-blooming, clustered flowers with a pronounced fragrance. Very free, hardy growth. Strong, dark green foliage.

**GOLD COAST Gr.** (H. Robinson; int. Jackson & Perkins '58) *Pinocchio* x *Peace.* Medium, ovoid buds. Clear yellow, non-fading, large, cupped, double flower of good lasting quality and strong fragrance. Resistant, leathery, glossy leaves on vigorous, upright plant with profuse, continuous bloom.

**GOLDIE F.** (E. S. Boerner; int. Jackson & Perkins '58) *Goldilocks* x *Pigmy Gold.* Ovoid, medium bud opens to large, full, double golden-yellow flower with lighter yellow at edges of petals. Very good lasting quality. Moderate fragrance. Abundant, resistant, leathery leaves. Many thorns on vigorous, upright, bushy plant. Abundant, continuous bloom. Greenhouse only.

**GOLDMARIE F.** (Wilhelm Kordes '58) *Masquerade* x *Golden Main.* Large, long-pointed buds open to pure orange-gold, semi-double, high-centered, very large flowers borne in clusters. Very good lasting quality, strong fragrance. Large, abundant, glossy, resistant foliage. Few thorns on very vigorous, upright bushy plant. Profuse, intermittent bloom. Tips freeze.

**GOVERNOR ROSELLINI Gr.** (R. V. Lindquist; int. Howard Rose Co. '58) *Baby Chateau* x *Tiffany.* Medium, ovoid buds. Full, red, high-centered, double blooms with good lasting quality. Borne singly and several together. Moderate raspberry fragrance. Abundant, dark green, leathery leaves mildew. Very vigorous, upright bush with abundant, continuous bloom.

**GREEN FIRE** F. (H. C. Swim; int. Armstrong Nursery '58) *Goldilocks* x unnamed seedling. Long, pointed, ovoid, medium bud. Yellow, semi-double, open flower with traces of pink in old flowers, particularly in cool weather. Good lasting quality. Slight fragrance. Semi-open, vigorous, upright growth. Resistant, semi-glossy foliage. Abundant, continuous bloom.

**HALALI** HM. (Mathias Tantau '56) *Marchenland* x *Peace*. Large, long-pointed buds. Clustered, very large, open, semi-double, pink-red bloom of very good lasting quality. Slight fragrance. Very vigorous, upright bush with abundant, large, leathery, resistant leaves. Few thorns. Profuse bloom for four weeks. Tips freeze.

**HANSESTADT BREMEN** F. (Wilhelm Kordes '58) *Ama* x *Fanal*. Very large, ovoid, crimson buds. Full, high-centered, double, clustered, deep salmon and reddish-pink blooms. Moderate fragrance. Very good lasting quality. Profuse, intermittent bloom. Large, leathery, abundant, resistant foliage on very vigorous, upright bushy plant.

**HEAT WAVE** F. (H. C. Swim; int. Armstrong Nursery '58) Unnamed seedling x *Roundelay*. Small to medium, long, pointed, ovoid bud. Clustered, orange-scarlet to cherry, double, open, cupped flower with good lasting quality. Slight fragrance. Abundant, continuous bloom on vigorous, upright bushy plant with many thorns and resistant, dark green, leathery foliage.

**HEIDELBERG** E. (Wilhelm Kordes '58) *Sparrieshoop* x *World's Fair*. Very large, long, pointed buds borne in clusters. Deep, fiery red, open, high-centered, very large, double bloom with very good lasting qualities. Moderate fragrance. Abundant, dark green, leathery glossy, resistant foliage on very vigorous, climbing, bushy plant. Profuse, intermittent bloom. A perpetual shrub rose.

**HEIN EVERS** F. (Mathias Tantau '57) *Red Favorite* x *Fanal*. Medium, long, pointed buds. Large, slightly-fragrant, open, semi-double, clustered, blood-red flower of very good lasting quality. Few thorns on vigorous, upright plant with abundant, leathery, resistant leaves.

**HENRY MORSE** F. (Wilhelm Kordes; int. E. H. Morse '58) Parentage not given. Clustered, deep blood-red and crimson, loose, semi-double bloom with slight fragrance. Very leathery foliage on hardy, free-growing plant.

**HI-FI** F. (C. Gregory & Son '58) *Independence* cross. Semi-double, brilliant orange-flame, clustered bloom with little fragrance. Very free-blooming and growing hardy plant with medium green, glossy leaves.

**HOBBY F.** (Mathias Tantau '55) *Red Favorite* x *Kathe Durig-neau.* Medium, long, pointed bud. Coral-pink, large, double, high-centered flowers with good lasting quality and slight fragrance borne in clusters. Large, abundant, resistant leaves. Few thorns on moderate, upright, bushy plant. Profuse bloom for five weeks. Tips freeze.

**HONEY GOLD F.** (E. S. Boerner; int. Jackson & Perkins '56) *Yellow Pinocchio* x *Fashion.* Large, semi-double, open, yellow flower, flushed with *Pinocchio*-pink at finish. Very good lasting quality, moderate fragrance. Resistant, glossy, normal green foliage. Vigorous bush. Abundant continuous bloom. Greenhouse only.

**HORIZON F.** (Mathias Tantau '56) *Crimson Glory* x *Tantau's Triumph.* Long, pointed, medium buds. Clustered, cinnabar-red, semi-double, open, medium blooms. Good lasting quality. Slight fragrance. Resistant, leathery foliage. Few thorns. Profuse bloom on upright vigorous bush.

**ICEBERG F.** (Wilhelm Kordes; int. McGredy & Son '58) *Robin Hood* x *Virgo.* Pure white flowers with miniature Hybrid Tea shape borne in clusters. Very free-blooming. Slight fragrance. Prolific, light green foliage on very free-growing, hardy bush.

**IVORY FASHION F.** (E. S. Boerner; int. Jackson & Perkins '58) *Sonata* x *Fashion.* Medium, ovoid bud. Large, semi-double ivory flowers change to clear white. Decorative yellow stamens. Good lasting quality. Moderate fragrance. Leathery, resistant leaves on vigorous, upright plant with abundant, continuous bloom.

**JEANIE HT.** (H. M. Eddie; int. Wyant '58) *Mme. Edmond Labbe* x *Condesa de Sastago.* Large, globular bud opens to large, double, full, high-centered bloom with base of petals yellow, both sides cream, pink near edge. Good keeping quality. Moderate fragrance. Abundant, intermittent bloom on vigorous, bushy plant. Resistant, glossy leaves. Tips freeze.

**JOLIE MADAME HT.** (Francis Meilland; int. Universal Rose Selection '58) *(Independence* x *Happiness)* x *Better Times.* Medium ovoid bud opens to medium, open, cupped, double flowers borne several together. Inside petal brilliant vermilion-red, with reverse dull geranium red. Long-lasting quality. Slight fragrance. Abundant, leathery, resistant leaves on vigorous, bushy plant. Continuous, abundant bloom.

**JUDY HART HT.** (T. E. Motose; int. Geo. B. Hart, Inc. '58) *VierLanden* x *(Florex* x *Senator)* Large, Tyrean-rose, ovoid bud. Very good lasting quality. Large, high-centered, double, Bengal-rose flower. Strong Centifolia fragrance. Abundant, leathery leaves.

Few thorns on vigorous bushy plant (3'). Profuse, continuous bloom. Freezes to 12". Greenhouse only.

**JUNE OPIE F.** (Wilhelm Kordes; int. H. Morse & Sons '58) *Masquerade* x unnamed seedling. Apricot shaded salmon-pink semi-double flowers with slight fragrance, borne in clusters. Very free-blooming. Thick, leathery leaves on very free-growing, upright, hardy plant.

**JUNE PARK HT.** (Bertran Park; int. Sanday Roses '58) *Peace* x *Crimson Glory*. Double, deep rose-pink flower borne singly. Fragrant. Vigorous plant, free from disease. Dark green foliage. Bloom 4½-5" when fully open.

**KORDES PERFECTA HT.** (Wilhelm Kordes; int. Jackson & Perkins '58) *Golden Scepter* x *Karl Herbst*. Large, urn-shaped buds. Very large, double, high-centered, abundant, continuous cream flower tipped with crimson, later flushed crimson. Vigorous, upright plant. Strong fragrance. Very good lasting quality. Dark green, resistant, abundant, leathery, glossy leaves. Many thorns.

**LAGER FEUER F.** (Mathias Tantau '58) *Red Favorite* x *Kathe Duvigneau*. Medium, long-pointed buds open to bright velvet-red, large, open, double blooms borne in clusters of good lasting quality. Slight fragrance. Large, resistant, dark green, leathery leaves. Few thorns on vigorous upright plant with profuse bloom for about five weeks.

**LAMPION F.** (Mathias Tantau '57) *Fanal* x *Kathe Durigneau*. Small, long, pointed buds borne in clusters. Large, single, open blood-red flower of good lasting quality. Slight fragrance. Abundant, dark green, resistant, leathery, glossy leaves on upright, bushy plant with moderate growth. Abundant blooms.

**LICHTERLOH HMsk.** (Mathias Tantau '55) *Red Favorite* x *New Dawn*. Medium, ovoid bud. Blood-red, semi-double, open, medium flowers with good lasting quality borne in clusters. Slight fragrance. Profuse bloom for four weeks. Few thorns on vigorous, upright bush with dark green, resistant, leathery leaves.

**LILA VIDRI HT.** (S. Dot '58) (seedling x *Prelude*) x *Rosa de Friera*. Medium, long, pointed buds open to high-centered, double, blue-violet flowers borne singly and several together. Good lasting quality. Little fragrance. Leathery, resistant foliage on compact, upright plant. Tips freeze. Abundant, intermittent bloom.

**LITTLE SCOTCH Min.** (Moore; int. Sequoia '58) *Golden Glow* x *Zee*. Large, long-pointed, soft butterscotch colored bud borne singly and several together. Very double, medium, full bloom becomes unusual near-white color. Good lasting quality, moderate tea-like fragrance. Small, abundant leaves on upright, bushy dwarf 12" plant with few thorns. Abundant, continuous bloom.

**LORNA MAY F.** (G. de Ruiter; int. Blaby Rose Gardens Ltd. '58) *Poulsen's Pink* x *Kathe Duvigneau*. Single crimson-red flower with white centers borne in very large clusters. Extremely free-blooming. Very bushy plant with light green foliage.

**LYS ASSIA F.** (Wilhelm Kordes '58) *Spartan* x *Horstmann's Brunette*. Large, long, pointed buds. Very large, open, high-centered, double blooms borne in clusters. Very good lasting quality. Slight fragrance. Resistant, abundant, glossy leaves on vigorous upright, bushy plant. Profuse, continuous bloom.

**MARCIA GANDY HT.** (J. Verschuren; int. Gandys Roses Ltd. '57) Cross of two unnamed seedlings. Very fragrant, full chrysanthemum-crimson-rose-red flower borne singly. Very free-blooming. Dark bronzy leaves on hardy, very free-growing bush.

**MARY JO HT.** (Joseph H. Hill '58) Unnamed seedling x *Queen Juliana*. Nasturtium-orange, medium short, pointed bud. Large, double, high-centered maize-yellow flower when newly opened, amber-yellow after three days. Very good lasting quality. Petals hang on. Slight fragrance. Resistant, abundant, leathery, spinach-green foliage. Very vigorous, upright plant. Abundant bloom. Greenhouse only.

**MAYDAY F.** (E. S. Boerner; int. Jackson & Perkins '56) *(Pinocchio* seedling x unnamed Hybrid Tea) x *Fashion*. Medium, ovoid buds borne singly and in clusters. Double, cupped flowers with petals white on inside, cameo-pink on outside. Very good lasting quality. Moderate fragrance. Medium, leathery, resistant foliage on vigorous, upright, branching plant. Abundant, continuous bloom. Greenhouse only.

**METEOR F.** (Wilhelm Kordes; int. S. McGredy & Son '57) Parentage not given. Miniature Hybrid Tea-type orange-scarlet flowers borne in clusters. Slight fragrance. Very free-blooming. Prolific, light green leaves on hardy, bushy, free-growing plant.

**MINK F.** (E. S. Boerner; int. Jackson & Perkins '55) *Pinocchio* x *Garnette* seedling. Small globular buds borne several together and in clusters open to very double, open medium orange-pink flowers of very good lasting quality. Moderate fragrance. Leathery, resistant foliage. Few thorns on vigorous, upright, bushy plant. Profuse, continuous bloom. Greenhouse only.

**MISS LIBERTY L.C.** (E. S. Boerner; int. C. W. Stuart '56)

*New Dawn* x *Cl. World's Fair.* Small, carmine, ovoid bud. Semi-double, open, cupped, Tyrean-rose bloom. Good lasting quality. Moderate fragrance. Abundant, leathery, resistant leaves. Many thorns on vigorous, climbing plant. Abundant, continuous bloom.

**MONCH F.** (Mathias Tantau '52) Unknown seedling x *Karl Weinhausen.* Medium, ovoid bud. Pure pink, clustered, double, open, large flower. Good lasting quality. Slight fragrance. Resistant, abundant, leathery leaves. Vigorous, upright bush.

**MÜNSTER S.** (Wilhelm Kordes; int. S. McGredy & Son '58) Parentage not given. Miniature Hybrid Tea-type soft pink flowers with deeper shading borne in clusters. Very free-blooming. Slight perfume. Light green, prolific foliage covers hardy, very free-growing plant.

**MY CHOICE HT.** (E. B. LeGrice; int. LeGrice Nurseries '58) *Wellworth* x *Ena Harkness.* Lemon-yellow buds heavily overlaid with scarlet-cerise open to soft clear pink blooms with pale yellow reverse borne singly and several together in the Fall. Very free-blooming. Very strong fragrance. Dark green leaves. Strong, free-growing plant.

**NAVAJO HT.** (M. Maladrone; int. Jackson & Perkins) *Hortulanus Budd* x *E. G. Hill.* Large, long-pointed bud. Large, double, high-centered dark red to rose-red flowers borne singly and several together. Good lasting quality. Strong fragrance.

**OLALA F.** (Mathias Tantau '56) *Fanal* x *Crimson Glory.* Medium, long-pointed bud opens to semi-double, large, open, clustered, bright blood-red flower. Very good lasting quality. Slight fragrance. Abundant, large, leathery, resistant foliage. Upright, bushy, very vigorous plant. Abundant bloom for four weeks.

**ORANGE Mist F.** (E. S. Boerner; int. Jackson & Perkins '55) *Ma Perkins* x unnamed Floribunda seedling. Ovoid, medium buds borne singly and several together. Cupped, double, geranium-pink flower. Very good lasting quality. Moderate fragrance. Leathery, normal foliage on vigorous, upright plant with few thorns and abundant continuous bloom. Greenhouse only.

**ORANGE RED SUPREME F.** (E. S. Boerner; int. Jackson & Perkins '58) *Spice* x *Garnette* seedling. Medium, ovoid buds open to open, double, orange-red flowers. Very good lasting quality. Very pleasing color, no blue in finished rose. Moderate fragrance. Abundant, medium, leathery, glossy, wrinkled foliage. Vigorous, bushy plant with abundant, continuous bloom. Greenhouse only.

**OREGON CENTENNIAL HT.** (G. J. Von Abrams; int. Peterson-Dering '59) *Charles Mallerin* x unnamed seedling. Medium, pointed bud opens to large, double, cupped, deep red flower. Good lasting quality. Moderate fragrance. Large, dark green, abundant, leathery foliage mildews. Compact, vigorous, upright bush. Abundant bloom.

**OUTSIDER F.** (Mathias Tantau '56) *Fanal* x *Red Favorite.* Medium, ovoid bud. Semi-double, open, medium flowers borne in clusters. Good lasting quality. Slight fragrance. Abundant, resistant, glossy foliage. Vigorous, upright plant with few thorns. Profuse bloom.

**PAPRIKA F.** (Mathias Tantau '58) *Marchenland* x *Red Favorite.* Long-pointed, medium bud. Clustered, semi-double, open, large, brick-red flower. Very good lasting quality. Slight fragrance. Resistant, abundant, leathery, glossy, dark green leaves. Few thorns on vigorous, upright plant with abundant bloom.

**PAULIEN VERBEEK HT.** (G. Verbeek '58) Cross of unnamed seedlings. 6″ orange-yellow flowers when fully open. Slight fragrance. Good freedom of bloom. Shiny, dark green foliage.

**PEGGY NEWTON F.** (E. S. Boerner; int. C. W. Stuart '57) *Golden Glow* x *Goldilocks.* Small, globular, sulphur-yellow buds open to medium, double, cupped primrose-yellow blooms, borne singly or in clusters. Medium lasting quality. Slight fragrance. Some petals hang on. Resistant, dark green, abundant, leathery, glossy, wrinkled leaves. Vigorous, bushy, spreading but not trailing dwarf plant (12-18″). Profuse, continuous bloom. Tips freeze.

**PERKY Min.** (Moore; int. Sequoia '58) (*Rosa wichuraiana* x *Floradora*) x *Oakington Ruby.* Small, long-pointed buds. Small, double, full, high-centered, pink flowers of good lasting quality and strong, sweet fragrance borne singly and several together. Very bushy, vigorous, compact 12″ plant with abundant, resistant, glossy leaves. Abundant, continuous bloom.

**PERLE von REMAGEN HT.** (H. Burkhord; int. Kordes & Son '57) *R.M.S. Queen Mary* x *Peace.* Very large, ovoid bud. Tender, pink, very large and double, high-centered flowers, borne several together. Very good lasting quality. Long stems. Moderate fragrance. Leathery, resistant leaves. Few thorns on vigorous, upright plant with profuse bloom.

**PETER NAY HT.** (N. V. Verschuren; int. Blaby Rose Gardens '58) *The Doctor* x *New Yorker.* Very full, large, velvety-scarlet flower, shaded crimson. Strong fragrance. Blooms freely-produced on long, strong stems. Very vigorous and free-growing. Large, leathery foliage.

**PHOENIX FIRST F.** (V. R. Kernovske; int. C. Langbeckery & Sons '59) *Our Princess* x *Pom Pom Beauty.* Small, ovoid, clustered buds. Small, very double, full, very dark red flower shaded to black. Very good lasting quality. Slight fragrance. Resistant, leathery foliage. Bushy plant has many thorns and free, continuous bloom.

**PICCOLO F.** (Mathias Tantau '57) *Red Favorite* x *Kathe Duvigneau*. Medium, ovoid buds borne in clusters. Very double, open, velvety black-red flower. Good lasting quality. Slight fragrance. Dark green, resistant, leathery, glossy foliage. Abundant bloom on bushy, dwarf plant of moderate growth.

**PINK CAVALCADE F.** (Carl Shamburger; int. C. W. Stuart '55) *Cavalcade* sport. Small, ovoid bud. Clustered, cupped, very double, large flower. Solferino red-mimosa yellow at base, silvery, iridescent white on tips and reverse. Resembles *Pinocchio,* only larger. Very good lasting quality. Strong, fruity fragrance. Dark green, leathery, glossy leaves. Few thorns. Upright, vigorous plant. Freezes to 18″. Abundant, continuous bloom.

**PINK GARNETTE SUPREME F.** (C. H. Perkins; int. Jackson & Perkins '57) Sport of *Garnette Supreme*. Medium, ovoid buds borne singly and several together. Double, cupped, Spinel-pink blooms. Very good lasting quality. Glossy, resistant foliage. Few thorns. Vigorous, upright plant. Continuous, abundant bloom.

**PINK MIST HT.** (Joseph H. Hill Co. '59) Sport of *Better Times*. Long, pointed, ovoid, medium bud. High-centered, large double flower phlox-pink when newly-opened turning to Rhodamine-pink after three days. Strong tea fragrance. Good lasting quality. Large, dark green, abundant, leathery, resistant foliage. Vigorous, upright plant. Few thorns. Greenhouse only.

**PINK PEACE HT.** (Francis Meilland; int. Conard-Pyle Co. '58) *(Peace* x *Monique)* x *(Peace* x *Mrs. John Laing)*. Medium, ovoid bud. Very double, full, cupped, rose-bengal flower. Very good lasting quality. Long stems. Strong tea fragrance. Leathery, large, resistant flowers. Very vigorous, upright, bushy plant. Abundant, continuous bloom.

**PORTLAND HT.** (Wm. Lowe & Son '58) Parentage not given. Rose-madder color. Medium fragrance. Very free-blooming. Well-shaped, hardy plant. Glossy, dark green, disease-resistant leaves.

**PRIMA BALLERINA HT.** (Mathias Tantau '57) Unknown seedling x *Peace*. Very large, long-pointed buds. Very large, full, double, cherry-pink flower. Strong fragrance. Long, strong stems. Very good lasting quality. Large, leathery, resistant foliage. Few thorns on very vigorous, upright plant. Profuse bloom.

**RAY BUNGE Cl.** (W. W. Bunge; int. Andrews Nursery '59) Sport of *Paul Neyron*. Large, long, pointed buds open to full, high-centered, double, purple-red flowers borne singly and in clusters. Very good lasting qualities. Moderate fragrance. Abundant, blackspot-resistant, leathery, glossy, dark green leaves. Many large thorns on very vigorous, upright plant. Profuse June bloom, then intermittent all Summer.

**REA SILVIA HT.** (Giacomasso '58) *Baiser* x *Peace*. Fire-red flower. Abundant leaves. Continuous, abundant bloom.

**RED BIRD HT.** (E. A. Manda, Jr.; int. Jackson & Perkins '58) *Better Times* sport. Large, ovoid buds. Deep red, large, double, high-centered flowers. Very good lasting quality. Strong fragrance. Dark green, leathery, resistant, abundant leaves. Vigorous, upright bush with few thorns. Abundant, continuous bloom. Greenhouse only.

**RED EMBLEM F.** (E. S. Boerner; int. Jackson & Perkins '59) *Garnette* seedling x *Pageant*. Medium, ovoid buds borne several together and in clusters. Large, open, double, deep red bloom. Very good lasting quality. Moderate fragrance. Vigorous, upright, bushy plant with abundant, leathery, resistant foliage. Abundant, continuous bloom. Greenhouse only.

**RED SPICE F.** (E. S. Boerner; int. Jackson & Perkins '58) *Spice* x *Garnette*. Medium, short, flat-top buds borne singly and several together. Full, very double, medium, solid dark red flower. Very good lasting quality. Moderate fragrance. Leathery, resistant, dark green leaves. Vigorous, bushy plant. Profuse, continuous blooms. Greenhouse only.

**RED WINGS F.** (E. S. Boerner; int. Jackson & Perkins '59) *Improved Lafayette* seedling x *Lavender Pinocchio*. Very vigorous, upright, bushy plant with medium, ovoid buds open to double, cupped, rich, dark red unfading flowers borne singly and several together. Very good lasting quality. Moderate fragrance. Abundant, dark green, leathery, resistant foliage. Continuous, abundant bloom.

**REVELRY F.** (E. S. Boerner; int. Jackson & Perkins '59) *Enchantment* x unnamed Floribunda seedling. Large, blood-red, ovoid bud changes to rose-red when half open and to rose-pink when very large, semi-double, open flower is fully open. Moderate fragrance. Very good lasting quality. Abundant, leathery, resistant, dark green leaves, on vigorous, upright, bushy plant. Profuse, continuous bloom. Greenhouse only.

**RIMROSE F.** (Francis Meilland; int. Universal Rose Selection '58) *Goldilocks* x *Perla de Montserrat*. Small, pointed buds darker than the medium, open, semi-double Indian-yellow flowers which turn lemon-yellow. Slight fragrance. Profuse, continuous, long-lasting blooms borne in clusters and several together. Abundant, leathery, resistant foliage on vigorous, compact, bushy plant with few thorns.

**ROSEMARY GANDY F.** (Jean Gaujard; int. Gandy's Ltd. '58) Parentage not given. Color similar to *Grand'mere Jenny*. Very free-blooming. Slight fragrance. Dark green, glossy foliage on very free-growing, hardy plant.

**ROSY JEWEL Min.** (Dennison Morey; int. Jackson & Perkins '59) Sport of *Dick Koster* x *Tom Thumb*. Small, ovoid buds. Small, semi-double, open rose-red flower with white center, reverse of petal lighter, borne several together and in clusters. Good lasting quality. Moderate fragrance. Light green, abundant, glossy leaves. Moderate, dwarf plant (6-8"). Abundant, continuous bloom.

**RUBY JEWEL Min.** (Dennison Morey; int. Jackson & Perkins '59) Sport of *Dick Koster* x *Tom Thumb*. Small, ovoid buds open to double, open, ruby-red flowers with lighter reverse, borne several together and in clusters. Moderate fragrance. Good lasting quality. Glossy, resistant foliage on moderate, dwarf plant (6-8"). Abundant, continuous bloom.

**RUBY LIPS F.** (H. C. Swim; int. Armstrong Nursery '58) *World's Fair* x *Pinocchio*. Clustered buds vary in size and shape (medium to small, long-pointed to ovoid). Medium, semi-double, open, very bright red, unfading flower. Good lasting quality. Slight fragrance. Short stems. Abundant, semi-glossy, resistant foliage on vigorous, upright, semi-open bush. Profuse, continuous bloom.

**S'AGARO HT.** (S. Dot; int. Pedro Dot '59) *(Angels Mateu x Radar)* x *Grand'mere Jenny*. Large, long-pointed buds. High-centered, double, geranium-red flower ending in Cochineal-carmine. Very good lasting quality. Slight fragrance. Dark green glossy leaves on compact plant with abundant, continuous bloom.

**ST. PAUL F.** (Wilhelm Kordes '58) *Masquerade* x *Spek's Yellow*. Very large, long-pointed crimson bud. Very large, semi-double, open, carmine-orange flowers borne in clusters. Moderate fragrance. Very good lasting quality. Abundant, glossy, dark green, resistant, large leaves. Very vigorous, upright, bushy plant. Profuse bloom.

**SALMON MARVEL F.** (G. de Ruiter; int. Blaby Rose Gardens '58) *Red Pinocchio* x *Signal Red*. Orange-scarlet flower like a carnation borne in clusters. Slight fragrance. Very free-blooming. Free-growing, hardy plant with glossy, dark green leaves.

**SALUTE F.** (S. McGredy & Son '58) *Masquerade* x *Lady Sylvia*. Semi-double, cherry and ochre bicolor, borne in clusters. Very free-blooming. Plenty of tough, dark green foliage on free-growing, hardy bush.

**SANTA ROSA F.** (William E. Silva '54) *Golden Salmon* x *Pinocchio*. Small, ovoid buds borne several together. Very double, globular, small, salmon-pink flower, strong brick at outer ends of petals. Very good lasting quality. Strong fragrance. Glossy, soft, bronze foliage. Vigorous, bushy plant with abundant, continuous bloom.

**SARAH COVENTRY F.** (E. S. Boerner; int. C. W. Stuart Co. '56) *Red Pinocchio* x *Garnette*. Medium, ovoid, purple-madder bud. Clustered, cupped, double, medium, chrysanthemum-crimson to cardinal red flowers. Very good lasting quality. Moderate fragrance. Abundant, glossy, resistant leaves. Vigorous, bushy, compact plant. Abundant, continuous bloom. Freezes to 8-12″.

**SATELLITE HT.** (J. L. Priestley '58) *Editor McFarland* x *William Harvey*. Large, long-pointed buds borne singly. Double deep crimson, unfading flowers. Strong fragrance. Profuse, continuous bloomer. Glossy, dark green, resistant foliage on vigorous plant (4-5′).

**SAYONARA HT.** (N. Grillo '59) Sport of *Sunnymount*. Long-pointed, large buds open to large, full double yellow-blend flowers with pink tones. Very good lasting quality. Sweet fragrance. Leathery, fringed leaves. Vigorous, upright plant. Abundant, free-blooming.

**SCARLET WONDER F.** (G. de Ruiter; int. Blaby Rose Gardens '58) *Signa Red* x *Fashion*. Full, orange-scarlet flowers borne in clusters. Very free-blooming. Slight fragrance. Glossy, dark green foliage on free-growing plant.

**SCHNEEWITTCHEN HMsk.** (Wilhelm Kordes '58) *Robin Hood* x *Virgo*. Large, long-pointed buds borne in clusters. Semi-double, open, large, pure white flower. Long, strong stems. Very good lasting quality. Strong fragrance. Large, light green, abundant, glossy, resistant foliage. Few thorns on vigorous, upright bushy plant with profuse, continuous bloom. Tips freeze.

**SIBELIUS HT.** (int. Blaby Rose Gardens '58) *New Yorker* x *Etoile de Hollande*. Velvety, crimson, full, pointed flower. Strong fragrance. Very free-blooming. Vigorous, hardy plant. Healthy foliage.

**SKYLARK F.** (Paul DeVor; int. C. Amling Roses, Inc. '58) Sport of *Carol Amling*. Small, urn-shaped, clustered buds. High-centered, double to very double, small flower with outer and inner petals Rhodamine-pink, base primrose-yellow. Petals hang on. Very good lasting quality. Slight fragrance. Abundant, glossy, resistant foliage.

Few thorns on vigorous, upright bush with abundant, continuous **bloom**.

**SOLO Cl.** (Mathias Tantau '56) Unknown seedling x *Crimson Glory*. Large, long-pointed buds borne in clusters open to very large, full, double, velvety, dark red bloom. Very good lasting quality. Moderate fragrance. Leathery, resistant foliage. Few thorns on vigorous, upright bush with profuse bloom. Tips freeze.

**STARFIRE Gr.** (Walter Lammerts; int. Germain's, Inc. '59) *Charlotte Armstrong* x unnamed seedling. Large, urn-shaped maroon-red buds borne singly and several together. Luminous, currant-red, open, high-centered, double flower. Very good lasting quality. Moderate fragrance. Abundant, leathery, glossy leaves on very vigorous, tall, compact bush (6'). Profuse bloom. Freezes to 12".

**STELLA Gr.** (Mathias Tantau '58) *Horstmann's Jubileumrose* x *Peace*. Clustered, large, ovoid buds. High-centered, very large, very double pink flower. Slight fragrance. Very good lasting quality. Vigorous, upright bush with few thorns. Leathery, dark green, resistant leaves. Abundant bloom.

**SUNSTONE HT.** (N. Fletcher; int. R. Tucker & Sons '57) *Bridget* x *Marcelle Gret*. Full, long bud opens to 6", clear yellow bloom splashed with red. Slight fragrance. Very free continuous bloom on vigorous, tall, hardy plant. Large glossy, bronze-green foliage.

**SWEET CARESS F.** (E. S. Boerner; int. Jackson & Perkins '59) *Pigmy Red* x *Demure*. Medium, ovoid buds on vigorous, upright bush. Very free and continuous rose-pink, full, very double blooms borne several together. Very good lasting quality. Moderate fragrance. Abundant, leathery, glossy, resistant leaves. Greenhouse only.

**SWEET SULTAN ClHT.** (S. Eacott '58) *Independence* x *Honour Bright*. Single, clustered, rich crimson flower shaded maroon. Very sweet fragrance. Perpetual-flowering on vigorous hardy plant.

**TAMBOURINE F.** (Alex Dickson & Sons '58) *Independence* seedling x *Karl Herbst*. Double, clustered, carmine-red and orange yellow bi-color. Slight fragrance. Very free-blooming strong, hardy, free-growing plant with large, dark green leaves.

**TAPESTRY HT.** (Gladys Fisher; int. Conard-Pyle '59) *Peace* x *Mission Bells*. Medium, pointed, ovoid bud. Large, cupped, high-centered, fire-red double flower overlaid with spirea-red showing amber-yellow in center. Strong, penetrating spicy fragrance. Glossy, dark green, resistant leaves. Moderately-free growth. Upright, bushy, much-branched plant with abundant, continuous bloom.

**TAURO F.** (F. Bofill; int. Rosas Torre Blanca '58) *Poinsettia* x *Alain*. Medium, globular bud opens to clustered, full, very double, large, dark red flower. Very long-lasting. Little fragrance. Petals hang on sometimes. Medium, glossy leaves on open, upright plant with abundant, continuous bloom.

**TEMPERAMENT F.** (Mathias Tantau '57) *Red Favorite* x *Kathe Duvigneau*. Large, ovoid buds borne in clusters open to large, double, open, scarlet pink-red flower. Very good lasting quality. Slight fragrance. Resistant, leathery leaves on vigorous, upright plant. Profuse bloom.

**THE QUEEN MOTHER F.** (E. W. Stedman '59) Sport of *Nymph*. Miniature Hybrid Tea-type bud. Double, soft rose-pink flower petals curve back on opening, borne in clusters. Sweetly-scented. Free-blooming. Hardy, vigorous plant with light green, glossy leaves.

**THUNDERBIRD F.** (Paul DeVor; int. Amling Roses Inc. '58) *Skylark* sport. Clustered, small, urn-shaped buds open to medium, high-centered, double rose-red flower with primrose-yellow base. Petals hang on. Very good lasting quality. Slight fragrance. Abundant, glossy, resistant leaves on vigorous, upright plant. Few thorns. Abundant, continuous bloom.

**TOKEN GLORY HT.** (N. Grillo '57) *Token Supreme* sport. Large, globular buds. Large, semi-double, full, open, orange flower. Good lasting quality. Moderate fragrance. Petals hang on. Bronzy, leathery, abundant, resistant leaves. Very vigorous, upright plant. Few thorns. Abundant, continuous bloom.

**TOPPER HT.** (Joseph H. Hill Co. '59) *Pink Bountiful* x *Sister Kenny*. Medium to small, short, Indian-lake bud opens to signal-red, large, semi-double, high-centered flower which turns crimson after three days. Very good lasting quality. Slight fragrance. Petals hang on. Abundant, leathery, resistant, parsley-green foliage. Vigorous, upright plant with abundant bloom. Greenhouse only.

**TORCH SONG HT.** (Francis Meilland; int. Conard-Pyle '59) *(Peace* x *Floradora)* x *Grand'mere Jenny*. Medium, ovoid buds. Large, open, high-centered, double, irridescent Dutch-vermilion flowers. Good lasting quality. Slight fragrance. Dark green, abundant, resistant, leathery foliage. Vigorous, bushy, upright plant. Abundant, continuous bloom.

**TRAUMLAND F.** (Mathias Tantau '58) *Cinnabar Improved* x *Fashion*. Medium, long-pointed buds borne in clusters. Tender, peach-pink, large, open, semi-double blooms. Very good lasting quality. Slight fragrance. Resistant, dark green, leathery foliage on a moderate-growing, upright, bushy plant. Abundant bloom.

**UNITY HT.** (W. H. J. Sansam '57) *Red Ensign* sport. Large, well-shaped, deep pink flower with outside petals slightly darker. Very fragrant. Strong, upright, hardy grower. Medium dark foliage. Free-flowering.

**VENEZUELA F.** (Wm. E. Silva; int. Booy Rose Nursery '57) *Joanna Hill* x *Pinocchio*. Salmon flower center edged with old-age brick. Abundant, resistant leaves. Very vigorous plant with profuse, continuous bloom.

**VICKY MARFA HT.** (S. Dot '58) *(Soraya* x *Ellinor Le Grice)* x *Henri Mallerin*. Large, long-pointed buds. Double, high-centered flower opens begonia-rose with golden-orange reverse and yellow base. Moderate fragrance. Leathery foliage on tall, upright, compact plant. Abundant, continuous bloom.

**WESTMONT Min.** (Moore; int. Sequoia '58) *(Rosa wichuriaiana* x *Floradora)* x *(Oakington Ruby* x *Floradora)* Small, pointed bud borne singly and several together. Bright red, open, semi-double flower similar to *Little Buckaroo*, but lacks white area in center. Resistant, abundant, glossy, leathery, dark green foliage on vigorous, bushy dwarf plant with free, continuous bloom.

**WHITE CHARM F.** (H. C. Swim and O. L. Weeks '58) *Pinocchio* x *Virgo*. Medium to small, long-pointed buds. High-centered, semi-double to double white flowers. Good lasting quality. Moderate fragrance. Leathery, resistant leaves on upright, bushy plant. Abundant, continuous bloom. Greenhouse only.

**WHITE QUEEN HT.** (E. S. Boerner; int. Jackson & Perkins '58) *Starlite* seedling x *Glacier* seedling. Large, long bud opens to large, cupped, flat, double, white flower borne singly and several together. Very good lasting quality. Moderate fragrance. Very vigorous, upright plant with many thorns and leathery, resistant leaves. Abundant, continuous bloom.

**YELLOW DAZZLER F.** (Sam McGredy; int. Jackson & Perkins '58) *Poulsen's Yellow* x unknown seedling. Deep gold, medium, ovoid bud, borne several together and in clusters. High-centered, double flower starts golden-yellow, finishes light yellow. Very good lasting quality. Moderate fragrance. Dark green, glossy, resistant foliage on vigorous, upright plant with abundant, continuous bloom. Greenhouse only.

**ZITRONENFALTER H.Msk.** (Mathias Tantau '56) *Marchenland* x *Peace*. Large, ovoid buds borne in clusters open to large, double, open, golden-yellow flowers. Good lasting quality. Slight fragrance. Resistant, leathery leaves on vigorous, upright, 4-5′ plant Few thorns. Tips freeze.

# New Rose Patents

1604. **KORDES' PERFECTA HT.** Issued to Wilhelm Kordes, Holstein, Sparrieshoop, Germany, assigned to Jackson & Perkins Co., Newark, N.Y., May 21, 1957.

1611. **SARAH COVENTRY F.** Issued to E. S. Boerner, Newark, N.Y., assigned to C. W. Stuart & Co., Newark, N.Y., June 25, 1957.

1624. **CALYPSO F.** Issued to E. S. Boerner, Newark, N.Y., assigned to C. W. Stuart & Co., Newark, N.Y., July 30, 1957.

1629. **FIRECRACKER F.** Issued to E. S. Boerner, Newark, N.Y., assigned to Jackson & Perkins Co., Newark, N.Y., Aug. 6, 1957.

1665. **ALLGOLD F.** Issued to Edward Le Grice, North Walsham, Norfolk, England, Dec. 10, 1957.

1667. **YELLOW DAZZLER F.** Issued to Samuel D. McGredy IV, Portadown, Ireland, assigned to Jackson & Perkins Co., Newark, N.Y., Dec. 10, 1957.

1671. **TOM TOM F.** Issued to Robert V. Lindquist, Hemet, Calif., assigned to Hemet Wholesale, Hemet, Calif., Dec. 24, 1957.

1672. **LAVENDER GIRL F.** Issued to Francis Meilland, Cap d.Antibes, Alpes Maritimes, France, assigned to Conard-Pyle Co., West Grove, Pa., Jan. 7, 1958.

1673. **BONICA F.** Issued to Francis Meilland, Cap d'Antibes, Alpes Maritimes, France, assigned to Conard-Pyle Co., West Grove, Pa., Jan. 7, 1958.

1675. **DUBONNET F.** Issued to Robert G. Jelly, Richmond, Ind., assigned to E. G. Hill Co., Inc., Richmond, Ind., Jan. 21, 1958.

1677. **THUNDERBIRD F.** Issued to Paul F. De Vor, Pleasanton, Calif., assigned to Clarence Amling Roses, Inc., Santa Ana, Calif., Feb. 4, 1958.

1678. **SKYLARK F.** Issued to Paul F. De Vor, Pleasanton, Calif., assigned to Clarence Amling Roses, Inc., Santa Ana, Calif., Feb. 4, 1958.

1682. **PEGGY NEWTON F.** Issued to E. S. Boerner, Newark, N.Y., assigned to C. W. Stuart & Co., Newark, N.Y., Feb. 11, 1958.

1683. **GOLD CUP F.** Issued to E. S. Boerner, Newark, N.Y., assigned to Jackson & Perkins Co., Newark, N.Y., Feb. 18, 1958.

1684. **ARLENE FRANCIS HT.** Issued to E. S. Boerner, Newark, N.N., assigned to Jackson & Perkins Co., Newark, N.Y., Feb. 18, 1958.

1687. **RED BIRD HT.** Issued to Edward A. Manda, Jr., Pleasant Hills, Mo., assigned to Jackson & Perkins Co., Newark, N.Y., Mar. 11, 1958.

1688. **IVORY FASHION F.** Issued to E. S. Boerner, Newark, N.Y., assigned to Jackson & Perkins Co., Newark, N.Y., Mar. 11, 1958.

1689. **THE ALAMO HT.** Issued to Francis Meilland, Cap d'Antibes, Alpes Maritimes, France, assigned to Conard-Pyle Co., West Grove, Pa., Mar. 11, 1958.

1690. **RENO Gr.** Issued to William E. Silva, Sebastopol, Calif., assigned to Peter J. Booy Rose Nursery, San Jacinto, Calif., Mar. 11, 1958.

1692. **ALWAYS HT.** Issued to Charles F. Leon, 1140 N.E. 42nd Ave., Portland, Ore., Mar. 18, 1958.

1694. **STARLET F.** Issued to Herbert C. Swim, Ontario, Calif., assigned to Armstrong Nurseries, Inc., Ontario, Calif., Apr. 8, 1958.

1709. **FUSILIER F.** Issued to Dennison H. Morey, Jr., Pleasanton, Calif., assigned to Jackson & Perkins Co., Newark, N.Y., May 20, 1958.

1711. **MERRY WIDOW HT.** Issued to Walter E. Lammerts, Livermore, Calif., assigned to Germain's, Inc., Van Nuys, Calif., May 27, 1958.

1715. **JUDY HART HT.** Issued to Thomas Edison Motose, Fairport, N.Y., assigned to George B. Hart, Inc., Rochester, N.Y., June 3, 1958.

1726. **LITTLE BUCKAROO Min.** Issued to Ralph S. Moore, Visalia, Calif., July 8, 1958.

1740. **DAWNLIGHT F.** Issued to Thomas Edison Motose, Fairport, N.Y., assigned to George B. Hart, Inc., Rochester, N.Y., Aug. 12, 1958.

1742. **STARFIRE Gr.** Issued to Walter E. Lammerts, Livermore, Calif., assigned to Germain's, Inc., Van Nuys, Calif., Aug. 12, 1958.

262  AMERICAN ROSE ANNUAL:

1757. **ORANGE MIST F.** Issued to Eugene S. Boerner, Newark, N.Y., assigned to Jackson & Perkins Co., Newark, N.Y., Sept. 23, 1958.

1758. **FIRE KING F.** Issued to Francis Meilland, Cap d'Antibes, Alpes Maritimes, France, assigned to Conard-Pyle Co., West Grove, Pa., Oct. 7, 1958.

1759. **PINK PEACE HT.** Issued to Francis Meilland, Cap d'Antibes, Alpes Maritimes, France, assigned to Conard-Pyle Co., West Grove, Pa., Oct. 14, 1958.

1760. **TORCH SONG HT.** Issued to Francis Meilland, Cap d'Antibes, Alpes Maritimes, France, assigned to Conard-Pyle Co., West Grove, Pa., Oct. 14, 1958.

1761. **SARABANDE F.** Issued to Francis Meilland, Cap d'Antibes, Alpes Maritimes, France, assigned to Conard-Pyle Co., West Grove, Pa., Oct. 14, 1958.

1762. **WHITE QUEEN HT.** Issued to E. S. Boerner, Newark, N.Y., assigned to Jackson & Perkins Co., Newark, N.Y., Oct. 14, 1958.

1763. **PINK MARVEL F.** Issued to Gerrit de Ruiter, Hazerswoude, Netherlands, assigned to Conard-Pyle Co., West Grove, Pa., Oct. 14, 1958.

1764. **GOLDIE F.** Issued to E. S. Boerner, Newark, N.Y., assigned to Jackson & Perkins Co., Newark, N.Y., Oct. 14, 1958.

1765. **SEVENTEEN F.** Issued to E. S. Boerner, Newark, N.Y., assigned to Jackson & Perkins Co., Newark, N.Y., Oct. 14, 1958.

1766. **MARY HAYWOOD Min.** Issued to Ralph S. Moore, Visalia, Calif., Oct. 28, 1958.

1767. **WHITE ASTER Min.** Issued to Ralph S. Moore, Visalia, Calif., Oct. 28, 1958.

1769. **MY CHOICE HT.** Issued to Edward Burton Le Grice, North Walsham, England, Nov. 11, 1958.

1770. **JUNE BRIDE Gr.** Issued to Roy E. Shepherd, Medina, Ohio, assigned to Edith C. Bosley, Mentor, Ohio, Nov. 11, 1958.

1771. **SCARLET MARVEL F.** Issued to Gerrit de Ruiter, Hazerswoude, Netherlands, assigned to Conard-Pyle Co., West Grove, Pa., Nov. 18, 1958.

1774. **PINK MIST HT.** Issued to Sidney Reece and Roy L. Byrum, Richmond, Ind., assigned to Joseph H. Hill Co., Richmond, Ind., Nov. 25, 1958.

# Index

OREGON CENTENNIAL HT

G. J. Von Abrams; introduced Peterson & Dering, Scappoose, Ore. Plant patent applied for. Described page 251.

RUBY LIPS F
H. C. Swim; introduced Armstrong Nurseries, Ontario, Calif. Plant patent
applied for. Described page 255.